Key Words in Education

Key Words in Education

K. T. Collins
L. W. Downes
S. R. Griffiths
K. E. Shaw

Longman

LONGMAN GROUP LIMITED
London
Associated companies, branches and
representatives throughout the world

First published 1973
ISBN 0 582 32705 9 (cased edition)
ISBN 0 582 32706 7 (paper edition)
Printed in Great Britain by
Hazell, Watson & Viney Ltd
Aylesbury, Bucks

Contents

Footnote   Words or phrases which are given in
bold in the text may be found elsewhere
as separate entries.

Introduction

The teacher of today is not regarded as 'trained' if he is merely conversant with the 'tricks of the trade'. He has moved a long way from his nineteenth-century forebears who were concerned largely with the presentation of predigested material to large groups of children and whose training was therefore limited to the absorption of academic subject matter and what was then called 'class management'. The teacher of today is a 'professional' in that his (or her) work has the accepted characteristics of a profession[1],

1 It involves skill based on theoretical knowledge.
2 It requires training *and* education.
3 It requires a demonstration of competence by passing an agreed test.
4 It insists on the maintenance of integrity by the establishment of and adherence to a code of conduct.
5 It provides a service for the public good.
6 It is organized as a professional body.

The authors of this compilation of *Key Words in Education* are concerned here with the first three of these professional characteristics. They believe that a profession cannot exist for long if its practice is not founded on a solid but dynamic and developing theoretical structure. This structure has grown, particularly since the turn of the century, into a subject in its own right which is called 'education'. It is very dependent for its growth and power on the established disciplines of philosophy, psychology, sociology and history (and in statistical areas of study, on mathematics)[2].

If education can also be thought of as a field where these other disciplines may meet and interact, then it can be said that this field is rapidly expanding under the impact of an increasing body of literature and research.

The institution of the BEd degree for teachers in colleges of education will make necessary a deeper study of educational theory in all its aspects. It is the one subject which all students must take to qualify for the degree. Yet courses in education are reputedly shallow and not very challenging. They have so far not compared favourably with the academic courses in established disciplines in most colleges.

The authors of *Key Words in Education* are lecturers in a College of Education but they are primarily experienced, practical teachers, who have taught in a wide range of schools from infant to sixth-form grammar schools and schools for the educationally subnormal. They have compiled this book because they want their students' practical expertise to be well informed and well motivated through wide reading and study of educational theory. They have found that students need guidance in their reading and frequent opportunities to discuss the meaning of words in the context of education.

The words selected for definition in this book are those which are most frequently needed by their students. No claim is made that the list is complete since selection is bound to be arbitrary. Nor will the definitions be completely acceptable to every teacher. The purpose has been to help particularly the new reader to find his way through educational literature when technical terms or abstract notions may be stumbling blocks.

The authors have also, where appropriate, tried to lead the student to further reading by quoting references to standard works. Again, the choice of these has been arbitrary, but in this they have tried to give references to those books which from time to time have been recommended to their own students in lectures, tutorials and seminars.

It is hoped that omissions and deficiencies may be put right in future editions. The authors would be very grateful for help in this from those who use the book. In particular they would welcome references to new material as it is published and which readers think should be included for the benefit of future students.

[1] G. Millerson, *The Qualifying Professions*, Routledge & Kegan Paul, 1964

[2] There is some dispute as to whether the contribution of philosophy to education should be described as educational philosophy or the philosophy of education. Similar distinctions seem to be made between educational psychology and the psychology of education; educational sociology and the sociology of education. But curiously no one seems to have made the same distinction between educational history and the history of education. History is regarded as a discipline with its own techniques and its own ways of thinking, but these are applied to the field of Education, just as in the history of mathematics they might be to the field of mathematics, or to any other subject area.

A

Abacus
A calculating device usually consisting of beads on a framework of parallel wires and using elementary ideas of place value. The abacus has appeared in many forms. It was used for calculation purposes in the ancient world and in medieval Europe, and it is still in considerable use in some eastern countries today.
E. M. CHURCHILL, *Counting and Measuring*, Routledge & Kegan Paul 1961
D. SMELTZER, *Man and Number*, A. and C. Black 1953

Aberdare Report (1881)
Report of the Departmental Committee on Intermediate and Higher Education in Wales. Terms of reference: To inquire into the present condition of intermediate and higher education in Wales and to recommend the measures which they may think advisable for improving and supplementing the provision that is now or might be made available for such education in the Principality.
Recommended the establishment of two more university colleges (at Cardiff and Bangor) and the provision of more places in non-denominational grammar schools.
J. STUART MACLURE, *Educational Documents 1816–1967*, 2nd edn, Chapman & Hall 1968

Ability grouping
The method of dividing pupils or students into separate homogeneous groups on the basis of tested or presumed ability in the subject or curriculum to be taught, in order to facilitate teaching.
See also **Streaming**; **Unstreaming**

Abitur
The final examination of the academic secondary schools in Germany, taken after the nine-year course of the gymnasium. It is an internal examination set by the gymnasium; but there is an abitur without Latin for pupils of Ober Realschule. The latter admits to some faculties of the university, the former to all faculties; the abitur also admits to teacher training colleges.
T. AULBENER *The Schools of West Germany*, New York Univ. Press

Abnormal
Differing from the **norm** or **average**: used more often in respect of some **personality** trait or **disposition** than of mental powers.
See also **Normality**; **Subnormality**

H. J. EYSENCK ed., *Handbook of Abnormal Psychology*, Pitman 1960
K. MENNINGER, *Man Against Himself*, Hart-Davis 1963
I. SKOTTOWE, *A Mental Health Handbook*, E. Arnold 1957
C. W. VALENTINE, *The Normal Child and Some of His Abnormalities*, Penguin (Pelican) 1967

Abreaction
The release of repressed emotion through the imaginative re-creation of the original experience.
M. HAMILTON, ed, *Abnormal Psychology*, Penguin 1967

Abstract
1. Existing apart from any particular concrete object, as a product of the mind; i.e. as a mental concept expressed in a word, symbol or pattern.
2. A brief summary of a thesis or dissertation, for the convenience of assessors; or of a published article.

Abstraction
The process of detecting the elements common to things or situations and developing them into a general concept, e.g. the child abstracts the common numerical element of 'fourness' from the four wheels of a car, the four legs of a dog, four fingers, four steps, four children, four dots, four bangs on the drum, etc.
P. H. MUSSEN, *The Psychological Development of the Child*, Prentice-Hall 1964

Absurdities test
A test purporting to measure **intelligence** in which the testee is required to detect incongruity in verbal or picture items, e.g. 'Bill Jones's feet are so big that he has to pull his trousers on over his head' (from **L. M. Terman** and **M. A. Merrill**, *Measuring Intelligence*, Harrap, 1937).
P. E. VERNON, *Intelligence and Attainment Tests*, University of London Press 1960

Academic
1. Pertaining to the realm of ideas, abstractions, theories; hence of education, that which embodies such an approach, and is suitable for older and abler pupils.
2. Term used to describe people, such as lecturers and professors, whose occupation is concerned with ideas and theories, rather than with actions.

Academic Board

The **Robbins Report** recommendation that colleges of education should come fully under the administrative and academic structure of universities was rejected by the Government, which then instructed a review of the government of Colleges in the form of a study group under the Chairmanship of Mr T. R. Weaver. Its report, published in 1966, gave governing bodies and academic staffs of colleges substantial responsibilities and freedom. Academic Boards varying in size from 12 to 25 members were set up after 1968 with responsibility and authority in the academic life of Colleges, and power to nominate three staff members, in addition to the Principal, to the governing body.

The powers of the Academic Board are defined by the Instrument of Government of each College; these vary, but generally allow substantial participation by staff in all major decisions likely to affect the academic work of the College.

In all essentials, the form of government proposed for Polytechnics set up as a result of Administrative Memorandum 8/67, is that proposed in the **Weaver Report**.

K. E. SHAW, 'A study of a college of education', unpublished PhD thesis, Bath University School of Management, 1973

Academic dress

The gown, hood and headgear worn by men and women graduates to denote the nature of their degree, university and academic standing. Usually required for ceremonial functions. The black gown only is worn for teaching. There is a curtailed costume for undergraduates in some universities.

Academic freedom

The right of the teacher and the student to use scholarly methods and teachings to discover knowledge in any direction and to make known their findings however popular or unpopular they may be. The dangers to academic freedom are mainly political, religious and administrative.

J. S. BRUBACHER ed., *Eclectic Philosophy of Education*, Prentice-Hall 1952

Academic method

Term sometimes applied to describe methods of teaching which do not involve active participation by the pupil.

See also **Chalk-talk**

Academic year

The period from September (or October) to June (or July) when most schools, colleges, universities are in session.

Academician

Member of an **Academy** in the sense of (2) below. In the UK for example, the title may refer to an artist who has achieved the distinction of election to membership of the Royal Academy. In the USSR, the title refers to the highest rank in the Soviet educational hierarchy.

Academy

1. Originally Plato's school of philosophy, from the name of the garden where he taught.
F. A. G. BECK, *Greek Education 450–350 B.C.*, Methuen 1964
E. B. CASTLE, *Ancient Education and Today*, Penguin (Pelican) 1969

2. A body of scholars, admission to whose ranks is a mark of eminent achievement in the field of learning, research or creative work; viz. Académie Française, American Academy of Fine Arts and Sciences, Royal Academy, etc.

3. One of the separatist schools and colleges established for Nonconformists after the Second Act of Uniformity (1665). These were initially staffed by teachers who, as a consequence of the Act, had been expelled from universities and grammar schools and by clergymen who had lost their livings. Their first intention had been to educate ministers, but many admitted young people who had no desire of becoming ministers. In many instances these 'dissenting academies' broke away from classical curricular traditions, e.g. introducing mathematics, science and modern studies.

4. Until recently in Scotland the word 'academy' was applied to selective schools only, but with the reorganisation of secondary education it may now also describe a comprehensive school.

Acalculia

Inability to perform mental operations which are concerned with number.
J. B. BIGGS, *Anxiety, Motivation and Primary School Mathematics*, National Foundation for Educational Research 1962

Acataphasia

Inability to link up words meaningfully.
See also **Aphasia**

Accelerated

1. A term applied to pupils whose attain-

ments are in excess of what their intelligence rating seemed to predict. This could be due to (*a*) underestimate of intelligence, and (*b*) overestimate of attainment. A more likely explanation lies in the idea that prediction on the basis of intelligence measurement is in terms of averages, i.e. on average, a child with a mental age of 8 will have a reading age of 8. Obviously it must also mean that some will have a greater and some will have a lesser reading age than their respective mental ages. The usefulness of this concept of prediction is that it will be very close to the truth for the great majority of children.
2. The term is also used to describe very intelligent children who are set work well in advance of their normal age group. The classes in which they are placed are sometimes called 'express' streams.
S. EVERETT ed., *Programs for the Gifted*, Harper & Row 1961

Accent
That quality of speech affecting particularly the vowel sounds, which is characteristic of a geographical area (e.g. Welsh or Scots accent), or of some stratum of society (e.g. working class accent, Oxford accent).
A. BULLARD, *Improve Your Speech*, Blond 1967
H. A. GLEASON, *An Introduction to Descriptive Linguistics*, rev. edn, Holt, Rinehart & Winston 1961
R. HOGGART, *The Uses of Literacy*, Chatto 1957; Penguin (Pelican) 1969
A. M. HORNER, *Spoken Words*, Phoenix House 1958

Acceptability, Social
The measure in which an individual or group is able to gain membership of normal social groups whether formal or informal. It depends principally upon factors such as personality, social and educational status, ethnic origin, etc.
K. M. EVANS, *Sociometry and Education*, Routledge & Kegan Paul 1962
C. M. FLEMING, *The Social Psychology of Education*, 2nd edn, Routledge & Kegan Paul 1959
O. A. OESER, ed., *Teacher, Pupil and Task*, Tavistock 1966

Accidence
A division of grammar, along with phonology (the study of sound changes and combinations) and syntax (study of rules for use of words, word order, etc.). Accidence deals with the changes in word forms, usually presenting them in patterned tables, called 'paradigms'. Accidence has assumed a large place in the grammatical study of non-romance and classical languages.
E. PARTRIDGE, *English; a Course for human beings*, Macdonald 1949
O. JESPERSEN, *The Growth and Structure of the English Language*, Blackwell 1948

Accident prone
Liable to sustain accidents more frequently than is normal.

Accidents in school
A teacher is **in loco parentis** to the children in his charge and the law requires only that he should act reasonably in this capacity, taking such care of his children as a careful parent would do. Unless the accident is of a trivial nature, the teacher should err on the side of caution – calling a doctor and possibly an ambulance, informing the child's parents, or alternatively accompanying the child to his home, and remaining there until the parent comes home.
In case of possible legal action arising from a school accident, the teacher should immediately consult his professional association.
G. R. BARRELL, *Teachers and the Law*, Methuen 1966, Ch. 11
G. TAYLOR and J. B. SAUNDERS, *The New Law of Education*, 7th edn, Butterworth, 1971

Accommodation
A term employed by **Piaget** to describe one of the mental processes in which existing schemas, or well defined mental actions, are modified as a result of new experiences.
See also **Assimilation**
J. PIAGET, *The Origin of Intelligence in the Child*, Routledge & Kegan Paul 1953
R. M. BEARD, *An Outline of Piaget's Developmental Psychology*, Routledge & Kegan Paul 1969

Accountancy
Several bodies grant membership of their professional organisation on examination after a period of practical work with a firm of Accountants. Two such bodies are:
Institute of Chartered Accountants, Moorgate Place, London, EC2
Society of Incorporated Accountants, Temple Place, Victoria Embankment, London, WC2

Acculturation
The process of assimilating a **culture** through participation in it.
S. N. EISENSTADT, *From Generation to Generation*, Collier Macmillan 1964, ch. 1
S. A. WEINSTOCK, 'Role elements', *British Journal of Sociology*, **14**, no. 2, June 1963

Accuracy
The quality of being exact as opposed to being approximate. In the nature of measurement generally, absolute accuracy is impossible since it is dependent upon essentially imperfect instruments and upon essentially imperfect observers.

ACE
An independent non-profit making organisation which seeks to help all who are interested in education; through its quarterly publication *Where?*; through its advisory service; and through courses which it organises for various groups (e.g. sixth formers).
Address: Advisory Centre for Education Ltd, 57 Russell Street, Cambridge.

Achievement
Skill or understanding acquired usually with reference to academic matters and particularly with reference to the **basic subjects**.
H. HECKHAUSEN *The Anatomy of Achievement Motivation*, Academic Press 1967

Achievement Quotient (or **AQ**)
An index of a person's **attainment** relative to his capacities, and is calculated by taking the ratio of his **attainment age** to his mental age and multiplying by 100, e.g.
$$\frac{\text{Reading age } 8.0}{\text{Mental age } 10.0} \times 100$$
gives an achievement quotient of 80 in reading. Some authorities however take the standpoint that for this purpose the attainment should be related to chronological age.
P. E. VERNON, *Intelligence and Attainment Tests*, University of London Press 1960

Achievement tests
Recent developments in this field are the *Bristol Achievement Tests*, by Alan Brimer *et al* (Nelson 1969). These cover English Language, Mathematics and Study skills. The age range tested is from 8.0 to 11.11 years, and there are Forms A and B to facilitate retesting.
See also **Age (3) Attainment age**

Achromatic vision or achromatism
Total colour blindness. In this extremely rare condition the person, who usually has additional visual defects, sees everything in black, white and various shades of grey.

Acoustics
The science of sound. The acoustic property of a room or theatre is its quality from the point of view of the listener, with regard to resonance, echo, etc.

Acquired
As opposed to what is inborn or innate. Much of a person's ways of thinking, feeling and doing can be traced to what he has acquired by his upbringing and education, while some of it can be attributed to inherited factors. This raises the problem of **heredity** and **environment** in relation to a person's general development and, in particular, to the development of intelligence.

Acquisitiveness
The desire to obtain property and possessions as a major purpose in life. Viewed with disfavour by the traditional morality of pre-industrial society, it is frequently claimed to be a characteristic of modern advanced communities. It is thought to pose moral and social problems to which educational agencies might offer possible solutions.
J. K. GALBRAITH, *The Affluent Society*, Hamish Hamilton 1958; Penguin (Pelican) 1962
R. H. TAWNEY, *The Acquisitive Society*, Bell 1921; Collins (Fontana) 1961

Activism
The theory which maintains that activity, physical and mental, is of primary importance in the learning process.

Activity methods
As opposed to 'passive learning'. The **Hadow Report** (1931), *The Primary School*, declared that 'the curriculum is to be thought of in terms of activity and experience rather than of knowledge to be acquired and facts to be stored' (p. 93). Activity methods imply mental and, where appropriate, physical activity leading to knowledge, understanding and appreciation rather than the passive acceptance of readymade answers or predigested evaluations from books or teachers. Obviously 'passivity' and 'activity' are a matter of degree, but it is plain, for example,

that a person's evaluation of a poem or a piece of music is shallow and insincere if he merely commits to memory the pronouncements of book or teacher, or that a child's attitude to, and appreciation of, geometry is healthier if he has been allowed to make, examine and discuss geometrical shapes rather than to have mechanically committed to memory Euclidean theorems and proofs.

M. V. DANIEL, *Activity in the Primary School*, Blackwell 1947

C. STURMEY, ed., *Activity Methods for Children Under Eight*, Evans 1949

D. THOMSON and J. REEVES, ed., *The Quality of Education*, Muller 1947

Acuity
Sharpness, normally of sensory perception (hearing, vision).

W. M. DEMBER, *Psychology of Perception*, Holt, Rinehart & Winston 1960

Adams, Sir John (1857–1934)
Scottish educationalist, who after work as a teacher, headmaster, lecturer and training college principal in Scotland, became Professor of Education in the University of London, 1902–22.
Publications include: *Herbartian Psychology Applied to Education* (1897); *The Evolution of Educational Theory* (1912); *The New Teaching* (1918); *Modern Developments in Educational Practice* (1922).

Adaptability
The capacity to modify response to suit change of situation or environment. As such it is sometimes regarded as evidence of **intelligence**.

A. D. WOODRUFF, *Psychology of Teaching*, 3rd edn, Longmans 1951, Part IV

Addition facts
The basic addition combinations (e.g. $4 + 5$, $3 + 6$). There are a hundred such facts when neither figure exceeds 9.
See also **Arithmetic fact**

L. W. DOWNES and D. PALING, *The Teaching of Arithmetic in Primary Schools*, Oxford University Press, Unesco Handbooks 1958

Addition process
The technique of finding the total of two or more quantities. When the basic addition facts are known the process usually consists of writing the quantities in vertical columns, having regard to **place value** and then adding

the units, tens and hundreds columns in turn.

L. W. DOWNES and D. PALING, *The Teaching of Arithmetic in Primary Schools*, Oxford University Press, Unesco Handbooks 1958

Addresses (of publishers, and other organisations supplying educational material)
See also **Treasure Chest** and Appendix IV

Adenoids
Part of the ring of protective tissue surrounding the throat. The mucus secreted by the tissue carries dust and infecting matter from the nose and secretes resistant antibodies. Infection produces enlargement of the tissue, which obstructs breathing and predisposes to infection of sinus and middle ear disease. Adenoids usually become smaller after childhood. Educationists are interested mainly because the condition is associated with school absence and sometimes with educational backwardness.

J. APLEY and R. M. KEITH, *The Child and his Symptoms*, 2nd edn, Blackwell Scientific 1968

D. PATERSON, *Sick Children* ed. Lightwood and Brimblecombe, Bailliere, 1963

Adequacy
The quality (in a person) which enables him to be equal to the demands, particularly intellectual or social, which are made of him.

M. F. CLEUGH, *Teaching the Slow Learner*, Methuen 1961

C. M. FLEMING, *The Social Psychology of Education*, 2nd edn Routledge & Kegan Paul 1959

A. E. TANSLEY and R. GULLIFORD, *The Education of Slow Learning Children*, Routledge & Kegan Paul 1960, Ch. 12

K. WALKER, *Patients and Doctors*, Penguin (Pelican) 1957

Adjustment
The process and condition of being in harmony with the physical and social environment in which an individual lives; indicated by the absence of symptoms of stress and by an ability to maintain good personal relationships.
See also **Maladjustment**
Growing up in a Changing World (Symposium), World Federation for Mental Health, 19 Manchester Street, London, W1.

L. F. SHAFFER and E. J. SHOBEN, *The Psychology of Adjustment*, 2nd edn, Constable 1956

Adler, Alfred (1870–1937)
A founder member of the Vienna Psycho-analytic Society who worked with **Freud** from 1902 to 1911. Finding Freud's great emphasis on sexuality largely unacceptable he developed his own school of psychotherapy under the name of **Individual Psychology**. Adler was particularly interested in the importance of social factors in personality development and his ideas have had con-siderable influence in the fields of education, criminology and medicine. The term **inferiority complex** was coined by Adler.
Translated works include: *The Practice and Theory of Individual Psychology* (2nd edn, Routledge & Kegan Paul 1929); *The Educa-tion of Children* (Allen & Unwin 1930); *Understanding Human Nature* (Allen & Unwin 1946).
LEWIS WAY, *Alfred Adler: an introduction to his psychology*, Penguin 1956
HERTHA ORGLER, *Alfred Adler: the man and his work*, 3rd edn, Sidgwick & Jackson 1963

Administration
1. In education, the business of running the machinery of Education, which involves finance and staffing at the County level and, for example, the kind of work connected with form-filling in the schools.
D. COOKE and J. DUNHILL, *A Short Guide to Educational Administration*, University of London Press, 1962
2. The administration of tests: in the case of standardised tests, the instructions concern-ing the method and time have to be adhered to strictly, according to the published stan-dardised procedure. Failure to do this renders the test invalid.
N. E. WHILDE, *The Application of Psychologi-cal Tests in Schools*, Blackie 1955

Admission to school
This is compulsory in the UK when the child is aged five, unless the parent(s) can give evidence that the child is receiving satis-factory education elsewhere. Every grant-aided school is required by the Secretary of State for Education and Science to keep an admission register. A pupil cannot be refused admission to a school except on reasonable grounds, e.g. he cannot be excluded because his brothers and sisters do not attend the school.
G. R. BARRELL, *Teachers and the Law*, Methuen 1966, Ch. 8

G. TAYLOR and J. B. SAUNDERS, *The New Law of Education*, 7th edn, Butterworth 1971

Admission to university
Each university or university college has minimal academic requirements for admis-sion to study for a degree (i.e. matriculation). Any faculty, school or department within the university may stipulate further require-ments for particular studies. Matriculation may not be required for studies other than those for a degree (e.g. for various diplomas). *See also* **UCCA**
K. BOEHM, Ed., *University Choice*, Penguin 1966
NATIONAL UNION OF TEACHERS, *University and College Entrance*
Which University? Cornmarket 1969

Adolescence
The period between puberty and maturity characterized by the development (at about 12–14 years) of secondary sexual charac-teristics and onset of mature functioning in sex organs. Girls normally reach adolescence earlier than boys. The end of adolescence in other than the physical sense is a less defined period in the late teens or early twenties.
C. M. FLEMING, *Adolescence*, 2nd edn, Rout-ledge & Kegan Paul 1963
A. T. JERSILD, *The Psychology of Adolescence*, 2nd edn, Collier-Macmillan 1963
F. MUSGROVE, *Youth and the Social Order*, Routledge & Kegan Paul 1964
J. M. TANNER, *Growth at Adolescence*, 2nd edn, Blackwell 1969
W. D. WALL, *The Adolescent Child*, new edn, Methuen 1948

Adult education
The education of persons beyond the school leaving age, and adults usually in evening classes and short courses, but outside the sphere of higher, further or professional education. Providing bodies are the Workers' Educational Association (**WEA**), the local education authority (**LEA**) in **evening institutes** and **university extension** courses.
NATIONAL INSTITUTE OF ADULT EDUCATION, *Year Book of Adult Education*
R. PEERS, *Fact and Possibility in English Education*, Routledge & Kegan Paul 1963
R. PEERS, *Adult Education: a comparative study*, 2nd edn, Routledge & Kegan Paul 1959

Advanced level (GCE, A level)
That stage of proficiency in the General Certificate of Education (**GCE**) following **O**

level, normally the level of work prepared during at least two years in the **sixth form**. There are five pass grades.

Write for information to the secretaries of the various **Examining Boards** (e.g. London, Oxford, Cambridge, Northern Universities) *See also* UCCA

E. BLISHEN, *Education Today*, BBC Publications 1963

Advisory Centre for Education *see* ACE

Advisory Councils
There are many advisory bodies concerned with official policy in Education.

Advisory Council on Education (*Scotland*) was set up by the Education (Scotland) Act of 1918. It assists the Scottish Education Department in matters of policy and administration.
Central Advisory Council for Education (*England*). Set up by 1944 Act to replace Consultative Committee to advise Minister on questions he may refer to them, and on such matters of the theory and practice of Education as they may think fit; but not educational administration. The term of office of members ended in 1966. No new members were appointed, despite provisions in the 1944 Education Act for the existence of such a body.
There is also an *Advisory Council for Education* (*Wales*). Set up in 1944 Act. See *Education 1964*, HMSO, for a review.
National Advisory Council on Training and Supply of Teachers. Set up in 1949 with members representing area training organisations, **LEAs** and various national associations of teachers. After 1968 it ceased to meet but was not formally dissolved.
National Advisory Council on Education for Industry and Commerce. Set up in 1948 as a result of the **Percy Report**.
Industrial Training Council
National Advisory Council on Art Education. Advises Secretary on all aspects of art education in all establishments of further education.
Secondary Schools Examination Council. A body set up in 1917 to advise the Board of Education in matters relating to the coordination of examinations taken in secondary schools.
Many Local Authorities also have advisory committees of teachers who may be consulted by Chief Education Officers on Education policy.

Advisory Council for Child Care
There are two councils (England and Wales, Scotland) set up in 1948 by the **Children Act** 1948, whose function is to advise the Home Secretary on matters relating to the care of children without the benefits of normal home life.
A. BOWLEY and L. GARDNER, *The Young Handicapped Child*, Livingstone 1969
Children in the Care of Local Authorities in England and Wales, HMSO 1956

Advisory services
Her Majesty's Inspectorate and local inspectors exist to advise schools; some Authorities employ advisory teachers; Authorities are obliged to employ a youth officer and school meals officer. Most advisers are in the fields of physical education, music, housecraft and handicraft.

Aesthetics
The systematic study of the beautiful, particularly in relation to the fine arts, involving the definition of beauty and the formulation of principles relevant to the production and evaluation of works of art.
W. ELTON, *Essays in Aesthetics and Language*, Blackwell 1954
H. READ, *Education Through Art*, 3rd edn, Faber 1958
F. E. SPARSHOTT, *The Structure of Aesthetics*, Routledge & Kegan Paul 1963

Aetiology (Amer. etiology)
The study of the causes or origins of a disease or abnormal condition.

Affect
Feeling or emotion, especially in its persisting state.

Aftercare
The statutory duty to provide supervision for young persons discharged on licence from approved schools, and some other offenders: was exercised until 1965 by the Home Office through welfare officers attached to approved schools. This duty is now exercised by Children's Departments of local authorities, and by the Probation Service.
Organisation of Aftercare, HMSO 1963

Age
1. CHRONOLOGICAL AGE, the actual age in years and months.
2. MENTAL AGE, the age at which on average

children get certain items right, or a certain overall score in a standardised intelligence test; e.g. if, on average, children aged 10 get a particular score in an intelligence test we can attribute a mental age of 10 to anyone who gets this score, irrespective of that person's chronological age.
See also **Binet, Terman.**

3. ATTAINMENT AGE (reading age, arithmetic age, etc.) is the age attributed to a person who gains a certain score in some field or other of mental activity when that score represents the average attainment of people of that chronological age; e.g. A child may have an arithmetic age of 8, although his chronological age is 10, because he scores at the level of the average eight-year-old.

P. E. VERNON, *Intelligence and Attainment Tests*, University of London Press 1960
P. E. VERNON, *Measurement of Abilities*, 2nd edn, University of London Press 1956

Age, skeletal. *See* **Carpal age**

Aggressiveness
A tendency to attack, usually in response to interference or opposition, or to take the initiative vigorously; **Freud**ian psychologists connect it with the operation of the **death instinct**, and **Adler**ian psychologists regard it as an expression of the will to power.

A. ADLER, *Guiding Human Misfits*, Faber 1946
K. Z. LORENZ, *On Aggression*, Methuen 1966
K. MENNINGER, *Man Against Himself*, Hart-Davis 1963

Agoraphobia
An inordinate fear of open spaces, e.g. a field, street, or park.

Agraphia
Inability to do handwriting as the result of brain lesion.

Agreed Syllabus
A syllabus of religious education which since the 1944 Education Act each **LEA** must draw up, or adopt, for use in its own **maintained schools** (*see* **Voluntary controlled schools**); a syllabus 'without any catechism or formulary distinctive of any particular religious denomination' (**Cowper-Temple clause**). The agreed syllabus in any LEA will have been adopted or will be the result of joint consultation among representatives of the various religious denominations, the teachers' organisation in the area, and the LEA itself.

G. R. BARRELL, *Teachers and the Law*, Methuen 1966, Ch. 10
G. TAYLOR and J. B. SAUNDERS, *The New Law of Education*, 7th edn, Butterworth 1971
See also the agreed syllabuses of particular LEAs, e.g. Cambridgeshire and West Riding of Yorks.

Agriculture, Colleges of
In addition to universities offering degree courses in agriculture there are eight Colleges of Agriculture in Great Britain which offer courses to diploma level. Entrance requirements are usually at least four **GCE** O level subjects. The colleges are residential and offer courses also in horticulture and dairying.

NATIONAL ADVISORY COUNCIL FOR INDUSTRY AND COMMERCE, *Lampard Vachell Report*, HMSO 1966
MINISTRY OF AGRICULTURE, *Further Education for Agriculture* (De La Warr Report), HMSO 1959

Aided school
A **voluntary school**, two-thirds of whose **managers** or **governors** are chosen by the voluntary body providing the school, the other third being appointed by the **LEA**. Under the 1967 Act the managers or governors have to meet 20 per cent of the cost of improving or enlarging the school buildings and the State pays the other 80 per cent. The LEA meets the bill for the running costs (particularly teachers' salaries). The managers or governors have large powers in the appointment and dismissal of teachers in the school. The foundation managers or governors control the religious education programme of the school.

G. R. BARRELL, *Teachers and the Law*, Methuen 1966
G. TAYLOR and J. B. SAUNDERS, *The New Law of Education*, 7th edn, Butterworth 1971

Aides, Teachers'
The **Plowden** Committee chose the term 'teachers' aides', rather than ancillary or auxiliary teachers. They recommended that teachers' aides should be trained and certificated as are nursery nurses, i.e. by a two year course leading to examination by a central examining body, and that the entrance requirements should be similar for the two services.

Plowden Report, *Children and their Primary Schools,* 1967, Ch. 26

AIMech E
Associate of the Institution of Mechanical Engineers
Institution of Mechanical Engineers, 1 Birdcage Walk, London, SW1

Aims of education
These have varied since ancient times according to period and culture. Today most educationists would subscribe to a statement which included (*a*) nurture of individual growth (*b*) the perpetuating of social skills and values.
See also **Philosophy of education**
G. H. BANTOCK, *Education in an Industrial Society*, Faber 1963
R. F. DEARDEN, *The Philosophy of Primary Education*, Routledge & Kegan Paul 1968
J. DEWEY, *The School and Society*, 2nd edn University of Chicago Press 1915
P. H. HIRST and R. S. PETERS, *The Logic of Education*, Routledge & Kegan Paul 1970
T. B. H. HOLLINS, ed., *Aims in Education*, Manchester University Press 1964
M. V. C. JEFFREYS, *Glaucon; an Inquiry into the Aims of Education*, Pitman 1950
R. S. PETERS, ed., *The Concept of Education*, Routledge & Kegan Paul 1967
D. THOMPSON AND J. REEVES, eds., *The Quality of Education*, Muller 1947
A. N. WHITEHEAD, *The Aims of Education*, Williams & Norgate 1929

Alalia
Absence of speech owing to psychogenic causes or delayed development of speech in childhood.
G. H. J. PEARSON, *Emotional Disorders of Children*, Allen & Unwin 1951

Albemarle Report (1960)
Report of the Departmental Committee on the Youth Service in England and Wales (Chairman: The Countess of Albemarle).
Terms of reference: To review the contribution which the Youth Service of England and Wales can make in assisting young people to play their part in the life of the community, in the light of changing social and industrial conditions and of current trends in other branches of the education service; and to advise according to what priorities best value can be obtained for the money spent.
As a result of the recommendation an Emergency Training College for youth leaders was established (at Leicester), a committee for the negotiation of salaries of youth leaders was set up and the Youth Service Development Council was founded.
Report on Youth Service in England and Wales 1960 *see* App. III
J. S. MACLURE, *Educational Documents*, Chapman & Hall 1968

Albino
A person having a congenital deficiency of pigment in the skin, hair and eyes. The typical albino has milk coloured skin, almost white hair and eyes with a pink or blue iris and a deep red pupil. The term is also used to describe similar pigment deficiency in plants and animals.

Alexander, Sir William P. (b. 1905)
General Secretary, Association of Education Committees since 1945. Former schoolmaster, Director of Education in Margate and Sheffield. Publications include *Intelligence, Concrete and Abstract* Cambridge University Press 1935 and *Education in England* 1954; 3rd edn, Newnes 1965. Represents the **LEAs** in teachers' salary negotiations.

Alexia
An inability to read as a result of suspected lesion in the brain. Often referred to as **word blindness** or dyslexia.

Algebra
Generalised arithmetic which uses symbols (e.g. a, b, c, x, y, z) to study the relationships between the numbers of a given number field and the results of operation on these numbers on the basis of accepted assumptions.
G. BIRKHOFF and S. MACLANE, *A Survey of Modern Algebra*, 3rd edn, Collier-Macmillan 1965
J. L. KELLEY, *Introduction to Modern Algebra*, Van Nostrand 1960

All-age school
Unreorganized school accepting children in both the primary and secondary age range; usually applied to country schools. The number of such schools is now negligibly small in the state sector, and the term is now obsolete.
See also **Reorganization**

Allport, Gordon W. (b. 1897)
American psychologist who has devoted much attention to the field of personality

study, in a series of volumes published since 1937. He is best known for his theory of **functional autonomy** of motives. This moves beyond the **Freud**ian position by asserting that in the adult, motives are independent of the infantile drives from which they develop.

G. W. ALLPORT, *Pattern and Growth in Personality*, Holt Rinehart & Winston 1961

G. W. ALLPORT, *Personality: a psychological interpretation*, Holt Rinehart & Winston 1937 (London, Constable)

Allowance
1. Extra remuneration paid to teachers who are the principal teachers of a subject in a school (Head of Department Allowance) or who have a particular responsibility for a subject (Special Responsibility Allowance), or who are headmaster/mistress or deputy headmaster/mistress. The system was replaced in 1971 by a new system of graded scales.
2. The term may also refer to **capitation allowances** and to book allowances, library allowances, etc.

Reports of **Burnham Committee**, *Salary Scales for Teachers*, HMSO

NATIONAL UNION OF TEACHERS, *Information for Teachers* 1972

Alma mater
Latin for 'kindly mother'. An expression sometimes used affectionately by an **alumnus** to describe his or her school, college or university.

Alpha and Beta army tests
The former, a group test (mainly verbal) used originally for classifing US army intake in 1917 in First World War. The latter, a non-verbal test, for the same purpose to complement the Alpha test and also to test draftees who were illiterate or whose normal language was not English.

P. E. VERNON, *Intelligence and Attainment Tests*, University of London Press 1960

Alphabetic method
A method of teaching reading in which the pupil spells the names of the letters of a word from left to right by calling them out aloud. The method is largely obsolete in state schools, which teach by **phonic** and/or **Look and Say** methods. Some children succeeded in learning by this method because they were forced to *look* at the whole word and *say* it

repeatedly so often that the word was easily recognizable. It is therefore probably more true to regard this method as a form of 'Look and Say'.

W. S. GRAY, *The Teaching of Reading and Writing*, Evans for Unesco 1956

Alpha-rhythm or waves
Electrical activity of the brain of a relaxed person revealed in rhythmic oscillations of 8 to 13 cycles per second and normally viewed on the **electroencephalograph**. This activity prevails over all the regions of the brain but is detected in its clearest form in the parieto-occipital parts.

D. HILL and G. PARR, eds, *Electroencephalography*, 2nd edn, Macdonald 1963

Alumnus
A pupil or student. Usage is obsolete or pretentious in Britain but more widely current in the USA.

AMA
1. Assistant Masters Association (Incorporated). Strictly, IAAM.
2. Assistant Mistresses Association (Incorporated).
See also **Joint Four**
Address: 29 Gordon Square, London, WC1

Ambiguity
Doubt or uncertainty attaching to a statement, question, or situation, e.g. as in a **questionnaire** item or in an **intelligence test** question.
In the process of **standardisation** all items which show ambiguity should have been eliminated.

Ambivalence
A condition in which opposite feelings or dispositions exist simultaneously, e.g. enthusiasm for and hostility towards a certain policy, or love and hate towards some person or thing.

I. D. SUTTIE, *The Origins of Love and Hate*, Penguin (Peregrine) 1960

Amentia
Mental deficiency. May also refer to the temporary confusional insanity which may follow certain infectious fevers.
Primary amentia: poor mental development as a result of prenatal factors, the cause of which is not fully understood.
Secondary amentia: poor mental develop-

ment as a result of poor environmental conditions, either prenatal, perinatal or postnatal.
I. SKOTTOWE, *A Mental Health Handbook*, Edward Arnold 1957 (Note on pp. 81–2)

Amnesia
A disorder, organic or functional, which results in a partial or complete loss of memory. Causes may be brain injury, shock, fatigue, fever or extreme repression. Retroactive or retrograde amnesia – a loss of memory of events immediately preceding a shock or trauma, e.g. as caused by an accident.
B. HART, *The Psychology of Insanity*, Cambridge University Press 1957

Amoral
Without a sense of moral responsibility; morally or ethically indifferent or neutral.
See also **Psychopath**

Analysis, Phonic
The division of words into their constituent sounds.
See also **Synthesis, phonic**
F. J. SCHONELL, *The Psychology and Teaching of Reading*, 4th edn, Oliver & Boyd 1961
A. J HARRIS, *How to Increase Reading Ability*, 4th edn, Longmans 1961, Chs 12 and 13

Analysis of Variance
1. A variety of procedures known as experimental designs.
2. Statistical techniques designed to be used with these procedures and which are concerned with the analysis of the total of the squared deviations from the mean into sums of squares due to: (*a*) the various experimental effects; (*b*) the interaction among them; (*c*) sampling error. These techniques facilitate tests of the significance of these experimental and interaction effects.
H. E. GARRETT, *Statistics in Psychology and Education*, Longmans 1964
E. F. LINDQUIST, *Statistical Analysis in Educational Research*, Boston, Houghton, Mifflin 1940
M. J. MORONEY, *Facts from Figures*, Penguin (Pelican) 1969

Ancillary staff
Those employed in an educational institution other than normal teaching and administrative staff, e.g. caretaker, cleaners, kitchen staff.
See also **Auxiliary teacher**

Anderson Report
Grants to Students 1960. *See also* Appendix IIIA

Animism
The belief, found especially amongst primitive people that inanimate objects and all living things are inhabited by some kind of soul, e.g. the ghosts of departed people. Or somewhat similar beliefs of young children that especially moving things, e.g. a cloud or a tree moving in the wind, are alive and possess a mind and a will of their own. Many references are to be found in the works of **Piaget**.
J. PIAGET, *The Child's Conception of the World*, Harcourt Brace 1929
J. PIAGET, *The Child's Conception of Physical Causality*, Kegan Paul 1930
J. PIAGET, *The Language and Thought of the Child*, Routledge & Keegan Paul 1959

Antenatal
Referring to the period preceding birth, i.e. to the foetal period.
A. GESELL, *The First Five Years of Life*, new edn, Methuen 1955

Anthropology
The systematic study of human communities through their institutions and of men in their social and cultural aspect, in their relations with one another in living communities. These communities are examined on the spot. Until the mid-twentieth century the communities studied were usually small-scale, preindustrial and preliterate societies whose kinship and legal systems, systems of social control and government, religious beliefs, aesthetic and social standards were studied on the spot. Since then the subject has developed rapidly to encompass similar aspects of large modern industrial societies. Anthropology differs from other allied social sciences chiefly in its greater emphasis on the descriptive and analytical approach to cultural factors, beliefs, values, etc., which are less amenable to quantitative and experimental study.
J. BEATTIE, *Other Cultures*, Routledge & Kegan Paul 1964
Address of the Royal Anthropological Institute: 21 Bedford Square, London WC1

Anthropomorphism
The attribution of human qualities, especially

of form, thought and feeling, usually to deities and to animals.

Aphasia
A disorder in which there is an inability to use or understand speech, possibly as a result of brain lesion, particularly in Broca's area of the dominant hemisphere, or as a result of emotional disturbance. In some definitions, also extended to cover the lack of ability to understand symbols or written language.
G. H. J. PEARSON, *Emotional Disorders of Children*, Allen & Unwin 1951 .

Aphrasia
A condition in which the individual is unable to speak connected phrases though he is able to speak single words.

Apparatus
Material(s) whose use promotes facility and skill to the area of learning for which they have been constructed. e.g. mathematical structural apparatus, or gymnastic apparatus.
See also **Audio-visual aids**

Apperception
A term employed by **Herbart** to denote the process by which new sense experiences are related to the existing mass of retained structured experience in the mind.
SIR J. ADAMS, *Herbartian Psychology Applied to Education*, 1897. Reprinted Heath.

Appreciation lessons
Lessons in which pupils or students are guided and stimulated into an awareness of the **aesthetic** qualities of some work of art, e.g. of a piece of music, of a painting, or of a poem.
G. HIGHET, *The Art of Teaching*, Methuen 1951; paperback 1963, pp. 242–6
S. MARSHALL, *Experiment in Education*, Cambridge University Press 1963
H. READ, *Education through Art*, 3rd edn, Faber 1958
G. SAMPSON, *English for the English*, Cambridge University Press 1970, pp. 88–109

Apprenticeship
The period spent in learning a group of skills under the direction of a qualified adult; normally applied to learning crafts, but is used more ambitiously in graduate apprenticeships in industry. It was the major method in training for teaching for many years.

See also **Pupil-teacher**
K. LIEPMANN, *Apprenticeship*, Routledge & Kegan Paul 1960

Approved schools
Boarding schools, *approved* by the Secretary of State for Home Affairs, for boys and girls who have been found guilty of an offence, are in need of care and attention, or are beyond parental control, and who have been judged by a court to be in need of removal from home for an extended period of education and training. They are paid for from public funds. From 1972 they are under the general supervision of the Department of Health and Social Security. Governing Bodies to be reconstituted as from 1973. They are generally run as schools, with trade instruction for children over the age of 15; staffed by teachers, instructors and housemasters who receive **Burnham scale** plus emoluments. Rarely of more than 100 places, they receive boys from **Classifying Schools**; the children may be licensed at discretion of managers to statutory **after care** not exceeding three years.
R. ADAM, *Careers-Approved Schools*, HMSO for Home Office 1964
G. ROSE, *Schools for Young Offenders*, Tavistock 1967
Report of the Work of the Children's Department, Home Office H.C.bi-ennial
SECRETARY OF STATE FOR THE HOME DEPARTMENT, *Children in Trouble*, Cmnd 3601, HMSO 1968
Statistics Relating to Approved Schools, HMSO, annually
G. TAYLOR and J. B. SAUNDERS, *The New Law of Education*, 7th edn, Butterworth 1971

Apraxia
Inability to manipulate objects satisfactorily because of possible brain lesion.

A priori knowledge
Knowledge which is not derived from experience but is deduced or 'recollected' independently of experience, from definitions, principles or revealed truths of religion which are supposed to exist in everyone or are self-evident. Logic and mathematics illustrate this kind of truth, and much ancient and medieval philosophy depended upon *a priori* reasoning. Scientific method and empirical verification have now largely displaced this form of belief and argument.
BERTRAND RUSSELL, *The Problems of Philosophy*, Oxford University Press 1967

Aptitude
As in the phrase 'age, ability and aptitude': a specific ability, e.g. for foreign language, music, mathematics, which may be partly innate, partly acquired, but which sometimes may have relatively little relationship to the person's general level of ability.
W. V. BINGHAM, *Aptitudes and Aptitude Testing*, Harper & Row 1937
O. K. BUROS, ed., *Mental Measurement Year Books*, New York, Gryphon Press
H. SCHOFIELD, *Assessment and Testing*, Allen and Unwin 1972

Aptitude test
A test designed to measure a person's potential ability in a specific field of activity. There is need for considerable refinement in aptitude testing but a number of tests have been successfully used in vocational guidance and personnel selection.
See also **Aptitude**

Aquinas, Thomas (1227–74)
Medieval scholar and Church Father from whose work springs the Catholic philosophical and theological system called Thomism. Moving away from the position of St Augustine that the soul interprets sense data by divine illumination, Aquinas sought to reconcile this with the classical Greek position that knowledge is organised by an active intellect, and thus made a synthesis between Medieval Christian theology and Classical Philosophy. This intellectual tradition was taken over by the Jesuits in their methods. Education is discussed in sections of the great *Summa Theologiae* (available in translation – several editions)
F. C. COPLESTON, *Aquinas*, Penguin (Pelican) 1955, 1970

Area college
One of the types of college providing further education. Though the functions of each overlap, more advanced work (e.g. **HNC** and **sandwich courses**) is done in area than in local colleges; but less degree level work is done than in **regional colleges**.
M. ARGLES, *South Kensington to Robbins*, Longmans 1964

Area Training organisation. *See* **ATO**

Aristotle (384–322 BC)
Greek philosopher, logician, moralist, psychologist, political thinker, biologist – pupil of **Plato**.
Works: *Politics*; *Ethics*, *Organon*, *The*

Physics, *The Metaphysics*; *De Anima*; *Rhetoric*, *Poetics*.
Complete works of Aristotle in English may be found in the Loeb Classics.

Arithmetic
That part of mathematics which is concerned with numbers: the science of numbers.
See also **Arithmetical fact**
L. W. DOWNES and D. PALING, *The Teaching of Arithmetic in Primary Schools*, Oxford University Press, Unesco Handbooks 1958
Teaching Arithmetic (Journal), Pergamon

Arithmetic age
The average age of pupils obtaining a particular score on a standardised arithmetic test. Such a score can then be used to indicate a child's arithmetic level measured in years. This will be the same as his own chronological age if his arithmetical ability is average. It will be higher (or lower) than his own age if his arithmetical ability is higher (or lower) than average.
P. E. VERNON, *Intelligence and Attainment Tests*, University of London Press 1960
F. J. SCHONELL, *Diagnostic and Attainment Testing*, Oliver & Boyd 1950

Arithmetical fact
The complete statement showing the result when two numbers are associated in a particular way. e.g. the numbers 6 and 3 may be considered as being associated in the following four ways $6 + 3 = 9$; $6 - 3 = 3$; $6 \times 3 = 18$; $6 \div 3 = 2$. Each of these statements is said to be an arithmetical fact.
L. W. DOWNES and D. PALING, *Teaching Arithmetic in Primary Schools*, Oxford University Press, Unesco Handbooks 1958

Arithmetic mean
A measure of central tendency computed by adding together a set of measures or scores and dividing the total by the number of scores in the set, e.g. the arithmetic mean of the following group of scores: 2, 4, 3, 4, 2, is 3.
H. P. GARRETT, *Statistics in Psychology and Education*, 5th edn, Longmans 1958
S. R. GRIFFITHS and L. W. DOWNES, *Educational Statistics for Beginners*, Methuen 1969

Arnold, Matthew (1822–88)
English poet, critic and essayist, son of Dr **Thomas Arnold**. Inspector of Schools, 1851–86, during which time he was also Professor of Poetry at Oxford University for

two periods of five years. At government request, he visited and made reports on the state of education in several continental countries. These reports showed up the deficiencies in English education of the time. He wrote widely in the fields of literature, politics, education and religion. During the last twenty years of his life he wrote almost exclusively on social problems.

W. F. CONNELL, *The Educational Thought and Influence of Matthew Arnold*, Routledge & Kegan Paul 1950

Arnold, Thomas (1795–1842)
Headmaster of Rugby from 1828 until his death. Pioneer of public school reform. He laid great emphasis on cultivating moral standards in his school and considered the Christian religion as the indispensable foundation for this development. He resigned from the Senate of the University of London because its studies and examinations did not 'satisfy the great principle that Christianity should be the base of all education in this country'.

Arnold's work at Rugby powerfully contributed to raising the moral standard of all the public schools, and of English education generally. The employment of monitors in the government of the school and the modernisation of the curriculum, are associated with his name. It may well be that many reforms attributed to Arnold should be attributed to Samuel Butler who was headmaster at Shrewsbury and had introduced many reforms at his school a number of years before Arnold became headmaster of Rugby.

J. W. ADAMSON, *A Short History of Education*, Cambridge University Press 1919

THOMAS ARNOLD, *On Education. A selection of his writings*, ed. T. W. Bamford, Cambridge University Press 1970

T. W. BAMFORD, *Thomas Arnold*, Cresset Press 1960

N. WYMER, *Dr Arnold of Rugby*, Hale 1953

Art college
Institutions of advanced art training offering specialist and professional courses to City and Guilds, National Diploma in Design, and (in 1966) Diploma in Art and Design (five-year course). Certain colleges (the **art training centres**) offer a one-year consecutive course to Art Teachers' Diploma, a **graduate equivalent** qualification. Admission to art

colleges requires similar qualifications to those for colleges of education, e.g. at least five **GCE O** levels.

Art training centres
Institutions which offer a one-year specialized professional course of teacher training for intending teachers of art which is consecutive to an academic course; they prepare students for a recognised qualification similar to the Graduate Certificate in Education.

DEPARTMENT OF EDUCATION AND SCIENCE, *Statistics of Education*, HMSO, Annual

ATCDE; *Handbook of Education for Teaching*, Methuen

Articles of Government
A constitution drawn up by an **LEA** under the 1944 Act, with the approval of the Secretary of State, relating to maintained county secondary schools (and, by an order of the Secretary of State, for secondary **voluntary schools**) having particular reference to the respective functions of **LEA**, head teacher, and **governors**.

G. R. BARRELL, *Teachers and the Law*, Methuen 1966

G. TAYLOR and J. B. SAUNDERS, *The New Law of Education*, 7th edn, Butterworth 1971

Arts Council
A council, assisting in the provision of adult education, to encourage the appreciation of art, music and drama. It is the Council for the Encouragement of Music and the Arts (CEMA) reconstituted; and receives its grant from the Treasury rather than from the **Department of Education and Science**. As a further encouragement to the Arts, the Government which was elected in 1964 appointed a Minister of Culture.

Ascertainment
The standard legal procedure for determining a child's need for special educational treatment because of his inability to profit by normal educational opportunities.

J. KERSHAW, *Handicapped Children*, 2nd edn, Heinemann 1966

NATIONAL UNION OF TEACHERS, *Ascertainment of Educationally Subnormal Children*, Schoolmaster Publishing Co. 1961

G. TAYLOR and J. B. SAUNDERS, *The New Law of Education*, 7th edn, Butterworth 1971

Ashby, Sir Eric, FRS (b 1905   )
Master of Clare College, Cambridge. Botanist. President of British Association 1962–63. (Important Presidential address 'Investment in Man' called for massive research into Education particularly at University level.) Author of *Scientist in Russia; Technology and the Academics*, Macmillan 1958; paperback 1963; *Community of Universities*, Cambridge University Press 1963.

Assignment
A task or series of tasks allocated to the pupil or student, usually as *'prep'* or homework or private study, and sometimes in the classroom situation, especially when work is on a group or individual basis.
See also **Winnetka Plan; Dalton Plan**
A. V. ROWE, *Education of the Average Child*, Harrap 1959
C. WASHBURNE, *A Living Philosophy of Education*, John Day Co, 1940

Assimilation
1. To digest so that it becomes part of one's self. In education usually the term is used of knowledge of facts, but more broadly used of the fusion between the individual and his social group(s).
2. In the work of Piaget the process of absorbing and organizing experiences into psychic schemes or patterns around the activities which produce them: a fundamental process of learning and growth. Assimilation however is always being modified by **accommodation**, which compels the child to make modifications in his existing ways of organising experience.
R. BEARD, *An Outline of Piaget's Developmental Psychology*, Routledge & Kegan Paul, 1969
N. ISAACS, *The Growth of Understanding in the Young Child*, Ward Lock 1964
J. L. PHILLIPS, *The Origins of Intellect: Piaget's theory*, Freeman 1969
I. E. SIGEL, *Logical Thinking in Children: research based on Piaget's theory*, Holt Rinehart & Winston 1968

Assistant
1. In higher education establishments (polytechnics, universities, colleges of education, etc.) the initial grade staff appointment. The career grade is regarded as that of lecturer, and the hierarchy is to lecturer, senior lecturer, head of department, or in universities to reader and professor.
2. The name given to a language teacher from another country who is seconded to a school for a period (usually an academic year) in order to give help in language education.
3. The term is also often used to distinguish between Heads and teachers in a school.
See also **AMA**

Association of Teachers in Colleges and [University] Departments of Education. *See* **ATCDE**

Association theory
The theory that in thinking, ideas combine into complexes through their regular meeting in time or place. It is one of the early theories of learning.

Assumed mean
An arbitrary or guessed average usually near to the middle of a **frequency distribution** chosen to simplify the computation of the mean or of measures deriving from the mean.
When using an Assumed Mean, the actual Mean is computed by finding the sum of the deviations from the A.M. and then adding the sum to the Assumed Mean itself

$$\left(M = A.M. + \Sigma\frac{D}{N} \right)$$

P. E. VERNON, *Measurement of Abilities*, 2nd edn, University of London Press 1956

Asthenia
Lack of strength or vigour.

Asthenic
The type of human physique characterised by a lean, long-limbed, narrow-chested body. In E. Kretschmer's work, *Physique and Character*, the term is associated with the shy, sensitive, aloof mental type, and in cases of mental disease with schizophrenia.
E. KRETSCHMER, *Physique and Character*, 2nd edn, Routledge & Kegan Paul 1936
P. E. VERNON, *Personality Tests and Assessments*, Methuen 1953

A stream
Usually denotes the most able stream in schools where the classes are differentiated by intellectual ability. But some schools denote their **streaming** arrangements by designating some classes by a number and others by a number followed by a letter

(e.g. 2, 2A, 2B). This can be misleading to parents and others.

Atavistic
A term describing the tendency in man to revert to behaviour characteristic of the race's remote ancestors.

Ataxia
Lack of coordination of parts of the body, particularly the lack of ability to coordinate voluntary muscular movements, as in certain types of cerebral palsy. Locomotor ataxia is a disorder of the nervous system caused by syphilis, characterised by peculiar gait and difficulty in coordinating muscular movement.

ATCDE
Association of Teachers in Colleges and [University] Departments of Education. The professional association of those concerned with teacher training.
Publications include:
Education for Teaching, 3 times a year.
Handbook on Training for Teaching, Methuen
Colleges of Education for Teaching annual.
The Association also collaborates with other professional bodies (e.g. British Psychological Society, British Film Institute) to produce literature which has relevance to the training of teachers.
Address: 151 Gower Street, London WC1

Athetoid
Afflicted with athetosis, a condition caused by a lesion of the older motor centres of the brain, as in cerebral palsy. Athetosis is characterised by writhing movements which are involuntary and irregular. These movements do not happen during sleep. Severe tension often accompanies the condition. Articulation of speech is usually poor and is sometimes affected very severely.
In contrast to spasticity, which inhibits voluntary movement, athetosis is characterised by involuntary movements.
E. P. FLOYER, *A Psychological Study of a City's Cerebral Palsied Children*, British Council for the Welfare of Spastics, 1955.

Athletic type
One of Kretschmer's three basic physical types, having broad shoulders, well-developed chest, thick neck, flat abdomen and large muscles.
See also **Asthenic type**; **Pyknic type**

E. KRETSCHMER, *Physique and Character*, 2nd edn, Routledge & Kegan Paul 1936

Athletics
Games and various physical activities (generally divided into field and track events) which may be practised in schools and colleges and which usually culminate in competition e.g. interhouse or interschool.
P. W. CERUTTY, *Schoolboy Athletics*, Stanley Paul 1963
G. F. D. PEARSON, *Athletics*, Nelson 1963

ATO
Area Training Organisation. Institute of education, an organisation whose functions include (*a*) the supervision of the initial training of teachers in **colleges of education** and in **university departments of education**, (*b*) the provision of part-time and full-time courses for in-service teachers, (*c*) research in matters pertaining to education. Each institute is regionally organised, usually in the geographical area based on a university. Each has a governing body consisting of representatives from the university, the colleges of education, serving teachers, the **LEAs**, and an assessor from the **Department of Education and Science**. The institute examines candidates for the Teacher's Certificate or Teacher's Diploma and to all intents and purposes makes the award. But see *Education: A Framework for Expansion*, H.M.S.O. Cmnd 5174, 1972
Year Book of Education 1953, Evans, Section 2 ch. 2

Atomism
1. In philosophy, the theory of the school founded by Democritus, that both mind and matter are composed of atoms and that these minute atoms, although varying in size, are indestructible.
2. In psychology, any theory that maintains that the elementary units making up a conscious state are of overriding importance.
W. H. KILPATRICK, *Source Book in the Philosophy of Education*, Collier-Macmillan 1963

Attainment age. *See* Age

Attainment quotient
An index of a person's attainment relative to his chronological age, usually calculated by finding the ratio of the attainment age (e.g. in reading or arithmetic) to the chronological age and multiplying by 100, e.g.

$CA = 10.0$; Reading age $= 9.0$; Reading Quotient $= \dfrac{9}{10} \times 100 = 90$.

P. E. VERNON, *Intelligence and Attainment Tests*, University of London Press 1960

Attendance Officer or Welfare Officer

The official of the local authority whose task is to enforce the law on school attendance by home enquiries about children where reasons for absence are not known or are queried by the school. His duties and influence have in recent years increased by liaison with **Children's Officer** and **Probation Officer**. He is therefore often known as School Welfare Officer.

P. ARCHER, ed., *Social Welfare and the Citizen*, Penguin (Pelican) 1957
G. TAYLOR and J. B. SAUNDERS, *The New Law of Education*, 7th edn, Butterworth 1971
Plowden Report, *Children and their Primary Schools* 1967, Appendix 8

Attention

The adjustment of the mind and sense organs to a specific stimulus or situation, when other stimuli or situations are excluded. Attention in children cannot be understood in isolation from other factors, e.g. the teacher-child relationship, the difficulty of the work, the degree of fatigue in the child, the inherent interest of the stimulus or situation, etc.

M. D. VERNON, *The Psychology of Perception*, University of London Press 1965; Penguin (Pelican) 1970
R. S. WOODWORTH, *Psychology: A Study of Mental Life*, 10th edn, Methuen 1935

Attention-seeking

Term used to describe people whose behaviour is designed to attract attention to an inordinate degree and which may therefore be indicative of some degree of abnormality.

A. A. STONE and G. L. ONQUE: *Longitudinal Studies of Child Personality (Abstracts with index)*, Harvard University Press 1959

Attention, Span of

The length of time during which the person can concentrate on some task, activity, or object.

N. L. MUNN, *Psychology*, 5th edn, Harrap 1966

Attitude

A personality disposition affecting conduct and belief in relation to some person, institution, situation or other object, revealing itself, for example, in love or hate in degrees of intensity from person to person.
See also **Attitude scale**

A. L. EDWARDS, *Techniques of Attitude Scale Construction*, Appleton Century Crofts 1957
M. JAHODA and N. WARREN, eds, *Attitudes*, Penguin 1966
P. E. VERNON, *Personality Tests and Assessments*, Methuen 1953, ch. 9

Attitude scale

Usually a series of statements which enable the investigator to measure the testee's **attitude** towards some object or idea when the latter has endorsed or rejected the various statements contained in the scale. Two commonly used kinds of Attitude Scale are (*a*) the Thurstone scale, in which all the statements have certain values ranging between extreme 'for' and extreme 'against'; (*b*) the Likert scale, in which the attitude under consideration, or some aspect of it, is scanned in each statement, the testee in each case being required to express his own attitude in terms of agreement, disagreement or neutrality, in respect of each statement.

The individual's score is computed and such a score is interpreted by comparison with other individual scores or with the average scores of various groups, notably the group of which the individual is a member.

A. L. EDWARDS, *Techniques of Attitude Scale Construction*, Appleton-Century Crofts 1957
M. JAHODA and N. WARREN, eds, *Attitudes*, Penguin 1966
P. E. VERNON, *Personality Tests and Assessments*, Methuen 1953, ch. 9
P. E. VERNON, *Personality Assessment: a critical survey*, Tavistock 1969

Audio

Pertaining to or used in the transmission or reception of sound, cf. video.

Audio-aid

Any device which relies on sound to facilitate the learning process, e.g. gramophone records, tape-recorder. The term is also frequently used to indicate the hearing aids specially made for those with hearing loss.

P. STREVENS, *Aural Aids in Language Teaching*, Longmans 1958
Write to: The National Committee for Audio-Visual Aids in Education, 33 Queen Anne Street, London, W1

Audiometer
An instrument used to measure the power, or acuity, of hearing. Various types of audiometer are in use but they fall into two main groups: those which use speech signals and those which use tone signals.

Audio-visual aids (AVA)
Learning or teaching aids, which are visual or aural in nature, e.g. a film or a tape recording, or a combination of aural and visual as in sound film and television.
Audio-Visual Aids Centre, Paxton Place, London SE27
E. A. TAYLOR, *A Manual of Visual Presentation in Education and Training*, Pergamon 1966
D. UNWIN, ed., *Media and Methods*, McGraw-Hill 1969

Authoritarianism
In education, the method in which the educator assumes complete control in setting tasks, prescribing procedures and evaluating results, without allowing any other person(s) a share in the decision making. Contrast laissez-faire and democratic methods.
J. S. BRUBACHER, *Modern Philosophies of Education*, McGraw-Hill 1969
R. S. PETERS, *Ethics and Education*, Allen & Unwin 1966, paperback 1970, ch. 9

Authority in education
The reliance in educational policy-making on an accepted source of opinion, especially a long-standing articulate cultural tradition embodied in social groups or institutions of high prestige.
G. H. BANTOCK, *Freedom and Authority in Education*, Faber 1970
W. BOYD, ed., *Plato's Republic for Today*, Heinemann 1962
J. S. BRUBACHER, *Modern Philosophies of Education*, 3rd edn, McGraw-Hill 1950
M. V. C. JEFFREYS, *Glaucon*, Pitman 1950
L. ARNAUD REID, *Philosophy and Education*, Heinemann 1962

Authority, Local, (LEA = Local Education Authority)
Education is administered locally by county, borough, or city councils which appoint an Education Committee and employ officers, usually the Director of Education, or Chief Education Officer and his staff. Large county authorities (e.g. Lancashire) are further internally broken down into 'divisions'.

Finance is derived from local rates plus a grant from central taxation. The local authority is, in the full sense, the teacher's employer, within the state system.
H. G. DENT, *The Educational System of England and Wales*, rev. edn, University of London Press 1969
G. TAYLOR and J. B. SAUNDERS, *The New Law of Education*, 7th edn, Butterworth 1971

Autistic children
Autistic children show symptoms of their handicaps from the beginning of life. These symptoms include extreme isolation and a strong desire to avoid change. In all such children there is a disability from their earliest days to relate to people or to situations. There is a rejection of reality, and a tendency to indulge in repetitive activities and to brood.
In 1961 a British working party under the Chairmanship of Dr Mildred Creek produced a report which included nine points which might be of diagnostic value in this area. The working party expressed the unanimous opinion that 'the heart of the matter was the presence of an impaired capacity for human relationships'.
The National Society for Autistic Children was established in 1962 and School in 1965. Address: 1A Golders Green Road, London NW1
B. FURNEAUX, *The Special Child*, Penguin (Educational Special) 1969
B. RIMLAND, *Infantile Autism*, Methuen 1965
P. T. B. WESTON, ed., *Some Approaches to Teaching Autistic Children*, Pergamon Press 1965
J. K. WING, *Early Childhood Autism*, Pergamon 1967

Autonomic nervous system
That part of the nervous system of mammals which regulates the involuntary processes of the body, e.g. breathing, circulation, glandular secretion. It plays an important part in the mechanism which helps to keep the body's temperature, fluid balance, chemical composition, etc., relatively constant.
W. B. CANNON, *Bodily Changes in Pain, Hunger, Fear and Rage*, Harper & Row (Torchbooks) 1929
K. WALKER, *Human Physiology*, rev. edn, Penguin (Pelican) 1964

Auxiliary teacher
A person who, though untrained, or having

followed only a short course of training, acts as an assistant to a teacher by performing routine duties under the teacher's supervision. The intention is to relieve the teacher of non-teaching duties.

AVA. *See* **Audio-visual aids**

Average
Medium in quantity or quality: a generic term for central tendency usually expressed as the **median**, the **mode**, or **arithmetic mean**, the last meaning being the more usual one.
S. R. GRIFFITHS and L. W. DOWNES, *Educational Statistics for Beginners*, Methuen 1969

Average deviation or **mean deviation**
A measure of dispersion, or spread, of scores or measures. A group of scores will yield a **mean** or **average** score and individual scores will deviate from this mean by varying amounts. The average of these deviations constitutes the average deviation. It is rarely used in the statistics of education or psychology because it cannot, as opposed to standard deviation, form the basis of further statistical calculations.
H. E. GARRETT, *Statistics of Psychology and Education*, Longmans 1964
S. R. GRIFFITHS and L. W. DOWNES, *Educational Statistics for Beginners*, Methuen 1969
P. E. VERNON, *Measurement of Abilities*, 2nd edn, University of London Press, 1960

Avoidance reaction
A negative reaction which enables a person to escape an unpleasant or threatening object or situation.

Award
A token of recognition for some achievement. Monetary grants made by some official body (e.g. **LEAs**) often to enable people to pursue a course of study.

Axon
The long narrow extension of a nerve cell which transmits impulses from the cell body towards the next cell.

B

BA
Bachelor of Arts: the initial degree which is normally taken in the *Humanities* in the Universities of England, Wales and Northern Ireland. The initial degree in Scotland is normally the **MA**.
See also **CNAA**

Baccalaureat
A matriculation examination granted by the Ministry of National Education in France. The examination is taken in two parts, usually at the ages of 17 and 18, by French children normally on completion of their secondary studies. It is controlled at university level and is regarded as a form of matriculation requirement by the universities. It is difficult to compare in standard with the English **GCE** A level because it involves a wide range of compulsory subjects and is largely factual in character.
E. J. KING, *Other Schools and Ours*, 3rd edn, Holt, Rinehart & Winston 1967

Bachelor
Bachelor of Arts/Sciences/Music/Education, etc., the first degree of English and Welsh universities. Bachelor of Science and Bachelor of Literature are higher degrees in Oxford.
See also **BA**; **BEd**; **BSc**

Backwardness
The condition in which children are achieving considerably less than others of the same age: often used interchangeably with 'retardation'. Usually refers to failure in the basic subjects. Schonell uses *backwardness* to refer to achievement falling distinctly behind that of children of similar age and *retardation* to the unrealised margin of intellectual power which can characterise dull, normal and even supernormal pupils.
BOARD OF EDUCATION, *Backward Children*, HMSO 1937
C. BURT, *The Causes and Treatment of Backwardness*, 4th edn, University of London Press 1952
F. J. SCHONELL, *Backwardness in the Basic Subjects*, Oliver & Boyd 1942
A. E. TANSLEY and R. GULLIFORD, *Education of the Slow Learning Child*, Routledge & Kegan Paul, 1960

Balfour Act
The Education Act of 1902 passed when A. J. Balfour was prime minister. A measure which abolished **School Boards** and gave the right to provide primary and secondary education to the elected county councils and to certain large borough councils. The Act encouraged local authorities to build secondary schools and to include a system of 'free places' in Grammar Schools for pupils from elementary schools.
S. J. CURTIS and M. E. A. BOULTWOOD, *An Introductory History of English Education since 1800*, 4th edn, University Tutorial Press 1966

Barlow Report
Scientific Manpower, 1946: *see* Appendix IIIA

Bartlett, Sir Frederick Charles (b. 1888)
English psychologist. Director of the experimental psychology laboratory at Cambridge from 1922. Professor of experimental psychology at Cambridge 1931–52. His outstanding work was done in the fields of learning and social psychology and among his best known books were *Remembering: a study in experimental and social psychology* (Cambridge University Press 1932) and *The Mind at Work and Play* (Allen & Unwin 1951). He was editor of the *British Journal of Psychology* from 1924 to 1948.

Basal age (Basic age)
Usually refers to the highest year group of intellectual tasks all of which the testee can perform successfully: thus in the **Terman-Merrill** **intelligence test** the psychologist, to save time, will tentatively start the testing at some point in the scale, but is prepared to administer the tests in the previous year group until that year group of tests is reached in which the child is completely successful.

Basic English
C. K. Ogden's attempt to devise a language of 850 words of English sufficient for communication, and thus to systematise language teaching. His work has been of value in increasing the efficiency of teaching English to foreigners, and has led to developments in the teaching of reading to English children through the selection of an essential graded vocabulary. Basic English has not reached the importance that was originally anticipated because the 850 words ignore the fact that idiom can use the same words in many different senses.
C. K. OGDEN, *Basic English*, Routledge & Kegan Paul 1948

Basic subjects
The fundamental (verbal and numerical) subjects of the primary school; reading, writing, spelling, elementary arithmetic.
F. J. SCHONELL, *Backwardness in the Basic Subjects*, Oliver & Boyd 1942

Battery of tests
1. A series of group tests, each measuring a different aspect of intelligence, and separately timed. The results are then combined to give a general score.
2. A term sometimes used to cover all the tests which might be administered to a subject to give his psychological profile. e.g. it might include tests of intelligence, attainment, personality, etc., and might be given at different times.
P. E. VERNON, *Intelligence and Attainment Tests*, University of London Press 1960

BEd
Bachelor of Education: the degree in Education recommended in the **Robbins Report** to be taken by a certain percentage (25 per cent suggested in that Report) of students in Colleges of Education on successful completion of a four-year course.
Write to Registrar of particular universities.
Higher Education, Robbins Report 1963, vol. 1
'Which?' A Guide to the New Degree in Education, Careers, Research and Advisory Centre, 25 St Andrew's Street, Cambridge

Bed-wetting
Enuresis. The involuntary passing of urine during sleep. Sometimes due to physical abnormalities, it is more usually considered a symptom of maladjustment and treated by psychological rather than medical procedures.
K. SODDY, *Clinical Child Psychology*, Bailliere 1960

Behaviourism
A psychological theory which seeks to interpret behaviour as objectively as possible in terms of the actual response of the organism to stimuli. Thus a strict behaviourist does not accept the part played by conscious forces such as purpose and will. The theory thus leads to the philosophy of **determinism**.
See also **Watson**; **Skinner**

Bell shaped curve. *See* **Normal curve**

Bell–Lancaster
Dr Andrew Bell and Joseph Lancaster independently developed the **monitorial system** of elementary education in operation during the period from 1808 to about 1862. Bell was supported by the National Society (for promoting the Education of the Poor in the Principles of the Established Church, C of E 1811) and Lancaster by the British and Foreign School Society (Free Church, 1808). These schools sought to teach the rudiments of religious knowledge and the **Three Rs** principally to children over the age of six. The teacher instructed selected older pupils, the 'monitors', who then instructed groups of pupils in their turn. In this way large numbers of children could receive instruction cheaply.
H. C. BARNARD, *History of English Education from 1760*, University of London Press 1961
D. SALMON, ed., *The Practical Parts of Lancaster's Improvements and Bell's Experiments*, Cambridge University Press 1932
See also **Madras System**

Beloe Report
Secondary Schools Examinations other than GCE, the Report of a committee under the chairmanship of R. Beloe, published in 1960, regards the Ordinary Level of the **GCE** as unsuitable for many secondary school pupils and recommends: (1) the setting up of examinations at a lower level, on a subject basis; (2) the main control of these examinations to be in the hands of about twenty regional bodies on which teachers should be represented.
As a result of this Report the Minister of Education declared himself in favour of a new school-leaving certificate to be called the Certificate of Secondary Education (**CSE**).
See also Appendix IIIA
SCHOOLS COUNCIL, various Bulletins, e.g. no. 1, *CSE: some suggestions*; no. 2, *CSE Experimental Examinations: Mathematics*, HMSO 1967

Bernstein, Basil
Sociologist and authority on social determinants of education especially in linguistic development as a limiting factor in educability. Director of the Sociological Research Unit at the London University Institute of Education.
As a major factor in transmission of learning and reinforcing, language is a key determinant of successful education. The social

structure influences speech habits and differential responses are set up, otherwise than as a result of intelligence; thus the social structure affects cognition. Secondary education requires for effectiveness an extended language with a planned, discriminating, sensitive and complex vocabulary and syntax.
B. BERNSTEIN, *Class, Codes and Control*, Vol. I Routledge and Kegan Paul 1971
A. H. HALSEY, *Education Economy and Society*, Collier-Macmillan 1961 ch. 24
D. LAWTON, *Social Class Language and Education*, Routledge & Kegan Paul 1968

Beta rhythm or waves

Electrical activity of a normal brain, mainly detected in the frontal and temporal regions, showing irregular rhythmic oscillations of 18 to 30 cycles per second.
D. HILL and G. PARR, eds, *Electroencephalography*, 2nd edn, Macdonald 1963

Bias

The tendency to weight some factor or situation in favour of certain ideas or values and thus under-represent others. e.g. it might appear in (*a*) a school curriculum which offers better opportunities in some subjects; (*b*) in methods of work which favour one approach or another; (*c*) in **sampling** where certain elements of the population are over-represented.
W. J. REICHMANN, *Use and Abuse of Statistics*, Penguin (Pelican) 1964

Bilateral school

A school which provides, by means of separate **streams**, for two types of secondary education; viz. grammar-technical; technical-modern; grammar-modern.
Secondary Education (**Spens Report** 1938) Ministry of Education Circular 144, 16 June 1947

Bimodal (stats)

Having two **modes**, e.g. a frequency distribution based on the results of a standardised test and which includes only the C and A stream classes, in a three stream school will usually show a bimodal effect, i.e. the respective peak frequencies of the A and C classes, with a depression in the middle where the B class frequencies would normally have appeared.
See also **Standardisation of tests**
P. E. VERNON, *Measurement of Abilities*, 2nd edn, University of London Press 1960

Binary system

A number using base 2 (as compared with the more usual base 10), e.g. two is represented as 10 (i.e. 1 two and no units); four is represented as 100 (i.e. 1 four, no twos, and no units); 111 would mean 1 four, 1 two and 1 unit (i.e. 7 in the denary (tens) number system).

Binary system of education

The division of **higher education** into two supposedly parallel systems, proposed by the Secretary of State for Education and Science in 1965. One part, mainly comprising polytechnics, colleges of education (other than voluntary colleges) and technical colleges, is controlled by the LEAs, under the general direction of the Department of Education and Sciences. The other part comprises the universities, which preserve their traditional independence. The concept is contrary to the spirit and proposals of the **Robbins Report.** It was opposed strongly by the colleges of education, under their organisation, the **ATCDE**, and also by many teachers in Further Education.
R. LAYARD, J. KING and C. MOSER, *The Impact of Robbins*, Penguin (Education Special) 1969

Binet, Alfred (1857–1911)

French psychologist who was amongst the first to provide a persuasive experimental study of intelligence. His Intelligence Scales (1905–11) using pencil and paper and simple apparatus activities remain a fundamental tool of child study as an individual clinical test. They have been adapted for USA by **Terman** and Merrill, and revised and amplified on several occasions subsequently in America and Europe.
L. TERMAN and M. A. MERRILL, *Measurement of Intelligence*, rev. edn, Harrap 1937
G. A. MILLER, *Psychology, The Science of Mental Life*, Penguin (Pelican) 1970

Birth rate (bulge)

The annual number of children born as ascertained by the Registrar General. The sudden increase in the postwar years, which subsequently fell back, is called the 'bulge'. This reached its peak in 1947, and fell back almost to prewar levels until 1955 when the trend upwards began afresh.
J. A. BANKS, *Prosperity and Parenthood*, Routledge & Kegan Paul 1954
R. K. KELSALL, *Population*, Longmans 1967

G. LEYBOURNE and K. WHITE, *Education and the Birth Rate*, Cape 1940
Statistics of Education, HMSO, annual

Birth trauma
1. Physical injury sustained in the course of birth.
2. The psychological shock involved in the process of birth which may reveal itself in later life in the form of neurotic illness.
J. APLEY and R. M. KEITH, *The Child and his Symptoms*, Blackwell 1968
A. A. STONE and G. C. ONQUÉ, *Longitudinal Studies of Child Personality: Abstracts with index*, Harvard University Press 1959

Biserial correlation
A measure of correlation to meet the situation in which both of the correlated variables are continuously measurable, but in the one case the division is in two categories only, e.g. we may know the individual **IQs** of a group of children but, in respect of their attainments in History, we know merely whether they have been successful or unsuccessful in a particular examination.
H. E. GARRETT, *Statistics in Psychology and Education*, 6th edn, Longmans 1966

Black Papers
Three publications which appeared between 1968 and 1970 in which modern trends and developments in education were attacked. The burden of these documents is perhaps best expressed in a sentence taken from 'Letter to Members of Parliament' written by C. B. Cox and A. E. Dyson which appeared in the first *Black Paper*: 'It is our belief that disastrous mistakes are being made in modern education, and that an urgent reappraisal is required of the assumptions on which *progressive* ideas, now in the ascendant, are based.'
Black Papers, nos 1, 2 and 3, The Critical Quarterly Society

Blank (interest)
A questionnaire designed by E. K. Strong to help in educational and vocational guidance by discovering the preferred activities of people.
P. E. VERNON, *Personality Tests and Assessments*, new edn, Methuen 1953

Blind (school)
Children who have no perception of light and cannot be taught by any method involving the use of sight, may be taught by non-visual methods in schools for the blind. Those whose condition, whilst defective, enables them to profit from special methods involving the use of sight, or whose vision would suffer from following the ordinary curriculum are educated in a Partially-Sighted School.
N. GIBBS, *The Care of Young Blind Children*, Royal National Institute for the Blind
W. LIGHTFOOT, *The Partially-Sighted School*, Chatto & Windus 1948

Block grant
The annual grant made by the central Government to a local authority in respect of all local public services for which it is responsible, including education.

Block practice
Teaching practice of solid duration, lasting up to a whole term, as opposed to teaching practice of one or two days per week over a longer period.
A. COHEN and N. GARNER, ed., *A Student's Guide to Teaching Practice*, University of London Press 1963; paper back 1968
L. W. DOWNES and K. E. SHAW, 'Innovation in teaching practice, *Trends in Education*, **12**, October 1968

Block release courses
An alternative to part-time day courses involving attendance in college for periods averaging eighteen weeks or less in a year. They may consist of two or more periods of full-time study, students resuming employment in the interim period(s). They may, on the other hand, consist of one or more short period of full-time study supplemented by study on the basis of part-time day courses during another part of the year.

Block timetable
A timetable organised in such a way that long periods (e.g. half a day or a whole day) can be devoted to the various subjects: as opposed to a timetable in which pupils may have to change subject several times per day.

Board of Education
A Government Department which preceded the Ministry of Education. Set up in 1900 as a result of the Board of Education Act 1899, to replace the Committee of the Privy Council on Education which had existed since 1839. It merged the powers formerly held by

the Education Department, the Science and Art Department, and some educational powers of the Charity Commission; was replaced by the **Ministry of Education** in 1945; the name was again changed in 1964 to the **Department of Education and Science**.

L. A. SELBY-BIGGE, *The Board of Education*, Putnam 1934

Board schools

An obsolete term describing elementary schools established from 1870 onwards by **school boards** in places where schools were not otherwise provided by any voluntary society, trust or person (e.g. *British schools*, *National schools*).

C. BIRCHENOUGH, *History of Elementary Education in England and Wales*, University Tutorial Press 1932

Boarding homes

Homes other than boarding schools, maintained by an **LEA** to supply board and lodging for handicapped or deprived children. Standards of cleanliness, repair and safety must be maintained in such establishments and they are open to inspection by representatives of the Secretary of State for Education and Science.

J. STROUD, *An Introduction to the Child Care Service*, Longmans 1965

G. TAYLOR and J. B. SAUNDERS, *The New Law of Education*, 7th edn, Butterworth 1971

Boarding school

A school which admits children for meals and/or full-time accommodation in addition to tuition. Day-boarders sleep at home. Full boarders remain in school during the entire term. Most public schools operate this system.

Borderline

A more or less broad zone around the pass mark in an examination, within which cases are given special scrutiny to ensure maximum fairness. Where the examination is for selection as in 11+, selection amongst borderline cases is particularly difficult.

P. E. VERNON, ed., *Secondary School Selection*, new edn, Methuen 1957

A. YATES and D. A. PIDGEON, *Admission to Grammar Schools*, Newnes for NFER 1957

Borstal

'Open' or 'closed' residential institutions under the general supervision of the Home Office for the training of offenders aged 16 and not over 23, judged suitable by a court. The training is of a vocational and general nature, and the regime is stricter than that of **Approved Schools**, but the intention is reformatory rather than punitive. The Borstal system dates from 1908, when the first institution was set up near the village of Borstal in Kent.

T. C. N. GIBBENS, *Psychiatric Studies of Borstal Lads*, Oxford University Press 1963

R. HOOD, *Borstal Reassessed*, Heinemann 1965

J. A. F. WATSON, *The Child and the Magistrate*, new edn, Cape 1950

Braille

A system of reading and writing for the blind based on touch evolved by Louis Braille (1809–52) though based on the older system of Barbier. The various letters of the alphabet are represented by various combinations of raised dots.

Brain

That portion of the central nervous system located in the skull. It is of paramount importance in thought process, voluntary muscular control, and in regulating functions basic to life, like respiration and circulation.

W. GREY WALTER, *The Living Brain*, Duckworth 1953; Penguin (Pelican) 1968

Brevet

The Brevet d'Etudes du Premier Cycle (BEPC) is the certificate awarded to pupils who have successfully completed secondary education in France but who do not take the Baccalaureat. It is awarded by examination. (It is in some respects similar in intention to the English **CSE**)

Bright

A term often used to described personality but also used to describe the band of intelligence quotients (therefore irrespective of age) which is well above average.

See also **Intelligence**

British and Foreign School Society

Founded to establish schools for the poor. Friends took over the work of the pioneer, Joseph Lancaster, in 1808, founded the Lancasterian Society in 1810, and gave it the title, British and Foreign School Society, after Lancaster had left, in 1814. Its schools became known as **British Schools**. It still provides schools and Colleges of Education and administers a number of educational trusts.

s. j. curtis and m. e. a. boultwood, *History of Education in England*, 4th edn, University Tutorial Press 1966

j. s. maclure, *Educational Documents 1816–1967*, 2nd edn, Chapman & Hall 1968

d. salmon, ed., *The Practical Parts of Lancaster's Improvements and Bell's Experiments*, Cambridge University Press 1932

British Association for the Advancement of Science

Colloquially known as the British Association. It has eleven sections each dealing with a separate branch of science, including Education. The Association was founded in 1831 at York and holds an annual conference which may be held in any part of the British Commonwealth. It also publishes a quarterly, *Advancement of Science*. 3, Sanctuary Buildings, Gt. Smith St., London SW1

British Council

An organisation for promoting British culture throughout the world and for facilitating arrangements for people from abroad to spend a period of study in Britain. It is an autonomous organisation receiving financial support direct from the Government. It is advised by voluntary expert committees and its officers are appointed by the Government. Address: 65 Davies Street, London W1

British Schools

As opposed to the **National Schools**, British Schools were non-denominational in character though, broadly speaking, they reflected a nonconformist approach.

See also **British and Foreign School Society**

s. j. curtis and m. b. a. boultwood, *History of Education in England since 1800*, 4th edn, University of London Press 1966

j. s. maclure, *Educational Documents 1816–1967*, 2nd edn, Chapman & Hall 1968

d. salmon, ed., *The Practical Parts of Lancaster's Improvements and Bell's Experiments*, Cambridge University Press, 1932

Broadbent, Donald E.

Psychologist and Director of Applied Psychology Unit of the Medical Research Council of Great Britain. A leading behaviourist, who insists on exact scientific verification, he has made a special study of auditory perception and has published a general sum-

mary of the achievements of the behaviourist approach to psychology.

Publications include: *Perception and Communication* (Pergamon 1958) and *Behaviour* (Eyre and Spottiswood 1961)

Broadcasting

Schools Broadcasting on sound radio was begun by the BBC in 1924. By 1960–61, forty-nine programmes weekly were produced, with special regional programmes. Registered schools numbered 29,000. After pilot projects, Schools' TV by BBC began in the Autumn of 1957 and by various independent TV companies from the same year. Policy is laid down by the **Schools Broadcasting Council** and other advisory bodies.

See also **Television**

Report of Committee on Broadcasting, Cmd. 1753, HMSO 1960

Broken home

A home in which the parents of small children have separated, usually by divorce, court order or desertion. It is frequently alleged that this situation contributes greatly to conduct disorders in the children; but this hypothesis has not been fully substantiated.

b. wootton, *Social Science and Social Pathology*, Allen & Unwin 1959

Brougham, Henry (1778–1868)

Whig politician, journalist and lawyer. He was instrumental in the setting up of a parliamentary committee in 1816 'to inquire into the education of the lower orders' and introduced a Parish Schools Bill 1820; schools were to be rate-maintained with parental contributions. The Bill was withdrawn. He helped to found the Society for the Diffusion of Useful Knowledge. He was a principal mover in the foundation of a University in London in 1828, a secular institution, now University College, London.

f. hawes, *Henry Brougham*, Cape 1957

Bryce Commission

The Royal Commission on Secondary Education set up in 1894 'to consider what are the best methods of establishing a well organised system of secondary education in England'. It was the first Commission to include women, and reviewed the period since the Schools Inquiry Commission of 1868. Reporting in 1895 the commission stressed the need for unity of control over secondary

schools, greater provision and a balanced curriculum, drawing attention to the prevailing lack of these, and other conditions.
See also **Spens Report:** *Report of Consultative Committee on Secondary Education,* 1938

BSc
Bachelor of Science: the initial degree normally taken in the Sciences in Universities in England, Wales, Scotland and Northern Ireland.
See also **CNAA, Bachelor**

Bühler, Charlotte (b. 1893)
Prominent Austro-American psychologist who has made special contributions to developmental psychology of children notably in the field of language, and in social and emotional development.
Her writings include *The First Year of Life* (Day, 1930), *From Birth to Maturity* trans. C. and W. Menaker (Routledge & Kegan Paul, 1935; Humanities Press 1954), *The Child and His Family*, trans. H. Beaumont (Harper & Row 1939), *Child Problems and the Teacher* (Holt, Rinehart & Winston 1952; Routledge 1953).

Bulge
A term used to describe a particular phenomenon connected with the **birth-rate** after the 1939–45 war when there was a sharp upswing in the birth-rate which reached its peak in 1947 and then fell back. As the children born at this time moved through the schools' system, their sudden extra numbers put great strain upon educational provision. This age group and the problems associated with its passage through the schools is known as 'the bulge'.
See also **Crowther Report,** *15–18* 1959

Burnham Committee(s)
Originally established in 1919 under the chairmanship of Lord Burnham. The Burnham Committees have the task of recommending to the Secretary of State for Education and Science salary scales for teachers in various educational institutions. Teachers and local education authorities (LEAs) are represented on the various committees whose chairman is selected by the Secretary of State and whose recommendations may be accepted or rejected but not modified by the Secretary of State. The Burnham Main Committee deals with

salaries of teachers i n primary and secondary schools. Committees other than Burnham deal with salaries in other branches of education, e.g. the Pelham Committee with salaries in **Colleges of Education**. Salary scales approved by the Secretary of State are made binding on LEAs.
G. TAYLOR and J. B. SAUNDERS, *The New Law of Education*, 7th edn, Butterworth 1971
G. R. BARRELL, *Teachers and the Law*, Methuen 1966

Burnham Scale. *See* **Burnham Committees**

Bursary
An award or grant as cash or remission of fees, to enable scholars to proceed to fee-paying schools or **higher education**; usually gained by examination.

Burt, Sir Cyril (1883–1971)
Psychologist to the London County Council Education Department 1913–32, probably the first such appointment in the world. Professor of Education and then Professor of Psychology at the University of London: Emeritus Professor from 1950.
Publications include: *The Distribution of Educational Abilities* (King & Son 1917, new edn, Staples Press, 1948); *Mental and Scholastic Tests* (1921, 4th edn, Staples Press 1964); *Handbook of Tests* (King & Son 1928); new edn, Staples Press 1948); *The Young Delinquent* (University of London Press 1925); *The Measurement of Mental Capacities* (P. S. King 1927); *How the Mind Works* (with E. Jones, E. Miller and W. Moodie) Allen & Unwin 1933); *The Subnormal Mind* (University of London Heath Clark Lectures) (Oxford University Press 1935); *The Backward Child*, 4th edn (University of London Press 1937); *Factors of the Mind* (University of London Press 1940); *The Causes and Treatment of Backwardness*, 4th edn (University of London Press 1952); *A Psychological Study of Typography*, (Cambridge University Press 1959).

Burt-Vernon Test
The **word recognition test** originally devised by **Sir Cyril Burt** and rearranged by P. E. Vernon in 1938, having a reading-age range from 4 to 15.
P. E. VERNON, *The Standardisation of a Graded Word Reading Test*, University of London Press 1938

Butler Act

The Education Act of 1944 which was passed when R. A. Butler was President of the **Board of Education**. It abolished the Board of Education, established instead a **Ministry of Education**, and authorised the appointment of a **Minister of Education**. The Act gave considerably greater scope and power to the Minister than the President had enjoyed previously. It sought to coordinate fully a national system of education to be organised in three successive stages – primary, secondary, further. The Act thus eliminated the concept of elementary education and introduced the idea of 'secondary education for all'.

G. R. BARRELL, *Teachers and the Law*, Methuen 1966

H. C. DENT, *The Educational System of England and Wales*, rev. edn, University of London Press 1969

W. O. LESTER SMITH, *Government of Education*, Penguin (Pelican) 1965

M. M. WELLS and J. B. TAYLOR, *The New Law of Education*, 7th edn, Butterworth 1971

C

Campus

American word for the grounds of an educational institution or of a related group of educational institutions on which the buildings are situated and which might contain other space in the immediate neighbourhood belonging to the institution.

CAP

Certificat d'Aptitude Pédagogique. The certificate awarded to the French primary or elementary school teacher (instituteur), at the end of the training course, and which attests his status as a qualified (titulaire) teacher for that branch of the educational system.

Capacity

Potential, usually in relation to mental activity. A person may be said, in this sense, to be working up to capacity or below capacity. In a more general sense it is the extent to which a person effectively accepts new tasks.

CAPES

Certificat d'Aptitude Pédagogique d'Etudes Secondaires. The certificate awarded to French graduate teachers which attests their status as trained graduates. Until 1965 it was awarded on the result of examination and inspection, but is now awarded after the end of a probationary period as the result of a favourable report by an inspector.

CAPET

Certificat d'Aptitude Pédagogique d'Etudes Techniques. A certificate similar to the above for graduate teachers in technical institutions.

Capitation allowance

A cash allowance given to a school at the rate of so much per head according to numbers on the register, to cover costs of books, apparatus and other expendable educational materials.

Cardinal number

A number indicating how many there are in any group or set of objects: as opposed to ordinal number which indicates the position of a particular member of a set or group, e.g. the cardinal number 5 indicates the total number in a particular set of objects. The ordinal number 5 indicates the fifth position when the set is considered in order.

E. CHURCHILL, *Counting and Measuring*, Routledge & Kegan Paul 1961
J. PIAGET, *The Child's Conception of Number*, Routledge & Kegan Paul 1952

Care and protection

Section 2 of the Children and Young Persons Act 1962 sets out the conditions under which a court may find a child who has not committed an offence to be in the need of care and protection: briefly such a child is seriously neglected, ill-treated or in moral danger. A Place of Safety Order will be taken out and the child brought before a Juvenile Court within 28 days, and may be taken into care of the local authority or a fit person.
See also **Fit Person Order**
W. C. HALL and A. C. L. MORRISON, *Law Relating to Children and Young Persons*, 7th edn, Banwell and Nicol (Butterworth) 1967
J. STROUD, *Introduction to Child Care Service*, Longmans 1965

Careers Research and Advisory Centre (CRAC). *See* Vocational Guidance

Caretaker

The person officially appointed to carry out and/or supervise the cleaning, heating and general maintenance of the school buildings and grounds.

Carnegie Trusts

Various trusts established by Andrew Carnegie who emigrated from Scotland to the USA in 1848. He amassed great wealth as an industrialist and retired in 1901 to devote himself to the distribution of his wealth by the formation of various financial trusts for social and educational advancement in the USA, Britain and the English-speaking world.

Carpal age

The bone development of an individual in comparison with that of people of similar chronological age as measured by the development of the wrist bones.
J. M. TANNER, *Growth at Adolescence*, 2nd edn, Blackwell 1969, ch. 4
J. M. TANNER, *Education and Physical Growth*, University of London Press 1961

CASE

Confederation for the Advancement of State Education. Its main aim as stated in a policy statement passed by the Annual General

Meeting in 1966 is as follows: 'The main aim of CASE is to secure the improvement and extension of all facilities and opportunities in the field of education which are wholly or in part financed from public funds.'
Address: National Secretary, 42 Meadow Hill Road, Birmingham 30

Case conference
A meeting of interested parties (e.g. teacher, social worker, house parent, doctor, psychologist, probation officer, etc.) to discuss and coordinate work on a current case (a person or family requiring assistance, care, supervision, remedial treatment, etc.)
J. KASTELL, *Casework in Child Care*, Routledge & Kegan Paul 1962, ch. 8
N. TIMMS, *Social Casework*, Routledge & Kegan Paul 1964

Case history
Detailed official report, usually following a chronological pattern, of the facts and circumstances concerning an individual under investigation; usually consisting of data of a medical, educational and personal nature, and intended to guide remedial or corrective treatment.
J. KASTELL, *Casework in Child Care*, Routledge & Kegan Paul 1962

Case load
The number of current cases (i.e. persons or families requiring professional assistance, interest, or supervision) undertaken by a social worker, probation or after care officer as his personal responsibility. The term is therefore used as a measure of the pressure of work on the individual social worker, or as a measure of the community's need or as a criterion for deciding whether new cases can be taken on.
J. KING, *The Probation Service*, Butterworth 1969, ch. 1
J. STROUD, *Introduction to the Child Care Service*, Longmans 1965

Casework (Social)
A professional method by which trained workers may assist individuals and families requiring support and guidance through home visits. The caseworker assesses the need and arranges for provision of social services, at the same time accepting a degree of personal responsibility for guiding the family.
J. KASTELL, *Casework in Child Care*, Routledge & Kegan Paul 1962

N. TIMMS, *Social Casework*, Routledge & Kegan Paul 1964

Catechetical (method)
Ancient method of teaching, based on rote learning and oral recitation of answers in response to set questions.
See also **Questioning**

Catharsis
1. The purging of feelings (e.g. fear and anger) in one who observes great tragedy on the stage (Aristotle).
2. The working off in play of natural impulses, which were once biologically important (aggression – fear) but which in the civilised state are irrelevant or requiring redirection.
3. In **psychoanalysis**, the process characterised by the release of repressed emotion by 'reliving' past experiences.
See also **Abreaction**.

Cathexis
A build-up of mental energy in relation to some idea, memory, course of thought, or action.

CAT
College of Advanced Technology. National CATS were set up to implement the White Paper *Technical Education* and the Ministry of Education Circular 305/56 in 1956. They were intended to form the apex of the Local-Area-Regional system of English Technical Education. Full-time and **sandwich** courses were provided leading to the award of Dip. Tech. As from 1st April 1962 all CATs became direct grant institutions and ceased to be maintained by LEAs. Following the recommendations in the **Robbins Report** on Higher Education, the Government accepted that these colleges should have university status.
M. ARGLES, *South Kensington to Robbins*, Longmans 1964
M. JAHODA, *The Education of Technologists*, Tavistock 1963
H. C. DENT, *Year Book of Technical Education and Careers in Industry*, A. and C. Black (annual)

Cattell, J. M. (1860–1944)
American psychologist who through his writings and research influenced psychology towards the use of objective methods, the study of individual differences and the use of mental tests.

Cattell, Raymond B. (b. 1905)

Research Professor in Psychology and Director of the Laboratory of Personality Assessment at the University of Illinois. Born in Devonshire, Cattell's first degree at London University was in chemistry. After spending some years working with such distinguished psychologists as **Spearman** and **Thorndike**, Cattell developed a special interest in the field of human motivation and personality study. He has written widely on these subjects and is dedicated to putting the study of personality on a firm quantitative and experimental basis. His works include *The Scientific Analysis of Personality*, Penguin (Pelican) 1965

CCTV (closed circuit television). *See* **Television**

CEG

Collèges d'Enseignement Générale. Secondary schools which in France replaced the **Cours Complémentaires** to provide secondary education of a less academic type than the **Lycées**. Pupils may take the Brevet d'Etudes du Premier Cycle (BEPC) or they may transfer to Lycée to take the **Baccalaureat**.

CEMA. *See* **Arts Council**

Central school

Prior to the reorganisation of elementary schools into primary and secondary stages, some large towns, notably London and Manchester, set up schools other than grammar and technical schools which gave a purely post-primary education. From their location these were called central schools.
SIR H. HADOW, *Education of the Adolescent*, HMSO 1926

Central tendency (stats)

The tendency of scores or measures in a distribution to cluster about a point usually near the mid point between the extremes of the distribution, its measure being expressed in **mode** or **(arithmetic) mean**, or **median**.
H. GARRETT, Statistics in Psychology and Education (Longmans) 1964
S. R. GRIFFITHS and L. W. DOWNES, *Educational Statistics for Beginners*, Methuen 1969
P. E. VERNON, *Measurement of Abilities*, 2nd edn, University of London Press 1940

K.W.E.—2*

Central Welsh Board

The coordinating body for the Welsh Intermediate Schools which were established by the Welsh Intermediate Education Act of 1889. It was succeeded by the Joint Welsh Board and this, in turn, by the Welsh Joint Education Committee in 1949.

Centre of interest

A unit of work arising naturally out of pupils' interest and experience which is pursued irrespective of subject boundaries, e.g. a local fair with its history, life of fairground people, nature of business and amusements, etc. It may therefore involve reading, writing, art, drama, music, mathematics. This kind of work is more easily carried out in primary schools because of non-specialisation and fluidity of timetable but it is not impossible at secondary level.
See also **Project**
B. ASH and B. RAPAPORT, *Creative Work in the Junior School*, Methuen 1957 (paperback 1968)
M. V. DANIEL, *Activity in the Primary School*, Blackwell 1947
K. RICHMOND, *Purpose in the Junior School*, Redman 1949
A. W. ROWE, *The Education of the Average Child*, Harrap 1959
E. B. WARR, *Social Experience in the Junior School*, Methuen 1951

Centres d'Apprentissage

Training centres for industrial operatives, under the French Ministry of National Education, set up in 1939. A free training, for three years, is offered which consists, in equal parts, of workshop and technical-general education. The course leads to the certificate of Professional Aptitude in a trade. There are also privately run centres.

CEP

Certificat d'Etudes Primaires. The certificate awarded to the pupil who successfully completes elementary education in France, and which is necessary to admit him to, for example, apprenticeship courses.

Cerebellum

Literally 'little brain'. The part of the brain which comes at the top of the spinal cord, above and behind the medulla.

Cerebration
Action of the **brain**, conscious or unconscious. Sometimes used loosely to mean 'thinking'. W. GREY WALTER, *The Living Brain*, Duckworth 1953; Penguin (Pelican) 1968

Cerebrum
The front and larger part of the **brain** which deals with the higher thought processes.

Certificat d'Aptitude *see* **CAP**; **CAPES**; **CAPET**

Certificat d'Etude Primaire *see* **CEP**

Certificate (Education)
An authentic statement of the nature and extent of the recipient's success in scholastic and/or professional achievement, e.g General Certificate of Education (**GCE**), or Certificate of Secondary Education (**CSE**).

Certificated teacher
A teacher who is recognised by the Department of Education and Science as fully trained and qualified as a result of completing a course of training (now normally three years) leading to the award of the certificate of a university institute of education. Training is usually at a college of education. Suitably qualified and 'mature' students may become qualified after a two-year course. Graduates and graduate equivalents normally take a one-year course at a college of educaton or at a department of education of a university.
ATCDE, *Handbook of Teaching*, Methuen, Annual

CES
Collèges d'Enseignement Secondaires. A new type of more comprehensive secondary school of which there were 15 in 1965; they are expected to increase rapidly to replace **CEG** within the French secondary school system.

Chair (professional)
A position of high academic eminence in a university. The occupant of a university chair has a professorial title and is normally head of a department or school.

Chalk-talk
The method of teaching which tends to rely excessively on 'passive' methods of learning, in which the teacher presents his subject matter in a predigested form (usually oral) and in which he underestimates the learner's need for **activity** in the learning situation.

Chance
The way things occur in the absence of plan or design, or are due to a complex of factors whose detailed operations are not understood. The way 'chance' factors operate is an important part of the study of **statistics**.

Chancellor (of university)
The nominal head of a university, usually a public figure such as a member of the Royal Family or a prominent politician: e.g. the late Sir W. Churchill was Chancellor of the University of Bristol.

Character
The integrating factor in personality. A structure of lasting characteristics which gives a person individuality; recognised in his activity, particularly in dealing with **conflict**. Character is manifested in the peculiar way in which a person brings to bear the instinctive, emotional and intellectual aspects of his personality on the performance of his various social roles – viz. as father, teacher, employer, citizen. This systematic conduct usually exhibits the influence of ethical code or set of values; hence character is usually related to moral judgement, and popularly assessed by the strength with which moral decisions are implemented and moral opinions held.
J. S. BRUBACHER, *Modern Philosophies of Education*, new edn., McGraw-Hill 1969
J. A. HADFIELD, *Psychology and Morals*, Methuen 1965

Charity Commissioners
The Board of Charity Commissioners set up by the Charitable Trusts Act 1853 took over the powers of the **Endowed Schools Commission** in 1874 to draw up schemes for the reform of individual endowed schools by altering foundation deeds that were clearly obsolete and an obstacle to the betterment of the school. They often used funds thus released to provide girls' schools. By 1894 the Commissioners (Endowed and Charity) had made 851 original and 127 amending schemes. They lost their powers to the Board of Education in 1899.
P. H. J. H. GOSDEN, *The Development of Educational Administration in England and Wales*, Blackwell 1966
Spens Report, *Secondary Education* 1938

Charity Schools

Schools founded for poor pupils by bene-factors, individual or group, under special statutes.

M. G. JONES, *The Charity School Movement*, Cambridge University Press 1938; new edn, Cass 1963

Check list

A list of points to be observed or investi-gated by a **field worker** (*see* **field work**); an aide-mémoire and rough method of stan-dardising observations, etc., carried out simultaneously by several workers, therefore making the observations amenable to quan-titative or statistical treatment.

Chi-square test (χ^2)

A single and direct test of **significance** where the observations can be classified into dis-crete categories and treated as frequencies. A useful method of comparing experimen-tally obtained results with those expected on the basis of some hypothesis, e.g. in testing a new method of teaching reading, two com-parable groups of children might be taught, one by the new method and one by a tradi-tional method, individual pupils after a period being divided into 'improved' and 'considerably improved'.

H. E. GARRETT, *Statistics in Psychology and Education*, 6th edn, Longmans 1966
C. MCCULLOUGH and L. VAN ATTA, *Statistical Concepts*, McGraw-Hill 1963

Chief Education Officer

The chief administrative officer of an **LEA** appointed by the LEA in consultation with the Secretary of State and subject to his approval.

Child and young person

The legal definitions of the terms (*a*) child and (*b*) young person, are given by the 1944 Education Act Section 114 as (*a*) a person who is not over compulsory school age, and (*b*) a person who is no longer a child but is under the age of eighteen years. (Section 8 of the 1946 Act extends the meaning of (*b*) so that, for the purposes of the Act, a person is deemed not to have reached the age of eighteen until the end of the term in which his birthday falls.)
See also **Children** Acts; Appendix II, Education Acts
G. R. BARRELL, *Teachers and the Law*, Methuen 1966

Child Care Officer

Field worker appointed to the staff of the Children's Department of a local authority and responsible to its **Children's Officer**. Before 1960, they were called Boarding Out Officers or Children's Visitors. They have many duties connected with the reception of children into the care of the local authority, boarding out, fostering, adoption and helping families where children are at risk.

J. STROUD, *An Introduction to the Child Care Service*, Longmans 1965

Child-centred

Governed by considerations of children's needs and interests. Child-centred, as opposed to teacher-centred, classrooms would be seen to involve activity and experience by the children rather than the passive accep-tance of factual material given to them by the teacher.

M. V. DANIEL, *Activity in the Primary School*, Blackwell 1947

Child development

The dynamic process of emergence and interaction of physical, psychological and social changes in the growing child. The study, accurate and systematic description, and the detection of patterns and stages in this process is a central interest of child psy-chology in the work, for example, of **Susan Isaacs**, **J. Piaget**, A. Gesell.

J. H. S. BOSSARD and E. S. BOLL, *Sociology of Child Development*, 4th edn, Harper & Row 1966
M. E. BRECKENRIDGE and M. N. MURPHY, *Growth and Development of the Young Child*, 8th edn, W. B. Saunders 1969
P. M. PICKARD, *Psychology of Developing Children*, Longman 1970

Child guidance. *See* Clinic, Child Guidance

Child neglect

Failure to provide a child adequately with care, shelter, food or discipline or similar failure on the part of a parent or guardian to meet his responsibilities to a child. In severe cases a criminal prosecution may ensue.

H. WILSON, *Delinquency and Child Neglect*, Allen & Unwin 1962

Child psychology

The branch of psychology that makes a special study of the behaviour and development of children in the period prior to adolescence and explains child growth and change in the light of the knowledge and principles discovered.

L. CARMICHAEL, ed., *Manual of Child Psychology*, 2nd edn, Wiley 1954
A. GESELL, *The First Five Years of Life*, new edn, Methuen 1955 (and other works)
K. LOVELL, *Educational Psychology and Children*, University of London Press 1969
P. M. PICKARD, *Psychology of Developing Children*, Longman 1970

Child study

The study of the growth and development of children on the assumption that the content and methods of education should be closely related to a thorough understanding of the nature, needs and interests of children.
See the series of books edited by the NATIONAL CHILDREN'S BUREAU (1 Fitzroy Square, London WC1) under the general title *Studies in Child Development*, published in association with Longman).

Child Study Movement

The British Child Study Association was founded in 1894 and in 1907 amalgamated with the Childhood Society, founded in 1896; a journal was published from 1899 to 1921. The movement is associated with the names principally of **C. Burt, Susan Isaacs**, and **C. W. Valentine**; and much valuable work was done in the field of psychological study of children, particularly their intellectual and social development.

L. S. HEARNSHAW, *A Short History of British Psychology 1840–1940*, Methuen 1964

Child welfare

The statutory responsibility for child welfare lies primarily with the parents. Where these cannot, for whatever reason, exercise this responsibility, it devolves on the local authority, e.g. the county or county borough council through a **Children's Committee** to which the **Children's Officer** is responsible. If children are brought before the courts for any reason, the responsibility may ultimately rest with the Home Office: e.g. when a child or young person is found guilty of an offence or for other reasons committed to an Approved School.

P. ARCHER, *Social Welfare of the Citizen*, Penguin 1957
J. STROUD, *Introduction to the Childcare Service*, Longmans 1965

Children Acts

Children Act 1908.
Children and Young Persons Act 1932 (amended 1952 and 1956).
Young Persons Act 1933.
Children Act 1948.
Children and Young Persons Act 1963.

H. ELGIN, *The Law and the Teacher*, Ward Lock 1967
A. E. IKIN, *Children and Young Persons Act 1933*, Pitman 1933
G. G. RAPHAEL, *Children and Young Persons Acts*, Eyre and Spottiswoode 1932

Children's Centre

The **Plowden Report** (ch. 9) recommended that Nursery provision for preschool children should be expanded through the use of units in which clinics or day nurseries should be set up with two or three nursery groups, each of about twenty places and staffed by trained nursery assistants under the ultimate supervision of a qualified teacher.

Children's Committee

A Committee of a County Council or County Borough Council whose function is to oversee the work of the **Children's Officer** and his/her staff in the execution of the Council's statutory duties in the field of child care, e.g. committal to care, reception, boarding out, long term residential care and adoption of children. The Committee is appointed under the Children Act 1948 (*see* Appendix II) which was a result of the **Curtis Report**. There are also, under this Act, two Advisory Councils for Child Care (one for England and Wales, and one for Scotland).

J. STROUD, *An Introduction to the Child Care Service*, Longmans 1965

Children's Department

A department of the Home Office responsible for the administration of the Child Care Service, **remand** homes and **approved schools**, supervision of adoption procedures and conditions of employment of children.
Report on the work of the Children's Department, HMSO 1964 and triennially.

Children's Departments (LEA)

Nationwide local organisations financed from both local and national funds to ensure at least minimum care for children lacking temporarily or permanently the care of a responsible adult, and who are unable or incompetent to look after themselves. Their duties are to receive into care, and act on behalf of the local Authority in the organisation and running of **children's homes** and **foster homes** and in the supervision of the work of **foster parents**. Under direction of **Children's Committee** and supervision of **Children's Officer**.

Children and Young Persons Act 1933; Children's Act 1948

KENNETH BRILL, *Children – Not Cases*, National Children's Home 1962

KENNETH BRILL, *Children in Homes*, Gollancz 1964

Report of the Work of the Children's Department, HMSO, Bi-ennial

Children's fears

A symptom of anxiety which shows itself as a form of withdrawal sometimes culminating in flight. The pattern of fears changes as the child develops, and is not consistent over large groups of children. It may be caused by a variety of external and internal psychological factors but their occurrence, unless excessive, is common enough to be considered normal. Common fears are of noise, loss of support, the unfamiliar, animals, darkness, being abandoned, mutilation, imaginary creatures, etc.

F. W. CLEMENTS and B. P. MCCLOSKEY, *Child Health*, E. Arnold 1964

L. CARMICHAEL, ed., *Manual of Child Psychology*, 2nd edn, Wiley 1954

B. SPOCK, *Baby and Child Care*, new rev. edn, New English Library 1969

C. W. VALENTINE, *The Psychology of Early Childhood*, 4th edn, Methuen 1950

Children's Home

A residential institution for children committed to the care of the local authority or voluntary body whether temporary or long term.

J. STROUD, *Introduction to the Child Care Service*, Longmans 1965

Children's Officer

Official of the **Children's Department**, of the LEA responsible for children who enter the care of the local authority, and for the organisation of a service to meet their needs: short-term residential care, placement and fostering, adoption, preventive and rehabilitative casework, supervision of non-residential and post-residential cases.

J. KASTELL, *Casework in Child Care*, Routledge & Kegan Paul 1962

J. STROUD, *The Child Care Service*, Longmans 1965

Chorea (St Vitus Dance)

A disease of childhood, associated with rheumatic fever, and giving rise to irregular purposeless muscular movements. Associated with emotional instability and changes in the cerebral cortex and central nervous system, the disease may present serious obstacles to the educational progress of the child.

D. PATTERSON, *Sick Children*, ed. R. LIGHTWOOD and F. S. W. BRIMBLECOMBE, Bailliere 1963

Chronological age

A person's age as computed from his date of birth as opposed to his **mental** or **attainment** age obtained from tests and similar measuring or estimating procedures.

CHUDE

Conference of the Heads of University Departments of Education.

Church school

A large majority of former denominational primary and secondary schools are now **controlled** or **aided** by the LEAs. Some of them are still loosely referred to as 'church' schools, particularly if they have Church of England foundations.

CID

Conference of Institute Directors, the semi-permanent body which enables directors of the university Institutes of Education to meet for discussions and to make decisions of common policy.

See also **Institutes of Schools or education**

City and Guilds of London Institute (for the Advancement of Technical Education.)

A public body founded 1878 (Royal Charter 1900) to advance technical and scientific education and to examine students within the technical and commercial field at further education level and usually at the craft, skilled operative, or clerical level. Its examinations are primarily directed to the needs of the industrial employee. General Regulations (annual) from 76 Portland Place, London, W1

M. ARGLES, *South Kensington to Robbins*, Longmans 1964

Civics

A school curriculum subject intended to

promote good and informed citizenship through the study of elementary economics, public administration, local and national government, etc.

J. DRAY and D. JORDAN, A Handbook of Social Studies, new edn, Methuen 1950

ASSOCIATION FOR EDUCATION IN CITIZENSHIP, Education for Citizenship in Secondary Schools, Oxford University Press 1946

CLASP
Consortium of Local Authorities Special Programme. A consortium of LEAs which cooperates with the Department of Education and Science and the Ministry of Public Building and Works. Two purposes led to the establishment of CLASP and succeeding Consortia (a) by pooling resources, to cheapen school building; (b) to rationalise building methods.

Class (sociological)
Large groupings of population, usually by occupation and education, in a status order ranging from unskilled workers to executives; used for classification by Registrar General, and by sociologists and others to describe social organisation.

E. E. BERGEL, Social Stratification, McGraw-Hill 1962

G. D. H. COLE, Studies in Class Structure, Routledge & Kegan Paul 1955

J. KLEIN, Samples from English Cultures, Routledge & Kegan Paul 1965

Class, Extramural (university)
Adult education class arranged by the extramural department of a university and taught by university teachers. Courses are academic but do not lead to a recognised qualification; they are usually cultural in content. Pamphlets which give information on extramural opportunities can normally be obtained by writing to the extramural tutor of the nearest university.

Class interval, or step interval
A statistical term indicating a range of values on a quantitative scale. The range is sufficiently narrow, however, for all the cases falling within its limits to be regarded as having the same central value without detriment to the degree of accuracy required in the exercise.

P. E. VERNON, The Measurement of Abilities, 2nd edn, University of London Press 1956

Class list
The results of first degree university examinations, published often in three or four divisions; a graduate is thus said to have a 'first', 'upper second' degree, etc.

The term is also used in schools to indicate the results of internal examinations.

Class teaching
Teaching all the members of the class simultaneously, as opposed to group teaching, or teaching on an individual basis. Activity methods in educating children have tended in recent decades to minimise the importance of class teaching.

Classes, size of
Since it is generally recognised that size of classes is related to the effectiveness of teaching some upper limit is held to be desirable. Classes tend to be smaller in direct grant schools than in maintained schools, and smaller still in private schools. In the industrial areas of the UK the tendency is for classes in state schools to be larger than in other parts of the country.

Plowden Report, Children and their Primary Schools 1967

Statistics of Education, HMSO, annual vol. 1

Classic
A standard work in any subject, e.g. Newton's Principia Mathematica, Darwin's Voyage of the Beagle

Classicist
One who is versed in the classics or devoted to maintaining their eminence in education.

Classics
(a) Greek, Roman or more modern writers of the first rank.

(b) Their written or recorded works.

(c) The study of the great works in Greek and Latin (including Ancient History).

AMA, The Teaching of Classics, Cambridge University Press 1961

Ministry of Education, pamphlet no. 37, Suggestions for the Teaching of Classics, HMSO 1959

Classification test
A mental test requiring the testees to indicate which objects (in the form of drawings or words) belong together, by crossing out the item(s) not belonging. Sometimes loosely used to mean a test, or tests, for putting

children into relatively homogeneous groups.
P. E. VERNON, *Intelligence and Attainment Tests*, University of London Press 1960

Classifying school
After a court appearance children who are made the subject of an **Approved School** Order are in the great majority of cases sent first to a classifying school. After observation and testing by the staff which includes teachers, psychologists and other specialists, they are transferred to an approved school with a suitable regime.

CLAW. *See* Consortia

Clearing house
Bodies acting as central agencies which exist to organize the admission of students to colleges of education and universities respectively by attempting to match applications and places available.
See also **ATCDE, UCCA**

Clearing House (Colleges of Education)
The Colleges of Education Clearing House was established by the Council of Principals in 1933 and its activities taken over by the **ATCDE** in 1943. It arose in order to eliminate the confusion arising from haphazard and simultaneous applications for college places. Roman Catholic and domestic science colleges entered the scheme in 1959.
Address: The Registrar, T.C.C.H., 151 Gower Street, London, WC1
See also **UCCA**

Clever Hans
A horse trained by Von Osten in Elberfield, Germany, which, it was claimed, could carry out difficult arithmetical operations. Many other horses were trained by Von Osten, and Krall trained still more later. It has been shown that these tricks depended, not on arithmetical ability, but on the ability to respond to certain signs given consciously or unconsciously by the trainer.
D. KATZ, *Animals and Men*, Penguin (Pelican) 1953 ch. 1

Clinic
A centre for diagnosis and treatment of some disorder – physical, mental, behavioural.

Clinic, Child Guidance
A centre for dealing with children suffering from educational or behavioural problems.

Such a clinic will normally have a team consisting of a psychiatrist, an educational psychologist, a psychiatric social worker and, sometimes, a remedial teacher.
W. M. BURBURY, E. M. BALINT and B. J. YAPP, *An Introduction to Child Guidance*, Macmillan 1945
M. F. CLEUGH, *Psychology in the Service of the School*, Methuen 1951, ch. 9

Clinical Psychologist
A psychologist whose qualifications and training fit him for work in a clinic, e.g. Child Guidance Clinic. Usually such a person holds a degree in psychology and has received suitable professional training, such as leads to a university diploma. Clinical psychologists are usually members of the British Psychological Society.

CNAA
The Council for National Academic Awards. The first non-university body in this country empowered to award degrees. Its predecessor was the **NCTA**, which awarded the Diploma in Technology. The Robbins report published in October, 1963, proposed that the CNAA, with powers to award degrees should be instituted, and in September, 1964, the Council received its Royal Charter.
The Governing Body of the CNAA is a Council comprising a Chairman and twenty-one appointed members, one-third drawn from the universities (including the former **CATS**), one-third from establishments of further education other than universities, and the remainder from industry, commerce and local authorities.
Colleges who wish students to study for the Council's degrees have to submit their courses for approval. The Council also has to be satisfied concerning the qualifications of the academic staff, the standard of work in the subject at the college, the available facilities, the curriculum of the proposed course, arrangements for practical training, the admissions standards and the arrangements for examinations.
Entry qualifications for these degree courses are five **GCE** passes, including two suitable subjects at A level, or four passes with three at A level or an equivalent qualification.
The Council's courses and awards overlap to some extent those of the London University external courses and degrees.
The council may also award higher degrees: MA, MSc, MPhil, and PhD.

Compendium of Degree Courses obtainable from 3 Devonshire St., London

Coaching
Special tuition, usually on an individual basis, designed to promote improvement in some skill.

Coaching effect
The improvement that is due to familiarisation by coaching. Thus, in intelligence tests, the reference is to improvement in score which is not necessarily an indication of an improvement in intelligence.

P. E. VERNON, *Intelligence and Attainment Tests*, University of London Press 1960

Code
1. *Revised Code.* A notorious administrative procedure introduced by R. Lowe in 1862 which made the subsidy payments and teachers' pay dependent on results obtained by pupils during tests administered by visiting inspectors. The **Payment by Results** system was gradually whittled away over the next 30–35 years.
2. A type of translation question often used as items in intelligence tests.

G. A. N. LOWNDES, *The Silent Social Revolution*, Oxford University Press 1937
B. SIMON, *Studies in the History of Education*, Lawrence & Wishart 1960

Coeducation
The education of boys and girls in the same school or environment.

R. R. DALE, *Mixed or Single Sex School?* Routledge & Kegan Paul 1969

Coefficient
An index of the degree in which some characteristic or relationship is present, as in **correlation** coefficient.

Cognition
The act or faculty of knowing, beyond mere awareness, usually as distinguished from willing and feeling (volition, affection). Cognitive theories of learning infer brain processes such as memories and expectations, and are in this way distinct from stimulus-response theories of learning.

B. R. BUGELSKI, *The Psychology of Learning*, Methuen 1963
R. BURGER and A. E. M. SEABORNE, *The Psychology of Learning*, Penguin (Pelican) 1966

E. R. HILGARD, *Theories of Learning*, 2nd edn, Methuen 1959, ch. 1

College
Name given to certain secondary schools especially in the private sector, e.g. Eton College; and to many institutions of further and higher education, e.g. technical colleges, colleges of further education; of aeronautics; of education; of commerce. It is also applied to **colleges of universities**.

Collèges d'Enseignement Générale, Secondaires. *See* CEG; CES

College of commerce
Municipal institution of **further** and **higher education** providing part- and full-time courses leading to university external, professional, and similar qualifications, in commerce and associated subjects, e.g. languages, economics, administration, law, etc.

College of education
Higher education institution offering courses in academic and professional studies to intending teachers, leading to the Certificate of Education of the university institute of education of which the college forms part, and to the Graduate Certificate in Education; from 1965 also to **B Ed** degree. Supplementary courses of varying duration are offered by many Colleges. The majority of Colleges of Education are maintained by LEAs, but a substantial number are controlled by Voluntary Bodies, e.g. the Church of England.

ATCDE, *Handbook of Training for Teaching*, Methuen, Annual
McNair Report, *Teachers and Youth Leaders*
Robbins Report, *Higher Education* 1963

College of Preceptors *see* Preceptors, College of

College of Advanced Technology *see* CAT

College of university
A number of large British universities are federations of constituent colleges which enjoy a large measure of autonomy. Colleges select their own students and appoint their own staff. They are in separate buildings and have a distinctive tradition and ethos, though varying greatly in size and wealth of endowment. Oxford, Cambridge and London are notable examples of this structure.
See also **Federal university**

Colour blindness
Inability to discriminate between certain colours. Usually a congenital weakness. In **achromatic** vision all colours appear as grey.
The Health of the School Child, HMSO, annual

Coloured progressive matrices
These tests are a modified form of the **Standard Progressive Matrices** and are designed for use with young children and old people. They consist of sets A and B of the SPM and a set, Ab, intermediate in difficulty, between Set A and Set B. Like the SPM, these tests are untimed and are intended to be used in conjunction with the **Crichton Vocabulary Scale** to assess general intelligence.
Publishers: H. K. Lewis & Co. Ltd.

Combined Cadet Force
Cadet corps in which the Army, Navy and Air Force are conducted jointly with some scope for appropriate specialization. These corps are attached to most public schools and to many secondary schools. They are the modern equivalent of the OTC (Officers Training Corps).

Comenius, Johann Amos (1592–1670)
Bohemian educationist who advocated, notably in the teaching of Latin, systematic and psychological methods in advance of his time, in particular in the sphere of rationale of textbook composition.
A bishop of the Moravian Church he believed that universal education on the plan of reform he advocated would lead to universal peace and the turning of energy from war to religious ends. He visited England in 1641–42 at the instigation of Samuel Hartlib who published several of Comenius's works. His most important work was *The Great Didactic*, trans. M. W. Keatinge.
S. J. CURTIS and M. E. A. BOULTWOOD, *A Short History of Educational Ideas*, 4th edn, University Tutorial Press 1965, ch. 8
C. H. DOBINSON, ed., *Comenius and Contemporary Education*, Unesco 1970
J. PIAGET, *John Amos Comenius*, Unesco 1957
R. R. RUSK, *Doctrines of the Great Educators*, 3rd edn, Macmillan 1965

Comics
In Britain, children's literature which formerly was devoted very largely to coloured comic-cartoon presentation of stories and which required very little reading ability but which, today, while still presenting some of its material with ample coloured cartoons, is much more substantial in content and treatment. Publications are broadly graded to meet the needs and interest of infant, junior and secondary levels.
JENKINSON, *What do Boys and Girls Read*, 2nd edn, Methuen 1946
Readership Survey, Hulton Press, annual
G. TREASE, *Tales out of School*, 2nd edn, Heinemann 1964

Committee of the Council on Education
A body set up in 1839 by Royal Prerogative from members of the Privy Council to supervise the intervention of the State into public education. Its Vice-President, first appointed in 1856, was the chief executive in the field of Education until 1899, when his office was replaced by that of President of **Board of Education**. The Committee was served by a branch of the Civil Service, the **Education Department**.
H. C. BARNARD, *A History of English Education from 1760*, University of London Press 1961
S. J. CURTIS, *History of Education in Great Britain*, University Tutorial Press 1967, ch. 7

Common Entrance Examination
An examination taken by pupils usually in **preparatory schools** with a view to admission to **public schools**. It is an examination devised by the public schools jointly and taken at the age of thirteen. The papers of individual pupils are marked by the school which they wish to enter and that school decides which candidates to admit.
Preparatory and Public Schools Yearbook (A. and C. Black)

Common Room (SCR, JCR)
The university or college rooms in which staff (Senior Common Room) and students (Junior Common Room) respectively meet socially, and which function as informal clubs.
In schools the staff-room is often referred to as 'the common room'.

Common school
The school which the great majority of children of all groups within a national community attend. In the USA common schools became the object of a nationwide movement in the period of reform after 1830 because of their assumed contribution to

national unity and democratic values. Cp. in France the 'école unique'.

R. WELTER, *Popular Education and Democratic Thought in America*, Columbia University Press 1963

Community Centre

A building devoted to recreational pursuits and providing rooms for meetings, with the object of promoting a richer community life in a given area, e.g. in a new town, village or suburb. Though some centres are autonomous, most are provided by the local authority.

R. N. MORRIS and J. MOGEY, *The Sociology of Housing*, Routledge & Kegan Paul 1965

Community school

In USA: in reaction to the 'child centred' approach, a movement in American education between the wars which strove to consider the children not merely as individuals but as members of a local community, and which used the buildings to serve all age groups in the community. The movement sought to integrate the school activity democratically with the locality, using its resources and serving its needs.

Plowden Report, *Children and Their Primary Schools*, 1967, para. 121

F. G. ROBBINS, *Educational Sociology*, Holt Co. 1953, ch. 15

Comparative education

The study of two or more national systems of education, as existing now and as historical developments, in order that differing approaches to similar problems may be described and evaluated.

Comparative Education, Pergamon, three times a year

Comparative Education Review: official organ of the Comparative Education Society (periodical appearing three times a year), Publication offices: 525 West 120th Street, New York.

I. L. KANDEL, *Comparative Education*, Houghton Mifflin 1933

N. HANS, *Comparative Education*, 3rd edn, Routledge & Kegan Paul 1958

International Yearbook of Education, Unesco International Bureau of Education, Geneva

E. J. KING, *Other Schools and Ours*, 3rd edn, Holt, Rinehart & Winston 1967

Compensation

A term used by **Freud** and **Adler** to describe an unconscious psychological defence mechanism which consists of substituting effort in a new direction of endeavour to make up for frustration encountered in another field of activity.

C. J. ADCOCK, *Fundamentals of Psychology*, 2nd edn, Methuen 1960, Penguin (Pelican) 1964

J. A. HADFIELD, *Dreams and Nightmares*, Penguin (Pelican) 1954, 1967

Compensatory education

Name given to special educational procedures devised to meet the needs of children who have undergone sustained cultural deprivation usually associated with poverty, slum-home conditions, discrimination, etc. and who have not received the basic culture patterns which are necessary for school learning.

B. S. BLOOM *et al*, *Compensatory Education for Cultural Deprivation*, Holt, Rinehart & Winston 1965

M. CHAZAN and C. DOWNES, *Compensatory Education and the New Media*, occasional publication, University College, Swansea

Children at Risk, occasional publication, University College, Swansea

Compensatory Education, Introduction, occasional publication: University College, Swansea

T. COX and C. A. WAITE, eds, *Teaching Disadvantaged Children in the Infant Schools*, University College of Swansea 1970

E. W. GORDON and D. A. WICKERSON, *Compensatory Education for the Disadvantaged*, College entrance examination Board, 475 Riverside Drive, New York 1966

Competition

The element of striving to achieve more than the other person – obvious in games. Introduced into academic school work to provide motivation as between individual groups or classes. More progressive thought points to the harmful effects of competition between individuals, since people are variously endowed with abilities. The modern trend is to encourage the pupil to improve on his own past performances.

Complementary addition

A method of estimating the difference between two quantities, e.g. What do I need to add to four to make it eight ? Used in some schools as part of the subtraction process, and in fairly general use in shopping situations where the shopkeeper adds on from the price of the article purchased until he reaches the value of the coin handed over the counter by the customer.

L. W. DOWNES and D. PALING, *The Teaching of Arithmetic in Primary Schools*, Oxford University Press, Unesco Handbooks 1958

Completion test
A test (of intelligence, general knowledge, personality) in which the items are incomplete (e.g. blank spaces in sentences) and are to be completed by the testee: this kind of test was originally devised by **Ebbinghaus**.

P. E. VERNON, *Intelligence and Attainment Tests*, University of London Press 1960

Complex
A group of ideas of an emotional nature which have been repressed and which are thus in the realm of the unconscious. They may exercise influence in the life of the individual to an abnormal degree, e.g. in the inhibition of learning and in the distorting of personality.

See also **Fixation**; **Inferiority complex**

J. A. C. BROWN, *Freud and the Post-Freudians*, Cassell 1963, Penguin (Pelican) 1969

D. STAFFORD-CLARK, *Psychiatry Today*, Penguin (Pelican) 1952

Composition
The making of sentences, oral or written, in relation to some topic or subject. Sustained expression in sentences with a degree of coherence and unity: the composition may be narrative, descriptive, analytic, imaginative, etc. Oral composition tends to be sadly neglected in schools generally.

H. BLAMIRES, *English in Education*, Bles 1951, ch. 2

D. HOLBROOK, *The Secret Places*, Methuen 1965

B. JACKSON and D. THOMPSON, *English in Education*, Chatto & Windus 1962

Comprehension
The ability to understand the spoken or printed word. Often meant in contradistinction to the ability merely to recognize printed words and the tendency to 'bark at print'.

See also **Comprehension Tests**

Comprehension tests
Tests whose aim is to assess the candidates' ability to read for meaning (as opposed to mere word recognition) as e.g. in the Burt (Rearranged) Word Reading Test or the

Holborn Reading Scale. Examples of Comprehension Test are those of F. E. Schonell: Silent Reading Test A (R3), Silent Reading Test B (R4); and that of Daniels and Diack: Silent Prose Reading and Comprehension Test (Test No. 10). It is of interest to note, too, that in the successive national surveys of reading which were carried out in the period 1948–64, the same test, of reading comprehension, was used on each occasion. The test is known as the Watts-Vernon test and is, of course, not available to anyone except those making the national surveys.

J. C. DANIELS and H. DIACK, *The Standard Reading Tests*, Chatto & Windus 1958
Progress in Reading, Education Pamphlet No. 50 HMSO 1966

F. J. SCHONELL and F. E. SCHONELL, *Diagnostic and Attainment Testing*, Oliver & Boyd 1950

Comprehensive school
Secondary schools which offer a wide range of subjects covering the grammar, technical and modern curricula; they have been set up in a growing number of areas, especially in London, to meet the shortcomings of the tripartite system and the 11+ examination, and to meet the needs of children of all abilities. They are one of the major educational experiments of our times.

T. BURGESS, *Inside Comprehensive Schools*, HMSO 1970

R. COLE, *Comprehensive Schools in Action* Oldbourne 1964

J. STUART MACLURE, ed., *Comprehensive Planning: a symposium on the reorganisation of secondary education*, Councils & Education Press 1965

NUT, *Inside the Comprehensive School*, Schoolmaster Publishing Co. 1958

R. PEDLEY, *The Comprehensive School*, 4th edn, Penguin (Pelican) 1969

Compulsory School Age
The period of a child's life when he is legally compelled to receive suitable education, normally in a school. In the UK a child is required by law to attend school from the beginning of the term following his fifth birthday. He is legally entitled (as from 1972) to leave school at the end of the school year following his sixteenth birthday. Thus the statutory period of schooling is eleven years.

Comte, Auguste (1798–1857)
French philosopher of the early nineteenth century. He considered that all human know-

ledge passes through three stages, the theological, the metaphysical and finally the positive. Positivism regards scientific knowledge as the only valid form of knowledge and the scientific method of observation and reasoning as the only valid approach to knowledge. Comte invented the term 'sociology' and considered that there was a hierarchy of knowledge with sociology as the 'queen', the others being subordinate. He believed that a positivist morality and religion could be set up through which social problems could be solved. Most modern sociologists would regard this as a naïve solution.

T. RAISON, ed., *The Founding Fathers of Social Science*, Penguin (Pelican) 1969

Conation
A striving or endeavour; a term used in psychology to describe acts of will. The term is important in instinctivist or 'drive' theories and is much used by **McDougall** and his followers.

Concentration
The focusing of attention on a task or on an experience. In the days of **faculty psychology** concentration was frequently regarded as a faculty under the control of the will. Modern psychology tends to link the problem of concentration with the whole problem of motivation.

Concept
A mental pattern, grouping or structure, arrived at by abstracting common elements from a variety of experiences, and usually expressed in words or symbols. All higher mental processes (reasoning, the use of symbols) depend upon concepts.
Piaget's work has a large and vital bearing on the study of children's conceptual growth and development.

J. S. BRUNER, *Studies in Cognitive Growth*, Wiley 1966

K. LOVELL, *The Growth of Basic Mathematical and Scientific Concepts in Children*, Oxford University Press 1961

P. H. MUSSEN, *The Psychological Development of the Child*, Prentice-Hall 1963

E. A. PEEL, *The Pupil's Thinking*, Oldbourne 1950

Concurrent training
The system of teacher-training under which professional studies (education, school and study-practice) are pursued over the whole period of the course, rather than separately at the end (cf. the consecutive course followed by most graduates).

ATCDE, *Handbook of Training for Teachers*, Methuen, annual

McNair Report, *Supply and Training of Teachers and Youth Leaders*, 1944

Newsom Report, *Half our Future* 1963

Conditions of Service for Teachers
The conditions of service for teachers are set forth in the Schools Regulations 1959, Schedule II, which states principally that there shall be a probationary year, that teachers shall be employed under a written agreement, defining conditions of service, of which each has a copy, etc.

NATIONAL UNION OF TEACHERS, *Handbook for Teachers*

G. TAYLOR and J. B. SAUNDERS, *The New Law of Education*, 7th edn, Butterworth 1971

Conditioning
A process by which a stimulus which was originally effective is replaced by a stimulus which was originally ineffective, in evoking a certain response. 'Conditioning' derives from 'conditioned reflex', connected particularly with the work of **Pavlov** and is now used to explain a wide range of complex behaviour. As an example of conditioned reflex Pavlov's dog, which salivated naturally when presented with food, later salivated at the mere sound of a bell which had in the meantime been deliberately linked with the presentation of food. But see also **Skinner**

I. P. PAVLOV, *Lectures on Conditioned Reflexes*, 2 vols, Lawrence & Wishart 1964

E. A. PEEL, *Psychological Basis of Education*, Oliver & Boyd 1956

J. B. WATSON, *Behaviourism*, rev. edn, University of Chicago Press 1958

B. B. WOLMAN, *Contemporary Theories and Systems in Psychology*, Part 1 (Harper & Row) 1960

Conference of the Heads of University Departments. *See* **CHUDE**

Conference of Institute Directors *see* **CID**

Configuration (Gestalt)
A conceptual structure which is arrived at by insight, not gradually built up of separate parts, and which marks an advance in learning. The **gestalt** theory holds that learning

experiences should take account of such wholes rather than proceed by piecemeal analysis and recombinations. It seeks to promote insight, the solution of problems by relatively sudden restructuring of experience and knowledge on the part of the pupil.
B. R. BUGELSKI, *The Psychology of Learning*, Methuen 1963
R. BURGER and A. E. M. SEABORNE, *The Psychology of Learning*, Penguin (Pelican) 1966
R. MORRIS, *The Quality of Learning*, Methuen 1951

Conflict
A condition of struggle or violent opposition of forces. In psychology, mental conflict often repressed into the unconscious is frequently considered to interfere with normal learning and responses. In sociology, conflict between social groups is nowadays considered less apprehensively than it was formerly. It is rather thought of as a possible source of creation and reassessment; as a condition to be managed rather than suppressed.
J. A. C. BROWN, *Freud and the Post-Freudians*, Cassell 1963; Penguin (Pelican) 1969
L. A. COSER, *The Functions of Social Conflict*, Routledge and Kegan Paul 1956
R. KNIGHT and M. KNIGHT, *A Modern Introduction to Psychology*, 7th edn, University Tutorial Press 1966

Congenital
Present or potentially present in the child at birth whether due to heredity, or to circumstances attending the intra-uterine period.

Conscience
The attitude characterised by guilt feeling which is induced in the individual when he is inclined to lapses from the moral standards which he expects of himself or which he thinks are expected of him by others. Cf. the **superego** of psychoanalysis.
R. R. DALE, *Mixed or Single Sex School?*, Routledge & Kegan Paul 1969
G. M. STEPHENSON, *The Development of Conscience*, Routledge & Kegan Paul 1966

Conscience clause
Term introduced by **Brougham** in 1820, and inserted into the Education Acts since 1870. The conscience clause enables parents to withdraw their children from religious instruction, if they wish. It is also part of any agreement about conditions of employ-ment for teachers, which stipulates that a teacher is free from the obligation to undertake the teaching of religious subjects or of attending religious services (e.g. worship in Assembly) if he does not so wish.
G. R. BARRELL, *Teachers and the Law*, Methuen 1966

Conservation
The Piagetian principle which establishes the invariance of e.g. mass, number, weight. Young children fail to conserve: they believe e.g. that the quantity in a ball of Plasticine becomes greater if the ball is squeezed into an elongated form; or that a set or collection of objects changes in number when there is a change in the relationship between the elements. The ability to conserve grows with experience and maturation.
R. M. BEARD, *An Outline of Piaget's Developmental Psychology*, Routledge & Kegan Paul 1969
M. BREARLEY and E. HITCHFIELD, *A Teacher's Guide to Reading Piaget*, Routledge & Kegan Paul 1966
J. PIAGET, *The Child's Conception of Number*, Routledge & Kegan Paul 1952

Consortia
Several consortia of local authorities collaborate with the Department of Education and Science and the Ministry of Public Works and Buildings in the design and building of schools and the design of school furniture. Examples of such consortia are:
CLASP Consortium of Local Authorities Special Programme
SCOLA Second Consortium of Local Authorities
SEAC South Eastern Architects Collaboration
CLAW Consortium Local Authorities, Wales
Education in 1964 Cmnd 2612, HMSO

Consultative Committee, The
Created in 1899 to advise the **Board of Education** on matters referred to it. It produced several major reports:
Hadow: *Education of the Adolescent*, 1926.
Hadow: *Primary Schools*, 1928–31.
Hadow: *Infant and Nursery Schools*, 1933.
Spens: *Secondary Education*, 1938.
The Consultative Committee was replaced in 1944 by two Central Advisory Committees and these were superseded by the **National Advisory Council**.
See also Appendix III, Reports.

Contract of service
A teacher is appointed under an agreement or minute covering the regulations and conditions of his employment, and a copy of which he is required to sign and return to his employer. This defines his terms of service.
G. R. BARRELL, *Teachers and the Law*, Methuen 1966
Handbooks of professional associations (NUT, NAS, etc.)

Contribution, pension
The teachers' superannuation scheme is governed by Acts of Paliament and administered by the Pensions Branch of the Department of Education and Science. The teacher contributes 6¾ per cent of gross salary and his employer approx. 10 per cent. Pension, lump sum and gratuity benefits are thus assured, the pension payable only from the age of sixty. Service in excess of forty years does not count. The lump sum is the average annual salary of last three years of service; maximum pension after forty years' service (including army, or national service) is half salary. A widows' pension scheme was fully embodied in 1972.
Handbooks of professional associations (NUT, NAS, AMA, etc.)

Control group
In experimental design, a group of subjects whose performance is used as a check in the evaluation or interpretation of the performance of a similar group which is being subjected to the experiment (i.e. the *experimental group*). For example, in an experiment to find the effectiveness of a new teaching method, an experimental group of children would be matched as closely as possible with a control group (in age, ability, socioeconomic background etc.) who would be taught by traditional methods. Subsequently, any difference of performance between the two groups would seem to be attributable to the different teaching methods.
W. R. BORG, *Educational Research*, McKay 1963
F. L. WHITNEY, *Elements of Research*, Prentice-Hall 1958

Controlled school
A voluntary school, financially completely maintained by the LEA, but whose managers retain certain rights in appointing the Head and in religious education. Two-thirds of the managing body are appointed by the LEA.

G. R. BARRELL, *Teachers and the Law*, Methuen 1966
G. TAYLOR and J. B. SAUNDERS, *The New Law of Education*, 7th edn, Butterworth 1971

Controlled vocabulary
The vocabulary of an early reading book (or series of books) in which new words are deliberately spaced out so as not to confront the learner with too heavy a load of new words on a page. Controlled vocabulary usually goes with careful repetition of new words.
A. I. GATES, *Improvement of Reading*, 3rd edn, Collier-Macmillan 1947
A. J. HARRIS, *How to Increase Reading Ability*, 3rd edn, Longmans 1956
F. SCHONELL, *The Psychology and Teaching of Reading*, Oliver & Boyd 1945

Convent school
A Catholic school for girls (and often mixed nursery and infant classes) staffed by nuns and frequently closely adjoining a convent.

Conversion table
A table for converting test scores or measures from one form into another, e.g. **percentiles** into **quotients**.

Cook, H. Caldwell (1886–1939)
English master at the Perse School, Cambridge (1911–33), where he carried out experiments designed to convert schoolwork into organised play. He was convinced that true education is hampered by the classroom system and the teaching of subjects.
H. CALDWELL COOK, *The Play Way*, an *Essay in Educational Method*, Heinemann 1917

'Cooling-out'
The series of procedures in American higher education designed to avoid the more serious aspects of individual failure in Institutions of Higher Education, where because of a liberal admission policy, many failures will occur. Pre-entrance testing, counselling, reorientation courses, feed back to the student of test scores, probation and finally redirection into a lower level course are typical 'cooling out' procedures.
B. R. CLARKE, 'The "cooling out" function in higher education', in A. H. Halsey *et al.*, *Education, Economy and Society*, Collier-Macmillan 1961

Coordinates
Of a point (in a place), representing graphically the perpendicular distances from the

vertical or y axis, and from the horizontal or x axis, respectively.

Coordination

The effective working together of eye and hand, or eye and muscles, or of various muscles, in the performance of some act.

Corner (reading, science, mathematics, etc.) Part of a classroom set aside for group or individual work in specialised study, or activity, and used on a rota basis by the pupils in the class either in or out of classroom hours.

Cornwell Test

An orally presented group test of intelligence. Teacher reads the items aloud and pupils record their answers on a sheet of paper. Takes a number of school periods to administer. Has standard scores for **IQ** norms.

J. CORNWELL, *An Orally Presented Group Test of Intelligence for Juniors*, new edn, Methuen 1952

Corporal Punishment

Physical chastisement. The 'power' to give stems from the teacher's position **'in loco parentis'** to the children in his charge, but it must be such as a reasonable parent might give. Local authorities frequently have rules governing corporal punishment and action may be taken by the **LEA** as well as by parents against a teacher who breaks them. Irregular forms of physical punishment are strictly forbidden and if given may lead to a prosecution for assault.

G. R. BARRELL, *Teachers and the Law*, Methuen 1966

NATIONAL FOUNDATION FOR EDUCATIONAL RESEARCH, *Rewards and Punishments in School*, Newnes 1952

Correlation (stats)

The extent to which two or more sets of scores derived from the same sample are related to each other.

Each individual's corresponding scores or measures in two or more distributions may vary together in relation to their respective group averages. If they vary in the same direction from their respective averages they are said to correlate positively, and if they vary in opposite directions from their respective averages they are said to correlate negatively. The degree of correlation can be calculated by use of suitable formulae and is usually expressed in the form of a correlation coefficient ranging from $0·0$ (no correlation) to $±1·0$ (complete correlation). In educational statistics, correlation between all activities requiring intelligence is positive.

S. R. GRIFFITHS and L. W. DOWNES, *Educational Statistics for Beginners*, Methuen 1969

P. E. VERNON, *Measurement of Abilities*, 2nd edn, University of London Press 1956

Correspondence school, or college

An organisation which undertakes to teach by postal lessons. Textbooks are prescribed, lesson notes supplied, tests are set and the student sends his scripts to a tutor prescribed by the school or college. The marked scripts are, usually, returned via the school which make a note of the student's progress. Students are prepared for a very wide range of examinations including external degrees of the University of London. Fees vary. Correspondence Colleges advertise widely in the Press and particularly in educational publications. See particularly *National Extension College*.

Report of Committee on Accreditation of Correspondence Colleges (from Secretary, Association of British Correspondence Colleges Ltd, 4–7 Chiswell Street, London EC1)

Correspondent

The honorary representative of a teachers' organisation (**NUT, NAS,** etc.) in an individual school or college whose task is to collect dues, propagate information, etc. It is also the title given to the person nominated by school managers of **voluntary schools** to deal with their secretarial work, e.g. writing to applicants for teaching posts.

Cortex, Cerebral

The outer surface of the **brain** which has an intricate folded appearance and is believed by neurologists to be the seat of higher mental processes and to control muscular and other activity.

Council for National Academic Awards. *See* **CNAA**

Counselling

A method of providing individuals, usually students and pupils, with help, advice and guidance in their personal problems, notably those concerned with adjustment and progress in school or college, and with employment and vocation. Group, as well as individual procedures are employed, and counselling may be extended to delinquents, adults having marital problems or needing rehabilitation, or requiring psychiatric assistance, etc.

E. HARMS and P. SCHREIBER, eds, *Handbook of Counselling Techniques*, Pergamon 1963

NATIONAL FOUNDATION FOR EDUCATIONAL RESEARCH, 'The counselling function: A symposium', *Educational Research* 9, no. 2, 1967

J. WARTERS, *Techniques of Counselling*, McGraw-Hill 1964

County college

Establishments of further education envisaged in the 1944 Education Act for young persons under eighteen, who have left school. Though considered at length and recommended in the **Crowther Report** they have not yet been established.

County Council

The elected body which, as local government, administers and regulates many public services (roads, police, education, etc.) within a county.

County schools

As a legal term, the phrase refers strictly to all schools provided and maintained by **LEAs** whether county councils or county boroughs.

There are however schools administered by LEAs other than city and county borough authorities which are sometimes informally and locally referred to as 'county' schools.

G. WELLS and J. B. SAUNDERS, *The New Law of Education*, 7th edn, Butterworth 1971

Cours complémentaires

A four-year course of post-primary education in France, leading to the **Brevet**, etc., similar to the instruction offered in secondary institutions, other than **Lycées**, but staffed by primary teachers. An interim system of unspecialized secondary education. This category of school has now been superseded by the **CEG**.

Course

Any sequence of lessons, lectures, activities, relating to some particular study or problem, or group of problems.

Court, Juvenile

A magistrates' court having jurisdiction over young persons under seventeen. After four-teen, young persons may elect for jury trial at Sessions, but rarely do. The magistrates are lay, often with special experience of young people. The court is much less formal than adult courts. Courts may employ fines, conditional discharge, probation, or may commit young persons to **approved schools**, **remand homes**, attendance or detention centres, or to the supervision of a **fit person**.

W. E. CAVENAGH, *Juvenile Courts, the Child and the Law*, rev. edn, Penguin 1967

A. E. JONES, *Juvenile Delinquency and the Law*, Penguin (Pelican) 1945

J. A. F. WATSON, *The Child and the Magistrate*, Cape 1965

Cowper-Temple Clause

Non-denominational schools (board schools) were set up by Foster's Education Act of 1870. In order to meet religious differences a conscience clause operated to allow parents to withdraw children from religious instruction if they wished; but it was provided that 'no religious catechism or religious formulary which is distinctive of any particular denomination shall be taught'. This clause was proposed by Cowper-Temple.

H. C. BARNARD, *A History of English Education from 1760*, University of London Press 1961

CRAC (Careers Research Advisory Council). *See* Vocational Guidance

Cram school, crammer

The process of intensive learning of some subject or other in a relatively short space of time usually with a view to taking an examination, the emphasis being on committing subject matter to memory rather than on understanding and appreciation, and on anticipating likely questions and learning suitable answers. Cram-school (or 'crammer') is an establishment specialising in this kind of activity.

Creaming off (11+)

Taking the best, usually in the academic sense, to form a group or institution comprising individuals of superior ability. Best known example is the process involved in selecting pupils for **grammar school** education at age **eleven-plus**.

Creative activity

In schools, usually means activity of a kind which allows for, and induces, the use of imagination and initiative rather than imitation or repetition.

B. ASH and B. RAPAPORT, *Creative Work in the Junior School*, Methuen 1957

M. V. DANIEL, *Activity in the Primary School*, Blackwell 1947

S. MARSHALL, *An Experiment in Education*, Cambridge University Press 1963

D. PYM, *Free Writing*, University of London Press for Bristol Univ. Inst. of Education 1956

Creative drama
Unscripted drama which may be more or less structured, i.e. it could be the dramatisation of a known story or it could be the spontaneous acting out of a given situation, but in any case it will contain original elements of speech and action.

P. SLADE, *Child Drama*, University of London Press 1954

P. SLADE, *Experience in Spontaneity*, Longman 1969

B. WAY, *Development through Drama*, Longmans 1967

Creative writing
Writing which incorporates children's original thinking and feeling, stimulated by experience and imagination. It should be considered in the wider context of creative expression in music, art and drama.

A. B. CLEGG, *The Excitement of Writing*, Chatto & Windus 1964

B. FORD, ed., *Young Writers, Young Readers*, rev. edn, Hutchinson 1964

B. MAYBURY, *Creative Writing for Juniors*, Batsford 1969

D. PYM, *Free Writing*, University of London Press for Bristol Univ. Inst. of Education 1956

Crèche
A nursery, catering for very young children up to the age of about $3\frac{1}{2}$, whose function is to enable mothers to return to employment. In the UK the term used is 'Day Nursery'.
See also **Kindergarten; Nursery school**

Cretin
A person whose mental development has been retarded by severe under-secretion of the thyroid gland in early life.

Crib
1. A readymade, and often published, translation usually of Greek or Latin literature used to facilitate the task of pupil or student in translating from the original.
2. To plagiarise.
3. Sometimes colloquially used to mean cheating in examinations.

Crichton Vocabulary Scale
An intelligence test designed for use with **Coloured Progressive Matrices** and to cover approximately the same range of intellectual development. Suitable for children under 11 years of age and also for use with persons of defective or impaired intelligence. The tester reads the words aloud and the testee is invited to supply 'definitions'. The test provides an index of general cultural attainments and, by inference, of intelligence.
The scale consists of 80 words arranged in two approximately parallel sets of 40 words each. Set 1 consists of the first 40 words of the **Mill Hill Vocabulary Scale**.

J. C. RAVEN, *Guide to Using the Crichton Vocabulary Scale*, H. K. Lewis 1961

Crime
Behaviour regarded with disapproval by society, in that it contravenes laws and status of the civil authority, and punishable by the courts. Juvenile crime is often called **delinquency**.

L. T. WILKINS, 'Crime, cause and treatment: recent research and theory', *Educational Research* **4**, no. 1, 1961 (NFER)

Criterion
A standard adopted as the basis for making quantitative or qualitative judgements or comparisons, e.g. a standardised reading test is a criterion by which to judge the reading ability of a child by comparing his performance with the average performance of children of similar age.

Critical ratio
Mathematically equal to the ratio of the difference between the mean scores of two sample groups to the **standard error** of that difference; the magnitude of the ratio will determine limits of **significance**, i.e. the degree of the probability that the difference between the sample groups represents a difference between their respective populations. A Table of t for determining the significance of *t* values is contained in most textbooks on statistics.

H. E. GARRETT, *Statistics in Psychology and Education*, Longmans 1964

S. R. GRIFFITHS and L. W. DOWNES, *Educational Statistics for Beginners*, Methuen 1969

P. E. VERNON, *Measurement of Abilities*, 2nd edn, University of London Press 1956

Cross Commission 1886–88

A Royal Commission set up to inquire into the working of the Elementary Education Acts (England and Wales). Reports led to some modification in the payment-by-results regulations, and to the growth of the idea of separate senior departments; also to a freer distributions of central funds by capitation grants. The work of this Commission also led to the universities taking up the training of teachers in day training colleges.

H. C. BARNARD, *A History of English Education from 1760*, University of London Press 1961

S. J. CURTIS and M. E. A. BOULTWOOD, *An Introductory History of English Education since 1800*, 4th edn, University Tutorial Press 1966

Crowther Report

15 to 18 (1959). Report of the Central Advisory Council for Education on the education of boys and girls between the ages of 15 and 18. The Report deals in detail, with secondary and further education with special attention to the sixth form, Technical Education, County Colleges, organisation and teacher supply. The Chairman of the Committee was Sir Geoffrey Crowther.

See also Appendix IIIA

CSE

Certificate of Secondary Education. A leaving certificate first proposed by the **Beloe Committee** (a subcommittee of the Secondary Schools Examination Council) in their report *Secondary School Examinations other than the GCE* (1960). This certificate is on a subject basis, and intended to cater for the top half of the secondary modern school's ability range. Various aspects of this theme are contained in the many publications under the heading *Schools Council Examinations Bulletin* (HMSO).

EXAMINATIONS BULLETIN no. 1, *The Certificate of Secondary Education*, HMSO 1963

Cuisenaire (Mathematic Apparatus)

Structural apparatus consisting of a set of rods in various colours, rectangular in shape with cross-section 1 sq. cm. and ranging in length from 1 cm to 10 cm. The colours are used consistently so that rods of the same length have the same colour. Shades of the same colour indicate interrelationships, e.g. rods of 2, 4, and 8 cm all have a red pigmentation.

Address: The Cuisenaire Co., Reading.

J. B. BIGGS, *Mathematics and the Conditions of Learning* (NFER) 1967

Culture

All that which is acquired by man as a member of society and retained in the tradition. Sociological: The established and learned way of doing things; the beliefs, ideas, language, institutions and procedures which characterise a specific community, viz. myths, religion, law, art forms, social relationships, notions about food, etc. By extension, the distinguishing ideas, outlooks, habits, etc., of smaller groups as gang, age cohort, village, etc.

M. MEAD, *Coming of Age in Samoa* (1928) Penguin (Pelican) 1943

MEAD, M., *Growing Up in New Guinea* (1931) Penguin (Pelican) 1963

P. MUSGRAVE, *The Sociology of Education*, Methuen 1965

W. F. OGBURN and M. F. NIMKOFF, *Handbook of Sociology*, 4th edn, Routledge & Kegan Paul 1960

Cumulative frequency column

A column whose entries are the sum of all the scores up to and including the entry under consideration: sometimes the addition is effected downwards in which case a particular entry represents the sum of scores down to and including that point, e.g.

Score	Frequency	Cumulative frequency
5	1	4
3	2	3
1	1	1

S. R. GRIFFITHS and L. W. DOWNES, *Educational Statistics for Beginners*, Methuen 1969

P. E. VERNON, *Measurement of Abilities*, 2nd edn, University of London Press 1956

Cumulative record card

A document of a highly confidential nature which contains a continuous record throughout one or more stages of a pupil's educational career. It contains information on abilities, progress, personality qualities, important medical factors, family size and composition and any other information deemed of importance in relation to the child and his education.

C. M. FLEMING, *Cumulative Records*, University of London Press 1946

W. GLASSEY and E. J. WEEKS, *The Educational Development of Children*, University of London Press 1950

A. S. WALKER, *Pupil's School Records*, Newnes 1951

Curriculum
A group of activities, studies, experiences planned deliberately to meet the educational needs of pupils or students whether the needs are expressed in terms of intellectual, emotional, and social growth, as for young children, or in terms of successfully passing examinations as for older people.

The Department of Education and Science has instituted, through the **Schools Council**, a series of curriculum studies in various subjects. The first of these was *Mathematics in Primary Schools* (HMSO 1965).

R. HOOPER, ed. *The Curriculum*, Oliver and Boyd 1971

SCHOOLS COUNCIL, *Curriculum Innovation in Practice; a Report by J. S. Maclure of the Third International Curriculum Conference, Oxford 1967*, HMSO 1968

Curriculum Study Group
In 1962 a group of administrators, inspectors and specialists working in close collaboration with teachers and local authorities, was set up in order to extend the advisory service offered by the Inspectorate. It carried out preliminary studies in educational problems especially those which cross boundaries of responsibility. Its main interests have been the preparation of evidence for the **Plowden Report**, and the **CSE**. The Group ceased to exist separately in 1964, the staff being made available to the **Schools Council**.

The Curriculum Study Group was originally set up inside the Ministry of Education. Because teachers and **LEAs** felt the situation to be a threat to their freedom the Schools Council was established instead.

Reports on Education, 9 March 1964, Ministry of Education

NATIONAL FOUNDATION FOR EDUCATIONAL RESEARCH, *Educational Research* (Journal) February 1962, Newnes

Curve of normal probability. *See* Normal curve

Cursive writing
Writing in which letters are joined together, as opposed to script.

Curtis Report
Training in Child Care (see App. IIIB) Under the Chairmanship of Dame Myra Curtis in 1945, the Report looked into ways of compensating children for lack of normal home life and recommended the setting up of two Advisory Councils for Child Care (one for England and Wales and one for Scotland). It also recommended that each **LEA** should appoint a Children's Committee and a Children's Officer.

Custody of children
A child may be removed from the care of his parents if he is, or is suspected to be, ill-treated or neglected or is in need of care and protection. He is removed to the custody of the local authority, to a children's society, or to relations. In many cases the child is brought before a juvenile court so that he may be committed by Court Order to the care of a **fit person**, i.e. an individual, local authority, voluntary organization, or an **approved school** (especially for girls in moral danger and needing training).

See also **Children and Young Persons Act 1933**

J. STROUD, *Introduction to the Child Care Service*, Longmans 1965

Cut-off point (stats)
The point at which in a **rank order** list or in a mark list arranged in ascending/descending order it is decided to limit some group, e.g. In **GCE** or **eleven-plus** examinations, it may be necessary to limit the numbers of passes. The level at which the pass mark may be set, may thus change from year to year.

Cybernetics
The theory and study of systems of control and communication in humans and machines especially computers.

M. ASHBY, *An Introduction to Cybernetics*, Methuen 1964

G. PASK, *An Approach to Cybernetics*, Hutchinson 1961

K. U. SMITH, *Cybernetic Principles of Learning and Educational Design*, Holt, Rinehart and Winston 1966

Cyclothyme
A personality type who very noticeably fluctuates in mood between elation and depression.

E. KRETSCHMER, *Physique and Character*, 2nd edn, Routledge & Kegan Paul 1936

P. E. VERNON, *Personality Tests and Assessment*, new edn, Methuen 1953, ch. 3

D

Dalcroze *see* **Jaques-Dalcroze**

Dalton Plan or Laboratory Plan

A reorganisation of the curriculum, devised by Helen Parkhurst and first tried in Dalton, Massachusetts in 1919–20. The aim of the method is twofold: (*a*) to break down rigid teaching groups, and (*b*) to individualise the instruction by throwing the responsibility on to the individual pupil.

The method is based on the contract system in which each pupil is given monthly assignments, or jobs, in each subject. Pupil–teacher conferences are held and the teacher is on hand to explain details of the assignment, give advice, demonstrate the use of apparatus, suggest methods of study and preserve an atmosphere of study. Progress is recorded on job cards. Special laboratories devoted to special subject areas are available for study and practical work. Under the Dalton system individual work usually takes place in the morning and group activities, e.g. gymnastics, games, singing, take place in the afternoon. The method, or modified forms of it, has been used in UK notably in Streatham.

See also **Winnetka Plan**
M. PARKHURST, *Education in the Dalton Plan*, Bell 1926
A. PINSENT, *The Principles of Teaching*, 3rd edn, Harrap 1969

Dance, Educational

The spontaneous portrayal of feelings through bodily movement, and therefore an art form: if education means the education of the whole child (mind, body, emotions) then it must include various art forms, among which educational dance is acquiring more and more recognition and prominence.
See also **Educational gymnastics**
V. PRESTON, *A Handbook for Modern Educational Dance*, Macdonald & Evans 1963

Dartington Hall

A *progressive independent school* situated near Totnes in Devon. Founded by Mr and Mrs Leonard K. Elmhirst in 1931 as part of an experiment which also includes model farming and a College of Art, Music, and Drama for adults.
V. BONHAM-CARTER, *Dartington Hall: the history of an experiment*, Phoenix House 1958
W. B. CURRY, *Education for Sanity*, Heinemann 1947

Darwin, Charles R. (1805–82)

English naturalist who established the theory of organic evolution in his monumental *Origin of Species*. His work along with that of **H. Spencer** was publicly championed by **T. H. Huxley** against the Church, represented by Bishop Wilberforce; this Science v Religion controversy significantly affected the position of the Church in late nineteenth century education and especially the teaching of religious knowledge.
S. J. CURTIS, *History of Education in Great Britain*, 7th edn, University Tutorial Press 1967

Data

A collection of facts or figures on the basis of which conclusions may be drawn or inferences made.

Day-dreaming

Indulgence in imaginative mental fantasies. Carried to excess, so that it interferes with normal performance (i.e. by causing consistent inattention), it may be a symptom of maladjustment, indicating a need to escape from reality, a preoccupation with internal conflicts, etc.
C. W. VALENTINE, *The Normal Child*, Penguin (Pelican) 1967

Day-release

The practice of releasing people from industry or commerce for a day at a time, or for the equivalent of one day a week, in order to pursue studies at an educational institution, often for purposes of preparing for examinations.
Crowther Report, 15–18, 1959
DEPARTMENT OF EDUCATION AND SCIENCE, *Report of the Committee on Day Release*, HMSO 1964. Chairman: Henniker Heaton

Day training college

A teachers' training college or college of education in which students are not resident, and, therefore, drawing its students from a relatively small catchment area. The London Day Training College established in 1890 as a result of the recommendations of the **Cross Commission** developed into a University Department of Education and later into the London University Institute of Education.
ATCDE, *Handbook of Training for Teaching*, Methuen, annual
S. J. CURTIS, *History of Education in Great Britain*, University Tutorial Press 1967

Deaf, Education of the

Children who are completely, or almost completely, deaf normally attend special schools, day or boarding, for deaf children. Thoes who have partial hearing may attend special school, or a special class for partially deaf children, or even ordinary schools, when such opportunities are not available or when the incidence of the handicap is slight and/or is sufficiently overcome by the use of a hearing aid. This special education is today much more positive than it used to be, as is shown by the substitution of the words 'partial loss of hearing' or 'total loss of hearing' for the former words indicating the categories of 'partially deaf' and 'deaf'.

DEPARTMENT OF EDUCATION AND SCIENCE, *Health of the School Child*, 1966–68, HMSO

SIR A. EWING, *The Modern Educational Treatment for Deafness*, Manchester University Press 1960

Dean

The person appointed in a college or university to organise its general discipline.

Dean of Faculty

1. The head and director of studies of a faculty.
2. Also, in Scotland, the President of the Faculty of Advocates.

Death instinct

Innate tendency to strive towards death and destruction – **thanatos**. The life and death instincts were, according to Freud, the two fundamental instincts which govern a person's behaviour.

H. CRICHTON-MILLER, *Psycho-analysis and its Derivatives*, 2nd edn, Oxford University Press (Home University Library) 1945

S. FREUD, *Beyond the Pleasure Principle and other works* (*1920–22*), Vol. 18 of Standard edn, Hogarth Press, 1955

Decibel

The practical unit for measuring the loudness of sound ($\frac{1}{10}$ of a bel).

Decile

One of the nine points that divide a frequency distribution into ten equal frequency groups: usually expressed as $D_1, D_2, \ldots D_9$. The decile D_5 is thus synonymous with the 50th **percentile** and with the **median**.

H. E. GARRETT, *Statistics in Psychology and Education*, 6th edn, Longmans 1966

P. E. VERNON, *Measurement of Abilities*, 2nd edn, University of London Press, 1956

Decimal

Relating to the number 10.

Decimal classification

The Dewey system of classification: a method used in libraries to classify books on the basis of dividing all knowledge into ten chief categories and then subdividing decimally.

W. L. SAUNDERS and N. FURLONG, *Cataloguing Rules*, School Library Association 1958

Decimal currency. *See* Decimal system

Decimal fraction

Usually refers to the part of a whole number written in the **decimal system** and using **place value**.

L. W. DOWNES and D. PALING, *The Teaching of Arithmetic in Primary Schools*, Oxford University Press, Unesco Handbooks, 1958

Decimal system

The number system which uses 10 as its base. One of the oldest number systems, having its origin in the ten fingers, which were used to assist computation. An increasing number of countries are changing to a decimal system of currency and measures. In the UK this has been advocated since the mid-nineteenth century. A commission reported its recommendations in 1963 and decimal coinage has been introduced.

Report of Committee of Enquiry on Decimal Currency (Chairman: Lord Habsbury), Cmnd 2145, HMSO 1963

A. C. AITKEN, *The Case against Decimalization*, Oliver & Boyd 1962

Decomposition method

One of the two basic methods of subtraction, in which a unit of higher denomination in the minuend is moved to a lower denomination in order to facilitate the process of subtraction e.g.

$$\begin{array}{r} \overset{2}{\cancel{3}} \ \overset{14}{4} \\ -1 \ \ 6 \\ \hline 1 \ \ 8 \end{array} \quad \text{or} \quad \begin{array}{r} \overset{2}{\cancel{3}} \ \overset{10}{4} \\ -1 \ \ 6 \\ \hline 1 \ \ 8 \end{array}$$

The minuend 34 is 'decomposed' becomes twenty-fourteen, as it were, in order to make the working easier.

See also **Equal addition**

L. W. DOWNES and D. PALING *Teaching Arithmetic in Primary Schools*, Oxford University Press, Unesco Handbooks 1958

Deduction
A process of reasoning usually consisting of two propositions and a conclusion made on the basis of those propositions e.g. All children in secondary schools are aged 11 years at least. Here is a class of secondary school children. We can therefore conclude that they are aged 11 years or more.

In logical form these statements would be set out even more formally but in every-day discussion and writing they are usually hidden away in less formal language and often with part of the argument merely implied.

SALMON W. C., *Logic*, Prentice-Hall 1963

L. S. STEBBING, *Logic in Practice*, Methuen 1943

Defect, Mental
This term is being replaced by terms like 'retardation' which carry the implication of a difference in degree and not of kind; i.e. individuals are regarded as being more or less retarded mentally rather than as being in the category of either normal or defective.

M. ADAMS, *The Mentally Subnormal Social Casework approach*, Heinemann Medical Books 1960

A. M. CLARKE and A. D. B. CLARKE, *Mental Deficiency, the Changing Outlook*, rev. edn, Methuen 1966

Defence mechanism
A device usually of a self-deceptive nature, whereby a person protects himself from the psychological stress occurring when there are conflicting tendencies at work in the mind. Typical defence mechanisms are repression, sublimation, rationalisation, withdrawal, projection. Some authors use the term 'mental mechanisms'.

H. CRICHTON-MILLER, *Psycho-analysis and its Derivatives*, 2nd edn, Oxford University Press (Home University Library) 1945

R. KNIGHT and M. KNIGHT, *A Modern Introduction to Psychology*, 7th edn, University Tutorial Press 1966, ch. 17

K. LOVELL, *Educational Psychology and Children*, University of London Press 1969, ch. 4

Degree
The qualification offered by universities and similar institutions to those successfully completing a course of study, usually of at least three years. Pass degrees are of a general type requiring the study of several allied subjects. Honours degrees normally require the study of a single subject, or two subjects, at depth and in great detail, though General Honours degrees exist requiring the study of more subjects. The list of awards is divided into three or four classes of merit. Higher degrees are awarded for success in further advanced study. Assessment is made on research undertaken (usually embodied in a thesis), or by examination or by a combination of both.; e.g. **MA, MSc, PhD**. Honorary degrees are frequently conferred on politicians and other well-known public figures.

See also **Post graduate degrees and qualifications**

Delinquent
A term usually employed to describe children and young persons found guilty of an offence by the courts.

D. FORD, *The Delinquent Child and the Community*, Constable 1955

J. A. F. WATSON, *The Child and the Magistrate*, Cape 1965

Dementia
Insanity characterised by the gradual weakening of all the mental faculties.

Senile dementia: mental deterioration outruns bodily deterioration.

Dementia praecox: a group of deteriorating disorders occurring mainly in persons still young (sometimes used as a synonym for **schizophrenia**).

M. HAMILTON, ed., *Abnormal Psychology: selected readings*, Penguin 1967

B. HART, *Psychology of Insanity*, 5th edn, Cambridge University Press 1957

D. STAFFORD-CLARK, *Psychiatry Today*, Penguin (Pelican) 1952

Demography
The systematic study by statistical analysis and description, of populations, their changes and the factors affecting them.

Annual Abstract of Statistics, HMSO (for current statistics, Great Britain)

P. R. COX, *Demography*, Cambridge University Press 1970

R. K. KELSALL, *Population*, Longmans 1967

Demonstration lesson
A lesson intended to demonstrate some technique(s) of teaching, normally to prospective teachers.

Dent, H. C. (b. 1894)

A versatile educationist whose scholarship and publications have had an important place in British education over a long period. One-time editor of *The Times Educational Supplement* and later Professor of Education and Director of the Institute of Education, University of Sheffield. He has held a wide variety of other educational positions of eminence. His publications include: *A New Order in English Education* (University of London Press 1942); *The Education Act* (University of London Press 1944); *Education in Transition* (Kegan Paul 1944); *To be a Teacher* (University of London Press 1947); *Secondary Education for all* (Routledge & Kegan Paul 1949); *Secondary Modern Schools* (Routledge & Kegan Paul 1958); *The Educational System of England and Wales* (University of London Press 1961; rev. edn, 1969); *Universities in Transition* (Cohen & West 1961); *British Education* (Longmans for British Council [pamphlet] 1962).

Dental Service (school)

Regular dental inspection takes place in all maintained schools and this is followed by treatment where necessary either in school or in dental clinics. Parents may opt for their children's dental treatment to be given by a private dentist working under the National Health Service.

The Health of the School Child, HMSO biennial
Your Children's Teeth, British Medical Association

Department of Education and Science (DES)

From 1 April 1964, the powers and duties of the former Minister of Education became those of the Secretary of State for Education and Science together with departmental responsibility for University matters in Great Britain. The Ministry of Education was renamed the Department of Education and Science and organised into two administrative units, one dealing with Universities in Great Britain and with Science, the other with schools, further education, teachers and kindred subjects in England and Wales. The Secretary of State for Scotland is responsible for Education in Scotland.

DES, *Education 1964*, HMSO 1965, ch. 1

Department of Science and Art

Originated by a Select Committee in 1835 to spread knowledge of arts and design especially to the manufacturing population, the Department was set up, with Lyon Playfair as a first Joint Secretary. A small school of design was set up in 1837, followed by a fully fledged Department of Science and Art (South Kensington) in 1853 which, jointly with the Education Department (Whitehall), were institutions under the Committee of the Council. With the Charity Commission as a third partner, they later encouraged elementary education to extend beyond the three R's by grants, payment by results, examinations, specimens, etc. particularly in the field of applied science. They were merged with the Board of Education, which came into being in 1899.

M. ARGLES, *South Kensington to Robbins*, Longmans 1964
DEPARTMENT OF SCIENCE AND ART, *Annual Report: 1899*

Department of Scientific and Industrial Research. *See* **DSIR**

Deprivation

A term used in psychology to describe the condition of a person who does not have the proper social relationships (usually with a parent) which are important to mental health. Hence a repudiated or motherless child may be said to suffer from maternal deprivation.

J. BOWLBY and M. FRY, *Child Care and Growth of Love*, Penguin (Pelican) 1970

Depth psychology

The system of psychology, associated with Freud and his followers, in which human behaviour and emotional reactions are explained in terms of mechanisms which operate in the unconscious, particularly the deep unconscious.

See also **Freud, Jung, Adler** and **Psychoanalysis**

H. CRICHTON-MILLER, *Psychoanalysis and its Derivatives*, 2nd edn, Oxford University Press (Home University Library) 1945
J. B. ROTTER, *Clinical Psychology*, Prentice-Hall (Foundations of Modern Psychology Series 1964)

DES. *See* **Department of Education and Science**

Detention

A method of punishment by keeping pupils at school beyond the time at which they would normally have been released from class, usually in order to perform some task or other. It is a method opposed by those in education who believe that staying in after normal school hours should logically be a reward and a privilege, if children are to be educated to like school.

NATIONAL FOUNDATION FOR EDUCATIONAL RESEARCH, *Survey of Rewards and Punishments*, Newnes 1952

Determinism

Philosophic doctrine usually modelled upon theories of knowledge in the natural sciences, which holds that all physical and mental occurrences are the result of prior causes and conditions; generally opposed to the doctrine of free will, and often arguing that choice is an illusion.

J. S. BRUBACHER, *Modern Philosophies of Education*, McGraw-Hill 1969

KENNETH WALKER, *Human Physiology*, Penguin (Pelican) 1943 (reissue 1968)

Developmental psychology

Developmental approach to educational psychology. An attempt to fill the gap between what is known of animal learning (e.g. sensorimotor conditioning) and human learning (esp. insight, learning from reasoning and representation) by an approach which seeks to trace stages of development in intellectual activity from **neonate** to adult. Physical, emotional, personality and social development can all be conveniently studied at the same time; this approach usually supplements the study of individual difference.

R. M. BEARD, *An Outline of Piaget's Developmental Psychology*, Routledge & Kegan Paul 1969

C. BÜHLER, *From Birth to Maturity*, Routledge & Kegan Paul 1935

J. H. FLAVELL, *The Developmental Psychology of Jean Piaget*, Van Nostrand 1963

B. R. MCCANDLESS, *Children, Behaviour and Development*, Holt, Rinehart & Winston 1967

N. L. MUNN, *The Evolution of Growth of Human Behaviour*, Harrap 1965

Deviation

The turning aside from a straight course, or variation from a norm. Used in psychology and sociology to describe variation from normal development or normal behaviour.

C. W. VALENTINE, *The Normal Child and some of his Abnormalities*, Penguin (Pelican) 1956

K.W.E.—3

L. T. WILKINS, *Social Deviance*, Tavistock 1964

Deviation, Average (AD) (stats)

A measure of the spread or dispersion of the scores in a distribution obtained by finding the average of the deviations of each score from the mean, i.e. $AD = \dfrac{\Sigma d}{N}$. The average deviation is less influenced by extreme scores than the **standard deviation** but is not so useful in computing correlation and other statistics.

S. R. GRIFFITHS and L. W. DOWNES, *Educational Statistics for Beginners*, Methuen 1969

P. E. VERNON, *Measurement of Abilities*, 2nd edn, University of London Press 1956

Deviation quotient

A **standard score** whose **mean** and **standard deviation** conform to those traditionally associated with intelligence quotients (i.e. those derived from **mental age** and **chronological age**). The term 'deviation quotient' is strictly speaking incorrect, but it is a useful way of expressing deviation scores in a way which is understandable and acceptable to those who are accustomed to using the term 'intelligence quotient'.

N. E. GRONLUND, *Measurement and Evaluation in Teaching*, Collier–Macmillan 1965

Deviation score

An individual's test score expressed in terms of the dispersion or scatter of a group of such scores.

Dewey, John (1859–1952)

American philosopher and educationalist. As a **pragmatist** he strove to reform the American educational practice in the direction of promoting learning through active problem solving, which provided direct experience necessary to growth and achievement of maturity. He also wished to redirect education in the light of continuous analysis of modern society, its aims and needs.

His philosophy of education (*School and Society*, 1899, and *Democracy and Education*, 1916) was very influential but came increasingly under attack, and some reaction away from his views has set in.

J. PASSMORE, *A Hundred Years of Philosophy*, Penguin (Pelican) 1968

A. G. WIRTH, *John Dewey as Educator*, Wiley 1966

Dextrality
A preference for an organ or limb on the right side of the body in performing some act: usually the reference is to **handedness**.
See also **Dominance; Laterality; Sinistrality**
M. M. CLARK, *Left-handedness*, University of London Press for Scottish Council for Research in Education 1957

Diagnosis
The process of discovering the causes of failure, e.g. in intellectual attainment or in personality adjustment.
G. M. BLAIR, *Diagnostic and Remedial Teaching*, rev. edn, Collier-Macmillan 1956
N. M. BURBURY, E. M. BALINT and B. J. YAPP, *An Introduction to Child Guidance*, Macmillan 1945
G. M. DELLA-PIANA, *Reading Diagnosis and Prescription*, Holt, Rhinehart & Winston 1968
F. J. SCHONELL, *The Diagnosis of Individual Difficulties in Arithmetic*, Oliver & Boyd 1942

Diagnostic test
A test designed to show exactly where a testee fails on a given task (e.g. as in Schonell's *Diagnostic Arithmetic Tests*, Oliver & Boyd 1957), and thus indicating possible remedial measures.
G. M. BLAIR, *Diagnostic and Remedial Teaching*, rev. edn, Collier-Macmillan 1956
F. J. SCHONELL, *Diagnostic and Attainment Testing*, Oliver & Boyd 1950
F. J. SCHONELL, *Backwardness in the Basic Subjects*, Oliver & Boyd 1942

Diary keeping
A method used by many teachers, especially in primary schools, to encourage children to write about matters which are important to them as individuals. Only the teacher reads the diary and, while he leaves evidence of having read the diary, he does not correct it in the normal way. This degree of privacy and the absence of corrections is thought to encourage fluency in writing.
See also **News period**

Dichotomy
A division into two parts; especially of concepts, viz. body–mind, nature–nurture, such that the two are opposed or mutually exclusive.

Dictation
1. A method of testing spelling in which the teacher normally reads aloud a passage of suitable difficulty at an appropriate speed, the pupil being required to write down the words.
F. J. SCHONELL, *The Essentials in Teaching and Testing Spelling*, Macmillan 1932
2. A method of testing a person's ability to write a rhythm or melody played on some instrument.
A. BENTLEY, *Musical Ability and its Measurement in Children*, Harrap 1966
R. SHUTER, *The Psychology of Musical Ability*, Methuen 1958

Didactic
Intended for instruction: having the character or manner of a teacher. The term is sometimes used to describe methods of instruction which are concerned with imparting facts rather than with inspiring ideas.

Dienes Apparatus
Structural mathematical aids, made mainly of wood, designed to facilitate children's acquisition of basic mathematical concepts. They range from ideas of number bases to elementary algebra.
Obtained from: *The National Foundation for Educational Research*, 79 Wimpole Street, London, W1
J. B. BIGGS, *Mathematics and the Conditions of Learning*, NFER 1967
Z. DIENES, *Building up Mathmeatics*, rev. edn, Hutchinson 1960

Difference, Significant (stats)
A statistical difference between sample means which is probably not due to chance factors of sampling, the level of probability being stated, e.g. 20:1, 100:1 (or as, respectively, 5 per cent, 1 per cent).
S. R. GRIFFITHS and L. W. DOWNES, *Educational Statistics for Beginners*, Methuen 1969
P. E. VERNON, *Measurement of Abilities*, 2nd edn, University of London Press 1956

Differences, Individual
Personal characteristics which differ in degree or combination from individual to individual; e.g. intellectual, emotional, physical differences; differences of personality and social background. Awareness of the nature and extent of these differences and of the appropriate methods of measuring them and dealing with them is an important part of a teacher's training.
C. J. ADCOCK, *Fundamentals of Psychology*, Methuen 1960, ch. 13–15

N. L. MUNN, *Psychology: The fundamentals of human adjustment*, 5th edn, Harrap 1966, ch. 3

Digraph

Two consonants or two vowels which together represent one sound, e.g. 'ch' as in 'chase' or 'ea' as in 'lean'.

E. V. DECHANT, *Improving the Teaching of Reading*, Prentice-Hall 1964

Diploma

A document granted by an education institution on the satisfactory completion of a course of study or training. The award of higher diplomas is gradually becoming the prerogative of universities and university institutes. The Diploma in Education is now generally a higher qualification taken by teachers after some years of service. Graduates who were formerly awarded a diploma at the end of their year's training, now normally take the Certificate of Education of a university institute.

Diploma in Art and Design

Major qualification in Art offered by Art Colleges and Schools, and equivalent to pass degree of university; introduced in 1961 to replace the National Diploma in Design. It is awarded after a five-year course.

National Council for Diplomas in Art and Design (16 Park Crescent, London, W1) *Memorandum no. 1*

Diplopia

Double vision of a single object which sometimes occurs in squint or cross-eyedness (**strabismus**).

E. V. DECHANT, *Improving the Teaching of Reading*, Prentice-Hall 1964

Direct grant schools

Independent schools in the private sector of education (mostly secondary grammar) which are partly financed from the Department of Education and Science directly, and not through **LEAs**. In exchange for this state aid the schools undertake to offer at least 25 per cent free places annually (based on previous years' admissions) to pupils who have attended a grant-aided primary school for at least two years. Also, at the request of the LEA, they may be required to reserve a further 25 per cent of annual admissions for pupils whose fees the LEA will pay. Such schools are regarded as having higher status,

since many of them have **public school** (HMC qualifications or aspirations.)

G. TAYLOR and J. B. SAUNDERS, *The New Law of Education*, 7th edn, Butterworth 1971

Direct method

The method of language teaching which avoids the use of the native tongue of the learner, and postpones grammatical analysis, etc, by question and answer activity and conversation in the language being learned. In vogue since the 1920s, its approach is now being rescrutinized and reactivated in connection with **language laboratories**.

INCORPORATED ASSOCIATION OF ASSISTANT MASTERS IN SECONDARY SCHOOLS, *The Teaching of Modern Languages*, 4th edn, University of London Press 1967

R. LADO, *Language Teaching*, McGraw-Hill 1964

SCHOOLS COUNCIL, *French in the Primary School* (Working Paper No. 8), HMSO 1966

Director of Education

The paid administrative head of the Education Committee of an **LEA** whose business is to carry out the instructions of the Education Committee. This is the legal designation for this post in Scotland, but in England and Wales it is tending to be replaced by the title 'Chief Education Officer'.

G. TAYLOR and J. B. SAUNDERS, *The New Law of Education*, 7th edn, Butterworth 1971

Directory (Education Authorities Directory and Annual)

A compendium of information for administrators published annually by The School Government Publishing Company, 98 Kingston Road, London, SW19

Discipline

1. A formal body of knowledge or accepted field of enquiry, systematically studied and taught, e.g. the classical disciplines of Greek and Latin; the discipline of mathematics.

2. Good order in the classroom, and the training which promotes it in schoolchildren through precept, example, rules and systems of reward and punishment. The emphasis in modern pedagogy is on self-discipline which arises in the children through interest and activity.

R. FARLEY, *Secondary Modern Discipline*, A. and C. Black 1960

NATIONAL FOUNDATION FOR EDUCATIONAL

RESEARCH, *A Survey of Rewards and Punishments*, Newnes 1952

Discovery approach (maths)
A method of learning mathematics in which the pupil himself discovers mathematical ideas and relationships, usually through the experience he gains in the carefully prepared situation provided by the teacher, e.g. if a child is invited to attempt to make a triangle out of two milk straws of equal length, one of which has been cut into two parts, he will be in a position to discover the single but important geometrical truth that any two sides of a triangle are together greater than the third side.
The 'discovery' approach, recommended in past centuries by writers like **Quintilian** and **Comenius**, was strongly advocated by enlightened educationists in the nineteenth century and permeates much of the theory and practice of modern infant schools. Its leading advocates today, particularly in the field of mathematics learning are Miss E. Biggs, HMI and the organisers of the Nuffield Mathematics and Science Projects.
SCHOOLS COUNCIL, *Primary School Maths*, by E. E. Biggs, Curriculum Bulletin no. 1, HMSO 1969
Nuffield Maths Project Bulletins

Discrete (stats)
Separate, as in the division of a group into male and female categories; incapable of gradual transition from one value to another as are values on a continuum.
H. E. GARRETT, *Statistics in Psychology and Education*, 6th edn, Longmans 1966
P. E. VERNON, *Measurement of Abilities*, 2nd edn, University of London Press 1956

Discussion method
As opposed to lecture method and private study. It may assume a variety of forms, e.g. the teacher can act as chairman during a class discussion: there can be leaderless discussions: or a class can divide up into relatively small groups for discussion and their respective leaders report back to a meeting of the whole class.
P. R. MORT and W. S. VINCENT, *Modern Educational Practice*, McGraw-Hill 1950

Dispersion (stats)
A term used to describe how widely the scores in a distribution are spread. The degree of dispersion is usually given by such quantitative measures as **range**, **average deviation**, or **semi-interquartile range** (or quartile deviation)
S. R. GRIFFITHS and L. W. DOWNES, *Educational Statistics for Beginners*, Methuen 1969
P. E. VERNON, *Measurement of Abilities*, 2nd edn, University of London Press 1956

Disposition
The tendency for an individual to undergo a particular type of conscious mental experience when placed in a particular situation. e.g. a disposition to attack. The term is also used to describe the aspect of personality which indicates an individual's total natural tendencies to act in certain ways, e.g. a quiet disposition.

Dissertation
An extended piece of written work on a specific topic, but usually not amounting to a **thesis**, required of a student or candidate for an educational qualification: a brief treatise.
R. BORG, *Educational Research*, Longmans 1963
D. J. FOSKETT, *How to Find Out: educational research*, Pergamon 1965
S. R. GRIFFITHS and L. W. DOWNES, *Educational Statistics for Beginners*, Methuen 1969, ch. 7

Distance
1. Social: Reserve or constraint in social behaviour between individuals belonging to groups of different social status, viz. vertical between doctor and orderly, Brahmin and outcast; or horizontal, between ethnic groups of equal status. It is not usually accompanied by aversion or hostility.
2. Safeguard: The degree of reserve, not amounting to aloofness, said to be required to protect the authority of a high status position in public. It is short between teacher and nursery school child; longer between teacher and older pupils.
KIMBALL YOUNG, *Handbook of Social Psychology*, 2nd edn, Routledge & Kegan Paul 1957
W. WALLER, *The Sociology of Teaching*, Wiley 1965

Distribution (stats)
The values of a variable arranged in sequence in the form of a table e.g. on the basis of

magnitude. Entries in a teacher's record book:

A 65
B 80
C 48
D 50

put in the form of a distribution becomes:

B 80
A 65
D 50
C 48

S. R. GRIFFITHS and L. W. DOWNES, *Educational Statistics for Beginners*, Methuen 1969
P. E. VERNON, *Measurement of Abilities*, 2nd edn, University of London Press 1956

Division
The arithmetical process by which:
(*a*) a set is split up into a given number of equal subsets in order to accomplish the task of equal sharing; the answer required is 'How many in each subset?' e.g. 12 objects are shared equally among 3 people. How many does each person have? The answer is 4 (objects). This aspect of the process is called 'Partition'.
(*b*) a set is split up into equal subsets of a particular size in order to find how many subsets or groups there are; e.g. To how many people can I give 3 objects if I have 12 objects? The answer is 4 (people). This aspect of the process is called 'Quotition'.
L. W. DOWNES and D. PALING, *Teaching of Arithmetic in Primary Schools*, Oxford University Press, Unesco Handbooks 1958

Division (administrative)
A unit of educational administration found in county authorities (but not in county boroughs) having a local committee (called a divisional executive) and a **divisional education officer** but functioning under the general supervision of the county authority. This arrangement was introduced by the 1944 Act.
G. R. BARRELL, *Teachers and the Law*, Methuen 1966
G. TAYLOR and J. B. SAUNDERS, *The New Law of Education*, 7th edn, Butterworth 1971

Divisional education officer
The education officer employed by the county council to administer the educational affairs of a **division** (and sometimes of more than one division). He has direct obligation to his divisional executive(s) but he also carries out duties for the **LEA** of which his division is a subordinate part.

G. R. BARRELL, *Teachers and the Law*, Methuen 1966
G. TAYLOR and J. B. SAUNDERS, *The New Law of Education*, 7th edn, Butterworth 1971

Dizygotic
Originating in two separately fertilised ova. See **monozygotic**.
See also **Monozygotic Twins**
T. HUZEN, *Psychological Twin Research*, Stockholm (Almquist)
J. SHIELDS, *Monozygotic Twins*, Oxford University Press 1962

Domestic science
That body of theory and practice which includes needlework, cookery, and housecraft. An expression which is more and more being replaced by 'home economics'.
M. WEDDELL, *Training in Home Management*, Routledge & Kegan Paul 1955

Dominance
1. Lateral: A condition in which there is use of one side of the body in preference to the other, as in handedness or eyedness. May be an important factor in reading, writing, sport and other manual activities.
M. CLARK, *Left-handedness*, University of London Press for Scottish Council for Research in Education 1957
2. Genetic: The appearance in all hybrid offspring of a characteristic of one parent to the exclusion of a contrasting characteristic of the other parent. Contrasted with *recessiveness*.
A. MONTAGU, *Human Heredity*, new edn, New English Library 1965

Dotting test
A test of the speed with which a person can tap with a pencil or stylus. Also a test used by McDougall to study factors like attention and fatigue, in which the testee is required to place dots in small circles moving across a slit of adjustable width, but appearing irregularly.
P. E. VERNON, *Personality Tests and Assessments*, Methuen 1953

Drama
Variously interpreted in schools but tends to take two main forms: (*a*) play reading and/or (*b*) a study of plays as part of the work in literature. There is a growing tendency in education, however, to think of drama as a therapeutic medium and as a means of

imaginative expression in the creative sense, in the dramatisation of known events and stories or in the invention of dramatic situations and dialogue. This tendency is away from public performance and from the conventions of stage production to drama in the round and without audience, every child taking part in the proceedings.

E. J. BURTON, *Teaching English through Self-expression*, Evans 1949

P. SLADE, *Child Drama*, University of London Press 1954

B. WAY *Development through Drama*, Longmans 1967

Draw a Man test

A test developed by F. L. Goodenough purporting to measure a child's **intelligence,** and further refined and developed by Dale Harris.

F. L. GOODENOUGH, *Children's Drawings as Measures of Intellectual Maturity*, revised by D. B. Harris, Harrap 1964

M. L. KELLMER PRINGLE and K. T. PICKUP, 'The reliability and validity of the Goodenough Draw-a-Man test', *British Journal of Educational Psychology* 23, no. 3, 1963

Dreams

Thoughts, images or fancies passing through the mind during sleep. Freudians usually consider the dream to be an expression of the baulked wishes and frustrated yearnings of waking life. They often interpret dreams in terms of unconscious motivation.

S. FREUD, *The Interpretation of Dreams*, trans. J. Strachey, Allen & Unwin 1955

J. A. HADFIELD, *Dreams and Nightmares*, Penguin (Pelican) 1963

See also **Freud, S.**

Drill

1. Repetition of mental or physical operation in order to achieve improvement in speed and/or accuracy.
2. Obsolete term which refers to an outmoded form of physical education.

Drive

A theoretical concept which is closely related to 'need'. It is the motivating force which becomes active when a need is present, e.g. hunger drive. It is losing popularity as a useful term, particularly in the field of animal behaviour.

DSIR

Department of Scientific and Industrial Research.

During the 1914–18 war there arose a great need for government control and stimulus of scientific and technical research and education. The Committee for Scientific and Industrial Research (afterwards **DSIR**) was set up in 1915 as a central administration. It influenced education by finding that the output of mathematics, scientific and technical graduates was inadequate, and that research facilities were insufficient for the national interest, for Government departments; the encouragement of industrial research and its application; and the encouragement of scientific and technological research, by giving grants, etc. to universities and colleges. The work of the DSIR was fully discussed by the **Robbins** Committee on Higher Education 1961–3.

DSIR, *Universities and Colleges 1956–60*, HMSO 1962

ADVISORY COUNCIL ON SCIENTIFIC POLICY, *Annual Reports*, HMSO

Dual System

Name given to the partnership between **voluntary bodies** (mainly the religious denominations), and **school boards** (later Local Education Authorities), set up by the Elementary Education Act of 1870 (**Forster Act**) to provide elementary public education. The dual system still exists, though **reorganisation** of all age schools led to difficulties which the 1936 Education Act sought to remedy. The situation was resolved in the 1944 Education Act by the creation of 'aided', 'special agreement', and 'controlled' voluntary schools.

H. C. BARNARD, *A History of English Education from 1760*, University of London Press 1961

S. J. CURTIS and M. E. A. BOULTWOOD, *Education in England since 1800*, 4th edn, University Tutorial Press 1966

Dualism

1. Any philosophical theory that maintains that there are two fundamentally different sorts of principles in the universe (e.g. natural–supernatural; mental–physical)
2. In psychology, the view that there is a distinction of some sort between mental and physical phenomena, even though they may not be fundamentally or metaphysically different.

Duke of Edinburgh Award

A scheme of awards introduced in 1956 for boys, and extended to girls in 1958, to encourage a wide variety of leisure activities. It had first been suggested by the Duke of Edinburgh (Prince Philip) in 1954. The awards are made on the basis of Rescue, Public Service, an Expedition, Physical Fitness, Pursuits and Projects. Candidates for the tests may be nominated by LEAs, schools, voluntary youth service organisations, industrial firms and the Services. 'Unattached' candidates may also enter the scheme. Bronze, silver and gold badges are awarded. The main principle of assessment is genuine sustained effort.

Guide to the Duke of Edinburgh's Award Scheme for Boys (Girls), 2 Old Queen Street, London, SW1; 10 Palmerston Place, Edinburgh, 12; 91 St Mary's Street, Cardiff.

Dull
An expression indicating mental capacity well below **average**.
K. LOVELL, *Educational Psychology and Children*, University of London Press 1969, ch. 12

Dunce (obs.)
A pupil who is regarded as having failed dismally in his class work. Ironically named after the medieval scholar, Duns Scotus.

Duodecimal system
The arithmetical notation on a base of 12 (rather than 10) which survived till 1971 in British coinage and measurement (shillings, pence; feet, inches). Some mathematicians consider that a duodecimal system would be superior to a decimal system because the number 12 has more factors than 10 and would thus facilitate division into fractional parts. Such a system would, of course, require the invention of two more symbols to take the place of 10 and 11.
A. C. AITKEN, *The Case Against Decimalization*, Oliver & Boyd 1962

Durkheim, Emile (1858–1917)
French pioneer sociologist and university lecturer; originator of the study of sociology in education. He brought the ideas of **Comte**, **Spencer** and the German sociological school into a highly developed system, which influenced profoundly the course of twentieth century sociology and anthropology. He founded and edited the influential journal, *L'Année Sociologique* for fifteen years.
His writings include *Moral Education* (Collier-Macmillan 1961), and *Education and Sociology* (Collier-Macmillan 1956)
R. A. NISBET, *Emile Durkheim*, Prentice-Hall 1965
T. RAISON, ed., *The Founding Fathers of Social Science*, Penguin (Pelican) 1969

Dyslexia. *See* **Word blindness**
M. CRITCHLEY, *Developmental Dyslexia*, Heinemann 1964

E

Ear training (tests)
Used mostly in relation to musical education and that branch of it which concentrates on the acquisition and testing of the ability to make fine aural discrimination in pitch, rhythm and harmony.

A. BENTLEY, *Musical Ability in Children and its Measurement*, 1966

J. B. BROCKLEHURST, *Music in Schools*, Routledge & Kegan Paul 1962, ch. 7

R. SHUTER, *The Psychology of Musical Ability*, Methuen 1968

Early leaving
Leaving school, on reaching statutory school-leaving age, but before the completion of the course of studies which the child had undertaken, e.g. leaving a grammar course before attempting GCE O level. The high incidence of early leaving in the 1950s led to an investigation into its sociological, educational and psychological origins.

MINISTRY OF EDUCATION CENTRAL ADVISORY COUNCIL, *Early Leaving*, HMSO 1954

Ebbinghaus, H. (1850–1909)
German psychologist who was one of the first to show that the methods of science could be applied to the 'higher thought processes'. Noted very particularly for his work on memory. Research in verbal learning still makes use of methods and materials developed by him. Was successively Professor of Psychology at the Universities of Berlin, Breslau and Halle. He later turned to work on colour vision and to the testing of children's intelligence.

J. B. STROUD, *Psychology in Education*, Longmans 1965

R. THOMSON, *The Pelican History of Psychology*, Penguin (Pelican) 1968, ch. 4

Echolalia
1. The child's repetition, in the normal course of development, of the speech of others.
2. A disorder in which the sufferer involuntarily repeats words spoken by others.

LORD BRAIN, *Speech Disorders*, 2nd edn, Butterworth 1965

J. S. MOLLOY, *Teaching the Retarded Child to Talk*, University of London Press 1969

G. SETH and D. GUTHRIE, *Speech in Childhood*, Oxford University Press 1935

Ecole Normale
French Institution for the education and training of non-graduate teachers (formerly

Instituteurs). Though at one time concerned only with elementary education, the EN now also supplies teachers for Colleges d'Enseignement Générale. It offers academic instruction to the **Baccalaureat** level with some professional training and opportunities for practice. Only a proportion of French teachers enter the profession via the Ecole Normale.

The Ecole Normale Supérieure is an institution in Paris, created by the Convention in 1795, and, re-established by Napoleon, has provided teachers for higher education in France.

E. CUBBERLEY, *The History of Education*, new edn, New York, Houghton Mifflin: London, Constable 1948

E. J. KING, *Other Schools and Ours*, Holt, Rinehart & Winston 1967

Economics, of education
The study of the allocation of revenue and resources by the community to educational institutions; the return obtained, the nature of the choices involved, methods of administering the allocations, and the reaction upon the rest of the economy of these measures.

M. BLAUG, ed., *Economics of Education*, 2 vols, Penguin 1968, 1969

J. VAIZEY, *The Economics of Education*, Faber 1962; Penguin 1962

J. VAIZEY, *Education for Tomorrow*, rev. edn, Penguin 1966

ECT. *See* Electro-convulsive therapy

Ectomorph
In Sheldon's classification of physique by anthropometric measurement, the fragile linear body type, with, typically, thin arms, legs, neck and trunk. The ectomorph is associated by Sheldon with the cerebrotonic temperament, characterised by sensitivity, shyness and introversion.

L. J. BISCHOF, *Interpreting Personality Theories*, Harper & Row 1964

W. H. SHELDON, *The Varieties of Temperament*, Harper & Row 1942

Edgeworth, Richard Lovell (1744–1817) and Maria (1767–1849)
British educationists, authors of *Practical Education*, 1798, and *Professional education*, 1808. A comfortably-off landlord of Irish extraction, R. L. Edgeworth mixed with eminent men such as Erasmus Darwin and

Joseph Priestley in the Birmingham Lunar Society, and met Rousseau and D'Alembert. He supervised the education of his eighteen children; with one of whom, Maria, later a successful novelist, he wrote the two major works. An able teacher, sincere and undogmatic, he set out in detail a humane and kindly method of teaching, addressed to female readers, and in sharp contrast with the classical prejudices of the times.

E. INGLES-JONES, *The Great Maria*, Faber 1959

Edinburgh Review

Review founded in 1802 by F. Jeffrey, Sidney Smith and H. Brougham, embodying reformist views on literature and politics. For example, arising from a consideration of the **Edgeworths'** *Practical Education*, an educational controversy was sustained which culminated in the two great works of **J. H. Newman** and **H. Spencer** representing broadly opposed conceptions of Education, the former catholic and classical, the latter scientific and modern.

J. H. NEWMAN, *The Idea of a Liberal Education*, ed. H. Tristram, Harrap 1952
Cambridge History of English Literature, vol. 12, ch. 6

Educable

Capable of learning from the opportunities supplied in ordinary or special schools.
See also **Ineducable**

Education

1. The process and manner in which a person has been brought up.
2. The systematic instruction and training given especially to the young in preparation for life.
3. The theoretical and practical discipline studied as part of their professional training mainly by intending teachers, as distinct from their other academic subjects. It consists of psychological and sociological principles applied to the learning process; systematic child study; methods of teaching the academic subjects, and the historical, philosophical and administrative considerations and assumptions which underlie the whole process.

W. O. LESTER SMITH, *Education: an introductory survey*, Penguin (Pelican) 1957
J. W. TIBBLE, *The Study of Education*, Routledge & Kegan Paul 1966

Education Committee

A committee of the local council, e.g. city, county borough or county, which is set up specially from amongst the councillors with the task of organising and administering maintained schools in the area of that authority.

H. C. DENT, *The Educational System of England and Wales*, rev. edn, University of London Press 1969

Education Department

1. The office set up under the Committee of the Privy Council in 1856 and lasting until 1899 (and absorbed with the **Board of Education** in 1900) to administer grant aid to Elementary Schools. At its head were the President and Vice-President of the Privy Council, whilst the Permanent Secretary frequently played a significant role. It was replaced by the **Ministry of Education**, now in turn, replaced by the **Department of Education and Science**.
2. The department in a university which is concerned with the training of teachers (usually for secondary schools). Most students are graduates taking a one-year course leading to the Certificate of Education. Education Departments may also offer a higher degree in education, MA(Ed) or M Ed.
3. The department in a College of Education concerned with the professional aspects of a teacher's course running concurrently with his study of other academic subjects.

McNair Report, *Teachers and Youth Leaders*, 1944

Educational aids

Any materials, objects or techniques that help and augment the more usual techniques of education. The aids may be auditory, visual or manipulative. If the material is helpful in the learning process to a child working on his own, it is often referred to as a 'learning' aid. If it is chiefly used by the teacher to facilitate instruction it is often called a 'teaching' aid. Certain structural apparatus in mathematics belong to the former while the latter would include film, television, radio, pictures, charts, etc.

E. J. D. DEVEREUX, *An Introduction to Visual Aids*, The Visual Aids Centre, 78 High Holborn, London, WC1
D. UNWIN, ed., *Media and Methods*, McGraw-Hill 1969

Educational guidance

The advice given in relation to possible further study, e.g. by a member of staff to a pupil or by a competent institution, like the National Institute of Industrial Psychology, or the Tavistock Clinic, on the basis of tests and an interview. The term may now also be used in the general sense of advice on the appropriate form of schooling for a particular child.

NATIONAL FOUNDATION FOR EDUCATIONAL RESEARCH, 'The counselling function: a symposium', *Educational Research* **9**, no. 2, Feb. 1967 (Newnes)
See also ACE

Educational gymnastics

Modern development in **PE** teaching which reacts against mechanical, dull regimentation and formation; uses ideas derived from dances, mime and allied fields of educational practice, notably the works of R. Laban. The emphasis is upon the individual child, activity and purposeful movement, with frequent opportunity for individual children to choose their activity, discover their body potential, and thus to attain their maximum development. The manner of teaching is informal; the teacher coaches and guides; stimulation and suggestion replace regimentation; emphasis on competition is discouraged; exercises are based on systematic analysis of movement and accommodated to natural learning processes.

LONDON COUNTY COUNCIL, *Educational Gymnastics*, London County Hall 1963
R. MORRISON, *A Movement Approach to Educational Gymnastics*, Dent 1969

Educational ladder

An educational system which provides successive levels of education. In the UK it can be looked at in two ways.
(*a*) The public system of education from Primary School to Secondary School to various forms of **higher education**;
(*b*) The private sector, from preparatory school to public school (or independent, non-public school) to various forms of higher education.

Educational priority area (EPA)

The **Plowden Report** recommended that certain areas of old housing with very inadequate school buildings, where teaching is carried on under severe difficulties, should be designated by the Secretary of State as educational priority areas, so that extra resources may be devoted to them to offset the deprivation suffered by the children living in them.

Plowden Report, *Children and Their Primary Schools*, 1967, ch. 5

Educational psychology

In Britain, educational psychology has its roots in the nineteenth century. **Charles Darwin's** *Biographical Sketch of an Infant* written in 1877 is noteworthy in this respect. The approach of his half-cousin, **Francis Galton**, however, was nearer to what is regarded today as educational psychology, since he studied children as individuals, showing their essential differences as well as their common biological inheritance.

James Sully, at the turn of the century, opened a psychological laboratory at University College, London, to which he invited teachers to bring their more difficult pupils for examination. The British Child Study Association, founded in 1894, whose first president was Sully, included a study of the effects of environment on children's development.

The appointment of **Cyril Burt** to the London County Council as the first educational psychologist working for a local authority is a landmark.

Educational psychology has in the public mind been strongly connected with educational selection. Its work on learning problems and in the use of tests for educational diagnosis and remedial teaching has become less well known as a result. Because of their efforts to understand and help delinquent and maladjusted children, educational psychologists have perhaps also come to be associated with a permissive approach to educating children. The work of educational psychologists like **Schonell** and **Piaget** is widely in evidence in the classrooms as exemplified in remedial techniques in the teaching of the basic subjects and in the development of organisational ideas to promote learning through individual and group activities rather than solely through class teaching.

Research and scholarships have provided theoretical understanding which has produced and reinforced techniques of teaching through programmed learning, through various methods of grouping, and through enlightened views on rewards and punishment.

The main focus of research in educational psychology is found in the universities and in large scale educational agencies like the NFER.

L. J. CRONBACH, *Educational Psychology*, Hart-Davis 1963

E. STONES, *Readings in Educational Psychology*, Methuen 1970

E. STONES and D. ANDERSON, *Educational Objectives and the Teaching of Educational Psychology*, Methuen 1972

Educational sociology. *See* **Sociology of education**

Educational visits/journeys
Visits organised from the school for their educational and cultural value. It is customary to prepare pupils for the experience (e.g. by consulting maps and making plans) and to follow up with discussion, writing, etc.

E. LAYTON and J. B. WHITE, *The School Looks Around*, Longmans 1948

E. B. WARR, *Social Experience in the Junior School*, Methuen 1951

Educationally subnormal. *See* **ESN schools**

Eduction of correlates
The process of discovering a missing term when the other term and the relationship between the two terms are known, e.g. in 'The opposite of black is ——?', the educed correlate is 'white'. Eduction of correlates is part of **Spearman's** definition of intelligence.

R. KNIGHT, *Intelligence and Intelligence Tests*, 5th edn, Methuen 1953

EEG. *See* **Electroencephalography**

Ego
In the Freudian triple division of the personality, the ego is the largely conscious and logical part which deals with percepts, reality and the outer world. One of its main functions is to maintain a balance between the forces of the id, the inhibiting influence of the superego, and reality. The main aim of psychotherapy is the strengthening of the ego.

H. CRICHTON-MILLER, *Psycho-Analysis and its Derivatives*, 2nd edn, Oxford University Press (Home University Library) 1945

A. FREUD, *The Ego and the Mechanisms of Defence*, Hogarth Press 1968

S. FREUD, *The Ego and the Id*, Hogarth Press 1962

D. STAFFORD CLARK, *What Freud Really Said*, Macdonald 1965

Eidetic imagery
The type of vivid imagery, chiefly in young children and rarely occurring after adolescence, in which the image is not localised within the head but is projected on to some external surface. Other features of the eidetic image are its intensity and its richness of detail.

G. W. ALLPORT, 'Eidetic Imagery', *British Journal of Psychology*, 1924, pp 99–120

R. N. HABER, 'Eidetic images', *Scientific American*, **220**, no. 4, April 1969

N. L. MUNN, *Psychology: the fundamentals of human adjustment*, 5th edn, Harrap 1966, pp. 381 f

Electroencephalography
The study by mechanical methods of the electrical activity of the brain in humans. The encephalograph is an instrument which amplifies the brain's electric currents (which are of the order of less than a millivolt), picking them up from electrodes on the scalp. The wave pattern is recorded on a moving roll of paper by ink-writing pens, and the patterns thus obtained are susceptible of analysis and interpretation for diagnostic and experimental purposes. Such a record of wave patterns is usually referred to as an electroencephalogram, or EEG.

D. HILL and G. PARR, eds, *Electroencephalography*, 2nd edn, Macdonald 1963

Electro-convulsive therapy (ECT)
A treatment for mental disorder. The patient is treated with anaesthetic and muscle relaxant drugs, supplied with oxygen, and a small electrical current is applied. The effect of the treatment, which may be repeated, is to relieve depression.

D. STAFFORD CLARK, *Psychiatry for Students*, 3rd edn, Allen & Unwin 1965

Elementary Code (1904)
This code, following the *Balfour Act* of 1902, contained changes designed to liberalise the elementary schools.

J. S. MACLURE, *Educational Documents 1816–1967*, 2nd edn, Chapman & Hall 1968

Elementary education
A term which came into common use to describe the system of basic studies centred on literary and simple number skills which

national systems of schooling offered when first instituted. Thus it came to mean the earliest stage of schooling. The term 'elementary school' tended to be used for state schools giving education between the ages of 5 and 14. It was discontinued after 1944 when 'secondary education for all' after the age of 11 was instituted. The term is now obsolete in the UK.

S. J. CURTIS and M. E. A. BOULTWOOD, *History of English Education since 1800*, University Tutorial Press 1966

Hadow Report, *Education of the Adolescent*, 1926

J. D. WILSON, *The Schools of England*, Sidgwick & Jackson 1928, ch. 3

Eleven plus

The selection examination for entry to selective secondary schools (usually **Grammar schools**) which children in fewer and fewer LEAs take after attaining their tenth or eleventh year, towards the end of the primary school course.

With increasing reorganisation of education at secondary level on comprehensive lines, the eleven-plus examination is being phased out. Its retention in some LEAs is associated with the selection of a small percentage of pupils to take up reserved places in **direct grant schools**.

See also **Special place examination**

W. MCCLELLAND, *Selection for Secondary Education*, University of London Press 1942

R. PEDLEY, *The Comprehensive School*, 4th edn, Penguin 1969

D. PIDGEON amd A. YATES, *Admission to Grammar School*, Newnes 1957

P. E. VERNON, *Secondary School*, Methuen 1957

Elite – theory of education

The view which holds that the best returns in Education can be obtained by concentrating educational resources on the few who are likely to contribute highly valued skills. Hence it aims at refining selective procedures and improving **higher education** for a privileged minority rather than distributing available resources over the whole educational system.

G. H. BANTOCK, *Freedom and Authority in Education*, Faber 1970

C. BROGAN, *The Educational Revolution*, Muller 1955

J. W. GARDNER, *Excellence*, Harper & Row 1961

K. MANNHEIM, *Man and Society: in an Age of Reconstruction*, Routledge & Kegan Paul 1940

R. WILKINSON, *The Prefects*, Oxford University Press 1963

Embryology

The branch of biology concerned with the study of a young organism in the early stages of development, for example as before hatching from the egg. In mammals the term 'embryo' is used to describe the organism in the earliest phase of its prenatal development. The term 'foetus' is applied to the organism in the later stages.

N. L. MUNN, *The Evolution and Growth of Human Behaviour*, 2nd edn, Harrap 1965

Emergency training

The critical shortage of teachers, caused by the war and by the decision to raise the school leaving age to fifteen, brought about the Emergency Training Scheme, designed to attract able men and women by offering them a year's intensive training. The first emergency training colleges opened in 1945 (there had previously been a pilot scheme) and the scheme closed in 1951, having produced 30,000 teachers. The colleges were set up and administered by the LEAs and were financed by the Ministry. Courses lasted thirteen months, including about six weeks vacation.

MINISTRY OF EDUCATION, *Challenge and Response*, HMSO 1950

Emile

Title of, and name of the principal character of the French philosopher, **J. J. Rousseau's** famous educational work of 1762. Emile is the pupil, Jean-Jacques is the Preceptor. Emile's upbringing and education are described in detail up to the moment when he becomes a father. The key idea, revolutionary at the time, was that the teacher should follow the child's natural development, treat the child as a child not as a miniature adult; the education should be 'negative', that is, not seeking deliberately to mould and fashion the child, by precept and discipline, but instead permitting the maximum of liberty and experience (though in a completely supervised and artificial environment).

G. H. BANTOCK, 'Emile reconsidered', *British Journal of Educational Studies*, 1953

W. BOYD, ed., *Emile for Today*, Heinemann 1956

H. M. POLLARD, *Pioneers of Popular Education*, Murray 1956, ch. 2

Emotion

The affective aspect of experience, innately primitive in form and developing by differentiation according to the environment, into the many recognised manifestations, e.g. love, fear, jealousy, rage, frustration, etc. Emotional states are closely bound up with motivation in learning school subjects. Emotional disorders are a feature of **maladjustment**. Emotional development is a product of both maturation and learning; the school's task in 'educating' children's emotions, is broadly that of avoiding or combating culturally disapproved manifestations (e.g. violent rage, phobic fears, jealousy) whilst promoting a harmonious, balanced development through aesthetic and social experiences, literature, drama and play.

G. H. BANTOCK, *Education, Culture and the Emotions*, Faber 1967

S. FREUD, *A General Selection from the Works of S. Freud*, ed. J. Rickman, Hogarth Press 1937

N. L. MUNN, *Psychology: the fundamentals of human adjustment*, Harrap 1966

M. PHILLIPS, *The Education of the Emotions*, Allen & Unwin 1937

Empathy

A word coined in 1912 to denote the power through which a person reacts to an experience, especially of the aesthetic type, by a particularly close identification with the performer, the part, or role played. The observer 'feels himself into' what is observed, assimilating the experience in a particularly direct way. A common example, among many, is when some spectators keenly watching a high jumper, themselves lift one of their legs from the ground, as though they themselves were involved in the jump. It is a particularly important quality in teachers who are trying to understand children's problems.

G. M. BLAIR, R. S. JONES and R. H. SIMPSON, *Educational Psychology*, New York, Macmillan 1954

Empirical

Term used to describe a result gained from practical experience or observation, rather than deduced from abstract principles. Hence applied to many educational and some psychological findings and procedures.

Empiricism

The doctrine which, rejecting speculative, metaphysical demonstrations, prefers confirmation of results by experiment and observation.

In philosophy it is notably a British movement (Locke, Berkeley, Hume).

A. J. AYER and R. WINCH, eds, *The British Empirical Philosophers*, Routledge & Kegan Paul 1952

Employment: children

Children's employment is governed by the Children and Young Persons' Act 1933, as variously amended, and by the bye-laws which it empowers Local Authorities to make. In general no child may be employed until he has reached an age which is two years below the upper limit of compulsory school leaving age: he may not be employed before the end of school hours or for more than two hours per day. There is a long list of prohibited occupations. The teacher's responsibility is to draw attention of the **LEA** to suspected infringements. But see amendments contained in local By-Laws which can be furnished by the Local Education Officer.

G. R. BARRELL, *Teachers and the Law*, Methuen 1966

G. TAYLOR and J. B. SAUNDERS, *The New Law of Education*, 7th edn, Butterworth 1971

Employment: school leavers

School leavers may be placed in employment either privately or through the Youth Employment Officer of the Department of Employment and Productivity or of the **LEA**. In most areas the latter visits the school regularly to interview leavers; frequently carries out vocational selection procedures and collaborates with the Careers master.

M. P. CARTER, *Home, School and Work*, Pergamon 1962

M. P. CARTER, *Into Work*, Penguin (Pelican) 1969

Crowther Report, *15–18*, 1959

Employment, teachers

Teachers in **maintained** schools are employed by the **LEA** and may be appointed (*a*) to the staff of a particular school (*b*) to the service of the authority, and therefore liable to be sent to any school in the authority's area. Other teachers may be employed on a 'temporary basis'; on a 'supply basis', i.e.

asked to teach in a school for a few days or weeks; or on a 'permanent supply basis' which may include service as a **peripatetic** teacher or as head-teacher in country schools.

G. R. BARRELL, *Teachers and the Law*, Methuen 1966

G. TAYLOR and J. B. SAUNDERS, *The New Law of Education*, 7th edn, Butterworth 1971

Endocrinology
The systematic study of the function of the endocrine glands, which assist in the regulation of body mechanisms by their chemical secretions into the bloodstream. Endocrine imbalance may affect children's capacity to profit from education.

V. H. MOTTRAM, *The Physical Basis of Personality*, Penguin 1944

A. S. MASON, *Health and Hormones*, Penguin (Pelican) 1960

Endomorph
The type of physique, according to Sheldon's theory, in which the digestive organs predominate giving an obese, flabby appearance. The Endomorph is associated by Sheldon with the viscerotonic temperament, characterised by joy of eating, joviality and relaxation.

L. J. BISCHOF, *Interpreting Personality Theories*, Harper & Row 1965, ch. 9

SHELDON and STEVENS, *The Varieties of Temperament*, Harper & Row 1942

Endowed Schools Commission
Set up by the Endowed Schools Act 1869, this Commission had powers to reform endowed grammar schools by altering their foundation deeds so as to release funds. Before losing their powers to the *Charity Commission* in 1874 they made 235 new schemes of school government.

S. J. CURTIS and M. E. A. BOULTWOOD, *An Introductory History of Education in England since 1800*, 4th edn, University Tutorial Press 1966

Spens Report, *Secondary Education*, 1938

English, Use of
1. Arising from the need to ensure a standard of English expression among (especially) science students, a number of Examining Boards have set up a paper in the 'Use of English' at **GCE A** level, which has been recognised for entrance requirements in several universities.

2. A magazine, edited by D. Thompson, published by Chatto & Windus.
National Association for Teachers of English, 41 Brooksly Road, Tilehurst, Reading, Berks.

English Association
An association founded in 1906 to promote knowledge and appreciation of the English language and literature and to uphold standards in written and spoken English. It publishes *English Essays and Studies* and *The Year's Work in English Studies*.
Address: 8 Cromwell Place, London SW7

Enuresis
Bedwetting, the involuntary release of urine during sleep. This is not particularly abnormal up to about age 5 in children, but at later ages may be symptomatic of emotional disturbance or maladjustment, if not due to physical defect.

J. APLEY and R. M. KEITH, *The Child and His Symptoms*, 2nd edn, Blackwell 1968

Environment
The general conditions (as opposed to inherited factors) of life, especially those of home, neighbourhood and school, that have a bearing on the growth and development of mind, personality and character.

Environmental studies
A subject taken at school or college of education, designed to give life to the formal curriculum by combining history, geography, social studies, etc., in a systematic examination of the environment, which is taken as the centre of interest. Projects, workbooks, visits and field work methods are frequently used in this teaching.

D. G. WATTS, *Environmental Studies*, Routledge & Kegan Paul 1969

H. A. T. GLOVER, *New Teaching for a New Age*, Nelson 1946

A. HAMMERSELY, F. JONES and G. A. PERRY, *Environmental Studies*, Blandford 1968

H. PHILLIPS and F. J. C. MCINNES, *Exploration in the Junior School*, University of London Press 1950

V. ROGERS, *The Social Studies in English Education*, Heinemann 1968

A. W. ROWE, *The Education of the Average Child*, Harrap 1959

G. MARTIN and E. R. A. TURNER, *Environmental Studies*, Blond 1972

EPA. *See* **Educational priority area**

Epistemology
The theory of knowledge: that branch of philosophy which deals with problems concerning the nature and validity of knowledge and belief.
J. S. BRUBACHER, *Modern Philosophies of Education,* McGraw-Hill 1969, Ch. 4,
B. RUSSELL, *An Inquiry into Meaning and Truth,* Allen & Unwin 1940, Penguin (Pelican) 1970

Equal addition
This is one of the methods of effecting subtraction (*see* **Decomposition** for another method). It is a method which can facilitate the process of subtraction by adding equally to the minuend and subtrahend, e.g.

$$\begin{array}{r} 4\ ^16 \\ -\ ^32\ 8 \\ \hline 1\ 8 \\ \hline \end{array}$$

In this instance ten units have been added to six, in the minuend, and one ten has been added to the twenty in the subtrahend. The actual problem has thus been transposed from 'forty-six subtract twenty-eight' to 'forty-sixteen subtract thirty-eight'.
L. W. DOWNES and D. PALING, *Arithmetic in the Primary School,* Oxford University Press, Unesco Handbooks 1958

Equality of educational opportunity
The political ideal that all children should have equal chances to develop their abilities and aptitudes to the fullest extent. Initially an attempt was made to overcome inequalities in parental wealth by the extension of the free place system. After 1944, inquiries into the working of 11+ selection led to an increased awareness of social-class learning. **J. Floud's** *Social Class and Educational Opportunity* made a turning point. It was increasingly felt that a Comprehensive system of Secondary Education would provide conditions of greater equality of opportunity than the Tripartite system. With the publication of the **Newsom** (1963) and **Plowden** (1967) **Reports,** the idea of compensating underprivileged children extended the notion of creating conditions of greater equality of opportunity, by suggesting increased spending in **Educational Priority Areas.**
See also **Parity of esteem**

DEPARTMENT OF EDUCATION AND SCIENCE, Circular 10/65, HMSO
J. W. B. DOUGLAS, *Home and School,* Mac-Gibbon & Kee 1964; Panther 1969
J. W. B. DOUGLAS and others, *All our Future,* Peter Davis 1968
P. MUSGRAVE, *Sociology of Education,* Methuen 1965

Erasmus (of Rotterdam: 1466–1536)
Renaissance scholar who travelled widely and wrote extensively, including works embodying Renaissance humanist attitudes in education, particularly with reference to the teaching of Latin. Best known are the *De Ratione Studii,* 1511 and *De Pueris Instituendis* 1529; he also revised Lilly's Latin grammar text, whilst in England. His educational work is mainly concerned with the duties of parents and tutors. He represents the transition between the early humanism of the Italian Quattrocento attitudes and the later European Renaissance. He also worked for reform, within the Church, by his satirical writing. Selections of his works in translation: *Essential Works,* Col. W. T. H. Jackson (Bantam Books 1968); *The Essential Erasmus,* ed. J. P. Dolan (Mentor Books 1968)
W. H. WOODWARD, *Desiderius Erasmus,* Columbia University Press 1964

Eroticism or **Erotism**
A term which, in the Freudian sense, includes sexual excitement derived at various stages of individual development from oral, anal and genital regions. It is also used to denote an excessive show of sexual feelings and reaction.

Escapism
The tendency or desire to evade duties, tasks or situations because they spell difficulty or unpleasantness. The process often involves **rationalisation** on the part of the 'escaper' which may be prompted by unconscious motives.

ESN schools
Schools for educationally subnormal children; one of the several types of schools for handicapped children.
Educationally subnormal children are 'pupils who, by reason of limited ability or other conditions resulting in educational retardation, require some specialised form of education wholly or partly in substitution

for education normally given in ordinary school' (Ministry of Education, *The Handicapped Pupils and Special Schools Regulations*, pamphlet no. 365, HMSO 1959).

Before proceeding to an ESN school a child is usually, but not necessarily, ascertained by his local authority as being in need of special educational provision. Recommendation for admission is made by a Medical Officer.

Minimum leaving age (as for all special schools) is sixteen.

ESN schools may be day or residential. Whether a child will proceed to one or the other will depend on his particular needs, the geographical nature of the catchment area for the particular school, and on the consent of the parents.

M. F. CLEUGH, ed., *Teaching the Slow Learner in the Special School*, Methuen 1961

S. JACKSON, *Special Education in England and Wales*, 2nd edn, Oxford University Press 1969

D. G. PRITCHARD, *Education and the Handicapped, 1760–1960*, Routledge & Kegan Paul 1963

ESP. *See* Extrasensory perception

Esperanto

An artificial 'international' language made up of words common to the chief European languages but which excludes sounds peculiar to any one language. It was devised by a Russian, Dr L. Zamenhof, who adopted the pseudonym 'Dr Esperanto' in 1887.

G. A. CONNOR, *Esperanto*, Bailey Bros (Yoseloff) 1959

Essay

1. A piece of continuous original prose composed by pupils on a given topic or subject.

J. A. CUTFORTH, *English in the Primary School*, Blackwell 1952

P. GURREY, *The Teaching of Written English*, Longmans 1954

B. JACKSON and D. THOMPSON, eds., *English in Education*, Chatto & Windus 1962

2. Literary composition which deals analytically or interpretatively with a subject from the personal viewpoint of the writer.

Essentialism

An educational theory which emphasises the authority which comes from tradition and which claims to distinguish the essential from the non-essential in school curricula.

In an article in *Foundations of Education* (Wiley 2nd edn, 1967), G. F. Kneller states the four basic principles of essentialism as follows:

(*a*) learning necessarily involves hard work and application;

(*b*) the initiative in education should be with the teacher rather than with the pupil;

(*c*) the heart of the educational process is the absorption of prescribed subject matter;

(*d*) the school should not abandon traditional methods of mental discipline.

J. S. BRUBACHER, *Modern Philosophies of Education*, McGraw-Hill 1969

Ethics

The systematised study of the principles of morally 'right' and 'wrong' behaviour.

A. MACINTYRE, *A Short History of Ethics*, Routledge & Kegan Paul 1967

R. S. PETERS, *Ethics and Education*, Allen & Unwin 1966

Ethics (professional)

The norms of correct conduct characteristic of, or laid down by, a profession, e.g. in teaching it would be considered unethical and unprofessional for a Head to make a report on a member of his staff to the LEA without first showing it to the individual teacher concerned.

Handbook of Information for Teachers, Schoolmaster Publishing Co.

Ethnic group

A racial, national or tribal group characterised by common manners, custom and beliefs.

Ethos

Greek word, 'custom'; the prevailing tone, the characteristic sentiments prevailing in e.g. a school or particular type of school. Thus 'the public school ethos' or 'grammar school ethos'.

Euclid

Greek mathematician who lived in Alexandria in the third century BC. He is best known for his *Elements* which became the basis for the study of geometry generally. The majority of non-Euclidean geometries are still based on his works.

T. L. HEATH, *History of Greek Mathematics*, 2 vols, Oxford University Press 1921

Eurhythmics
A system developed by **Jaques-Dalcroze** in which the appreciation and interpretation of music, especially on the rhythmic side, is learnt through physical movement.
E. JAQUES-DALCROZE, *Rhythm, Music and Education*, New York, Dalcroze Society 1967

Evening institutes
Establishments usually housed in day schools and supported by the **LEA**, which provide Further Education and purposeful leisure time study and occupation for people of all ages from school leaving age upwards during the autumn and winter months. Modest fees are charged; courses include vocational and educational subjects, arts, crafts and music.
MINISTRY OF EDUCATION, Pamphlet no. 28, *Evening Institutes*, HMSO 1956

Evening School
Usually a school conducted in the evenings on day-school or college premises for purposes of **further education**; nowadays more frequently termed **evening institute**.

Examining Boards for GCE
1. Associated Examining Board for the General Certificate of Education
2. Cambridge Local Examinations Syndicate
3. Joint Matriculation Board (The Universities of Manchester, Liverpool, Leeds, Sheffield and Birmingham)
4. University Entrance and School Examinations Council, University of London
5. Oxford and Cambridge Schools Examination Board
6. Oxford Local Examination
7. Southern Universities Joint Board for School Examinations (Universities of Bristol, Exeter, Reading, Southampton and Surrey)
8. Welsh Joint Education Committee

Examination
A formal written, practical or oral test to appraise students' progress, ability or knowledge, e.g. the Eleven plus selection examination for selective secondary schools, **GCE, CSE, Internal examinations**.
P. HARTOG and E. C. RHODES, *Examination of Examinations*, Macmillan 1936
J. MONTGOMERY, *Examinations: an account of their evolution as administrative devices in England*, Longmans 1965
S. WISEMAN, *Examinations and English Education*, Manchester University Press 1961

Excepted district
A municipal borough or urban district, not forming part of the normal administrative arrangements of an **LEA**, but allowed its own administration (under the Education Act 1944) provided the population was not less than 60,000, or the school population was not less than 7000, and provided also that the agreement of the Department of Education and Science is obtained. There are approximately forty such excepted districts.
H. C. DENT, *The Education Act of 1944*, University of London Press 1944

Exceptional children
Children whose education, because of giftedness or because of mental or physical handicap, may be considered to require special provision.
See also **Mentally gifted; Handicapped**

Exchange of teachers
A scheme enabling teachers to be seconded for one year to teach in some other Commonwealth country or in the United States, their own places being filled by teachers from these same countries.
Write: Central Bureau for Educational Visit and Exchanges, 55a Duke Street, Grosvenor Square, London, W1

Exercise
A task designed to give a pupil the opportunity to practise a specific skill or to reproduce information, with the object of increasing his ability and enabling the teacher to assess his progress. Traditional textbook layout takes the form of an expository section followed by exercises closely related to it, with general revision exercises at longer intervals.

Exhibitionism
An abnormal degree of behaviour designed to attract attention: in the classroom, usually symptomatic of some acute need or deprivation.
H. CRICHTON-MILLER, *Psychoanalysis and its Derivatives*, 2nd edn, Oxford University Press (Home University Library) 1945

Existentialism
A system of philosophy, resembling an introspective humanism, in which emphasis is placed on the individual's goal in life and the values he has discovered for himself. The individual's own existence is of prime impor-

tance. Since the war Existentialism has attracted the attention of many young people, particularly in France.

W. BARRETT, *Irrational Man*, Mercury Books 1961

W. KAUFMANN, *Existentialism from Dostoievsky to Sartre*, World Publishing Co 1965

Experience
The acquisition of knowledge, understanding, skills and attitudes through active participation. Modern educational thinking and practice place great stress on the value of experience in the educational process. This principle is found *par excellence* in infant classes but tends to give way more and more to verbal instruction, the older the children become. Experience can be direct, or second-hand, e.g. through pictures or through experiences recounted by a writer or speaker.

S. MARSHALL, *An Experiment in Education*, Cambridge University Press 1963; paperback 1966

MELLOR, E., *Education through Experience in Infant School Years*, Blackwell 1950

Experiential
Pertaining to experience.

Experimental group
Normally considered in conjunction with **control group**. In any investigation into the effects of a particular factor on the development (physical, intellectual, etc.) of children, or other persons, it is necessary as far as possible to isolate this one factor, e.g. two groups can be studied, matched in all respects except that one group is left-handed. The difference in performance (e.g. speed of writing) may then be attributed possibly to that factor. The group into which this factor is introduced is called the 'experimental' group and the group carrying on normally is called the 'control' group.

W. R. BORG, *Educational Research: an introduction*, McKay 1963

F. L. WHITNEY, *Elements of Research*, 3rd edn, Prentice-Hall 1950

Experimental psychology
The study of various aspects of human and animal behaviour through the use of laboratory techniques.

W. M. O'NEIL, *Method in Psychology*, Melbourne University Press 1962

C. E. OSGOOD, *Method and Theory in Experi-* *mental Psychology* Oxford University Press 1952

C. W. VALENTINE, *An Introduction to Experimental Psychology*, University Tutorial Press 1947

See also **Psychology**

Extended course
A course going beyond the statutory school leaving age. Such courses frequently, but not always, prepare pupils for **CSE** or **GCE O** level examinations. **Crowther Report**, *15–18*, 1950, ch. 5

External degree
An initial or a higher degree of a university which can be taken by candidates who may have prepared their work outside that university, e.g. by private study or during attendance at some other educational institution. External initial degrees can be taken only in the University of London but *higher degrees* are awarded by many universities without a residence requirement.

Address: External Registrar, University of London, Senate House, Malet Street, London, WC1

External examinations
Examinations set and administered by an institution which does not take part in the teaching or training of candidates, e.g. the external examinations of the University of London for its degree, or those set by the various examination boards for **GCE**.

R. J. MONTGOMERY, *Examinations: an account of their evolution as administrative devices in England*, Longmans 1965

Extracurricular
A term used to describe those activities carried out under the aegis of the school (though not necessarily supervised or deliberately organised) which are not within the time devoted to lessons and **PE** – e.g. drama, debating, games, rambling, canoeing, excursions social activities, etc.

Extramural
Term used to describe academic work, at the **higher education** level, conducted outside the university or college responsible for it; usually lectures, seminars, practical sessions, etc. Most universities have an Extramural Department whose tutors organise and staff the work. Extramural courses are advertised and are open to the public.

Extrapolation
1. The calculation of values of a function beyond the range provided by tabulated data, e.g. supposing the given top 'raw' score in a table of norms in an intelligence test corresponds to a particular **IQ**, it would be necessary, if the 'raw' score of a particular candidate goes above this, to extrapolate in order to estimate the appropriate IQ.
2. The confirmation of a curve beyond the point for which there are data, on the assumption that the curve will continue to be regular.

Extrasensory perception (ESP)
Perception which, it is claimed, takes place outside the normal sensory channels. Used by some psychologists to explain such powers as telepathy and clairvoyance, which cannot be explained scientifically. Sometimes expressed in the abbreviated form – ESP.
J. B. RHINE, *New Frontiers of the Mind*, Penguin (Pelican) 1950

Extrovert
Jung postulated two personality types, the introvert (shy, retiring) and the extrovert (outgoing, uninhibited). Experimental work by Eysenck established this as a continuum of measureable responses, and as one of the major empirical dimensions of personality, as measured by a question-and-answer technique such as the Maudsley Personality Inventory (MPI).
H. J. EYSENCK, *The Structure of Human Personality*, 3rd edn, Methuen 1970

Eyedness
See **laterality**. The preferential use of one eye rather than the other in tasks requiring the use of one eye only, and affecting vision generally if involved in cross-laterality, i.e. where a person is right-eyed and left-handed, or vice versa.
C. BURT, *The Backward Child*, 4th edn, University of London Press 1937

M. CLARK, *Left-handedness*, University of London Press 1957

Eye movement
A phrase usually found in a context relating to movements of the eye during reading. The eye moves along the level of print and periodically pauses. These pauses are known as 'fixations' and the distance between the 'fixations' is known as 'the eye-span'. Good readers usually make few fixation pauses from the beginning to the end of a line of print, while poor readers make many more. But poor and irregular eye-movement is not the cause of poor reading. It is the reflection of reading inability. A child who has poor eye-movement in reading needs to be given simpler material which interests him and on which he can succeed.
A. I. GATES, *The Improvement of Reading*, 3rd edn, Collier-Macmillan 1947
A. J. HARRIS, *How to Increase Reading Ability*, 3rd edn, Longmans 1956

Eye-span
The number of words, measured in letters or letter-spaces, read during one fixation pause of the eyes.
I. H. ANDERSON and W. F. DEARBORN, *The Psychology of Teaching Reading*, Ronald Press 1952

Eye-voice span
The distance between the word being read (silently) and the actual word being uttered, this distance usually being described in numbers of letters.
I. H. ANDERSON and W. F. DEARBORN, *The Psychology of Teaching Reading*, Ronald Press 1952

Eye-hand span
In typewriting the distance in number of words (usually about $1\frac{1}{2}$ words) between what the typist is reading and what is being typed.

F

Face to face group

Primary groups in which individuals are in frequent contact with one another directly: family, village, school, work, recreational groups.

P. W. MUSGRAVE, *The Sociology of Education*, Methuen 1965

W. J. H. SPROTT, *Human Groups*, Penguin (Pelican) 1967

Factor (in cognitive abilities)

1. A general factor is the mental ability which is brought into play whatever the nature of the intellectual tasks or tests and it accounts for the positive association or inter-correlation between them. It is much in evidence in a test of general intelligence consisting of a variety of subtests involving e.g. verbal elements, numerical elements, logical elements.

2. A group factor is a mental ability within the wider context of the general factor, but independent of it. It accounts for a positive association between tasks or tests within a more limited range. Verbal ability is an example of a group factor and is revealed in the intercorrelation between the various reading and writing skills.

3. A specific factor is that element in intellectual performance which accounts, in isolation from the general factor or any group factor, for success in particular tasks or particular parts of a task. For example, the power of visual imagery might help in the solution of certain kinds of tasks or problems but it does not reveal positive association with other specific factors.

P. E. VERNON, *Measurement of Abilities*, 2nd edn, University of London Press 1956

Factor analysis

The statistical techniques which analyse test correlations in order to find which are the most important factors involved.

J. P. GUILFORD, *Psychometric Methods*, 2nd edn McGraw-Hill 1954

D. N. LAWLEY and A. E. MAXWELL *Factor Analysis as a Statistical Method*, Butterworth 1963

G. H. THOMSON, *The Factorial Analysis of Human Ability*, University of London Press 1939

Factor theory, of intelligence

The theory which was developed in opposition to **Spearman's** two-factor theory. Spearman contended that human intellectual ability could be broken down into two com-ponents, namely, a factor of general ability (designated 'g') and a specific ability linked with the particular activity being attempted (designated 's'). Later investigators, particularly Thurstone, found the concept of general ability unacceptable and broke down intelligence into a number of group factors which overlap, e.g. verbal, numerical, spatial ability. More recently Guilford in California, using the technique of factor-analysis, has broken down intellectual ability into over forty factors.

J. P. GUILFORD, *The Nature of Human Intelligence*, McGraw-Hill 1967

G. H. THOMSON, *Instinct, Intelligence and Character*, Allen & Unwin 1924, ch. 20

L. L. THURSTON, 'Theories of intelligence', *Scientific Monthly*, **62**, 1946, 101–12

P. E. VERNON, *Measurement of Abilities*, 2nd edn, University of London Press 1956

Faculty psychology

During the nineteenth century it was believed that the mind was composed of specific faculties (memory, imagination, reasoning, etc.), located, improved and developed by teaching, and procedures were devised with this in view. With the appearance of the theories of general intelligence, faculty psychology ceased to be regarded as useful.

R. S. WOODWORTH and R. M. SHEEHAN, *Contemporary Schools of Psychology*, 3rd edn, Methuen 1965

Family

The fundamental social institution; a primary group based on socially sanctioned sex relationships. The mother, father and children constitute the nuclear family. With other relations, usually married offspring, they constitute the extended family. Diverse classifications of the family are used by anthropologists.

J. H. S. BOSSARD and E. S. BOLL, *Sociology of Child Development*, Harper & Row 1966

R. HOGGART, *Uses of Literacy*, Chatto 1957; Penguin (Pelican) 1969

M. MEAD and K. HEYMAN, *Family*, Collier-Macmillan 1965

P. MUSGRAVE, *The Sociology of Education*, Methuen 1965

W. J. H. SPROTT, *Human Groups*, Penguin (Pelican) 1958, ch. 4

Family system (grouping)

1. A system employed particularly in residential schools for children who are delinquent

or disturbed or partially sighted, etc., under which the pupils live in small groups (eight to twelve in each) with a housemother and perhaps housefather. This is thought to promote intimacy, security and a feeling of belonging in a domestic atmosphere.
2. The family system, or family grouping, is also used in some progressive infant schools (notably in Bristol) where the children are not grouped in classes according to age but in small groups, ranging from 5 to 7 years. Brothers, sisters, cousins, etc. of varying ages may or may not be included in the same 'family'. The organisation is sometimes referred to as 'vertical classification'.
L. RIDGWAY and I. LAWTON, *Family Grouping in the Primary School*, Ward Lock Educational 1968
L. RIDGWAY and I. LAWTON, *Family Grouping in the Infants' School*, Ward Lock Educational 1965

Fantasy
Imaginative activity where images arise at the whim or pleasure of the individual. The fantasy stage is passed through in the normal development of most young children and is only to be thought of as dangerous if indulged in excessively as a form of escape.
It is often used diagnostically in projective techniques to explore aspects of personality.
N. L. MUNN, *Psychology: the fundamentals of human adjustment*, Harrap 1966
K. BÜHLER, *The Mental Development of the Child*, Routledge & Kegan Paul, 1930
S. ISAACS, *Childhood and After*, Routledge & Kegan Paul 1948

FAP. *See* Fixed action pattern

Fatigue
Weariness from labour of body or mind. In psychological literature the term is often used to indicate a decreasing efficiency which may be due to physical, mental, nervous or sensory factors. The subjective element in fatigue is boredom due to repetition of the same activity or from lack of motivation.
N. L. MUNN, *Psychology: the fundamentals of human adjustment*, 5th edn, Harrap 1966
M. D. VERNON, *The Psychology of Perception*, University of London Press, 1965; Penguin (Pelican) 1972

Favouritism
The tendency, conscious or unconscious, for a teacher to show special consideration for some pupil or pupils and for this to reveal itself in various forms of preferential treatment.

Federal university
A university comprising a number of colleges in different places, possessing considerable degrees of autonomy, conducting their own courses and examinations, but linked together by certain common factors and interests and holding one joint university charter. The only example in Britain is the University of Wales.
See also **College of university**

Feeble-minded
According to the pre-1959 classification of mental defectives the category which was above that of **idiot** and **imbecile**. This classification has now been discontinued.

Feedback
Term derived from the science of servo-mechanics and control systems to describe the return to a system, of part of its output, so as to correct instability or mistakes. It was used to describe **cybernetic** regulatory systems, and is now loosely used in learning theory to describe any measure of check on the efficiency of teaching by a partial monitoring or testing of the learner's responses. Thus a teacher may, during a lesson, regard the wrong answers to his questions as 'feedback' which will indicate the need for a change in approach or the use of a different technique of teaching.
See also **Programmed learning**
W. SLUCKIN, *Minds and Machines*, rev. edn, Penguin (Pelican) 1960
K. U. SMITH and M. F. SMITH, *Cybernetic Principles of Learning*, Holt, Reinhart & Winston 1966
D. UNWIN, ed., *Media and Methods*, McGraw-Hill, 1969, p. 1.

Fernald-Keller method
A method of teaching reading which stresses the value of writing and tracing, and the articulatory impressions from saying words. Some teachers use the method to supplement other techniques when teaching slow-learners.
G. M. FERNALD and H. KELLER, 'The effect of kinaesthetic factors in the development of word-recognition in the case of non-readers',

(*Journal of Educational Research*, no. 4, Dec. 1921.)

F. J. SCHONELL, *Backwardness in the Basic Subjects*, Oliver & Boyd 1942, ch. 10

Field cognition theory

A theory, relevant to learning and problem solving, which stresses the total situation within which an activity is performed, usually considered as a system of forces and obstructions. A developed form of this theory is that of **Kurt Lewin**.

L. CARMICHAEL, *Manual of Child Psychology*, 2nd edn, Wiley 1954, ch. 15

K. LEWIN, *Principles of Topological Psychology*, McGraw-Hill 1936

B. B. WOLMAN, *Contemporary Theories and Systems in Psychology*, Harper & Row 1960, ch. 13

Field work

Practical work, outside the laboratory or library, involving first hand study of a problem; the collection of data by observation, survey, interview, measurement and similar research techniques in order to generate or validate hypotheses, assess change, or reveal suspected conditions.

G. A. LUNDBERG, *Social Research*, Longmans 1948

C. SELLTIZ et al., *Research Methods in Social Relations*, Methuen 1960

Filial regression

The genetic principle, first expounded by **Galton**, according to which children tend (e.g. in height, or intelligence) to move statistically from the group to which their parents belong, towards the average; thus tall people tend to have children, who, as adults, become shorter than themselves and short people tend to have children who, as adults, tend to become taller than themselves.

J. COHEN, ed., *Readings in Psychology*, Allen & Unwin 1964, ch. 3

Finance of education

Public expenditure on primary, secondary and further education is shared between the local authority, which raises money by the rates, and the Central Government which raises money by national taxation. The government makes a block grant to each local authority to help finance social services of which education is one. The private sector depends upon fees. University education is mainly financed by the central government through the University Grants Committee UGC. A statement of financial details is published in the Department of Education and Science's annual report and notably in *Statistics of Education*.

M. BLAUG, ed., *Economics of Education*, Penguin, 2 vols., 1968–69

Statistics of Education: Vol. 5. Finance and Awards, HMSO

J. VAIZEY, *The Economics of Education*, Faber 1962

J. VAIZEY, *The Control of Education*, Faber 1963

J. VAIZEY, *Education for Tomorrow*, rev. edn, 1966, pp. 115–18

Finger painting

The technique used by young children at the nursery and infant stage of tracing-out patterns, designs or pictures with the finger on wet paint which has already been spread on the paper.

C. LANDRETH, *Education of the Young Child*, Wiley 1942, ch. 15

First school

The name suggested by the **Plowden Report** for schools catering for the 5–8 years age group. First schools are replacing Infant schools in many LEAs.

Plowden Report, *Children and Their Primary Schools* 1967

See also **Middle School**

Fisher Act

Education Act of 1918 which aimed at the establishment of 'a national system of public education available for all persons capable of profiting thereby'. Called for extension of nursery schools, fixed the leaving age at 14 without exemptions, abolished 'half-timers', provided for **central schools** and strove to set up compulsory further education. The financial restriction of the 1920s government nullified many of its intentions. H. A. L. Fisher, a Vice-Chancellor of the University of Sheffield, was appointed President of the Board of Education by Lloyd George.

S. J. CURTIS and M. E. A. BOULTWOOD, *History of English Education since 1800*, 4th edn, University Tutorial Press 1966, ch. 8

T. L. JARMAN, *Landmarks in the History of Education*, 2nd edn, Murray 1963, chs 17, 18

Fisher, Sir Ronald Aylmer (b. 1890)

Statistician. Educated at Harrow and Gonville and Caius College, Cambridge. Taught in Public Schools. Galton Professor of Eugenics, University College, London, 1933–43; Professor of Genetics, University of Cambridge, 1943–57. Many other academic distinctions.

Publications include: *Statistical Method for Research Workers* (13th edn, 1963); *Statistical Tables* (6th edn, 1963); *The Design of Experiments* (8th edn, 1966); *Statistical Methods and Scientific Inference* (2nd edn, 1959), all published by Oliver & Boyd.

Fit-person order
An order of court which commits a child or young person to the care of a person, other than the child's parents, fit to exercise such responsibility. Often the local authority is designated as 'a fit person'. Frequently used when the child or young person has committed an offence, or is deemed to be in need of care and protection, or is beyond control.
Children and Young Persons' Act, 1933

Five-point scale
An assessment scale ranging from the lowest grade, E, to the top grade, A. It is sometimes refined by the inclusion of pluses and minuses.
S. R. GRIFFITHS and L. W. DOWNES, *Educational Statistics for Beginners*, Methuen 1969

Fixation
1. The arrest of development of the personality, particularly the emotional aspect. Fixation is typified by childish actions, overdependence on others and self-centredness, although the intelligence of the person may be average or above. In Freudian psychoanalysis the term is frequently used to describe certain aspects of psychosexual development.
2. Mother fixation, over-attachment to the mother. Sometimes used as a synonym for the **Oedipus complex**.
S. FREUD, *A General Selection from the Works of S. Freud*, J. Rickman, ed., Hogarth Press 1937
J. NUTTIN, *Psychoanalysis and Personality*, Sheed & Ward 1954
3. The pause which is made by both eyes for the purpose of perception, e.g. when scanning a line of print in reading, the eyes normally pause at fairly regular intervals.
G. M. BLAIR, *Diagnostic and Remedial Teaching in Secondary Schools*, rev. edn, Collier-Macmillan 1956

Fixed action pattern (FAP)
A pattern of behaviour, particular to a species. Although such behaviour is rigid

and stereotyped, it is the climax of a series of instinctive actions, which, earlier in development might have had a degree of flexibility.
K. LORENZ, *King Solomon's Ring*, Methuen 1952
N. TINBERGEN, *Behaviour in Animals*, Methuen 1965

Flannel graph
A flat board over which flannel cloth is stretched. Paper or card outlines, to which strips of flannel are fixed, will adhere readily to the board. It thus facilitates rapidly changing displays. Used, mainly in infant and primary education, as a visual aid.
E. J. P. DEVEREUX, *An Introduction to Visual Aids*, Mathews, Drew & Selbourne 1964
Consult also: Visual Aids Centre, 78 High Holborn, London WC1.

Flash card
A card, showing a unit of meaning in reading or arithmetic, which is held up for the child to read for a very short space of time. The technique is designed to encourage the perception of meaningful units (e.g. a word, phrase or sentence, or a number fact like $6 \times 7 = 42$) rather than the elements, e.g. the individual letters of a word.
It is often used, in self-corrective form, as a device to encourage the necessary repetition of facts, in a pleasant way through **games**.
L. W. DOWNES and D. PALING, *The Teaching of Arithmetic in Primary Schools*, Oxford University Press, Unesco Handbooks, 1958, ch. 15

Fleming Report
A committee was set up by R. A. Butler in 1942 'to consider means whereby the association between the Public Schools and the general educational system could be developed and extended . . .' Their Report (*The Public Schools and the General Education System* 1944) recommended bursaries, and reserved places in the Public Schools for children who might profit irrespective of parental income. The suggestion has been accepted but rarely implemented. See also Report of the Public Schools Commission 1968-70, Appendix IIIA.
W. O. LESTER SMITH, *Education: an introductory survey*, Penguin (Pelican) 1957, ch. 7

Floud, Jean E.
Leading authority on the sociology of education with particular interests in selec-

tion procedures, social mobility as determined by schooling and the role of the teacher. Formerly lecturer and Reader in Sociology of Education at the Institute of Education, University of London; Fellow of Nuffield College, Oxford.

J. E. FLOUD, A. H. HALSEY and F. M. MARTIN, *Social Class and Educational Opportunity*, Heinemann 1956

A. H. HALSEY, J. E. FLOUD and C. A. ANDERSON, *Education, Economy and Society*, Free Press Glencoe 1961

Foetus (Amer. fetus)

The young organism in the womb, or in the egg, particularly in the later stages of development. In reference to man the term 'embryo' is used to describe the organism during the first three months and the term 'foetus' is applied from the end of the third month to birth.

Folk high school

A residential school offering courses to adults which are intended to increase their cultural, rather than academic or vocational skills. Flourishing in Scandinavia, they have been seen as a solution to many social problems and adult education shortcomings.

H. BEGTRUP, H. LUND, and P. MANNICHE, *The Folk High Schools of Denmark*, 4th edn, Oxford University Press 1949

J. LAUWERYS, ed., *Scandinavian Democracy*, Copenhagen 1958

Footrule (Spearman's)

A shortened version of **Spearman**'s 'rank order' formula for determining correlation.

The formula is $R = 1 - \dfrac{6\Sigma(g)}{N^2 - 1}$, where R is the correlation coefficient, g is the gain, if any, in rank in the second of the two series of ranks, and N is the number of cases.

Forecast

A statement of intended or projected lessons or activities. In some areas head teachers sometimes require their staff to submit a forecast of work for the immediate future period, e.g. for the week, or term.

Form board

A device used to test performance, and thus an aspect of intelligence, requiring the person tested to fit pegs or shapes into corresponding holes in a board. Frequently used with very small or severely retarded children, since it requires no verbal or written skills (e.g. Seguin Form Board).

A. ANASTASI, *Psychological Testing* 3rd edn, Collier-Macmillan 1968

Form entry

The usual number of classes which make up the annual intake of pupils into a school: hence a school may be described as 'three-form' or 'five-form entry'.

Formal approach

The approach to teaching which stresses rules and principles, analysis and deduction, technical vocabulary and drill methods, rather than creative activity, discovery and spontaneity. Its curricula and methods of teaching are academic, bookish, often tied to needs of examinations. It is characteristic of education which is teacher centred rather than child centred.

Formula

A concise statement, verbal or in mathematical symbols, of a structural or functional relationship. More loosely, it is a statement of a law, principle or set of conditions which might lead to the solving of an administrative problem.

Forster Act

Elementary Education Act 1870, introduced by W. E. Forster, MP for Bradford and Vice-President of the Education Department in the recently returned Liberal Government. He was a Quaker Radical, a son-in-law of Arnold of Rugby and keenly interested in education. The Bill established school districts (civil parishes or municipal boroughs). Where a deficiency of school provision was revealed by an Education Department survey, the religious denominations were given six months' grace to remedy them, and could apply for parliamentary grants in aid, but no local rate aid. Failing this, school boards were to be set up elected by ratepayers to 'fill up the gaps'. The Act created a system complementary to the existing voluntary system, (cp the '*dual system*') but left education neither completely free nor compulsory. In the next six years $1\frac{1}{2}$ million school places were provided, two-thirds by voluntary bodies, one-third by school boards.

H. C. BARNARD, *A History of English Education from 1760*, University of London Press 1961, ch. 13

S. J. CURTIS and M. E. A. BOULTWOOD, *An Introductory History of English Education since 1800*, 4th edn, University Tutorial Press 1966

Foster parent

An adult who accepts parental responsibility for a child not his or her own for a temporary period, but without adopting the child; usually through a **fit person order**.

J. STROUD, *Introduction to the Child Care Service*, Longmans 1965

G. M. TRASLER, *In Place of Parents*, Routledge & Kegan Paul 1960

Frame

1. Each picture in a motion film or film strip.
2. Each unit of instruction in a teaching-machine programme.
3. Climbing frame: a piece of apparatus used in physical education mainly for juniors and infants.

Frame of reference

1. Mathematical figure consisting of lines used as axes and a point (or points) of reference.
2. Principles, concepts, attitudes and values which have been organised into a system. The individual (or group) consciously or unconsciously accepts this system, interprets facts, and behaves accordingly. His behaviour is not always determined by the particular situation he is in, but by the frame of reference which he holds and into which the situation fits.

C. W. SHERIF and H. CANTRIL, *The Psychology of Ego Involvement*, Wiley 1947

Franks Report

A Commission of Inquiry was appointed by the Hebdomadal Council of Oxford University in 1964, under the Chairmanship of Lord Franks, Provost of Worcester College, Oxford, with the following terms of reference: To inquire into and report upon the part which Oxford plays now and should play in the future in the system of higher education in the United Kingdom, having regard to its position as both a national and international University; and in the light of its findings on this subject to consider 'various particular matters relating to the University.' The inquiry was triggered off by the publication of recommendations and criticisms in the **Robbins Report** which affected Oxford.

UNIVERSITY OF OXFORD, *Report of Commission of Inquiry*, 2 vols, Oxford University Press, 1966

Fraternal twins

Dizygotic (two-egg) twins; siblings who happen to be born at the same time, with different genetic endowment.

See also **Twins**

I. M. LERNER, *Heredity, Evolution and Society*, Freeman 1968

A. MONTAGU, *Human Heredity*, Mentor 1965, ch. 8

Freedom, Academic

The right of teachers at all levels to carry on their work without threats to their salary, tenure, or promotion prospects, or to their civil liberty, which might arise from attempts to force them to favour special political or religious beliefs in their teaching.

LORD BEVERIDGE, *A Defence of Free Learning*, Oxford University Press 1959

W. O. LESTER SMITH, *Education; an introductory survey*, Penguin (Pelican) 1957, ch. 6

Frequency (stats)

The number of times a score or measure appears in a set of marks or measures, e.g. if the following marks in a test are obtained by various members of a small class: 4, 9, 6, 5, 5, 4, 5, 6, 3, 5, 7 , 4, 2; the frequencies can be represented in the following manner:

```
                             –
                      –  –  –
Frequency   –  –  –  –  –  –        –
Score       1  2  3  4  5  6  7  8  9
```

It can be seen that the Mark 5 has the greatest frequency.

S. R. GRIFFITHS and L. W. DOWNES, *Educational Statistics for Beginners*, Methuen 1969

Frequency curve

The graphical curve described by a distribution of marks or measures showing how many times each particular mark has been scored.

See also **Normal curve**

S. R. GRIFFITHS and L. W. DOWNES, *Educational Statistics for Beginners*, Methuen 1969

P. E. VERNON, *Measurement of Abilities*, 2nd edn, University of London Press 1956

Frequency distribution

Values of a variable (such as test scores) arranged in order of size and showing the frequency with which each score occurs. In the following group of scores, 8, 4, 7, 5, 6, 4, 3, 7, 6, 6, 6, 6, 5, 7, the frequency distribution would be as follows:

Score	Frequency
8	1
7	3
6	4
5	2
4	2
3	1

Freud, Anna
The youngest of **Sigmund Freud's** children, Anna, became a famous psychoanalyst in her own right. Four of her lectures were published as *Introduction to Psycho-analysis for Teachers* (Allen & Unwin 1931); her major work, written in collaboration with D. Burlingham, is *Infants Without Families* (2nd edn, Allen & Unwin 1965).

Freud, Sigmund (1856–1939)
Founder of the theory of psychoanalysis. He practised in Vienna, working as a neurologist after reading medicine. His work in psychoanalysis developed from his studies of hysteria under J. Charcot, and took shape from about 1895. He spent his last years in England. His many works include (in translation by J. Strachey): *The Interpretation of Dreams* (Allen & Unwin, 1955), *Outline of Psychoanalysis* (Hogarth Press, 1969), *The Psychopathology of Everyday Life* (Benn, 1966), *Totem and Taboo* (Routledge 1950). A standard edition of *The Complete Psychological Works*, trans. J. Strachey and A. Freud, has been published by the Hogarth Press in 24 vols. A useful selection is *A General Selection from the Works of Sigmund Freud*, ed. J. Rickman (Hogarth Press 1937).
E. JONES, *The Life and Work of S. Freud*, 3 vols, (Chatto 1953–57) abr. edn, 1962, Penguin (Pelican) 1967
D. STAFFORD-CLARK, *What Freud Really Said*, Macdonald 1965; Penguin 1967

Frieze (school)
A decorative and illustrative sequence of pictures and designs shown as a broad band on the wall: normally on cloth, paper or painted on to the wall.
S. MARSHALL, *Experiment in Education*, Cambridge University Press 1963

Froebel, Friedrich (1782–1852)
German educational philosopher who began as a follower of **Pestalozzi** and later turned to the education of the very young child of Kindergarten age. He strongly advocated that education should promote development from within the child, guarding, encouraging and protecting.
The Education of Man published in German, 1826, and in English, 1887. The first English kindergarten was opened by two of his pupils in 1851; the Froebel Society was established in 1875. In 1938 this became the National Froebel Foundation (2 Manchester Square, London, W1) which issues certificates to teachers trained under its auspices.
S. J. CURTIS and M. E. A. BOULTWOOD, *A Short History of Educational Ideas*, 4th edn, University Tutorial Press 1965, ch. 14
V. JUDGES, *Freedom: Froebel's Vision and on Reality*, National Froebel Foundation
E. LAWRENCE, ed., *Friedrich Froebel and English Education*, rev. edn, Routledge & Kegan Paul 1969
B. PRIESTMAN, *Froebel Education Today*, new edn, University of London Press 1955
R. R. RUSK, *Doctrines of the Great Educators*, Macmillan 1965

Frustration
The condition of unease or distress which ensues when a wish, drive, intention, etc., repeatedly fails to find an outlet or is continuously prevented from being realised. Sustained frustration is inevitable in social life (e.g. of sex drive), but in some individuals it contributes to nervous illness and maladjustment.
J. A. C. BROWN, *The Social Psychology of Industry*, Penguin (Pelican) 1970, ch. 9
C. T. MORGAN, *Introduction to Psychology*, McGraw-Hill 1956, ch. 5
N. L. MUNN, *Psychology, the fundamentals of human adjustment*, 5th edn, Harrap 1966, ch. 8

Fugue
An abnormal psychological condition in which the sufferer, forgetting his identity, flees from a situation to which he cannot adjust.
R. KNIGHT and M. A. KNIGHT, *Modern Introduction to Psychology*, 7th edn, University Tutorial Press 1966, ch. 16
N. I. MUNN, *Psychology, the fundamentals of human adjustment*, 5th edn, Harrap 1966, ch. 9

Functional autonomy
The theory advanced by **G. W. Allport** that habits tend to continue, initiating behaviour in their own right, even though the motives

which led to their acquisition no longer exist. Two examples might be: (*a*) a person who has experienced hunger for a long period may become acquisitive for objects which have no relation to hunger for food; (*b*) a student may study well merely to pass examinations but gradually he may begin to study for sheer pleasure.

G. W. ALLPORT, *Pattern and Growth in Personality*, Holt, Rinehart & Winston 1961, ch. 10

G. W. ALLPORT, *Personality*, Holt, Rinehart & Winston 1961

L. J. BISCHOF, *Interpreting Personality Theories*, Harper & Row 1965

Further education
Education beyond the school-leaving age received elsewhere than at an institution of **secondary education** and leading to general, craft, or commercial qualifications rather than professional qualifications. Further Education includes activities which have recreational and cultural purposes.

See: *Education: a Framework for Expansion*, HMSO 1972

H. J. EDWARDS, *The Evening Institute*, National Institute of Adult Education

LONDON COUNTY COUNCIL, *On from School*, LCC 1962 pamphlet

A. J. PETERS, *British Further Education*, Pergamon 1967

D. SIBBERSTON, *Youth in a Technical Age*, Max Parrish 1958

G

G factor
General factor (as opposed to specific factor and group factor), a general intellectual ability which is supposed to show in all the tests in a battery and in all subjects.
See also **Spearman**
C. SPEARMAN, *The Abilities of Man*, Macmillan 1927
P. E. VERNON, *Measurement of Abilities*, 2nd edn, University of London Press 1956

Galton, Francis (1822–1911)
Scientist, some of whose work analysed famous families and laid stress on the hereditary factor in ability. It is now thought that his hypothesis was, at least, partially self-validating and his conclusions in this field are no longer widely accepted. Modern thinking and research would suggest that he underrated the effects of social environment in the development of the individual.
F. GALTON, *Hereditary Genius*, 1869, Fontana 1962
R. THOMSON, *The Pelican History of Psychology*, Penguin (Pelican) 1968, ch. 5

Games
Activities carried on under the aegis of the school within or without school hours in which various sports are pursued by pupils of the school concerned and in which elements of coaching and teaching are involved. At primary level the supervision will probably be done by the class teacher and at secondary level by the games master or **PE** specialist.
C D. JOYNSON, *A Guide for Games*, Kaye & Ward 1969
J. B. PICK, *The Phoenix Dictionary of Games*, new edn, Phoenix 1965

Gamete
A mature germ cell; the ovum of the female or the spermatozoon of the male.

Gang
A highly cohesive informal group of children usually of a similar age, which sometimes, especially in the older groups, becomes aggressive, predatory or delinquent. The 'gang age' is usually taken to be the period from 9 to 13 years. Many gangs are benevolent and help children to develop by providing support and example during the period of emergence from childhood.
A. K. COHEN, *Delinquent Boys: the culture of the gang*, Collier-Macmillan 1955

ARYEH LEISSNEV, *Street Club Work in Tel Aviv and New York*, Longman in Association with the National Bureau for Cooperation in Child Care 1969
F. M. THRASHER, *The Gang*, University of Chicago Press 1963
L. YABLONSKY, *The Violent Gang*, Collier-Macmillan 1963; Penguin (Pelican) 1967

Gattegno, Caleb G.
One of the most prominent exponents of the use of the **Cuisenaire** mathematical **structural apparatus**. Also closely connected with **Words in Colour**, an approach to learning reading and writing.
Address: Cuisenaire Company, Reading, Berks.

GCE
The General Certificate of Education, which in 1951 replaced the School and Higher School Certificate Examinations. The examination is on a subject basis (i.e. a candidate can pass in one or more subjects) and there are eight Examining Boards. The Ordinary (O) level is usually taken at 16 after a five-year secondary course, and the Advanced (A) level usually at 18.
R. J. MONTGOMERY, *Examinations*, Longmans 1965
S. WISEMAN, *Examinations and English Education*, Manchester University Press 1961

Gene
The physical unit of heredity located on a giant molecule in the chromosome, thought to consist mainly of deoxyribonucleic acid (DNA). Genes have the ability to reproduce themselves and also the ability to produce the proteins which speed the chemical processes in the cell.
A. MONTAGU, *Human Heredity*, Mentor 1965

General Certificate of Education. *See* GCE

General degree
A first degree of British universities, e.g. an ordinary degree as distinct from honours. A combination of subjects is studied at varying levels; a common pattern is:
1st year: 4 subjects to intermediate level
2nd ,, 3 ,, ,, general ,,
3rd ,, 2 ,, ,, special ,,
but many permutations are possible and requirements vary from university to university. Some (e.g. Exeter) award general degrees at honours level. Intending students

should apply for prospectuses and calendars of appropriate universities and colleges.

K. BOEHM, ed., *University Choice*, Penguin (Pelican) 1966

General education
Those aspects of education which should be characteristic of all educated people, irrespective of specialisation.
See also **Literacy**; **Numeracy**

General studies
1. In technical and similar colleges, an element in the part-time courses for craftsmen, technicians and other students. It includes teaching of English and physical education, and is designed to help young workers to find their way successfully about the world as consumers and citizens, to form standards and moral values, to train and develop activities and pursuits begun at school and improve basic education. Up to three hours a week may be devoted to this aspect of the course.

MINISTRY OF EDUCATION, *General Studies in Technical Colleges*, HMSO 1962
Crowther Report: *15–18*, ch. 25
2. *G.C.E.* 'O' and 'A' level examination paper pioneered by Professor R. A. C. Oliver of the Univ. of Manchester, and the N.U.J.M.B. to test general knowledge in arts, social and natural sciences. At 'A' level this subject attracts the largest entry of candidates in the Board's area.

G. M. FORREST et al., *General Studies and academic aptitude*, N.U.J.M.B. Occasional pubs. No. 30. 1970

Genetics
The branch of biology dealing with the manner in which inherited differences and resemblances come into being between similar organisms.

M. I. LERNER, *Heredity, Evolution and Society*, Freeman 1968
ASHLEY MONTAGU, *Human Heredity*, Mentor 1965
L. S. PENROSE, *Outline of Human Genetics*, 2nd edn, Heinemann 1963

Genius
In common usage has two meanings:
1. As applied to people of extremely high creative ability who have made a unique contribution in a particular field of study or creative activity. It is generally held that the intelligence of highly talented people is exceptionally high.
2. As applied to people of high intellectual ability as measured on a standardised test of intelligence.

The **IQ** level at which the term genius should be applied varies, according to the investigator, from 140+ to 180+. 'Gifted' is becoming a more popular term for this meaning of genius.

F. GALTON, *Hereditary Genius*, 1869
L. S. HOLLINGWORTH, *Children Above 180 I.Q.*, New York, World Book Co. 1942
L. M. TERMAN et al., *Genetic Studies of Genius* (*1925–47*), Stanford University Press, vol. 5, 1959

Genotype
A term coined by the Danish botanist, W. Johannsen, to describe the internal control, the hereditary element of an individual plant or animal which in reaction with environment gives the external or observed character of the organism. 'Genotype' determines the potentialities of the organism. It is handed down unchanged from generation to generation; fluctuations in the visible character of the organism from environmental causes do not affect it. The changeable visible character is termed the 'phenotype'.

C. D. DARLINGTON, *Genetics and Man*, (rev. edn. of *Facts of Life*, 1953), Allen & Unwin 1964
J. E. MEADE and A. S. PARKES, *Biological Aspects of Social Problems*, Oliver & Boyd 1965

Geography
The science of the earth including a study of land, water, air, the distribution of plant, animal, and human life, industry and commerce, and the interrelations of these factors.

G. J. CONS, *Handbook for Geography Teachers*, 4th edn, Methuen 1960
G. DAVIES, *Teacher's Handbook of Geography for the Primary School*, Longman
INCORPORATED ASSOCIATION OF ASSISTANT MASTERS IN SECONDARY SCHOOLS, *The Teaching of Geography in Secondary Schools*, 5th edn, Cambridge University Press 1967
UNESCO, *Unesco Source Book for Geography Teaching*, Longmans/Unesco 1965

Geographical Association
Founded 1893 to further the knowledge of geography and the teaching of geography in all categories of educational institutions in

the UK and abroad. Membership (now 7000) is open to all who are interested in geography or in education. Privileges of full membership include the receipt of the magazine *Geography* (four issues a year), use of library, books and periodicals. Facilities exist for student, school and college membership at special rates, and local branches exist for the organisation of lecture and excursion programmes for members in their vicinities.
Address: 343 Fulwood Road, Sheffield 10, Yorks.

Gestalt
A German term designating an integrated whole, not merely the sum of the independent parts which make up the whole.
The concept gives its name to a school of psychology, known as Gestalt psychology, originating in Germany during the early part of this century. Its main contention is that the organism behaves and reacts as a whole, even when stimuli are specific, and that therefore mental processes and behaviour cannot usefully be analysed into specific elements. In its early days it was concerned largely with the psychology of perception but has gradually extended to cover many aspects of the learning process. For example it is quoted in support of global methods of learning to read (Look and say, Sentence method etc.).
See also **Configuration, Kurt Koffka**
W. D. ELLIS, *A Sourcebook of Gestalt Psychology*, Routledge & Kegan Paul 1938
D. KATZ, *Gestalt Psychology*, Methuen 1951
R. MORRIS, *The Quality of Learning*, Methuen 1951
R. THOMSON, *The Pelican History of Psychology*, Penguin (Pelican) 1968, ch. 13

Gifted children. *See* **Mentally gifted**

Girls, Education of
It is mainly in the private sector of education that the education of girls is organised separately from that of boys: most preparatory schools and public schools are single-sex schools. Also at secondary level there is a greater tendency for direct grant schools than for maintained secondary schools to be single sex. The influence of the single-sex tradition is more in evidence at the Universities of Oxford and Cambridge than in other universities.
J. HEMMING, *Problems of Adolescent Girls*, Heinemann 1967

I. KAMM, *Hope Deferred*, Methuen 1965
NATIONAL UNION OF TEACHERS, *Higher Education Journal*, Summer 1969
J. NEWSOM, *The Education of Girls*, Faber 1948
K. OLLERENSHAW, *Girls' Schools*, Faber 1967

Gittins Report
(*Primary Education in Wales* 1967): the Welsh counterpart of the **Plowden Report** compiled under the chairmanship of Professor Gittins of the University College of Swansea. It was published simultaneously in English and Welsh.
On many fundamental issues the two Reports put forward similar recommendations but on certain matters their conclusions differ.
The Gittins Report devotes a substantial section to bilingualism in Wales and deals with the Handicapped Child and Child with Learning Difficulties in the Ordinary School at some length. See Appendix IIIA.

Glueck, Sheldon (b. 1896)
Roscoe Pound Professor of Law of Harvard University. An outstanding American authority on juvenile delinquency. He has, in conjunction with his wife, Dr Eleanor Glueck, made a number of field studies of delinquency and has contributed much of value to the literature on the subject. Their works include:
Unravelling Juvenile Delinquency (Harvard University Press, 1950); *Delinquents in the Making* (Harper & Row 1952); *Delinquents and Non-delinquents in Perspective* (Harvard University Press 1969); *Family Environment and Delinquency* (Routledge & Kegan Paul 1962).

Governing body
Under the Education Act 1944, state schools (voluntary schools, if maintained, are state schools) are conducted by a governing body appointed under an Instrument of Government and Articles or Rules which set out the functions of headmaster, the governing body, and the **LEA**. The governing body of primary schools is called 'the managers'; that of secondary schools and institutions of higher and further education is called 'the governors'.
Managers and governors of schools are nominated by the LEA except that in the case of voluntary primary schools and in the case of voluntary secondary schools, certain proportions will be 'foundation' managers

and governors, respectively, i.e. managers and governors appointed otherwise than by the LEA.

In the case of Institutions of **higher education**, governing bodies include members from the professions, the Universities, the **LEAs** and the teaching staffs. Student representation on governing bodies is also becoming the normal practice.

G. TAYLOR and J. B. SAUNDERS, *The New Law of Education*, 7th edn, Butterworth 1971

Governor

A member of a board of governors, nominated or co-opted, which is charged with the overall control of and responsibility for a secondary school or college. Their duties usually include the appointment of the headmaster, and, with his advice, of assistant staff, and may extend to that of raising funds. They include the educational policy of the school but not its day-by-day functioning.

G. TAYLOR and J. B. SAUNDERS, *The New Law of Education*, 7th edn, Butterworth 1971

Grade

1. A rating or assessment of intelligence, attainment or of some personality trait, usually on a **five point scale**.
2. (USA) A group of pupils working together in the same year or section of the curriculum.

Grading

The process of presenting a subject or task in very fine steps so that, ideally, every learner can easily and inevitably move from one stage to the next. This is the basis of **programmed learning** as applied to **teaching machines**.

Graduate Certificate of Education

A qualification offered to intending graduate teachers by English and Welsh universities and by some colleges of education. The duration of the course is one year, and it normally includes study of the theory and the practice of education, and teaching practice. A teacher so qualified is recognized as consecutively trained.

Write: The Registrar of particular universities or colleges, or: Association of Teachers in Colleges and Departments of Education, 51 Gower Street, London, W1

ATCDE, *Handbook of Education for Teaching*, Methuen annual

Graduate equivalent

A person who, while not a graduate, holds qualifications which are deemed to be of graduate standard. The matter arises mainly in two but not unrelated contexts: (*a*) acceptability for a one-year course of Professional Training in Education; (*b*) payment of graduate allowances in teachers' salaries.

In the former case the **institutes of education** exercise powers of discretion in interpreting various qualifications. In the latter case, qualifications or combinations of qualification which are considered to be of graduate standard and which entitle their holders to graduate allowances are listed in a booklet compiled after each **Burnham** settlement by the **Department of Education and Science**, *Scales of Salaries for Teachers in Primary and Secondary Schools, England and Wales*, HMSO.

Qualifications considered for payment of graduate allowances but which are not contained in this list are subject to negotiation between the DES and the LEA concerned. In cases of difficulty, teachers should consult their professional union.

Grammar

The study of language relating to the different classes of words, their interrelations, and their functions in sentences. This study is said to be less important in schools than hitherto, the emphasis on *usage* tending to replace it.

W. G. BEBBINGTON, *An English Handbook*, rev. edn, Schofield & Sims 1962

E. PARTRIDGE, *English; A Course for Human Beings*, Macdonald 1949

Grammar schools

Selective secondary schools which cater for the most able portion of the child population, offering a markedly academic course leading to **GCE**; usually controlled by **LEA**, but a small proportion (the **direct grant G.S.**) are partly financed from the **Department of Education and Science**. Cf. French *Lycée*, German *Gymnasium*.

R. DAVIS, *The Grammar School*, Penguin (Pelican) 1967

R. KING, *Values and Involvement in a Grammar School*, Routledge & Kegan Paul 1969

MINISTRY OF EDUCATION, *The Road to the Sixth Form: some suggestions on the curriculum of the grammar school*, Pamphlet no. 19, HMSO 1951

H. A. RÉE, *The Essential Grammar School*, Harrap 1956

Grandes Ecoles

Autonomous institutions of higher learning in France, which have the highest academic status. They are advanced specialised institutions, whose pupils will aim at the higher academic qualifications rather than first degrees, but in particular fields such as engineering, technology, Army education, etc. Grandes Ecoles, such as the Ecole Polytechnique, Ecole Normale Supérieure, St Cyr, Ponts et Chaussées, etc. are the peak of the French system of higher education.

Grant-aid

Grants of money from central government funds are made to a variety of bodies responsible for educational provision. A general grant is made to **LEAs** in respect of educational expenditure, but grants are also made to **ATOs**, to universities through the University Grants Committee, to special schools and establishments, direct grant grammar schools and voluntary colleges of education, as well as other bodies.

G. TAYLOR and J. B. SAUNDERS, *The New Law of Education*, 7th edn, Butterworth 1971

Gregarious tendency (instinctive)

The urge to come together in groups (*grex*, a flock), said to be particularly characteristic of human beings.

Groos, Karl (1861–1946)

German philosopher, psychologist and authority on children's play. His theory stresses the biological utility of play, and its imitative nature, and concludes that play is a preparation for mature life. His published work includes (in translation) *The Play of Man* (Heinemann 1901).

Group

1. Peer: an informal gathering of children or young people of similar age.
2. Social: any subsection of the national community whose members feel themselves united by a common bond or interest (e.g. similar employment, economic or educational status) yet not large enough to be a social class.
3. Reference: (i) the group to which a person aspires, with which he identifies himself and whose values, status, attitudes and standards he desires, though not necessarily belonging to it. (ii) the group, in a test situation, whose scores are used to establish norms.

J. H. S. BOSSARD and E. S. BOLL, *Sociology of Child Development*, Harper & Row 1966
D. CARTWRIGHT and A. ZANDER, ed., *Group Dynamics*, 3rd edn, Tavistock 1968
P. MUSGRAVE, *The Sociology of Education*, Methuen 1965
W. H. J. SPROTT, *Human Groups*, Penguin (Pelican) 1958

Group examination

An examination, such as the former School Certificate Examination and many matriculation and technical examinations, e.g. National Certificate, in which the candidates must take a given number of subjects, some compulsory and others from a set of optional subjects, in a prescribed proportion; all the required subjects must be taken at one and the same time. The opposite type is called a 'subject examination', e.g. the present **GCE**.

Crowther Report, *15–18*, Para. 130
H. MONTGOMERY, *Examinations*, Longmans 1965

Group therapy

Treatment for mental or social disturbance or illness, which takes the form of group discussion or activity, guided by a qualified person who seeks to bring members to deeper insight and understanding of their condition, and to alleviate it.

S. A. FOULKES and E. J. ANTHONY, *Group Psychotherapy*, 2nd edn, Penguin (Pelican) 1965
M. JONES, *Social Psychiatry in Practice*, Penguin (Pelican) 1968
D. V. MARTIN, *Adventure in Psychiatry: social change in a mental hospital*, new edn, Faber 1968

Group work

A term used to denote activities when the children are not organised as a class or as individuals but in small groups. For example when the class has undertaken a project they may subdivide, so that each group deals with a different aspect of the work. The teacher may use sociometric techniques to group children who work easily together. Alternatively (e.g. in written work in mathematics) the teacher may want to divide the class into several homogeneous groups working at different levels of ability.

J. C. GAGG, *Common Sense in the Primary School*, Evans 1951

S. MARSHALL, *Experiment in Education*, Cambridge University Press 1963

Guardian

1. An adult who undertakes some legal responsibility for a child without fostering or adopting it.
2. In Plato's *Republic*, the governing group.

Guess Who

A sociometric technique which seeks to establish the evaluation by a social group of its members' conduct, and hence to deduce possible personality traits. A word picture, e.g. 'Here is someone who talks a lot, always has something to say' is presented to the group, and each member writes down whom they think the description fits, including themselves if necessary. The data from several similar questions can then be interpreted in the light of facts emerging from a **sociogram**.

R. CUNNINGHAM, *Understanding Group Behaviour*, Teachers' College, Columbia University 1952

K. M. EVANS, *Sociometry and Education*, Routledge & Kegan Paul 1962

P. E. VERNON, *Personality Tests and Assessments*, new edn, Methuen 1953

Guidance

1. Educational: the study and practice of the techniques (diagnostic and administrative) designed to help the student progress to further courses and study. It is highly developed in America.
2. Vocational: a service provided to young people about to leave school and afterwards which advises upon suitable employment, frequently after applying tests and examining school reports. Usually performed by the careers master and the **Youth Employment Service** working together.

P. J. EDMONDS, *Careers Encylopaedia*, 6th edn, Macmillan and Cleaver 1969

The Directory of Opportunities for School Leavers, Cornmarket Press

NATIONAL FOUNDATION FOR EDUCATIONAL RESEARCH, 'The counselling function: a symposium' (*Educational Research* **9**, no. 2, 1967 Newnes)

Gymnasium

1. German classical secondary school corresponding to **lycée** or **grammar school**, and which prepares for university entrance through the matriculation examination, the Abitur.
2. In English schools, the centre for **PE**.

E. J. KING, *Other Schools and Ours*, 3rd edn, Holt, Rinehart & Winston 1967

H

Habit
Learned behaviour, usually of repetitive patterns of activity, which frequently becomes automatic. Directly purposive habits which are deliberately practised are **skills**. How habits are acquired and changed is a topic central to the experimental study of learning.
N. L. MUNN, *Psychology: the fundamentals of human adjustment*, 5th edn, Harrap 1966
O. L. ZANGWILL, *An Introduction to Modern Psychology*, new edn, Methuen 1950

Habituation
A synonym for 'adaptation' or 'accommodation' rather than for the process of habit formation.

Hadow Reports
The Consultative Committee to the Board of Education (Chairman Sir W. Henry Hadow) issued a number of Reports, notably three on *The Education of the Adolescent*, in 1926, advocating a break at 11 so that **elementary** education would be divided into **primary** and **secondary** stages; in 1931 on *The Primary School* (1931), and *Infant and Nursery Schools* (1933).
See also Appendix IIIA

Haemophilia
A condition occurring only in males, in which the blood fails to clot and which is therefore characterised by excessive bleeding even from small cuts. Children suffering from haemophilia will therefore attend ordinary schools at great hazard. In many cases they will receive **home tuition**. The condition is hereditary, being transmitted through the female members of families in which the disease occurs.

Half-timers
The Factory Act 1844 introduced the principle that children might alternate three days, or six half days, of work and school in the week. By the Education Act 1902 a position had been reached in which children were permitted to leave school for half of the school day to take up work, provided that by the age of thirteen they had achieved a certain educational standard. This provision was abolished as a result of the Fisher Education Act of 1918 and came to an end in 1927.
S. J. CURTIS and M. E. A. BOULTWOOD, *An Introductory History of Education in Great Britain since 1800*, 4th edn, University Tutorial Press 1966

Hall of Residence
A residential unit for university students which includes study-bedroom, common rooms and recreation rooms, refectory, etc. but not teaching rooms. It is under the supervision of a warden.

Hall, Stanley (1844–1924)
American pioneer of psychology who established the first Institute of Child Psychology at Clark University, USA. He was an important contributor to the scientific study of child development and education. His main works include: *Adolescence*, 1904 and *Youth*, 1907.

Halo effect
The tendency to attribute excellence to a person in respect of work or conduct as the result of his reputed high level in other departments of work, conduct or social standing. The tendency is particularly noticeable in subjective marking (e.g. of essays) where the candidate's identity is known.
P. E. VERNON, *Personality Assessment*, Methuen 1964

Handwriting
The production, by hand, of visual symbols to be read. As a subject, given special time in the school curriculum, it has declined in recent years. This has probably been caused by the invention of the typewriter, and the tape-recorder, and by the increasing recognition in school of the greater importance of oral communication. Handwriting, however, has regained considerable popularity in art education.
A. INGLIS and E. H. GIBSON, *The Teaching of Handwriting*; *Primary*, Nelson 1961–62
M. RICHARDSON, *Writing and Writing Patterns*, Teachers' Book, University of London Press 1935

Handedness
The more frequent use of one hand rather than the other in a task where the use of one hand only is needed.
See also **Dextrality; Dominance; Latorality; Sinistrality**
M. M. CLARK, *Left-handedness*, University of London Press for Scottish Council for Research in Education 1957

Handicapped children

Children who suffer in a significant degree from some physical, emotional or mental abnormality. Though there are many conditions, some of which overlap, and though some children suffer from a multiplicity of handicaps, the ten administrative and educational categories are as follows: Blind; Partially sighted; Deaf; Partially hearing; Physically handicapped; Delicate; Maladjusted; Educationally subnormal; Epileptic; Speech defect.

See also **Gittins Report**

Association for Special Education, Conference Report: *What is special education?* 1966

H. J. BAKER, *Introduction to Exceptional Children*, 3rd edn, Collier-Macmillan 1959

Statistics of Education, HMSO, annually

J. D. KERSHAW, *Handicapped Children*, 2nd edn, Heinemann 1966

D. G. PRITCHARD, *Education and the Handicapped (1760–1960)*, Routledge & Kegan Paul 1963

Handwork

A term used formerly to indicate a subject at the elementary level, concerned mainly with practical work (sewing and paper-cutting, paper-folding, etc.). Compare with handicrafts (e.g. woodwork, metalwork, pottery) and **domestic science** at mainly the secondary level.

F. T. DAY, *Coloured Paper Craft for Infant Schools*, Newnes 1950

S. ROBERTSON, *Creative Crafts in Education*, Routledge & Kegan Paul 1952

Hawthorne effect

A term used to indicate a situation where experimental conditions are such that the results are affected by the mere fact that the subjects in the experiment are receiving more attention than the **control group**. The **experimental group** may improve their performance not because they are using superior materials or because of experimental changes in the conditions, but because of changes in their own attitude arising from the novelty of the materials and from a feeling that they are regarded as important. This poses difficulties for psychologists attempting to measure the effectiveness of a new teaching method or medium. The term is so named from a production study at the Hawthorne works of the Western Electric Company in America.

W. R. BORG, *Educational Research*, McKay 1963

F. J. ROETHLISBERGER and W. J. DICKSON, *Management and the Worker*, Harvard University Press 1939

D. H. STOTT, *Roads to Literacy*, W. and R. Holmes 1964

Headmaster/mistress

The principal teacher of a school responsible to a **Governing body, Managers**, etc. (frequently the **LEA**) and appointed by them. Supervises the general running of the school, teaching, discipline, organisation and administration. Once appointed, the headteacher in Britain has a remarkable degree of freedom and autonomy.

B. ALLEN, ed., *Headship in the 1970s*, Blackwell 1970

G. R. BARRELL, *Teachers and the Law*, Methuen 1966

G. TAYLOR and T. B. SAUNDERS, *The New Law of Education*, 7th edn, Butterworth 1971

N. D. F. TOSH, *Being a Headmaster*, Glasgow, McClellan 1964

Headmasters' Conference (H.M.C.)

Conference of public school headmasters which has met regularly since 1869; promotes the interests of these schools by affording the opportunity for discussion and joint action. Membership of the Conference is taken to imply high prestige for the headmaster and his school which will regard such membership as conferring on itself the title 'public school'.

Address: 29 Gordon Square, London, WC1

Health education

A group of studies whose emphasis is on the care of the mind and body, both in terms of the individual and in terms of public health.

R. W. B. ELLIS, *Health in Childhood*, Penguin (Pelican) 1960

D. PIRIE and A. J. DALZELL-WARD, *A Textbook of Health Education*, Tavistock 1962

Health visitor

In addition to a highly specialised nursing training, health visitors, usually women, undergo a general training in social work. They attend children's clinics and visit homes of all children under two years of age, as part of the service of postnatal care. They maintain a link between medical and non-medical social services.

P. ARCHER, *Social Welfare and the Citizen*, Penguin (Pelican) 1957

Hebb, D. O. (b. 1904)
Canadian psychologist who has sought to produce a theory linking neurological and psychological explanations of mental activity and behaviour. He first drew the distinction between Intelligence A (genetic potentiality) and Intelligence B (present mental efficiency). Publications include: *The Organization of Behaviour*, Wiley (1949); *A Textbook of Psychology*, 2nd edn, Saunders (1966).
See also **Intelligence**; **Intelligence Tests**

Hedonism
The ethical theory which maintains that the highest good or the chief value of life is the enjoyment of pleasure, and that whatever we desire to do, or to become, is desired for the happiness we expect to derive therefrom. The theory received great support from Jeremy Bentham and John Stuart Mill in the nineteenth century.
H. SIDGWICK, *The Methods of Ethics*, 7th edn, Macmillan 1907; paperback 1963

Herbart, Johann Friedrich (1776–1841)
German philosopher, whose work influenced psychology and educational theory. Instead of referring to mental faculties such as memory, reason, etc., he explained mental events and learning by reference to laws of combination and interaction of sensations, ideas, images, in a similar vein to the 'associationist' theory of earlier psychology. His educational theory thus aims at correct combinations of experience by systematic and planned teaching; and hence his five steps; preparation, presentation, composition and abstraction, generalisation, application. See his *Allgemeine Pädagogik* (1806) trans. as *The Science of Education* (1893), D. C. Heath.
SIR J. ADAMS, *Herbartian Psychology applied to Education* (1897 reprinted D. C. Heath)
S. J. CURTIS and M. E. A. BOULTWOOD, *A Short History of Educational Ideas*, 4th edn, University Tutorial Press 1965

Heredity
1. The process of biological transmission of characteristics from one generation to the next, through **genes** in the sperm and egg cells. Since the effects of heredity are invariably influenced by environment (i.e. situation and culture) few characteristics (except for diseases like haemophilia, phenylketonuria) can be explained completely by heredity. The basic questions of personality, learning, behaviour, almost always involve the interrelationship of hereditary potentiality and the limiting factors of the environment.
ASHLEY MONTAGUE, *Human Heredity*, Mentor Books 1965
M. I. LERNER, *Heredity, Evolution and Society*, Freeman 1968
2. **Heredity** (social)
The process by which the cultural traits of one generation are passed to the next. The means of transmission are education, indoctrination and social control. Social 'transmission' is a more acceptable term.

Heterosexuality
The tendency to make the normal sexual love relationships with persons of the opposite sex as contrasted with **homosexuality**.
H. HAVELOCK ELLIS, *Psychology of Sex*, Heinemann 1933; Pan 1959
O. SCHWARZ, *The Psychology of Sex*, Penguin (Pelican) 1956

Heuristic method
An educational method in which the student is placed in the position of an original investigator and endeavours to discover laws and principles for himself. A great advocate of the method at the end of the nineteenth century was H. E. Armstrong and his work greatly affected the teaching of chemistry and physics, and subsequently other subjects.
H. C. BARNARD, *An Introduction to Teaching*, University of London Press 1952
A. PINSENT, *The Principles of Teaching Method*, 3rd edn, Harrap 1969

High flyers
Term used to describe pupils or students who are in the top range of ability and attainment.
J. W. GADNER, *Excellence*, Harper & Row 1961
The Year Book of Education, Evans 1961
P. A. WITTY, *The Gifted Child*, Heath 1951

High frequency deafness
Inability to hear sounds caused by vibrations of high audio frequency, e.g. the letters S and T. This results in a blurred aural impression of spoken words, a tendency to reproduce orally the imperfect impression and often a tendency to misinterpret the speech of others. Many children with this defect are now being helped by the provision of special hearing aids.

A. W. G. EWING, *The Modern Educational Treatment for Deafness*, Manchester University Press 1960

High school

1. American: Post-elementary or secondary school, sometimes divided into junior and senior, offering a six- or eight-year course, arranged on a three-three, four-two, or four-four year pattern.
2. British: (*a*) A term used in some areas to describe grammar schools.
(*b*) *Leicestershire Plan*. The intermediate school attended by all children after primary school, and which offers full secondary education to 15 for that proportion of children who do not elect to proceed to grammar school.
E. J. KING, *Other Schools and Ours*, 3rd edn, Holt, Rinehart & Winston 1967
W. MASON, *Leicestershire Plan and Experiment*, Councils Education Press 1963

Higher degree

In England and Wales generally a degree awarded subsequently to a first degree (or, in certain cases, subsequently to a Diploma in Education). Examples of such degrees are MA, MSc, MLitt, MEd, PhD. In Scottish universities the MA is a first degree. At Oxford the BLitt, the BSc, and the BCL are higher degrees.
For information write to the Registrar of particular universities.

Higher education

Education received at the age of 18+, usually at a university, polytechnic, or college of Education, and leading to a degree or professional qualification.
Robbins Report, *Higher Education*, 1963

Higher grade school

Urban schools which came into existence after the 1870 Act to offer education beyond the elementary level to children staying on beyond the leaving age, and to pupil teachers.
G. A. N. LOWNDES, *The Silent Social Revolution 1895–1965*, 2nd edn, Oxford University Press 1969

Higher National Certificate. *See* HNC and HND

Higher National Diploma. *See* HNC and HND

Histogram (stats)

A column graph showing the frequency distribution of a continuous variable. The width of each column represents the particular class interval and the height of the column represents the frequency within each class.
S. R. GRIFFITHS and L. W. DOWNES, *Educational Statistics for Beginners*, Methuen 1969
D. M. MCINTOSH, *Statistics for the Teacher*, 2nd edn, 1967
P. E. VERNON, *Measurement of Abilities*, 2nd edn, University of London Press 1956

Historical Association

An association at local and national level for collecting and distributing information relating to the study and teaching of history. Address: 59a Kennington Park Road, London, SE11.

Historigram (stats)

A graph showing the changes in a variable over a period of time. The values of the variable are plotted along the Y-axis and the time intervals are plotted along the X-axis.
L. R. CONNOR and A. J. H. MORRELL, *Statistics in Theory and Practice*, 4th edn, Pitman 1957

History

The field of study concerned with the recording and interpretation of past events.
W. H. BURSTON, *Principles of History Teaching*, Methuen 1963
P. CARPENTER, *History Teaching; the Era Approach*, Cambridge University Press 1964
M. V. C. JEFFREYS, *History in Schools*, Pitman 1959
E. M. LEWIS, *Teaching History in Secondary School*, Evans 1960
R. J. UNSTEAD, *Teaching History in the Junior School*, 3rd edn, A. and C. Black 1963

HMI

His (Her) Majesty's Inspector of Schools. Civil servants in the **Department of Education and Science**, appointed by the Crown, and specialising in some subject or aspect of education, charged with the work of visiting schools to advise on, and inspect their condition and administration.
There is also a local authority inspectorate. There is no administrative connection between these two services.
E. L. EDMONDS, *The School Inspector*, Routledge & Kegan Paul 1962
P. WILSON, *Views and Prospects from Curzon Street*, Blackwell 1961

HNC and HND
Higher National Certificate and Higher National Diploma which follow, in most subjects, Ordinary National Certificate and Ordinary National Diploma respectively. Originally instituted by the Board of Education and Institute of Mechanical Engineers in 1921. The award now offers a qualification at 'higher' level in a wide range of technical and commercial subjects. They are academically superior to the City and Guilds Certificate and may lead to membership of the respective institutes which is regarded as a professional qualification (e.g. AIMechE). HNC and HND are comparable awards, but the former is granted to part-time students and the latter to full-time students.

Holborn Reading Test
A reading scale, produced by A. F. Watts, consisting of 33 sentences graded in difficulty and having a reading-age range from 5·9 to 13·9.
A. F. WATTS, *The Holborn Reading Scale*, Harrap 1948

Holidays
In the course of a school year (1 August to 31 July) school must be open for forty weeks during the year. The twelve weeks of holidays are, in general, arranged by the **LEA** but the granting of **occasional closures** (not exceeding twenty sessions, i.e. equivalent to ten days), over and above such holidays, can be granted at the discretion of **managers** or **governors**.
G. R. BARRELL, *Teachers and the Law*, Methuen 1966
G. TAYLOR and J. B. SAUNDERS, *The New Law of Education*, 7th edn, Butterworth 1971

Holiday classes
These may be included along with camps, playing fields and centres, etc. among the provisions which the **LEA** may provide as part of its duty to ensure that there are adequate facilities for recreation and for social and physical training for children.
G. TAYLOR and J. B. SAUNDERS, *The New Law of Education*, 7th edn, Butterworth 1971

Holiday home
Any establishment providing board and lodging for pupils during holidays on basis of payment by the **LEA**.
G. TAYLOR and J. B. SAUNDERS, *The New Law of Education*, 7th edn, Butterworth 1971

Hollerith machine
A machine designed to sort cards punched with coded information such as are used in large-scale surveys and similar investigations which call for mechanised data processing. Such a machine was invented in the USA in the nineteenth century but it was developed there by H. Hollerith at the beginning of the twentieth century.

Home
The physical building in which a family lives, and the conditions of which influence profoundly the early years of childhood. The home has not only the function of providing warmth and shelter but becomes the centre of powerful emotional attitudes, and, in part, conditions the individual's expectations, standards, status, etc.
See also **Plowden Report**, *Children and Their Primary Schools*, 1967
J. H. S. BOSSARD and E. S. BOLL, *The Sociology of Child Development*, 4th edn, Harper & Row 1966
D. CHAPMAN, *The Home and Social Status*, Routledge & Kegan Paul 1955

Home Office
Government department responsible, among other things, for the general supervision of the approved schools service, probation and after-care agencies, and national child-care services.
Report of the Care of Children Committee, HMSO 1961

Home tuition
If an **LEA** considers that, for some special reason, a child or **young person** cannot attend school to recive education it can, with the approval of the Secretary of State for Education and Science, provide suitable education at the child's home.
F. J. SCHONELL, J. A. RICHARDSON and T. S. MCCONNEL, *The Subnormal Child at Home*, Macmillan 1958
G. TAYLOR and J. B. SAUNDERS, *The New Law of Education*, 7th edn, Butterworth 1971

Home visit
Visits to pupils' homes which teachers, or teachers in training, might carry out in order to understand their pupils better and then be in a position to be more effective teachers.
Newsom Report, *Half our Future*, 1963
C. SEGAL, *Backward Children in the Making*, Muller 1942

C. SEGAL, *No Child is Ineducable*, Pergamon 1967

Homework
Work done by pupils outside school hours; usually not by pupils under the age of eight. Homework is more frequently done by pupils in selective secondary schools, those working for public examinations, and those in Further Education, and varies from half an hour to two or more hours daily.
See also **Prep.**

Homosexuality
The tendency to make sexual love relationships with members of the same sex. In women it is known as Lesbianism. It is a 'normal' stage of development in adolescence. If it takes an active form between males it is regarded as a perversion punishable by law, unless between consenting adults.
B. MAGEE, *One in Twenty*, 2nd edn, Secker & Warburg 1968
O. SCHWARZ, *Psychology of Sex*, Penguin (Pelican) 1956
G. WESTWOOD, *A Minority*, Longmans n.d.
Wolfenden Report, *Departmental Committee on Homosexual Offences and Prostitution*, HMSO 1957

Homunculus
Literally 'little man'. The child regarded as a miniature adult.

Hooky
As in 'playing hooky', meaning 'playing truant'.

Hormone
A chemical compound manufactured by an endocrine or ductless gland and secreted into the blood stream. The hormone, when transported to another organ, may stimulate or inhibit the activity of that organ.
A. S. MASON, *Health and Hormones*, Penguin (Pelican) 1960

Hospital school
A school operating within a hospital, usually by tutorial methods, for the education of long-stay child patients. Hospital teachers receive one extra salary increment.
MINISTRY OF EDUCATION, *Education of the Handicapped Pupil, 1945–55*, Pamphlet no. 30, HMSO 1956

MINISTRY OF EDUCATION, *The Health of the School Child*, HMSO 1960

Housemother/father
In residential homes and schools the persons who seek to perform as far as possible the functions of parents, caring for the children in small groups in a domestic atmosphere. The term is usually used only in residential homes or schools set up for deprived or handicapped children.

Hull, C. L. (1884–1952)
Author of a systematic theory of learning which emphasises the place of drive reduction in promoting learning. He sought to use quantitative methods of research, and, accepting Pavlov's theory of conditioning, added an elaborate theory of reinforcement deriving from consideration both of the total situation of the learner and of his inner drives. His theory is expounded in *Principles of Behaviour*, Appleton-Century-Crofts 1943.
W. F. HILL, *Learning*, University of London Press 1963

Humanism
1. A sixteenth-century Renaissance movement which sought to rediscover and study classical antiquity, especially its language, literature and thought. It thus promoted and systematised the teaching of classical languages and literature.
W. BOYD, *The History of Western Education*, 6th edn, D. and C. Black 1952, ch. 6
2. A doctrine which, rejecting theology and religious belief in the Divine, exalts the human spirit and its achievements; and holds its development to be the ultimate aspiration of mankind.
M. KNIGHT, *Humanist Anthology*, Barrie & Rockliff 1961

Humanities
Branches of learning concerned with man, but defined more strictly as literature, belles-lettres, history, etc., in particular Greek and Latin literature. The teaching of the humanities, particularly to less able children, is often regarded by teachers as difficult and un-rewarding. **The Schools Council** set up a project to investigate and report on this problem.
SCHOOLS COUNCIL, *Humanities for the Young School Leaver: an approach through Classics*, HMSO 1967

SCHOOLS COUNCIL, *Humanities for the Young School Leaver: an approach through English*, HMSO 1968

SCHOOLS COUNCIL, *Raising the School Leaving Age*, Working Paper no. 2, HMSO 1965

Huxley, Thomas Henry (1825–95)

Biologist; Fellow of the Royal Society. As a member of the London School Board (1870–72) he profoundly influenced the new system of national elementary education by his insistence on progressive methods in teaching, and on the place of physical training, aesthetic subjects and physical science in the curriculum. He carried into effect many of the proposals and much of the spirit of **H. Spencer's** educational writings. A volume of his essays *Man's Place in Nature* was published in 1863.

D. S. L. CARDWELL, *The Organisation of Science in England*, Heinemann 1957

Hypermetropia (Hyperopia)

Farsightedness: an eye condition in which parallel rays are brought to a focus behind the retina and in which vision for distant objects is better than for nearer objects.

Hysteria

Derived from the Greek word for 'womb', this disease was thought to be exclusively feminine until soldiers developed similar symptoms owing to battle strain. The sufferer may take refuge from anxiety or conflict situations by a flight into incapacity, e.g. symptoms may be: loss of hearing or sight; paralysis, tremors, speech disorders, vomiting, diarrhoea, amnesia, etc. Hysteria is a form of psychoneurosis requiring psychiatric treatment.

E. JONES, *The Life and Work of S. Freud*, 3 vols, Chatto & Windus 1953–57; abr. edn 1962; Penguin (Pelican) 1967

J. D. PAGE, *Abnormal Psychology*, McGraw-Hill 1942

D. STAFFORD-CLARK, *Psychiatry Today*, Penguin (Pelican) 1952

I

IAPS
Incorporated Association of Preparatory Schools.
Secretary: L. P. Dealtry, 31 Melbury Court, Kensington, London, W8

IAAMSS
Incorporated Association of Assistant Masters in Secondary Schools.

Id
In Freudian psychoanalysis, one of the three main divisions in the structure of personality. It is the supposed seat of the instincts, contains all the repressed ideas and is the source of the energy associated with the instincts, the **libido**. It is unconscious, illogical, amoral and infantile. Freud later considered that the ego extended its organisation over part of the id, in the sense that passions, impulses, are in a degree subject to rational control.
H. CRICHTON-MILLER, *Psycho-Analysis*, 2nd edn, Oxford University Press (Home University Library) 1945
E. JONES, *What is Psychoanalysis?* Allen & Unwin 1949

Ideal type
A technique in sociological theory which consists in constructing from verified details a representative model for an institution, role or function which enables it to be distinguished clearly, its varieties classified, etc. Research then leads to refinement and sharper discrimination within the ideal type so that significant details of individual cases become more apparent.
H. H. GERTH and C. WRIGHT MILLS, *From Max Weber*, Routledge & Kegan Paul 1948, Preface

Idealism
A movement in philosophy in the nineteenth century which emphasised mind and thought in the motivation and explanation of philosophic dilemmas in contrast to empirical or scientific explanations. This movement influenced educational thinking profoundly through the work of Kant, Fichte, **Herbart**, **Froebel** and their successors.
S. J. CURTIS, *An Introduction to the Philosophy of Education*, 2nd edn, University Tutorial Press 1965, ch. 3
J. PARK, *Selected Readings in the Philosophy of Education*, 3rd edn, Collier-Macmillan 1968 New York

Ideation
A term used to describe the process by which, in the absence of sensory stimulation, the mind forms and manipulates ideas. The term ideational learning is used to cover the acquisition of mental associations and concepts, as distinct from motor learning.

Identical twins
Monozygotic (one egg) twins, who have the same genetic constitution. They can provide a source for the study of the effects of environment, upbringing, etc., in isolation from biological endowment.
J. SHIELDS, *Monozygotic Twins*, Oxford University Press 1962
See also **Twins**

Identification
An important process in development in which the young tend to imitate attitudes and general behaviour of older persons they hold in esteem. Momentary identification such as that experienced by spectators watching a game must be differentiated from true identification when one person puts himself in another person's shoes and sees things through the second person's eyes. Earliest identification is usually with the mother and later identification may be with teachers, the gang or even an institution.
S. FREUD, *A General Selection from the Works of Sigmund Freud*, J. Rickman, ed., Hogarth Press 1937

Ideology
A belief, doctrine or affirmation which, even if it is in contradiction to scientific or otherwise established fact, continues to be propagated for the sake of its supposed political or social utility, usually relying heavily on propaganda. Once established, the ideology of a group or community serves to regulate the behaviour of its members.
D. KRECH, R. S. CRUTCHFIELD and E. L. BALLACHEY, *The Individual in Society*, McGraw-Hill, 1962, ch. 11
K. MANNHEIM, *Ideology and Utopia*, Routledge & Kegan Paul 1966, ch. 2

Idiot
According to pre-1959 Mental Health Act, the lowest grade of mental deficiency. *See also* **imbecile** and **moron**. These terms are now obsolete.

D. G. PRITCHARD, *Education and the Handicapped*, (*1760–1960*), Routledge & Kegan Paul 1963

Illegitimacy
The condition of a child born out of wedlock, indicated by birth certificate (if in full form). The abbreviated form of certificate omits reference to illegitimacy.
D. DEWAR, *Orphans of the Living*, Hutchinson 1968
V. WIMPERIS, *The Unmarried Mother and her Child*, Allen & Unwin 1960
M. WYNN, *Fatherless Families*, Michael Joseph 1964

Illiteracy
A relative term denoting a level of scholarship, learning, and reading ability, far below that which is normal. This obviously will vary in relation to adults, on the one hand, for whom a generalised average level is assumed, and to children, on the other hand, whose average level of literacy will vary according to their chronological age. An adult whose reading age is below seven years is regarded as illiterate.
R. A. DENTLER and M. E. WARSHAUER, *Big City Drop-outs and Illiterates*, Praeger (Pall Mall) 1968
M. M. LEWIS, *The Importance of Illiteracy*, Harrap 1953
MINISTRY OF EDUCATION, Pamphlet no. 18: *Reading Ability* (HMSO) 1950
MINISTRY OF EDUCATION, Pamphlet no. 32, *Standards of Reading 1948–56* (HMSO) 1957

Illustrations. *See* Visual aids

Imagery
The experience of sounds, sight, taste, smell, movement, and imagination, usually stimulated by the sight or sound of words, e.g. in poetry.
A. PINSENT, *Principles of Teaching Methods*, 3rd edn, Harrap 1969

Imbecile
According to pre-1959 Mental Health Act, the middle grade of mental deficiency, with IQ approximately 25 to 50.
See also Idiot and Moron
D. G. PRITCHARD, *Education and the Handicapped* (*1760–1960*), Routledge & Kegan Paul 1963

Imitation
The process of copying the behaviour of another person or creature.
See also Identification; Mimesis

Immigrants, Teaching of
This is becoming an increasing problem in areas of the UK such as Greater London, the West Midlands and Yorkshire where the concentration of immigrants is high. For the teacher the problem of communication, particularly where a variety of nationalities can be found in one class, is very complex and special teaching skills are needed. But it is only part of the greater social and economic problem of integration. It is being recognised that the schools may be the vital factor in dealing with the problem.
LONDON COUNCIL OF SOCIAL SERVICE, *The Immigrant and the Teacher*, 1966
NATIONAL ASSOCIATION OF SCHOOLMASTERS, *Education and the Immigrants*, Hemel Hempstead, Educare 1969
SCHOOLS COUNCIL, *English for the Children of Immigrants*, HMSO; *Teaching English to West Indian Children*, Evans and Methuen 1970

Imprinting
Soon after birth, the young of many species of animals, but particularly birds, will follow any moving object, usually the mother. There is a critical period, quite brief, during which this behaviour can be established with great strength and resistance to change. The term was introduced by Lorenz, in 1935. It has been suggested this is a very special form of stimulus-response learning which can be seen in the human infant's attachment and response to its mother. It may thus be regarded as an important factor in later emotional development.
B. M. FOSS, *Determinants of Infant Behaviour*, 4 vols, Methuen 1961–69
K. Z. LORENZ, *King Solomon's Ring*, Methuen 1952
N. TINBERGEN, *Social Behaviour in Animals*, 2nd edn, Methuen 1965

In loco parentis
'In the place of the parent': the law expects that the teacher will take such care of his pupils as a careful parent would take of his children, since he is legally *in loco parentis*.
G. R. BARRELL, *Teachers and the Law*, Methuen 1966

Incentives

Factors motivating or inciting to action and improvement. In education a wide variety of incentives is used to stimulate children to do good work. A problem occupying the attention of educationists is the provision of appropriate incentives for the less able at the secondary level.

See also **Newsom Report**

A. PINSENT, *The Principles of Teaching Method*, Harrap 1969

J. E. SADLER and A. N. GILLETT, *Training for Teaching*, Allen & Unwin 1961

C. WASHBURNE, *A Living Philosophy of Education*, Day 1940

Increment

The amount by which an employee's salary is increased, usually annually, in recognition of service, training or qualifications.

See also **Burnham Scales**

NATIONAL UNION OF TEACHERS, *Handbook of Information for Teachers*, Schoolmaster Pub. Co., annual

Incorporated Association of Preparatory Schools. *See* IAPS

Indictable offence

A contravention of the law of a serious kind, other than such minor offences as can only form the subject of summary procedings before a magistrate. Juvenile courts may try indictable offences. Indictable offences are classified in the Criminal Statistics.

G. H. F. MUMFORD, *A Guide to Juvenile Court Law* 6th edn, Jordan 1968

Individual differences

Just as there are individual differences between people in physique so, psychology (and, indeed, commonsense) points out, there are equally basic differences between people in respect of mental powers and temperament.

K. LOVELL, *Educational Psychology and Children*, University of London Press 1969

C. E. SKINNER, *Essentials of Education Psychology*, Prentice-Hall 1959

L. E. TYLER, *The Psychology of Human Differences*, 3rd edn, Appleton Century Crofts 1947

Individual test

Any test which is necessarily administered to one person at a time. e.g. Wechsler Intelligence Scale for Children (**WISC**), or **Schonell** Graded Reading Vocabulary Test.

Induction

The method of forming general conclusions or principles on the basis of particular instances. Ordinarily there is an examination of a sample (or of samples) and the inference will represent an attempt to express a generalisation concerning *all* instances.

W. C. SALMON, *Logic*, Prentice-Hall 1963

L. S. STEBBING, *Logic in Practice*, Methuen 1943

Industrial Training Act 1964

The aims and intentions of the 1964 Act are set out in the White Paper *Industrial Training* (HMSO 1962; Cmnd 1892). The major aims are: to ensure an adequate supply of trained men and women; to improve the quality of industrial training; to share the cost of this training more evenly among firms. Industrial training boards are set up for each major industry with powers to obtain information, raise money by levies and make grants to firms providing satisfactory training.

FEDERATION OF BRITISH INDUSTRIES, *Education in Transition*, 1965

Ineducable

Incapable of being educated. A narrow and obsolescent concept which interpreted education as closely related to proficiency in *basic* subjects, caused severely subnormal (SSN) children to be described and thought of as 'ineducable'. The provision for these children was therefore made the responsibility of Health Departments rather than of the Education Departments of Local Authorities. The institutions this provided were called occupation centres and, later, training centres. It was gradually realised that the concept of educability for these children could and should be widened to embrace their social and emotional development so that they could be helped to live more easily with others. To this end, from 1971 the responsibility for the majority of SSN children has devolved upon the LEAs.

H. C. GUNSBERG, *The Social Rehabilitation of the Subnormal*, Bailliere, Tindall and Cox 1960

Mental Health Act 1959 (HMSO)

F. J. SCHONELL *et al.*, *The Subnormal Child at Home*, Macmillan 1958

S. SEGAL, *No child is ineducable*, Pergamon 1967

Infant school

The lower division of the primary schools for children between five and seven years; about one third of such schools are in buildings separate from the junior school with a separate head teacher.

E. R. BOYCE, *Today and Tomorrow*, 3 vols, Macmillan 1962

Infant and Nursery Schools, HMSO 1933

E. MELLA, *Education Through Experience in the Infant School Years*, Blackwell 1950

Plowden Report, *Children and Their Primary Schools*, 1967

See also **First school**

Infantile sexuality

Freud and the psychoanalytical school drew attention to the primacy of sex in human motivation. They pointed out the sexual manifestations in the behaviour of even very young children, and showed how this forms the basis of the adult pattern of sexual behaviour.

L. CARMICHAEL, *Manual of Child Psychology*, Wiley 1954

H. J. EYSENCK, *Fact and Fiction in Psychology*, Penguin (Pelican) 1965

S. FREUD, *Two Short Accounts of Psychoanalysis*, Penguin (Pelican) 1962

Inferiority complex

A **complex** which is rooted in a conflict in the unconscious between the desire for personal recognition and the fear of the distress which is associated with situations of real or imagined personal failure in the past. The result, in the main unconsciously determined, is defensive, compensatory and even aggressive behaviour.

In-group

A term used by W. G. Sumner to characterise a group which has internal loyalty, comradeship and 'we feeling' amongst its members; each member identifies very closely with the group. Examples are teams, certain work groups such as dockers' gangs, some families.

R. K. MERTON, *Social Theory and Social Structure*, Free Press 1956; new edn, 1965

W. G. SUMNER, *Folkways*, new edn, Dover-Constable 1959

Inhelder, Barbel

Swiss psychologist, Professor at the University of Geneva, and collaborator with **Jean Piaget** in a number of the latter's researches and publications; she has adapted Piagetian developmental stages to the diagnosis of degrees of mental subnormality in her book (as yet untranslated), '*Le Diagnostique du raisonnement chez les débiles mentaux*'.

J. H. FLAVELL, *The Developmental Psychology of Jean Piaget*, Van Nostrand 1963

B. INHELDER and J. PIAGET, *The Growth of Logical Thinking from Childhood to Adolescence*, Routledge & Kegan Paul 1958

Inhibition

A condition in which there is inner interference, physical or mental, with free expression or activity, and which thus prevents their manifestation.

Inhibition, Retroactive

In the theory of forgetting, refers to the blocking which occurs in the recall of original material by some subsequent learning interpolated between the original learning and recall.

K. LOVELL, *Educational Psychology and Children*, University of London Press 1969, ch. 9

N. L. MUNN, *Psychology: the fundamentals of human adjustment*, 5th edn, Harrap 1966, ch. 12

Initial teaching alphabet. *See* **ita**

Innate

Inherited, as opposed to 'acquired' or 'learnt'. Synonym for 'in-born'.

Innate releasing mechanism

The means by which animals release responses, such as feeding, mating, fighting behaviour, in other members of the same species. They may be acoustical (e.g. song, croaking, chirping), chemical (e.g. scents, touch); displays (e.g. posturing, dancing); visual (e.g. colouring or shape). Studied by K. Lorenz, and N. Tinbergen. Some biologists consider the term to be obsolete.

N. TINBERGEN, *Social Behaviour in Animals*, 2nd edn, Methuen 1965

Insight

1. In the field of learning, and particularly as used by the *Gestalt psychologists*, the perception of relationships leading to a sudden solution of a problem.

R. MORRIS, *The Quality of Learning*, Methuen 1951

2. In psychotherapy the appreciation by the

subject, without self-deception, of his own mental condition.

C. THOMPSON, *Psychoanalysis, Evolution and Development*, Allen & Unwin 1952

Inspection. *See* HMI

Instinct
An attempted explanation of patterns of behaviour which suggests that they arise not from learning and experience, but are partly or wholly innate or inherited. The major theory is **McDougall**'s (1908). This theory was severely criticised during the inter-war period by Malinowski and others, who stressed the effect of environment as a determinant of behaviour, and by Allport in his theory of functional autonomy of motives. A modified instinct theory has been restated by Lorenz and Tinbergen.

R. FLETCHER, *Instinct in Man*, 2nd edn, Allen & Unwin 1968

F. V. SMITH, 'The status of instinct' in *Readings in General Psychology*, ed. P. Halmos and A. Iliffe, Routledge & Kegan Paul 1959

N. TINBERGEN, *The Study of Instinct*, Oxford University Press 1951

Institute of Linguists
A British body which was founded in 1940 to encourage the study of foreign languages and to unite professional linguists in a learned association.

Journal: *The Incorporated Linguist*
Address: 3 Craven Hill, London, W1

Institutes or Schools of Education
Bodies proposed in the **McNair Report** 1944 and adopted by English universities, except Cambridge and some recent foundations, to bring teacher-training institutions and universities into a closer relationship. Their responsibilities include the organization of in-service training for teachers, the coordination of examining for member colleges, provision of Academic Diploma course, etc. It is proposed in the **Robbins Report** that they shall become university schools of education undertaking broader functions.

ATCDE, *Colleges of Education for Teaching*, ATCDE annually

CONFERENCE OF DIRECTORS OF INST. OF EDUCATION, *The Education and Training of Teachers*, Camelot Press 1962

S. J. CURTIS, *History of Education in Great Britain*, 7th edn, University Tutorial Press 1967

C. MORRIS, *The Universities and the Teaching Profession*, NUT 1960, pamphlet

Institutionalisation
The state of being overadapted to a physical and social environment of the closed type, (hospital, prison, old persons' home) such that the institutionalised person finds it difficult or impossible to lead an independent life outside. The condition arises as the result of an extended period of dependence when the person is shielded or prevented from taking personal decisions.

J. BOWLBY, *Maternal Care and Mental Health*, Geneva, World Health Organisation; (Bailey Bros; New York 1966)

Instructor
One who gives information and shows how some operation should be performed, without necessarily giving the reasons why.

Insurance
Teachers are not covered by Workmen's Compensation Acts, and, if injured in the course of duty, must bring an action against their employers (e.g. in state schools against the **LEA**), who would be insured against such injuries.

G. R. BARRELL, *Teachers and the Law*, Methuen 1966

Integrated day
A school day in which the various activities of the pupils are linked and interrelated meaningfully in and around a common theme or themes. Subject boundaries are thus transcended. The idea of the integrated day is part of a larger educational philosophy in which experience and activity are more prominent in learning situations, in which learning rather than teaching is stressed, in which the teacher's role is that of guide rather than that of instructor, and in which the limitations of subject teaching are avoided. Such a school day will often be in the context of a longer period of integrated work, lasting perhaps a week or even a term. On the other hand, the integration may be on the basis of project work taking up only part of each day for a period of weeks.

M. BROWN and N. PRECIOUS, *The Integrated Day in the Primary School*, Ward Lock Educational 1968

S. MARSHALL, *An Experiment in Education*, Cambridge University Press 1963

P. R. MORAN, 'The Integrated day'; *Educational Research*, **14**, no. 1, 1971

Intelligence

Variously defined as general mental ability, the power of reasoning, the capacity to profit from experience, the ability to learn, the ability to make successful adaptations to new situations, the capacity for abstract thinking, the ability to see relationships and educe correlates. No definition meets with universal acceptance by all psychologists. Some of the most interesting work in the field of intelligence since the war has been carried out by **J. Piaget** and by **D. O. Hebb.** Piaget is particularly intested in child development and the growth of concepts, while Hebb's approach to intelligence is physiological. It is to Hebb that we are indebted for the concepts, Intelligence A, innate potential, and Intelligence B, present mental efficiency. (Vernon added the concept of Intelligence C, that which is measured by intelligence tests and therefore greatly influenced by schooling.)
See also **Intelligence tests; IQ**

D. O. HEBB, *Organization of Behaviour*, Wiley 1949

J. PIAGET, *The Pyschology of Intelligence*, Routledge & Kegan Paul 1950

P. E. VERNON, *Intelligence and Attainment Tests*, University of London Press 1960

Intelligence Quotient. *See* IQ

Intelligence, Social

The ability to deal with social relationships and make a satisfactory adjustment to the social environment. This concept is increasingly being regarded as important by educationists, particularly where less able children and adults are being considered.

N. L. MUNN, *Psychology: the fundamentals of human adjustment*, 5th edn, Harrap 1966, ch. 7

Intelligence tests

An **intelligence** test seeks to measure or assess intellectual capacity with minimal emphasis on attainment. 'Intelligence test' may be said to begin with the 'mental test' developed by James McKeen Cattell in the USA in 1890 for testing College students individually. A more definitive landmark is the work of A. Binet and T. Simon whose scale for testing intelligence was adapted and revised in the USA and is best known in the revision supplied by L. Terman and M. Merrill under the title *Measuring Intelligence*. The latter is being superseded by the Wechsler Intelligence Scales (*see* **WAIS, WISC**).

Over a long period, intelligence tests have developed under the headings of:
A. Individual tests: (1) verbal; (2) non-verbal
B. Group tests: (1) verbal; (2) non-verbal
Increasingly doubt is being expressed about the nature of intelligence and about the ability to discriminate between potential and attainment. This is reflected in the tendency in the UK more and more to use verbal reasoning tests, especially for purposes of educational selection, and in the USA to use 'classification and screening tests'.

In the UK, test material, including intelligence tests, are in the main produced by the **NFER,** by Moray House in Edinburgh, and by the University of Bristol.

D. PIGEON and A. YATES, *An Introduction to Educational Measurement*, Routledge & Kegan Paul 1969

L. M. TERMAN and M. A. MERRILL, *Measuring Intelligence*, new edn, Harrap 1960

P. E. VERNON, *Intelligence and Attainment Tests*, University of London Press 1960

Interaction

The reciprocal influence and activity, both verbal and physical in which persons participate within groups, and which groups bring to bear on each other. Purposeful conduct of two or more people towards one another.

D. CARTWRIGHT and A. ZANDER, *Group Dynamics*, 3rd edn, Tavistock 1968

C. M. FLEMING, *Teaching: A psychological analysis*, 2nd edn, Routledge & Kegan Paul 1968

Interest blank

A test of an individual's interests devised by E. K. Strong: used in **vocational guidance** to advise on the suitability of a person's interests to various occupations.

D. FRYER, *Measurement of Interests*, Holt, Rinehart & Winston 1931

Intermediate BA, BSc, etc

A first examination as part of an initial degree scheme at a university.

Intermediate school

In Wales maintained selective secondary schools were known as intermediate schools as the result of the Welsh Intermediate

Education Act of 1889. They were intermediate in the sense of being a link between the elementary schools and university and higher education, thus anticipating some of the provisions of the 1902 Education Act. The word is still used in Northern Ireland.

Internal degree

A degree granted to a student who has registered as an internal student and who has successfully followed regular courses at a degree-granting institution, in the case of first and some research degrees, by full-time attendance.

Other internal research degrees may be gained by research without an attendance requirement.

NATIONAL UNION OF TEACHERS, *University and College Entrance*, pamphlet, Hamilton House, 10th edn 1968

See also **External degree**

Internal examinations

Examinations set and marked by the staff of an educational institution designed to assess their own students' progress, as opposed to those set by external bodies (e.g. the **GCE**)

See also **CSE**

J. MONTGOMERY, *Examinations: an account of their evolution as administrative devices in England*, Longmans 1965

P. E. VERNON, *The Measurement of Abilities*, 2nd edn, University of London Press 1956

Internalisation

1. The process of mentally carrying on speech or actions that previously were overt. See various works of **Piaget**.
2. Accepting as part of one's personality principles, attitudes and values which one has considered or experienced.

C. S. HALL, *A Primer of Freudian Psychology*, Allen & Unwin 1956

International Reading Association. *See* **IRA**

Interpolation

The calculation of intermediate values of a function between any two known values, e.g. on a thermometer if the reading of the temperature at 10.0 a.m. is 10°C and at 10.20 a.m. it is 12°C, it might be assumed by interpolation that the temperature at 10.10 a.m. was approximately 11°C.

P. E. VERNON, *Measurement of Abilities*, 2nd edn, University of London Press 1956

Inter-quartile range (stats)

The difference between the 75th and 25th percentiles, or between the first and the third quartile of a frequency distribution. *See* semi-interquartile range.

H. E. GARRETT, *Statistics in Psychology and Education*, 6th edn, Longmans 1966

D. M. MCINTOSH, *Statistics for the Teacher*, Pergamon 1963

P. E. VERNON, *The Measurement of Abilities*, 2nd edn, University of London Press 1956

Interview

A meeting between candidate and selectors for the purpose of assessing the former's quality in respect of a vacancy or post; or between consultant and inquirer in relation to the same problem.

R. C. OLDFIELD, *The Psychology of the Interview*, 4th edn, Methuen 1951

P. E. VERNON, *Personality Tests and Assessments*, rev edn, Methuen 1953

Introjection

The turning into the self of feelings towards others which give rise to conflict or aggressive impulses. In this way dislike of another person may be repressed and introjected in the form of suicidal tendencies. In early life parental prohibitions and demands develop into the superego by introjection.

S. FREUD, *A General Selection from the Works of Sigmund Freud*, ed. J. Rickman, Hogarth Press 1937

Introspection

Observation of one's own mental processes; self-analysis. Early psychologists relied heavily on introspection for their information about the mind but satisfactory objective introspection of the emotions or motives is almost impossible. Where it is used in modern experimental psychology introspection is usually immediate retrospection, i.e. reporting on mental states or reactions brought about by particular stimuli.

Introvert

A type of personality designated by **C. G. Jung** as the one which is concerned with the self and the subjective psychological processes rather than with the object and the objective processes. He proposes four main categories of introverts: thinking, feeling, sensation and intuition.

H. J. EYSENCK, *The Scientific Study of Personality*, Routledge & Kegan Paul 1952

C. G. JUNG, *Psychological Types*, trans. H. G. Baynes; Routledge & Kegan Paul 1923

Inversion

The act of reversing the natural order of anything. Sexual inversion – the assumption of the character and role of the opposite sex. In psychoanalysis used as a synonym for homosexuality.

IQ

Intelligence Quotient: The term first used by Stern in which the mental age of an individual is expressed as a percentage of his chronological age, i.e. $IQ = \dfrac{MA}{CA} \times 100$.

The average IQ is therefore 100. This conventional formula is not completely satisfactory when dealing with children and is unsatisfactory when dealing with adults. Another way of obtaining IQ is to compare the level of intelligence of an individual with that of other people in his own age group. This is done by **standardisation of a test**, i.e. by giving it to large numbers of people, and drawing up tables of **norms** from which standard scores for particular individuals may be obtained. These approximate to IQs and are sometimes called 'deviation quotients'.

K. LOVELL, *Educational Psychology and Children*, University of London Press 1969
P. E. VERNON, *Measurement of Abilities*, 2nd edn, University of London Press 1956

IRA

International Reading Association: an American body devoted to the dissemination of knowledge about reading and reading ability at all levels. It also initiates research and published bulletins.

Address: P.O. Box 119, Newark, Delaware, USA

See also **UKRA**

Isaacs, Susan Sutherland (1885–1948)

British educational psychologist with a particular interest in child development. Psychologist to the London Clinic of Psychoanalysis, 1931–48; Principal, Malting House School, Cambridge, 1924–27; connected with the teaching of psychology in the University of London, 1916–43.

Publications include: *The Nursery Years* (2nd edn, Routledge & Kegan Paul 1932); *Intellectual Growth in Young Children* (Routledge & Kegan Paul 1930); *The Children We Teach* (University of London Press 1932); *Social Development in Young Children* (Routledge & Kegan Paul 1934); *The Psychological Aspects of Child Development* (rev. edn, Evans 1950).

Isolate

An individual who is not accepted as a member of existing groups or who refuses to join. Isolates sometimes display symptoms of psychological disturbance.

K. M. EVANS, *Sociometry and Education*, Routledge & Kegan Paul 1962

ita

Initial teaching alphabet, invented by Sir James Pitman to enable beginners to learn to read on the basis of forty-three visual symbols. The system seeks to avoid the difficulties normally associated with early stages in reading when the child has to cope with the irregularities of English orthography. It is intended only for the early stages in reading. Transition to traditional orthography appears to be much easier than people at one time feared.

For literature write to: The ita Foundation, 9 Southampton Place, London, WC1

J. DOWNING, *Evaluating the Initial Teaching Alphabet*, Cassell 1967
F. W. WARBURTON and V. SOUTHGATE, *ita – an independent evaluation*, R. Chambers 1969

Item

1. Any question or unit in a questionnaire, intelligence or attainment test or personality inventory etc.
2. Item, forced choice. In a questionnaire, intelligence or attainment test or similar instrument, a question which compels the respondent to select one or other of two or more possible alternatives presented to him, but does not permit him to write in any other alternative he may have composed.
3. Multiple choice. In a questionnaire or similar instrument, but more frequently in a 'new style' examination paper, a question which presents the respondent with a series of possible answers, from amongst which he is required to select the appropriate one.

P. E. VERNON, *Intelligence and Attainment Tests*, University of London Press 1960

J

James Committee
This was a Committee set up under the Chairmanship of Lord James of Rusholme by the Secretary of State for Education and Science, Mrs M. Thatcher, in November 1970.
The Committee's terms of reference were 'to inquire into the present arrangements for the education, training and probation of teachers in England and Wales, and in particular to examine:
i. what should be the content and organisation of courses to be provided
ii. whether a large proportion of intending teachers should be educated with students who have not chosen their careers or chosen other careers;
iii. what, in the context of i and ii above, should be the role of the maintained and voluntary Colleges of Education, the Polytechnics and other further education institutions in local education authorities, and the Universities,
and to make recommendations.'
The Committee proceeded in the light of the (Edward Short) review already being undertaken by the Area Training Organisations and of the evidence already published by the Parliamentary Select Committee on Education and Science (1970)
Education: A Framework for Expansion, Cmnd 5174, HMSO 1972
S. HEWETT, ed., *The Training of Teachers – a factual survey*, University of London Press 1971
See: **White Paper** (1972)

James, William (1842–1910)
Psychologist and philosopher in USA; brother of novelist Henry James. After medical training and lecturing in psychology, he wrote *The Principles of Psychology* (1800) which established his reputation in the field. A textbook based upon it profoundly influenced generations of students, as did his *Talks to Teachers* (1899). He later turned more deeply to the examination of religion and ethics, e.g. *Varieties of Religious Experience* (1902) and became the leader of the philosophical movement called **pragmatism**, of which **John Dewey** was an adherent.
M. KNIGHT, *William James*, Penguin (Pelican Philosophy series) 1950

Jacques-Dalcroze, Emile (1865–1950)
Swiss composer and teacher of musical **eurhythmics**. His great contribution to the field of education lay in the application of eurhythmics to physical education and modern dance.
E. JACQUES-DALCROZE, *Rhythm, Music and Education*, New York, Dalcroze Society 1967

JCR. *See* **Junior Common Room**

Job card
A card on which is written a task to be completed individually or by a group of school children; often used in project work. A series of graded job cards is a primitive method of programming instruction.
A. D. ROWE, *Education of the Average Child*, Harrap 1959

Joint Four
A committee of representatives from the following four professional associations of secondary school teachers and heads: AHM (Association of Head Mistresses); IAHM (Incorporated Association of Head Masters); **IAAM** (Association of Assistant Mistresses); **AMA** (Association of Assistant Masters).

Journals of education, etc. *See* Appendix IV

Jukes
A family much quoted in early studies of heredity and environment in an effort to prove that their poor heredity, as opposed to the favourable heredity of the Darwins, resulted in poor intellectual and social achievements. But if the Jukes and Darwin studies had anything valid to pronounce about the effects of heredity as compared with the effects of environment, it would have been necessary for the children to grow up in similar environments.
A. SCHEINFIELD, *The Basic Facts of Human Heredity*, Pan Books 1963

Jung, Carl Gustave (1875–1963)
Swiss doctor, psychiatrist and philosopher, who, after a number of years working in association with Sigmund Freud, rejected the latter's theory concerning the sexual causation of psychoneurosis and broke away to form his own school of analytical psychology, which classified people into introverted and extroverted types. The unconscious mind to Jung included both a personal individual unconscious and a disposition inherited from ancestors which he called the 'collective unconscious'.
His many works (in English translation)

include: *Contribution to Analytical Psychology* (Routledge & Kegan Paul 1928); *Psychological Types* (Routledge 1923); *Modern Man in Search of a Soul* (Routledge & Kegan Paul 1933); *Essays on Contemporary Events* (Kegan Paul 1947); *Development of Personality* (Routledge 1954).

F. FORHAM, *An Introduction to Jung's Psychology*, Penguin (Pelican) 1953

Junior Common Room (JCR)

The common room used for recreational facilities by the student body of a College or University and, by extension of meaning, synonymous with the student body using it, e.g. all the undergraduates.

Junior high school

1. A major institution of secondary education in the USA. The junior high school developed after the 1914–18 war, offering a more valuable alternative to the upper elementary grades. It is a three-year school leading on to high school, so that the twelve-year pattern of education may be 6–3–3. This pattern involving the junior high school is not universal in the USA.

H. G. GOOD, *A History of American Education*, 2nd edn, Collier-Macmillan 1962

2. The term 'high school' is also used to describe the first part of the Leicestershire Comprehensive Plan. It is a school catering for *all* children after the age of eleven; a proportion of these, however, go on to grammar school provision at the age of fourteen to fifteen.

S. C. MASON, *The Leicestershire Experiment and Plan*, Councils and Education Press 1957 (pamphlet)

Junior school

The upper division of the primary schools for children between seven and eleven. The large majority have infant schools adjacent.

Gittins Report, *Primary Education in Wales*, 1967

MINISTRY OF EDUCATION, *Primary Education: Handbook of suggestions*, HMSO 1959

Report of Consultative Committee on Primary School, HMSO 1931

A. ROSS, *The Education of Childhood*, Harrap 1960

Seven to Eleven: Your Child at School, HMSO 1949

Plowden Report, *Children and their Primary Schools*, 1967

Juvenile

Persons not considered as adults for the purpose of disposal by the courts: (*a*) Children aged 10 and not yet 14; (*b*) young persons aged 14 and not yet 17.

The age of criminal responsibility was raised to 10 in 1964, having formerly been 8. Children who commit crimes before the age of criminal responsibility may be subjects of a **fit person** order and then may still be committed to **approved schools**, though without a finding of guilt.

See also **Court, Juvenile**

J. A. F. WATSON, *The Child and the Magistrate*, Cape 1965

K

K factor
The spatial factor in **intelligence**. Spatial ability, the capacity to manipulate shapes imaginatively, is linked with mechanical ability to give the K:M factor.
A. A. H. EL KOUSSY, *The Visual Perception of Space, British Journal of Psychology*, Supplement 20, 1935

Kay-Shuttleworth, Sir James P. (1804–77)
Doctor and, from 1835, Assistant Commissioner of Central Poor Law Board, a post which led to an interest in pauper children and in education as a means to combat their conditions. He was led to study, amongst others, the Scottish and Dutch educational systems, taking his idea of a **Normal School** from the latter. In 1839 he became First Secretary to the Committee of the Council on Education, and, in the same year, was joint founder of Battersea College of which he was Principal for two years in addition to the former post. His pioneer work was one of the most important factors in the development of teacher-training in the nineteenth century.
J. W. ADAMSON, *English Education 1789–1902*, Cambridge University Press 1965
H. M. POLLARD, *Pioneers of English Popular Education*, Murray 1956

Keller, Helen (1880–1968)
An American blind deaf-mute who learned to read, write and talk. Graduated in 1904. At nineteen months, suffered a severe illness which caused her to lose sight and hearing: soon became mute. Miss A. M. Sullivan undertook her education when H. Keller was seven years old. The amazing achievements of this partnership must be attributed to both pupil and teacher. She wrote her own account as *The Story of My Life*, Hodder & Stoughton 1951

Key words
Basically important words (e.g. in learning to read). Several analyses have been made of children's literature to establish which words appear with the greatest frequency and which are therefore fundamental in children's reading skill. The best known analysis in this country is that by McNally and Murray.
G. E. R. BURROUGHS, *A Study of the Vocabulary of Young Children*, Oliver & Boyd 1957
J. MCNALLY and N. MURRAY, *Key Words to Literacy and the Teaching of Reading*, Schoolmaster Publishing Co. 1968

Kinaesthesia
The sense connected with the muscles, tendons and joints which makes one aware of the position of one's body without the aid of vision or touch.

Kinaesthetic method
A method of teaching children to spell or learn number concepts by making the child trace with the finger the written word or number fact at the same time as he is saying it.
See also **Fernald-Keller method**

Kindergarten
A private school for children between two and seven years. The name was coined by **Froebel**. In the state system they are usually referred to as **nursery schools**. The expression is widely used in the USA.

Kinesiology (or Kinaesiology)
The systematic application of the principles of anatomy, physiology and mechanics to the study of movement. In recent years, in the field of physical education, kinaesiology has been extended to include the study of mechanical principles which apply to various techniques in sport.
K. F. WELLS, *Kinesiology*, Saunders 1966

Kinsey Report
Surveys which resulted in two books by A. C. Kinsey, American zoologist and student of sexual behaviour: *Sexual Behaviour in the Human Male* and *Sexual Behaviour in the Human Female* (Saunders 1948 and 1953). The books are based on 18,500 interviews of American adults. Criticism has been directed against the statistical techniques and ethical problems raised by the methods used in the investigation.

Klein, Melanie
A psychologist who, after practising psychoanalysis in Germany for seven years, came to England in 1926. Here she became the leader of one of the two groups of British Freudian psychoanalysts. The other group was led by **Anna Freud**, the daughter of Sigmund Freud. Klein and her followers were of the opinion that, even with young children, the analyst should attempt to uncover the instinctual conflicts which exist and interpret them immediately to the subject. By observing children as young as three, playing with

toys and dolls, she claimed that it was possible to see which instinctive forces were at work.

Her publications include *Contributions to Psychoanalysis* (Hogarth Press 1948); *The Psycho-analysis of Children* (3rd edn, Hogarth Press 1959).

Knight, Rex and Knight, Margaret
Late Professor and Senior Lecturer respectively in Psychology at the University of Aberdeen; co-authors of *A Modern Introduction to Psychology* (7th edn, University Tutorial Press 1966). Rex Knight's *Intelligence and Intelligence Testing* was for many years considered to be an authoritative British book on the subject and Margaret Knight's *William James* was the first book in the Pelican Philosophy series (Penguin 1950). Mrs Knight became a centre of controversy in the 1950s following a series of broadcasts on 'Morals without religion'.

Koffka, Kurt (1886–1941)
German born psychologist and one of the founders of **Gestalt** psychology with M. Wertheimer and **W. Kohler**. His psychology is an attempt to deal with the problems of perception by the concepts of configurations – meaningful wholes rather than elements – and consequently opposes **behaviourism**.

Publications include (in translation): *Growth of the Mind* (2nd edn, Routledge & Kegan Paul 1928); *Principles of Gestalt Psychology* (Routledge & Kegan Paul 1935).

W. D. ELLIS, *A Source Book of Gestalt Psychology*, Routledge & Kegan Paul 1938

Kohler, Wolfgang (b. 1887)
German psychologist and leading figure in the **Gestalt** school, who conducted far-reaching research into the nature of learning processes in anthropoid apes. An opponent of Nazism, he became a US citizen in 1946. His most famous work was *The Mentality of Apes* (2nd edn, Routledge & Kegan Paul 1925).

W. D. ELLIS, *A Source Book of Gestalt Psychology*, Routledge & Kegan Paul 1938

Kohs' Blocks
Kohs' Block design test. Originally constructed in 1923 by S. C. Kohs, the test offers a non-verbal test of performance. From 4 to 16 coloured blocks have to be arranged in a series of ten patterns.

P. E. VERNON, *Intelligence and Attainment Tests*, University of London Press 1960

L

Lancaster, Joseph. *See* **Bell–Lancaster**

Land grant colleges
The Morrill Act (USA 1862) granted public land to the states so that colleges might be maintained to promote liberal and practical education. Many have a marked agricultural or technical bias, but others are now state universities.
H. G. GOOD, *A History of American Education*, 2nd edn, Collier-Macmillan 1962

Language laboratory
An electronic system for the teaching of modern languages consisting of booths each equipped with a modified tape-recorder and linked to a console controlled by the teacher. Students are able to follow prepared tapes through headphones and record their responses, either as a group or individually; the teacher may monitor or direct this process. Slides or film strips may be used in conjunction with the tapes, which are programmed commercially or prepared individually by the teacher.
J. B. HILTON, *The Language Laboratory in School*, Methuen 1966
E. M. STACK, *The Language Laboratory and Modern Language Teaching*, 2nd edn, Oxford University Press 1966
J. D. TURNER, *Introduction to the Language Laboratory*, University of London Press 1965
D. UNWIN, ed., *Media and Methods*, McGraw-Hill 1964

Laplace-Gaussian curve. *See* **normal curve**

Latent learning
Learning which takes place, seemingly without motivation or reinforcement, and which is not displayed in behaviour until some time has elapsed after the stimulus.

Laterality
The preferential use of the organs on one side of the body rather than those on the other, e.g. the use of one hand rather than the other in a situation where the use of one hand is required. In cross-laterality there is a mixture of preferences, e.g. a left-handed person may use his right eye rather than his left. Some psychologists think cross-laterality may be one of the causes of backwardness, since the condition may increase the difficulty of hand and eye coordination.
See also **Dextrality; Dominance; Handedness; Sinistrality**

M. M. CLARK, *Left-handedness*, University of London Press for Scottish Council for Research – Education 1957

Law as it affects teachers
The English educational system is established by law, and the teacher's employment is subject to the terms of a contract depending upon statutes and regulations made under their authority. He is also *in loco parentis* under common law, and must take account of local authority rules. The statute law is interpreted by the courts and much that affects teachers exists as case law or precedent. The teacher's main safeguards are in his headmaster and his **professional association** which should be contacted immediately if problems arise which are likely to affect his professional standing because of possible legal implications.
G. R. BARRELL, *Teachers and the Law*, Methuen 1966
G. TAYLOR and /. B. SAUNDERS, *The New Law of Zducation*, 7th edn, Butterworth 1971

LEA
Local education authority, usually the county, city or borough council acting through its education committee and officers.
G. R. BARRELL, *Teachers and the Law*, Methuen 1966
Education Authorities Directory and Annual, The School Government Publishing Co.
G. TAYLOR and J. B. SAUNDERS, *The New Law of Education*, 7th edn, Butterworth 1971

Learning
Adaptive change in behaviour as a result of experience; includes conditioning, training, learning of motor skills, cognitive learning, the latter being the process of mentally retaining complex experiences by imposing structural patterns (concepts) upon them.
B. R. BUGELSKI, *The Psychology of Learning*, Methuen 1957
E. R. HILGARD, *Theories of Learning and Instruction*, University of Chicago Press 1965
J. HOLT, *How Children Learn*, Pitman 1968
N. L. MUNN, *Psychology: the fundamentals of human adjustment*, 5th edn, Harrap 1966, ch. 7
K. A. O'CONNOR, *Learning: an introduction*, Macmillan 1968

R. S. WOODWORTH and R. M. SHEEHAN, *Contemporary Schools of Psychology*, 3rd edn, Methuen 1965

Lecture method
The lecture method of teaching in **higher education** was derived from classical origins and adopted widely in western medieval universities when books were scarce. It is economical of manpower and has been retained in modern times to provide an introduction to a field of knowledge through the medium of a living personality, to arouse interest, promote individual comprehension and to offer a foundation and guidance for further independent study. It can be criticised when used as an all-purpose teaching method in that it pays little regard to individual differences among students, requires a higher standard of performance in the lecturer, frequently fails to engage attention, and encourages passivity in the audience. Such a method of teaching needs to be linked with other techniques such as seminars, workshops, individual guidance and judicious use of the printed word.
J. MCLEISH, *The Lecture Method*, Cambridge Institute of Education 1968
D. A. BLIGH, *What's the Use of Lectures*, Penguin 1972

Left-handedness. *See* Sinistrality

Leicestershire Plan
A scheme for the reorganisation of secondary education on an area basis; all children between eleven and fourteen go to unselective secondary schools (high schools) and then either remain for a final year or proceed to grammar school for a full-time course to 16+. This avoids some of the problems of the 11+ selection. The scheme has operated since 1957.
S. C. MASON, *The Leicestershire Experiment and Plan*, Councils & Education Press 1957 (pamphlet)

Lesbianism
The tendency in women to make sexual love relationships with other women; a **sexual perversion**.
See also **Homosexuality**
HAVELOCK ELLIS, *Psychology of Sex*, Heinemann 1934; Pan 1959
B. MAGEE, *One in Twenty*, 2nd edn, Secker & Warburg 1968

O. SCHWARZ, *The Psychology of Sex*, Penguin (Pelican) 1949

Lesson notes
The notes which the teacher, or student on teaching-practice, has made to guide and support him in the conduct of a lesson. His preparation leads the teacher to project himself imaginatively into the actual teaching situation: he therefore structures his subject matter, plans the sequence and the emphases of the lesson, gathers together what apparatus he might need, and generally anticipates, as best he can, the reactions of the pupils to the various parts of the lesson.
A. COHEN and N. GARNER, *A Student's Guide to Teaching Practice*, University of London Press 1968

Level of aspiration
The goal(s) or level(s) of achievement or excellence to which the individual person aims: this can be the result of a complex of factors, but one of the most powerful influences is the family's **level of expectation** in relation to the individual's future.

Level of expectation
The degree of success in any sphere of activity, but particularly that of scholarship, expected or hoped for by a person of himself or in respect of him by his parents or teachers. A knowledge of this level becomes important to a teacher in considering the psychological and sociological factors involved in the learning process.

Lewin, Kurt (1890–1947)
German born, American **Gestalt** psychologist and originator of **field theory**. He defines behaviour as locomotion caused by forces, and seeks to express this concept in mathematical, especially geometrical and topographical language. He has drawn special attention to the role of perception in learning and he has contributed to the understanding of **group dynamics**. His publications include *Principles of Topological Psychology* (McGraw-Hill 1936); and *Field Theory in Social Science* (Harper & Row 1951; Tavistock 1963).
B. B. WOLMAN, *Contemporary Theories and Systems in Psychology*, Harper & Row 1960

Liberal arts
1. In earlier times, the higher branches of learning which were suitable for free men

(*artes liberales*). These are: grammar, rhetoric, logic i.e. the *trivium*; geometry, arithmetic, music and astronomy i.e. the *quadrivium*.
2. Nowadays, those branches of learning other than those which are strictly technical or professional.

Liberal arts college

1. An American institution of higher learning offering a four-year course to first degree in arts subjects, often with music, fine art, etc.
2. One of the major divisions of a university (USA) including the arts and associated departments.

Liberal education

Education, irrespective of subject, that liberates the mind and the spirit. **Aristotle** indicated it as being education which enables a person to pursue contemplative activities rather than those of recreation and occupation. More generally in the Greco-Roman world it meant the education befitting the 'liber' as opposed to the slave. In the Middle Ages it was thought that a liberal education was best achieved through the seven **liberal arts**. At the present day the reference is to a broad education, avoiding the dangers of narrow specialisation, which has in view the preparation for life rather than for a particular occupation or profession.
R. LIVINGSTONE, *Education for a World Adrift*, Cambridge University Press 1943
C. P. SNOW, *The Two Cultures and the Scientific Revolution*, Cambridge University Press 1959.

Libido

In **psychoanalysis** the term for basic psychic energy. For Freud it was 'the energy of those instincts which have to do with all that may be comprised under the word "love".' Others, particularly **Jung**, use the term to cover the total strivings of the individual.
A. CRICHTON-MILLER, *Psychoanalysis and its Derivatives*, 2nd edn, Oxford University Press (Home University Library) 1945
S. FREUD, *A General Selection from the Works of Sigmund Freud*, ed. J. Rickman, Hogarth Press 1937

Library period

A lesson period allocated to the use of the library. Pupils need to develop skills and techniques in the use of a library and to learn acceptable codes of behaviour appropriate to the library. This work needs to be thought-fully organised. The ideal should be to get pupils to want to use the library in connection with their work in general.
LIBRARY ASSOCIATION: Address: Chaucer House, Malet Street, London, WC1
R. G. RALPH, *The Library in Education*, 2nd edn, Phoenix House 1960
SCHOOLS LIBRARY ASSOCIATION: Address: Premier House, 150 Southampton Row, London, WC1

Licentiate

The general title given to holders of first degrees of West European continental universities, e.g. Licence, Licenciado; originated in the licence to teach, granted by the Church in the medieval period. In Great Britain it is used to indicate the professional qualification of some grades of dentist, doctor and musician. It is also awarded by the **College of Preceptors** to teachers.

Life chances

The members of a particular social class have the same 'life chances', that is, the same probability of securing the good things of life such as freedom, a high standard of living, deference, status and whatever is esteemed within a society. Life chances are increasingly influenced by educational opportunity.

Likert Scale

Attitude tests with multiple-choice answers are sometimes referred to as Likert-type, in contrast to Thurstone-type. Likert was not the originator of this type of test but he did develop a statistical technique for weighting the responses.
A. L. EDWARDS, *Techniques of Attitude Scale Construction*, Appleton-Century-Crofts 1957
P. E. VERNON, *Personality Tests and Assessments*, new edn, Methuen 1953

Linguistics

The science of languages and therefore concerned with matters like grammar, etymology and phonetics.
D. HYMES, *Language in Culture and Society* Harper & Row 1967
SIMEON POTTER, *Our Language*, Penguin (Pelican) 1950

Lipreading

The technique developed by the deaf and those with partial hearing for understanding speech by observation of the speaker's lip movements. Some children, particularly the most intelligent, can often conceal their deafness from teachers by their lipreading facility.

A. W. G. EWING, ed., *Educational Guidance and the Deaf Child*, Manchester University Press 1957

A. W. G. EWING amd I. R. EWING, *New Opportunities for Deaf Children*, University of London Press 1958

Literacy
The quality of being able to communicate by means of the written word, or, more simply, the ability to read and write. This is a matter of degree, hence the term 'semi-literate'.

M. M. LEWIS, *The Importance of Illiteracy*, Harrap 1953

MINISTRY OF EDUCATION, Pamphlet no 18, *Reading Ability: some suggestions for helping the backward*, HMSO 1950

MINISTRY OF EDUCATION, Pamphlet no. 32, *Standards of Reading 1948–58*, HMSO 1957

Literature, English
Published writings in English which have quality and style. That branch of English as a subject of study which concentrates on the prose and poetic works of acknowledged worth.

H. BLAMIRES, *English in Education*, Bles 1951, ch. 3

B. FORD, *The Pelican Guide to English Literature*, Penguin Books, 7 vols, 1957–69; library edn, published by Cassell

B. JACKSON and D. THOMPSON, eds, 'Use of English': *English in Education*, Chatto & Windus 1962

L–M Intelligence Test
The 1937 revision of the 1916 'Stanford Revision of the Binet Scale' is sometimes referred to as the L-M Test due to the fact that this 1937 revision included two alternative forms of the test, form L and form M respectively.

L. M. TERMAN and M. A. TERMAN, *Measuring Intelligence*, new edn, Harrap 1937

Load (vocab.)
The rate at which new material is introduced into a book, lesson, or lecture, e.g. the vocabulary 'load' of a book intended for pupils learning to read is the rate, or gradient, at which new words are introduced.

A. F. WATTS, *The Language and Mental Development of Children*, Harrap 1944

P. WITTY, *Reading in Modern Education*, Harrap 1949

Local authority. *See* **Authority, Local**

Local education authority. *See* **LEA**

Locke, John (1632–1704)
English philosopher whose educational work *Some Thoughts concerning Education*, 1693, influenced Rousseau and was admired by Leibniz. His essay on education is a characteristic mixture of the conventional, strict, stoical and conservative attitude to child-rearing, and progressive elements of a liberal type, e.g. his advocacy of example, not rules, in moral training, his hostility to Greek and corporal punishment, and his interest in play methods.

SIR J. ADAMS, *Evolution of Educational Theory*, Macmillan 1928

S. J. CURTIS and M. E. A. BOULTWOOD, *A Short History of Educational Ideas*, 4th edn, University Tutorial Press 1965

Long division
That method of division in which the working is shown in full and in which therefore the process of subtraction under the partial dividends is written in full, e.g.

$$4)\overline{\begin{matrix} 94 \\ 376 \\ 36 \\ \hline 16 \\ 16 \\ \hline \end{matrix}}$$

If compound quantities of money, length, etc., were being divided, the multiplication involved in reduction and the adding on of smaller units would be shown.

See also **Division** and **Short Division**

L. W. DOWNES and D. PALING, *The Teaching of Arithmetic in Primary Schools*, Oxford University Press, Unesco Handbooks 1958

Look and Say
A method of teaching reading in which the learner in the very early stages is invited to respond to the total visual pattern of the word rather than attempt to first read the separate letters and then blend the sounds to make up the word.

BRISTOL UNIVERSITY, *A Second Survey of Books for Backward Readers*, University of London Press 1962

F. J. SCHONELL, *The Psychology and Teaching of Reading*, Oliver & Boyd 1945

v. SOUTHGATE and G. R. ROBERTS, *Reading—Which Approach?* U.L.P. 1970

Lower case letters
Sometimes abbreviated as 'lc letters': small letters as opposed to capital, or **upper case letters**.

Lowe's Code. *See* **Revised Code**

Luria, A. R.
Leading Soviet psychologist concerned with the application of experimental method to the problems of behaviour, with a wide interest especially in child development and language development. His work has influenced the linguistic theories of **B. Bernstein.**
Publications (in translation) include: *The Role of Speech in the Regulation of Normal and Abnormal Behaviour* (Pergamon Press 1961); *The Human Brain and Psychological Processes* (Harper & Row 1966); and (with F. I. Yudovitch) *Speech and Development of Mental Processes in the Child* (Staples Press 1965).

Lycée
In France, the prestige-conferring school at secondary level, approximating loosely to the traditional British grammar school or public school. Entry is highly selective and the curriculum is narrowly academic. In recent years, however, there have been a series of developments of a **comprehensive** nature which may change the character of French Secondary education.
E. J. KING, *Other Schools and Ours*, rev. edn, Holt, Rinehart & Winston 1963

M

MA

Master of Arts. A second academic **degree** in England and Wales for which a dissertation and/or passes in certain examinations are required in Universities, other than Oxford or Cambridge. At Oxford or Cambridge after a certain lapse of time following the taking of **BA** or **BSc** and the payment of a fee the MA degree is granted. In the Scottish universities MA is an initial degree. In some universities a Master's Degree in Education may be awarded after the completion of further courses to appropriate holders of an Advanced Diploma in Education.

McDougall, William (1871–1938)

British psychologist. After training in science and medicine became Reader in mental philosophy at Oxford University 1904–14. Served in Royal Army Medical Corps from 1914–19 and became Professor of Psychology at Harvard University 1920–27. From 1927 until his death was Professor of Psychology at Duke University. Well known for his attempts to prove the Lamarckian Hypothesis that acquired characteristics can be inherited. Strongly attacked behaviourism and introduced his 'hormic psychology' which emphasised the purposive aspect of behaviour. Publications include: *Introduction to Social Psychology* (Methuen 1908); *The Group Mind* (Methuen 1920); *Psychoanalysis and Social Psychology* (Methuen 1936); *The Riddle of Life* (Methuen 1938).

Mace, Cecil Alec (b. 1894)

Professor of Psychology, Birkbeck College, University of London, 1944–61. Particularly interested in the applications of psychology and philosophy in industry. For some years Editor of the Pelican Psychology series and of Methuen's Manuals of Psychology. Publications include: *The Principles of Logic* (Longmans 1933); 'Some trends in the philosophy of mind' (in *British Philosophy in the mid-century* (Allen & Unwin 1957); *The Psychology of Study*, Penguin (Pelican, 1962); *A Symposium* (Methuen and Penguin, 1962)

McMillan sisters, Margaret (1860–1931) and Rachel (1859–1917)

Scottish educationists who were pioneers in demanding regular medical inspection of school children and in stressing the need for physical education in school. Margaret founded the first open-air nursery school for children from two to five years in 1914, and later founded the Rachel McMillan Training College for nursery school workers in memory of her sister. Margaret McMillan's publications include: *Education Through the Imagination*, Swan Sonnenschien 1904); *The Nursery School* (Dent 1919).

S. J. CURTIS and M. E. A. BOULTWOOD, *A Short History of Educational Ideas*, 4th edn, University Tutorial Press 1965, ch. 8
D'ARCY CRESSWELL, *Margaret McMillan*, Hutchinson 1948

McNair Report

Teachers and Youth Leaders, 1944 *see* Appendix IIIA

Madras System

The **monitorial system** of teaching developed by Andrew Bell during his chaplaincy of the Military Male Orphan Asylum in Madras in the late eighteenth century, and published in his work *An Experiment in Education*. Bell introduced the system into Great Britain at about the same time as Lancaster was introducing his.
See also **Bell–Lancaster**
S. J. CURTIS, *History of Education in Great Britain*, 7th edn, University Tutorial Press 1967
D. SALMON, *Lancaster's 'Improvements' and Bell's 'Experiment'*, Cambridge University Press 1932

Magazine, Class or School

The collected, selected, edited, and published literary contribution of a class or of a school. If a class magazine, it is not usual to reproduce copies, but a school magazine is usually reproduced for general distribution.
D. MATTAM, *The Vital Approach*, Pergamon 1963

Maintained schools

Schools maintained by the state, and therefore normally administered through the **LEAs**. They include **aided schools, voluntary controlled schools, special agreement schools** and **county schools.**
G. TAYLOR and J. B. SAUNDERS, *The New Law of Education*, 7th edn, Butterworth 1971

Maintenance grant

A grant made (e.g. by an **LEA**) to a student to support him during his period of studies. The amount of the grant usually varies with the income of the student's parents or, in respect of a married person, with his family commitments.

MINISTRY OF EDUCATION, *Grants to Students*, HMSO 1960

Maladjustment
A condition in which an individual is failing to adjust satisfactorily to his environment with consequent emotional ill-effects and behaviour problems.
M. F. CLEUGH, *Psychology in the Service of the School*, Methuen 1951
Underwood Report, *Report of Committee on Maladjusted Children*, 1955, *see* Appendix IIIA.

Managers, School
A body of people appointed under an Instrument of Management to supervise the general affairs of a *primary* school. Powers are divided between the Managers, the Head and the **LEA** as defined by the Rules of Management.
G. R. BARRELL, *Teachers and the Law*, Methuen 1966
G. TAYLOR and J. B. SAUNDERS, *The New Law of Education*, 7th edn., Butterworth 1971

Mannheim, Karl (1893–1947)
Sociologist. Born in Budapest. Educated at various European universities before becoming Professor of Sociology in the University of Frankfurt, 1930. Came to England in 1933 and was lecturer in Sociology at the London School of Economics 1933–45. Professor of Education, University of London, 1945–47. Editor, International Library of Sociology and Social Reconstruction (Routledge & Kegan Paul).
Publications include: *Essays on the Sociology of Knowledge* (Routledge & Kegan Paul 1952); *Man and Society in an Age of Reconstruction* (Routledge & Kegan Paul 1940); *Diagnosis of our Time* (Routledge & Kegan Paul 1943).
I. MORRISH, *Disciplines of Education*, Allen & Unwin 1967
T. RAISON, ed., *The Founding Fathers of Social Science*, Penguin (Pelican) 1969

Manual (test)
A book describing the nature of a test, its administration, the method of marking, and supplying **norms**. The term is also used, particularly in America, to describe any book of instructions to accompany a course or a piece of apparatus.

Marks
An indication of the merit which the teacher or examiner wishes to attribute to a piece of work submitted by pupil or student. Marks usually are expressed in the form of a number or of a percentage, or in the form of an alphabetical letter (e.g. **B** on a five point scale means the second grade out of a possible five grades).
S. R. GRIFFITHS and L. W. DOWNES, *Educational Statistics for Beginners*, Methuen 1969
D. M. MCINTOSH, D. A. WALKER and D. MACKAY, *The Scaling of Teachers Marks and Estimates*, 2nd edn, Oliver & Boyd 1962
F. J. SCHONELL, *Backwardness in the Basic Subjects*, Oliver & Boyd 1942
P. E. VERNON, *Measurement of Abilities*, 2nd edn, University of London Press 1956

Maslow's Scale of Needs
A. H. Maslow has arranged human needs into an hierarchy or priority test of five levels, beginning with those of highest priority: (1) physiological; (2) security; (3) love; (4) esteem in terms of self-approval as well as the good opinion of other people; (5) self-expression.
A. H. MASLOW, 'A theory of motivation', *Psychological Review*, **50**, 1943
A. H. MASLOW, *Motivation and Personality*, Harper 1954

Masochism
An abnormal inclination of a sexual nature which makes pain or suffering gratifying, particularly when inflicted by a loved person. Contrasted with **sadism**.
J. A. HADFIELD, *Psychology and Mental Health*, Allen & Unwin 1950

Mass media
The main organs of communication affecting the mass of the population; notably press, radio and television.
J. A. C. BROWN, *The Techniques of Persuasion*, Penguin (Pelican) 1963
R. HOGGART, *The Uses of Literacy*, Chatto & Windus 1957; Penguin (Pelican) 1969
V. PACKARD, *The Hidden Persuaders*, Longmans 1957

Master of Arts. *See* **MA**

Master (Mistress) of Method
An obsolescent term describing the position of the tutor in the former teacher-training colleges, who was mainly responsible for the 'professional' aspects of the student's educa-

tion, as distinct from the tutors who were concerned with 'academic' subjects. The term still survives, e.g. in the University College, Swansea.

LANCE JONES, *The Training of Teachers*, Oxford University Press 1923

Masturbation
Behaviour in which persons obtain sexual gratification by fondling or manipulating their sexual organs; usually accompanied by erotic fantasies. This practice is usually associated with feelings of anxiety. It is these and their consequent effect on personality rather than the physical effects which constitute the principal problems. Recent investigations show that the practice is and always has been, so widespread as to be relatively normal. It is also part of normal behaviour in some animals.

S. FRANKENBURG, *Commonsense in the Nursery*, Penguin 1946
O. SCHWARZ, *The Psychology of Sex*, Penguin (Pelican) 1969
K. SODDY, *Clinical Child Psychiatry*, Bailliere 1960

Matched pairs technique
A method of experiment or of investigation in which, as far as humanly possible, variables between two groups of, e.g., pupils, are held constant by selecting pairs of pupils alike in terms of sex, age, intelligence, social background, etc., and observing the differences, if any, in them as a result of different treatment (or teaching methods).
See also **Control group**; **experimental group**

Maternal deprivation
The absence of normal mother care and love in a child's life. It is generally considered that this can have a serious detrimental effect on personality development. Hence the family system in orphanages and the efforts to 'foster out' children who come into **child care**.
J. BOWLBY and M. FRY, *Child Care and the Growth of Love*, Penguin (Pelican) 1953
B. WOOTTON, *Social Science and Social Pathology*, Allen & Unwin 1959
See also **Paternal deprivation**

Mathematical Association
An Association consisting mainly of teachers at secondary, grammar, college and university level whose fundamental aim is 'to promote good methods of mathematical teaching'. It has a journal, the *Maths*

Gazette and has published many reports. In recent years it has instituted a Diploma, the minimum entry qualifications being a pass in **GCE** A level Pure Mathematics, or the successful completion of a third year **supplementary course** at a college of education.
Address: Gordon House, 29 Gordon Square, London WC1

Mathematics, 'New' or 'Modern'
The term given to a movement in the mathematical world which is attempting to break away, particularly at the teaching level, from traditional content and traditional methods. It is inspired by the feeling that mathematical knowledge and technological applications are advancing so rapidly that much of the material taught to previous generations is no longer relevant. Thus 'modern' mathematics will introduce fresh material, such as groups, rings, fields, finite geometries, sets, logic, Boolean algebra and matrices. It will also find new ways of tackling some of the more traditional material.
T. J. FLETCHER, ed., *A Handbook on the Teaching of 'Modern Mathematics'*, Cambridge University Press 1965
D. PALING and A. FOX, *Elementary Maths: a modern approach*, Parts 1 and 2, Oxford University Press 1965, 1969
SCHOOLS COUNCIL, *Primary Mathematics* by E. E. Biggs, Curriculum Bulletin No. 1, HMSO 1969

Matrices, Progressive
Prepared by J. C. Raven, Director of Psychological Research at the Crichton Royal, Dumfries. A non-verbal test of mental ability complementary to the **Mill Hill Vocabulary Scale**. While the MHVS was designed to assess a person's ability to recall acquired information, the Progressive Matrices purport to test people with respect to their immediate capacities for observation and clear thinking. There are five sets, or subtests, and there is no time limit.
J. C. RAVEN, *Extended Guide to Using the Mill Hill Vocabulary Scale* (1958); *Guide to the Standard Progressive Matrices* (1960); *The Progressive Matrices Scale* (1960), all H. K. Lewis.

Matrilocal
A term used to describe the custom in a society of a married couple living at the home of the wife or her kinsfolk. Contrasted with patrilocal.

M. YOUNG and P. WILLMOTT, *Family and Kinship in East London*, Routledge & Kegan Paul 1957; Penguin (Pelican) 1969

Maturation
The process of biological development leading to changes both in behaviour, and in potential for learning. A child can 'mature' imperceptibly so that. at one stage he is not 'ready' for a particular piece of learning, while at the next stage he learns very quickly without any apparent teaching having intervened. There is much argument, at present, among psychologists, about the interplay of biological and experiential factors in promoting maturation.
N. L. MUNN, *Evolution and Growth of Human Behaviour*, 2nd edn, Harrap 1965, chs 7 and 10

Mature State Scholarship
Scholarships, tenable at university and intended for people over twenty-five, men and women, 'for courses in liberal studies rather than those of a technical or vocational nature'. The intention of the scholarships is that they shall help those who have not previously had the chance to benefit from **higher education**.
Details from: Department of Education and Science (Awards), 13 Cornwall Terrace, London, NW1

Mature student
In a university, a student who because of age and experience and general level of proficiency, may be admitted without the usual academic entry qualifications. In a **college of education** a student who, because of age and experience and a higher standard of qualifications at admission, is allowed to qualify in a shorter period of time than is normal. e.g. in one or two years instead of three.
ATCDE, *Handbook of Colleges and Departments of Education*, Methuen, annual

Maturity
The stage when general development (physical, mental, emotional, etc.) is completed. In human beings maturity is said to be reached when the individual is fully adult.
K. LOVELL, *Educational Psychology and Children*, University of London Press 1969

Maze test
A test requiring the testee to trace with a pen or pencil the most direct path to the terminus

through a figure having dead ends and false tracks. Such tests usually purport to measure elements of intelligence.
P. E. VERNON, *Intelligence and Attainment Tests*, University of London Press 1960

Mean (stats)
Usually the arithmetic mean or arithmetic average, found by adding all the values in a set of data and dividing by the number of cases. As a measure of central tendency it is strongly influenced by extreme values in the set.
H. E. GARRETT, *Statistics in Psychology and Education*, 6th edn, Longmans 1966
S. R. GRIFFITHS and L. W. DOWNES, *Educational Statistics for Beginners*, Methuen 1969
P. E. VERNON, *Measurement of Abilities*, 2nd edn, University of London Press 1956

Measurement, Educational
The techniques which attempt to quantify potential or achievement in the field of learning. These would include tests of intelligence, aptitude, and attainment in such subjects as reading and mathematics.
F. J. SCHONELL, *Diagnostic and Attainment Tests*, Oliver & Boyd 1950
P. E. VERNON, *Measurement of Abilities*, 2nd edn, University of London Press 1956

Mechanism, Mental
Semi-automatic reaction patterns resulting from repressed emotional systems and having their direction determined unconsciously. *See also* **defence mechanism**.
R. KNIGHT and M. KNIGHT, *A Modern Introduction to Psychology*, 7th edn, University Tutorial Press 1966, ch. 7

Median (stats)
A measure of central tendency. The median is the middle score or measure in a distribution arranged in order of size, or the number score or measure that would represent a point between the two middle ones.
H. E. GARRETT, *Statistics in Psychology and Education*, 6th edn, Longmans 1966
D. M. MCINTOSH, *Statistics for the Teacher*, 2nd edn, Pergamon 1967
P. E. VERNON, *Measurement of Abilities*, 2nd edn, University of London Press 1956

Medical inspection (School)
Regulations of the Department of Education and Science prescribe the minimum number of medical inspections in maintained schools:

(1) as soon as possible after the date of admission of the child, (2) during the last year at primary school, (3) during the last year at secondary school. Medical inspections are not optional: parents should attend if at all possible since they can often supply the doctor with valuable information.

DEPARTMENT OF EDUCATION AND SCIENCE, *The Health of the School Child*, HMSO, biennial

J. NEWSOM, *The Child at School*, Penguin (Pelican) 1950

Memory

Awareness of something previously known, learnt or experienced, and may reveal itself in **recognition** (as with words in listening or reading) or in **recall** (as with words in speaking or written composition).

See also **Rote learning**

F. C. BARTLETT, *Remembering: a study in experimental and social psychology*, Cambridge University Press 1932

I. M. L. HUNTER, *Memory, Facts ond Fallacies*, Penguin (Pelican) 1957

Menarche

The onset of menstruation occurring at puberty in girls.

J. M. TANNER, *Growth at Adolescence*, Blackwell 1969

Menopause

In women, the cessation of menstruation: the 'change of life'. It is often accompanied by temporary emotional instability.

O. SCHWARZ, *The Psychology of Sex*, Penguin (Pelican) 1969

Mental age. *See* Age, Mental

Mental defective

A child whose mental powers are so inadequate that he is unable to profit by normal methods of teaching in school, or an adult who, because of his poor mental equipment is markedly handicapped in his endeavours to earn a living. The old classification of such people was as feeble-minded (or **moron**), **imbecile**, **idiot**. Since the Mental Health Act of 1959 the classification has been changed to 'mentally subnormal'; 'severely mentally subnormal'.

Mental hygiene/health

The teaching profession generally is becoming more aware of the importance of mental health in education. The Schools Psychological Service which provides the aid of qualified educational psychologists and of child guidance clinics is available in most **LEAs** and is in process of expanding and developing.

National Association of Mental Health, 39 Queen Anne Street, London, W1

Mentally gifted

Persons whose intellectual calibre is well above average – 'high fliers'. **Terman** has conducted classic longitudinal studies of gifted children the results of which have appeared in a series of books published by Stanford University Press:

L. M. TERMAN et al., *Mental and Physical Traits of a Thousand Gifted Children* (1926); C. M. COX, *The Early Mental Traits of Three Hundred Geniuses* (1926); L. M. TERMAN et al., *The Promise of Youth* (1930); L. M. TERMAN and M. H. ODEN, *The Gifted Child Grows Up* (1947); L. M. TERMAN and M. H. ODEN, *The Gifted Group at Mid-life* (1959).

M. E. FREEHILL, *Gifted Children: their psychology and education*, New York, Macmillan 1961

H. J. BAKER, Introduction to *Exceptional Children*, 3rd edn, Collier-Macmillan 1959

D. G. HAAN and H. HAVIGHURST, *Educating Gifted Children*, University of Chicago Press

M. HUTCHINSON and C. YOUNG, *Educating the Intelligent*, Penguin (Pelican) 1969

P. WITTY, ed., *The Gifted Child*, Harrap 1951

Mesomorph

In Sheldon's classification of physique by anthropometric measurement, the type in which there is a prominence of bone and muscle. Associated by Sheldon with the Somatotonic temperament characterised by general assertiveness, competitive aggressiveness, noisiness and love of physical adventure.

C. T. MORGAN, *Introduction to Psychology*, 2nd edn, McGraw-Hill 1961

W. H. SHELDON, *The Varieties of Temperament*, 3rd edn, Harper & Row 1965

Metaphysics

A prori speculation on questions which cannot be answered by experimental or other scientific methods, as, for example, what kinds of things there are and the mode of their being. In the modern period metaphysical thought flourished among the German idealists Fichte, Schelling, Schopenhauer and Hegel. Philosophical suspicion of

metaphysics has been prominent amongst logical positivists and analytic philosophers such as E. Mach, G. E. Moore and L. Wittgenstein. A brief and pungent account of such criticism appears in A. J. AYER'S *Language Truth and Logic* 1936, (rev. edn, Gollancz 1946).
See also W. H. WALSH, *Metaphysics*, Hutchinson 1963

Metric system
The system of weights and measures using a base of ten produced by the French Academy of science and given legal recognition by the Constituent Assembly of France in the early days of the revolution. Many other countries have changed or are changing to a metric system of measures (particularly of currency.) The scientific world has, for many years, expressed its observations in metric form. International Athletics Competitions also use the metric system exclusively.
Report of the Committee of Inquiry on Decimal Currency, HMSO 1963

Metronome
A mechanical device used mainly in music but also in the psychological laboratory, which can be regulated to establish any predetermined tempo.

Middle class
Broadly speaking the socio-economic group which is considered to lie socially somewhere between the manual workers and the nobility. It is comprised mainly of professional, executive and management personnel at the upper levels and of 'white-collar' workers at the lower socio-economic levels.
A. MAUDE and R. LEWIS, *The English Middle Classes*, Penguin (Pelican) 1953
J. RAYNER, *The Middle Classes*, Longmans 1969

Middle school
The name suggested by the **Plowden Report** for schools catering for the 8–12 years age group. Currently middle schools vary across the age ranges 8–12, 9–12, 9–13, and 10–13. But the age range 9–13 appears with greatest frequency among the various **LEAs** who are establishing middle schools.
See also **First school**
DEPARTMENT OF EDUCATION AND SCIENCE, Education Pamphlet no. 57, *Towards the Middle School*, HMSO 1970

Plowden Report, *Children and their Primary Schools*, 1967

Midlands Maths Experiment
A title adopted by a group of teachers working on a scheme of new topics in mathematics from September 1962.
The Director of the Experient is Cyril Hope, OBE, The College of Education, Worcester.
See also **Mathematics, New**
C. HOPE, *Midlands Maths Experiment* (Report), Harrap 1963–5

Mill Hill Vocabulary Scale
A synonym test designed by J. C. Raven to record a person's present recall of acquired information and ability in verbal communication. It is intended to be used alongside his progressive matrices tests in order to obtain a general estimate of a person's intellectual powers. The scale consists of eighty-eight words divided into two parallel series of forty-four words. It can be applied orally to non-readers and in a written form to those who can read and write.
See also **Matrices (progressive); Standard progressive matrices**
J. C. RAVEN, *Extended Guide to Using the Mill Hill Vocabulary Scale with The Progressive Matrices Scales*, H. K. Lewis 1958

Mill, John Stuart (1806–1873)
British philosopher and economist, son of philosopher and economist, James Mill. Educated at home by his father, he was a child prodigy who by the age of fourteen was well-read in English, Greek, Latin and mathematics and had mastered all the economic theory then known. Spent thirty years in the India Office and after retirement was active in social reform movements. His *Principles of Political Economy with some of their Applications to Social Philosophy* (1848) was the leading economics textbook for many years.
M. ST J. PACKE, *John Stuart Mill*, Secker & Warburg 1954

Mimesis
The general tendency in individuals, particularly children, to imitate consciously or unconsciously the modes of action, feeling and thought of others.
P. NUNN, *Education: its data and first principles*, 3rd edn, Arnold 1962

Minister of Education
The title given to the member of the Government who was responsible for directing and promoting the education of the people of England and Wales between 1944 and 1964. Previously there had been a Board of Education presided over by the President of the Board of Education. In 1964 the Ministry of Education and the Ministry of Science were amalgamated to form the **Department of Education and Science**. There was also a corresponding change from 'Minister of Education' to 'Secretary of State for Education and Science'.

Ministry of Education
The Government Department of Education, which replaced the Board of Education 1944, and headed by the Minister of Education. In 1964 it was renamed the **Department of Education and Science**.

Mirror writing
Handwriting executed in reverse and legible when read from a reflection in a mirror. Found more frequently in abnormal and in retarded than in normal people.
C. BURT, *The Backward Child*, 4th edn, University of London Press 1937

MLA. *See* **Modern Languages Association**

Mnemonic
Any device which facilitates recall, e.g. the letters of 'roygbiv' provide the initial letters of the colours of the spectrum in the correct sequence.

Mobility, Social
The movement from one social group to another. The term is more often used to describe the vertical movement whereby the person moves up or down the social status scale. The expression 'horizontal social mobility' is sometimes used to describe movement within the same social status scale. Education is considered to be one of the chief means of social mobility.
D. V. GLASS, *Social Mobility in Britain*, Routledge & Kegan Paul 1954
A. H. HALSEY, J. E. FLOUD and C. A. ANDERSON, eds, *Education Economy and Society*, Part III, Free Press of Glencoe 1961
VANCE PACKARD, *The Status Seekers*, Longmans 1959

Mode (stats)
One form of **average** or **central tendency**. In a distribution of scores, it is the most 'fashionable': it is the score which appears with the greatest frequency. The modes gives a quick, but sometimes rough, estimate of average or central tendency, e.g.

x	f
5	1
4	3
3	5 – Mode
2	1
1	0

H. E. GARRETT, *Statistics in Psychology and Education*, 6th edn, Longmans 1966
S. R. GRIFFITHS and L. W. DOWNES, *Educational Statistics for Beginners*, Methuen 1969

Model
As used in the formulation of theories, the word denotes the illustration of a theory by three-dimensional constructions, by diagrams, by mathematical symbols or by verbal propositions. Its purpose is always to try to make clearer and more intelligible a complex theoretical formulation by structuring it and creating analogies. For example a complex economic system, real or theoretical, may be illustrated by a mathematical model.
J. R. LAWRENCE, ed, *Operational Research and the Social Sciences*, Tavistock 1966
J. STAFFORD BEER, *Decision and Control*, Wiley 1966
S. TOULMIN, *Philosophy of Science*, rev. edn, Hutchinson University Library 1967

Moderator (in education)
An experienced but disinterested person appointed to ascertain that the standards observed by internal examiners are consistent as between individual pupils or students, and in relation to standards observed more generally by other examiners.
D. R. MATHER, N. FRANCE and G. T. SARE, *The CSE: a Handbook for Moderators*, Collins 1965

Modern languages
Any languages now being spoken but more particularly that small group of languages which have greatest currency and which are taught as second languages in schools, e.g. French, German, Spanish, Russian, Italian.
F. L. BILLOWS, *The Techniques of Language Teaching*, Longmans 1961
UNESCO, *The Teaching of Foreign Languages*, Amsterdam 1965

Modern Languages Association
An association founded to assist teachers and students of modern languages and to secure due recognition for modern languages as instruments of general educational and cultural value.
Address: 2 Manchester Square, London W1

Modern school
A type of secondary school brought into prominence by the **tripartite system** of **secondary education** outlined in the White Paper, *Education Reconstruction* (1943) and intended to cater for the needs of children of non-academic bent, as opposed to those who might attend a **grammar school** or a **technical school**. Many modern schools are being merged into **comprehensive schools**, others are developing academic streams and encouraging children to stay at school to take the **GCE** or **CSE** examinations.
J. B. DEMPSTER, *Purpose in the Secondary Modern School*, Methuen 1956
P. KNEEBONE, *I Work in a Secondary Modern School*, Routledge & Kegan Paul 1957
W. TAYLOR, *The Secondary Modern School*, Faber 1963

Mongolism
A condition of mental retardation, described in the mid-nineteenth century by the English physician, Langdon Down. The distinguishing characteristics are, a general Mongolian facial appearance and specific peculiarities in the size of head, shape of eyes and ears, length of fingers and laxity of the joints. It is now thought that the cause is genetic and is concerned with abnormalities or aberrations in the number of chromosomes. Older women are more likely to produce mongoloid children than are younger women.
C. O. CARTER, *Human Heredity*, Penguin (Pelican) 1962

Monitor
A pupil to whom has been assigned some minor routine duty or duties in the general running of the school, e.g. supervising behaviour, distribution of exercise books, etc.
See also **monitorial system.**

Monitorial system
A method of mass teaching, introduced independently by Joseph Lancaster and **Andrew Bell** by means of which able children,

monitors, were taught by a master and proceeded to teach the same lesson to groups of other children. The system persisted into the latter part of the nineteenth century.
See also **Madras system**
See also **Bell–Lancaster**
D. SALMON, ed., *The Practical Parts of Lancaster's Improvements and Bell's Experiments*, Cambridge University Press 1932

Monoplegia
Cerebral palsy which causes motor disability in one limb only.
M. L. J. ABERCROMBIE, 'Perceptual and Visuomotor Disorders in Cerebral Palsy', *Little Club Clinics in Developmental Medicine, 11*, Heinemann 1964
K. S. HOLT and J. K. REYNELL, *Assessment of Cerebral Palsy*: vol. 1, *Muscle Function Locomotion and Hand Function*; vol. 2, *Vision, Hearing, Speech, Language, Communication and Psychological Function*, Lloyd-Luke 1967

Monozygotic
Resulting from one and the same ovum which divides after fertilization. Children born from such a division (twins, triplets, quadruplets), carry identically the same genetic structures; therefore, e.g. identical twins.
See also **Twins**
J. SHIELDS, *Monozygotic Twins*, Oxford University Press 1962

Montessori, Maria (1870–1952)
Italian doctor and educator. After receiving the first medical degree awarded to a woman in Italy in 1894, became interested in abnormal children and their training and also the training of normal children in the lower age groups. The first Montessori school was opened in Rome in 1907. After her schools were closed in Italy in 1934 she lived in Spain and later the Netherlands. She invented and made great use of various forms of sensory apparatus.
Though her work has liberality and compassion, there is a strong authoritarian element in her writing and the methods she advocated. Publications (in translation) include: *The Montessori Method* (Heinemann 1912, 2nd edn, 1920; Bentley 1964); *The Secret of Childhood* (Longmans 1936).
L. COLE, *A History of Education: Socrates to Montessori*, Holt, Rinehart & Winston 1950
E. M. STANDING, *Maria Montessori: her life and work*, Hollis & Carter 1957

Montessori System

A system of primary education based on the system developed by Séguin. The essence of the method is reputed to be spontaneity, freedom and interest, leading to the breaking down of artificial rules and repressive discipline. The children are encouraged to acquire educationally significant motor skills as well as the 'three Rs'. Each child works at his own speed and attacks his work as though it were play. All the activities have social value and only when behaviour becomes antisocial is it stopped.

Morant, Robert (1863–1920)

A very able civil servant who played a large part in reshaping English education at the very beginning of the century. He took an important part in drafting the Bill which became the Education Act of 1902. He later became Permanent Secretary to the Board of Education, and his influence was very considerable in the interpretation and application of the provisions of this Act. He reorganised the Board of Education with three branches – Elementary, Secondary, and Technical. In *Regulations for Secondary Schools* (1907) and *Code for Elementary Schools* (1904) he indicated clearly his conception of the nature and function of these two types of school respectively. His *Handbook of Suggestions for Teachers* (Cmnd 2638, HMSO, 1905) became the basis of later and enlarged versions.

More, Hannah (1745–1833)

One of the five sisters, living in or near Bristol, who concerned themselves with 'good works' all their lives. Hannah, the best-known, established schools for the poor in the Mendip villages, wrote tracts to counter the possibility of the spread of revolutionary ideas coming from France and those deriving from Paine's *The Rights of Man*, and many books of a moral and religious character. She could be described in the language of her day as evangelical in religion, a high Tory in politics but, according to her lights, a reformer.

M. G. JONES, *Hannah More*, Cambridge University Press 1952

Moreno, J. L. (b. 1892)

American psychologist best known as the originator of psycho-drama and the technique of sociometry, and for his work with small groups. His major work is *Who Shall Survive? Foundations of sociometry, group psychotherapy and sociodrama* (1934; 3rd edn, Beacon House 1953) which gives a full account of the development of sociometric method. See also his *New Introduction to Psycho-drama* (Beacon House 1963).

K. M. EVANS, *Sociometry and Education*, Routledge & Kegan Paul 1962

Moron

Used in a very general sense to indicate a person suffering from a pronounced degree of mental dullness, but in USA is used to describe persons who in this country attend schools for the educationally subnormal, and therefore who are superior to those categories that we used to designate 'idiot' and 'imbecile'.

Motivation

The process of arousing interest in some activity and the regulation and sustaining of a desire to pursue this activity. One of the main tasks of the educator is to create motivation in pupils by presenting learning situations which are interesting at the particular stages of the children's development. Rewards and praise are a widely used method of supplying motivation.

N. L. MUNN, *Psychology: the fundamentals of human adjustment*, 5th edn, Harrap 1966

NATIONAL FOUNDATION FOR EDUCATIONAL RESEARCH, *Survey of Rewards and Punishments*, Newnes 1952

A. H. MASLOW, *Motivation and Personality*, Harper 1954

MSc

Master of Science. A higher degree granted in universities, other than Oxford or Cambridge, for advanced studies and/or dissertation. In some universities it is possible to register for MSc (e.g. in Psychology) after taking an appropriate diploma.

Multilateral school

A school which by means of separate streams provides for all types of secondary education; differs from a *comprehensive school* in that the streams are kept separate.

MINISTRY OF EDUCATION, Circular 144, *Organization of Secondary Education*, 16 June 1947

Spens Report, *Secondary Education*, 1938

Multiple choice test

A test in which the respondent is offered the choice of a number of alternative answers (among which is the correct one) to each test item.

P. E. VERNON, *Intelligence and Attainment Tests*, University of London Press 1960

Multiplication

Continuous addition of the same quantity (e.g. $3 \times 4 = 4 + 4 + 4$) and thus the rapid calculation of such additions through the use and memorization of multiplication facts, e.g. $3 \times 4 = 12$.

L. W. DOWNES and D. PALING, *Teaching Arithmetic in Primary Schools*. Oxford University Press, Unesco Handbooks 1958

Munn, N. L.

American psychologist, principally interested in the developmental approach to the study of children's behaviour; author of standard reference book, *The Evolution and Growth of Human Behaviour* (Harrap 1955), and of *Psychology: the fundamentals of human adjustment* (5th edn, Harrap 1966)

Music

A subject which in schools at one time was almost exclusively devoted to singing but which is now expanding to include the elements of reading and writing music, musical appreciation, orchestral work, and music linked with movement.

School Music Association: 4 Newman Road, Bromley, Kent.

Musical Ability

Ability as vocalist or instrumentalist but more broadly, skill in rhythm, pitch, conducting or composition.

H. D. WING, *British Journal of Psychology*, Monograph Supplement, No. xxvii republished 1968

Myopia

Short or near-sightedness. In serious cases children suffering from this condition may be educated in schools for the **partially sighted** and may be technically referred to as 'high myopes'.

W. LIGHTFOOT, *The Partially-sighted School*, Chatto & Windus 1948

Myth

Usually, but not invariably, a story of events and persons related to important issues, but which did not take place in history. Often a primitive story invented to account for phenomena which were important and whose origin was not understood, e.g. the myths in the early chapters of Genesis to explain the origin of human life or the origin of diversity of languages. Myths often embody profound spiritual beliefs, e.g. that God created man in his own image.

M. ELIADE, *Myth and Reality*, Allen & Unwin 1964

F. FORDHAM, *An Introduction to Jung's Psychology*, Penguin (Pelican) 1953

N

Narcissism
An inordinate love and admiration of one's self. A concept postulated by *Freud* to explain the dual nature of man's sexuality.
ERNEST JONES, *The Life and Work of Freud*, 3 vols Chatto 1953–57; abr. edn, 1962; Penguin (Pelican) 1969

NAS
National Association of Schoolmasters; a professional organization of men teachers which broke away from the NUT in October 1922 over the question of equal pay which had come to the forefront in union affairs during the 1914–18 War. NAS members were opposed to equal pay.
Address: 59 Gordon Square, London WC1

National Association for the Teaching of English [NATE]
A body set up to promote interest in the teaching of English.
Write to Hon. Sec., E. A. R. Jones, 41 Brooksby Road, Tilehurst, Reading.

National Association of Schoolmasters. *See* NAS

National Certificate/Diploma
National Certificate originally instituted by the Board of Education and by professional institutes and offers a qualification at the 'Ordinary' or 'Higher' level in a wide range of technical subjects usually following part-time courses. They are at a more advanced level than the City and Guilds Certificates and may lead to membership of the various institutes, which is regarded as a professional qualification (e.g. AIMechE). National diplomas (OND and HND) represent comparable levels to the corresponding certificates but are taken after full-time courses.
CENTRAL OFFICE OF INFORMATION, *Technical Education in Great Britain*, Pamphlet 21, HMSO
P. F. VENABLES, *British Technical Education*, Longmans for the British Council 1959

National Council for Technological Awards. *See* NCTA

National Diploma in Design
The main qualification offered by art colleges and schools. The course is of five years, usually from 16 plus, and may include fine art, graphic and three-dimensional design, and work in a variety of media such as wood,

metal, pottery, glass, etc. Replaced by the graduate equivalent qualification Diploma in Art and Design from 1965–6.

National Extension College. *See* NEC

National Foundation for Educational Research. *See* NFER

National Froebel Foundation
A society which promotes educational ideas of **Friedrich Froebel** and examines teachers who seek qualifications to educate very young children. A number of colleges prepare students for the Certificate of Education and certificate of the National Froebel Foundation but the best known is the Froebel Educational Institute at Roehampton, close to London.
Address: The National Froebel Foundation, 2 Manchester Square, London, W1

National schools
Early elementary schools founded and run by the National Society for Promoting the Education of the Labouring Poor in the Principles of the Established Church, founded 1811. Where such schools still exist, they are probably known as *voluntary schools*.
G. R. BARRELL, *Teachers and the Law*, Methuen 1966
S. J. CURTIS and M. E. A. BOULTWOOD, *History of English Education since 1800*, Univ. Tutorial Press 1964

National Union of Students. *See* NUS

National Union of Teachers. *See* NUT

Nature–Nurture controversy
The argument, extending over many years, as to whether nature (heredity) or nurture (environment) is more important in determining various facets of personality, and in particular intelligence. A leading environmentalist of the eighteenth century in France was Claude Adrien Helvetius (1715–71); the outstanding English hereditarian was **Francis Galton** (1822–1911). In recent years investigators have used various statistical devices to analyse the relative contributions of heredity and environment to aspects of human development. In the study of intelligence it is now generally held in the West that the upper limit to intellectual development is set by heredity but that the realiza-

tion of this innate potential is dependent on a stimulating environment.

SIR PERCY NUNN, *Education: its data and first principles*, 3rd edn, Edward Arnold 1945

Newsom Report, *Half Our Future*, HMSO 1963

K. RICHARDSON et al (ed.), *Race, Culture and Intelligence*, Penguin 1972

A. R. JENSEN, *How much can we boost I.Q. and scholastic achievement?*, Harvard Educ. Review, Vol. 39, No. 1 1969

Nature study
The unspecialized general course usually associated with primary school work which includes an introduction to the elements of botany, biology and zoology.

I. FINCH, *Nature Study and Science*, Longmans 1971

K. S. N. KIRBY, *Nature Study for Schools*, Methuen 1958

H. PHILLIPS and F. J. C. MCINNES, *Exploration in the Junior School*, University of London Press 1950

E. PROCTOR, *Nature Study for Primary Schools*, Evans 1962

NCTA
National Council for Technological Awards, set up in 1955 to design an award of honours degree standard and to decide the conditions under which technical Colleges could conduct courses leading to this award. It instituted the Diploma in Technology. Following the **Robbins Report** of October 1963, the NCTA was replaced by the *Council for National Academic Awards* in September 1964, with a Royal Charter to award degrees.

Neale Reading Tests
Tests designed to ascertain the reading standards of children from six to twelve, taking account of reading speed, accuracy and comprehension.

M. D. NEALE, *Analysis of Reading Ability*, Text Booklet and Manual, Macmillan 1958

NEC
National Extension College. Founded in 1963 by the Advisory Centre of Education 'to pioneer a College of the Air and to bring new techniques and new standards to the neglected field of correspondence education. It aims to add to normal correspondence courses the stimulus of face-to-face discus-

sion between student and tutor and of television and radio, thus helping to break down the home student's sense of isolation.' The NEC is non-profit-making.
Address: Shaftesbury Road, Cambridge.

NEF
New Education Fellowship. An international organization founded in 1915 'to promote the exchange and practice of ideas in education that advance a world civilization'. Generally associated with progressive tendencies in education. Has sections and groups in twenty-two countries which organise courses and conferences.
Publication: *The New Era in Home and School* (monthly)
Address (in England): 1 Park Crescent, London, W1

Neonate
The term usually applied to the child between birth and the age of two weeks. Extended by some authorities to the period between birth and four weeks.

Neurosis
Sometimes psychoneurosis. As contrasted with **psychosis**, it is a milder form of mental illness for which usually no organic basis can be found. The neurotic person may suffer from mannerisms, tics, anxiety, phobias or obsessions, and, although his illness is not usually sufficient to require hospitalization, the disruption to his mental processes is great enough to make his adjustment to his environment unsatisfactory.

D. STAFFORD CLARKE, *Psychiatry Today*, Penguin (Pelican) 1952

J. A. HADFIELD, *Psychology and Mental Health*, Allen & Unwin 1950

New Education Fellowship. *See* **NEF**

Newcastle Commission
Royal Commission appointed in 1858 under the chairmanship of the Duke of Newcastle, 'to inquire into the state of public education in England and to consider and report what measures, if any, are required for the extension of sound and cheap elementary instruction to all classes of people'. Report in 1861 led to Lowe's **Revised Code 1862**.

S. J. CURTIS, *History of Education in Great Britain*, 7th edn, University Tutorial Press 1967

Newman, Cardinal John Henry (1801–1890)
Ordained into the Anglican Church in 1824,
was a leader of the Tractarian Movement
and tutor at Oriel. Received into the Roman
Church in 1845; rector of the new Catholic
University in Dublin 1854–58. This led to his
publishing a book of lectures *The Idea of a
University* (ed. M. J. Svaglic, Holt, Rinehart
& Winston 1960) an educational classic as an
analysis of the meaning of intellectual culture
and the role and methods of higher education in pursuing it. See also *The Idea of a
Liberal Education* H. Tristram, ed. (Harrap
1952).

News Period
A technique used, usually with young children, in which items of news of immediate
interest are discussed, the teacher possibly
writing up the key words or phrases on the
blackboard, the children then reading these
words aloud and possibly copying them in
chalk or pencil. At a more advanced level
the children might be invited to write down
their own individual items of news.
See also **Diary keeping**

Newsom Report, 1963
Half our Future see Appendix IIIA.

Newsom Report, 1968
Report of the Public Schools Commission (*see*
Appendix IIIA), a body set up in December
1965 by the Department of Education and
Science under the Chairmanship of Sir John
Newsom, to consider and report on possible
methods of bringing about the integration of
independent boarding and **public day schools**
with the **maintained schools** system.
J. C. DANCY, *The Public Schools and the
Future*, 1966
Fleming Report, *The Public Schools and the
General Educational System*, HMSO 1944

NFER
The National Foundation for Educational
Research, in its own words, 'is a partnership
for all those concerned with public education in England and Wales, and is concerned
with the study of problems arising at all
levels within the national educational system'.
Membership includes **LEA's**, national
teachers' organisations, universities and
university institutes, colleges of advanced
technology, H.M. Forces and associated
educational organisations. Its basic income

derives from membership subscription and
the **Department of Education and Science**
makes an annual grant. It undertakes major
research programmes of its own, develops
collaboration between bodies undertaking
educational research, nationally and inter-
nationally, and provides information and
consultative services for teachers and others
concerned with the practical problem of
primary, secondary and tertiary education.
Address: NFER, The Mere, Upton Park,
Slough, Bucks.
Address for Test Services: 79 Wimpole
Street, London W1
Annual report: *Notes on the work of the
National Foundation for Educational Research
in England and Wales.*
Journal: *Educational Research*

Noegenesis
The term used by **Spearman** to describe the
principles of cognition, noegenetic principles; namely, apprehension of experience,
eduction of relations and eduction of correlates

Noesis
The working of the intellect or reason;
cognition.
C. SPEARMAN, *The Nature of Intelligence and
The Principles of Cognition*, Macmillan 1923
C. SPEARMAN, *Abilities of Man*, Macmillan
1927

Non-academic. *See* **Academic**

Non-parametric (stats)
A term to describe those statistical techniques which may be applied to a set of data
regardless of the shape of the distributions
of the data, e.g. in computing **median, rank
order correlation**, and in **chi-square** calculations.
S. SIEGEL, *Nonparametric Statistics for
Behavioural Science*, McGraw-Hill 1956

Norm
A standard of development or attainment,
usually based on the average or median
attainment of a large group, e.g. a particular
age group.

Norms, Development
Tables, based on data collected from large
numbers of children, which show what
behaviour, or psychological development,
can be normally expected to appear in child-

ren at various chronological age levels.
C. BUHLER and H. HETZER, *Testing Children's Development*, Allen & Unwin 1935
M. SHERIDAN, *The Developmental Progress of Infants and of Young Children*, HMSO 1960

Norms, Tables of
The tables of scores used with standardised tests which enable individual performance to be compared with that of the population, or of a particular age-group, usually by translating the raw score into a percentile or quotient.
P. E. VERNON, *The Measurement of Abilities*, 2nd edn, University of London Press 1956

Normal (probability) curve
That distribution of scores or measures which gives a bell-shaped curve and in which the **mean, median** and **mode** all coincide. The curve satisfies certain mathematical conditions deriving from the theory of probability and represents a distribution which is approximated in practice but never actually achieved. Otherwise known as the Gaussian curve and as the Curve of normal distribution.
See also **Standard Deviation**
H. E. GARRETT, *Statistics in Psychology and Education*, 6th edn, Longmans 1966
D. M. MCINTOSH, *Statistics for the Teacher*, Pergamon 1963
P. E. VERNON, *Measurement of Abilities*, 2nd edn, University of London Press 1956

Normal school/college
An institution for the training of teachers. The term is of French origin (Ecole Normale), adopted in USA. Such institutions do not, up to the present, offer degrees.
L. COLE, *A History of Education: Socrates to Montessori*, Holt, Rinehart & Winston 1950

Normality
1. Correspondence to what is general and usual, especially in respect of physique, mental powers and personality development.
2. The statistical distribution conforming to that of the **normal probability curve**.
C. W. VALENTINE, *The Normal Child*, Penguin (Pelican) 1967

Norwood Report
Curriculum and Examinations in Secondary Schools, a report issued by the **Secondary Schools Examinations Council** under the Chairmanship of Sir Cyril Norwood in 1943. The first section of the report considered the principle of '**child-centred** education' and the nature of **secondary education**, and recommended three types of secondary schools (grammar, technical and modern). This tripartite division was implemented by the 1944 Act. On examinations, the report recommended changes in the old **School Certificate** so that it would become an internal examination, foreshadowing the present **CSE**, and in the old Higher School Certificate so that it would be held twice a year and serve the twofold purpose of a university entrance test and of meeting the requirements of the various professional organisations.
The recommendations were heavily criticized mainly because they implied a tripartite classification of human ability but changes did come about as a result of the SSEC's findings in 1947.
See also Appendix IIIA.
S. J. CURTIS and M. G. A. BOULTWOOD, *An Introductory History of Education since 1800*, 4th edn, University Tutorial Press 1966, ch. 9

Nuffield Foundation
The result of Lord Nuffield's biggest gift. It was established in 1943 as a trust with a capital valued at £10 million. Its four main objects are stated in the Trust Deed:
1. The advancement of health
2. the improvement of social wellbeing
3. the advancement of education
4. the care and comfort of the aged
In the main, the Foundation's activities relate to Great Britain but the Foundation supports research within the whole British Commonwealth and provides training fellowships and scholarships for students from the Dominions.
Well-known examples of work carried out, or in process of being carried out, in the advancement of education (No. 3 above) are
– The Science Teaching Project, Junior Mathematics Project, Language Teaching Materials Project, Programme in Linguistics and English Teaching, Society and the Young School Leaver, Resources for Learning.
Address: Nuffield Lodge, Regents Park, London N.W.1

Null hypothesis (stats)
The thesis that two or more samples under consideration could have been drawn from the same **population** and that therefore a

difference between their respective means is due to chance factors of sampling.

The function of an experiment or of an investigation might be to produce data to challenge or to support this hypothesis. For example, the null hypothesis may state, that in a particular mixed school there is no difference between the mathematical abilities of the girls and those of the boys. If a random sample of boys and of girls is taken in this school any difference in average score might be due to chance factors. But the bigger the difference between these average scores and the bigger the size of the samples the more powerfully will the null hypothesis be challenged (i.e. the greater the possibility that the difference is real).

W. R. BORG, *Educational Research*, New York, McKay 1963

H. E. GARRETT, *Statistics in Psychology and Education*, 6th edn, Longmans 1966

Number base

The structure in counting numbers in which the next higher denomination is increased by one when an agreed number has been reached: this can be seen, e.g. on the abacus when, using base ten, ten units accumulated on one bar are cancelled out and recorded as one item in the next bar up, i.e. ten units are replaced by one ten; ten tens are replaced by one hundred, etc., ad infinitum. Any number above 1 can form a number base. Electronic computers use the binary system, i.e. a number base of two in which 'eight' would be written as 1000.

D. E. MANSFIELD and others, *Mathematics: a New Approach*, Chatto & Windus, 2 series, 1965–69.

D. PALING and J. L. FOX, *New Mathematics for Primary Teachers*, Oxford University Press, 4 books, 1968–69

Numeracy

A word first publicly introduced in the **Crowther Report** meaning the minimum knowledge of mathematics and scientific subjects which any person should possess in order to be considered educated.

ATCDE, *Supply of Mathematics and Science Teachers*, Methuen 1954

Nursery school

A school before the **primary** stage for children between the ages of two and five. Children in this age group may be admitted to a nursery class which is attached to a primary school

See also **Kindergarten**

S. ISAACS, *Social Development in Young Children*, Routledge & Kegan Paul 1933

Plowden Report, *Children and their Primary Schools*, 1967, vol. I

W. VAN DER EYKEN, *The Pre-School Years*, 2nd edn, Penguin 1969

Nursery School Association: 89 Stamford Street, London, SE1

White Paper. *Education: A Frame-work for Expansion*, Cmnd 5174, HMSO 1972

NUS

National Union of Students, an association formed to promote the interests of students, with branches in most universities and **colleges of education**.

Address: 3 Endsleigh Street, London, WC1

NUT

National Union of Teachers: a professional society or association open to all teachers, but whose members are predominantly primary and secondary modern teachers. It is the largest of the teachers' organisations and provides a wide range of services including publication of *The Teacher*, a weekly paper. It also produces a *Handbook of Information for Teachers* (Schoolmaster Publishing Co., annual).

Address: Hamilton House, Mabledon Place, London, WC1

O

Object lessons
1. Lessons in which the teacher based his instruction on the use of an actual object (e.g. an apple). This is a slightly archaic meaning since the use of objects for purposes of demonstration and illustration has become commonplace.
2. A brilliant example of how to do something, e.g. an object lesson in story-telling.

Objective marking
Marking carried out in such a way that all competent markers can arrive, as nearly as possible, at the same score, for example, in marking spelling, or mathematical exercises on the basis of right/wrong. **Standardised tests** are accompanied by objective marking schedules. Cf. **Subjective marking**.
D. R. MATHER, *The CSE, A Handbook for Moderators*, Collins 1965
P. E. VERNON, *Measurement of Abilities*, 2nd edn, University of London Press, 1940

Oblivescent
Receding from the memory.

Observation, participant
A method of studying the activities and interaction of small social groups by joining them and performing a role as participant. This enables changes to be engineered for the purposes of studying the results (as by nominating a new leader, suggesting a new activity, etc.) and is adapted to the condition of teachers and youth leaders.
J. KLEIN, *Working with Groups*, Hutchinson 1966
C. SELLTIZ *et al*, *Research Methods in Social Relations*, Methuen 1960, Section 6

Occasional closures
Holidays which can be granted during term time, e.g. half-term holidays, and not added to the main holidays, at the discretion of managers or governors. These closures must not exceed ten days per school year and they count as days on which a school meets and as part of the forty weeks of school opening which is necessary to qualify for grant.
G. R. BARRELL, *Teachers and the Law*, Methuen 1966
G. TAYLOR and J. B. SAUNDERS, *The New Law of Education*, 7th edn, Butterworth 1971

Occupation therapy
Treatment carried out by professional personnel employed in hospital schools, in schools for the physically handicapped, and in hospitals for adults (especially those concerned with mental and emotional illness).
M. S. JONES, *Approach to occupational Therapy*, Butterworth, 1964
E. M. MACDONALD, ed., *Occupational Therapy in Rehabilitation*, 2nd edn, Bailliere 1964

Oedipus complex
A psychoanalytic concept of **Freud** which suggests that an unconscious sexual attachment develops in a boy for his mother alongside a jealousy of his father. This is supposed to result in guilt feelings and emotional conflict.
H. J. EYSENCK, *Fact and Fiction in Psychology*, Penguin (Pelican) 1965
S. FREUD, *Introductory Lectures in Psycho-Analysis*, 2nd edn, Allen & Unwin 1929
C. W. VALENTINE, *The Normal Child*, Penguin (Pelican) 1956

Ogive (stats)
The curve which graphically represents a cumulative frequency distribution, usually expressed in percentages.
H. E. GARRETT, *Statistics in Psychology and Education*, 6th edn, Longmans 1966

Ordinary level (GCE O level)
The stage of proficiency reached in one or more subjects in the **GCE**. The examination is taken normally after five years of secondary schooling, and is conducted by various **Examining Boards**.

Oligophrenia
A term used especially in Russian educational/psychological literature to denote mental subnormality due to serious brain pathology during intra-uterine or early life. (The Russian view denies the theory that mental subnormality can be due to inherited factors.)
A. R. LURIA, *The Mentally Retarded Child*, Pergamon Press 1963

ONC and OND
Ordinary National Certificate and Ordinary National Diploma.
See also **National Certificate/Diploma**.

Only child
The child in a family who has no brothers or sisters: verbally such children tend to be superior but socially they tend to be less mature.

D. W. WINNICOTT, *The Child and the Family*, Tavistock Press 1957

D. W. WINNICOTT, *The Child, the Family and the Outside World*, Penguin (Pelican) 1969

Open plan

The expression refers to schools in which the architectural arrangements are such that traditional classroom areas have been replaced by an arrangement of space – teaching areas, learning bays, etc. – which lends itself to learning and teaching situations which are flexible and informal. Such considerations are usually linked with progressive ideas such as **family grouping** and **integrated day**. Open plan education is mainly associated with Primary education, but increasingly there are Secondary Schools which show similar architectural features and which share the basic educational philosophy which they imply.

W. VAN DER EYKEN, 'Thinking in concrete', *New Education*, May 1965

Open University

An independent autonomous university whose courses are aimed at adult students on the basis of correspondence courses supplemented by radio and television courses and by residential vacation courses and seminars. It prepares students for its own first degree and for its own higher degree. No formal academic qualifications are required for registration as a student. The degree is granted by accumulating 'credits' in individual courses. Assessment is effected by a combination of continuous assessment and examination.

The Open University, Report of the Planning Committee to the Secretary of State for Education and Science, HMSO 1969.
Address, Walton, Bletchley, Bucks

Opportunity class

A class to which a child has been allocated temporarily in order to repair his deficiencies in some branch of skill or learning; the implied intention is that he shall then return to his normal class. The term is sometimes used as a euphemism for a permanent backward class.

Oracy

The skills of speech and listening (cf **literacy**, **numeracy**). The development of powers in the spoken language, the cultivation deliberately of adequate verbal expression in speech, is recognised by the **Newsom Report** as one of the central concerns of education; it is a factor in the development of personality, and in social and intellectual growth.

NATIONAL ASSOCIATION FOR THE TEACHING OF ENGLISH, Bulletin no. 2, *Some Aspects of Oracy*, 1965

A. M. WILKINSON, 'Spoken English', *Educational Review*, **18**, no. 3, 1966 (University of Birmingham)

A. M. WILKINSON, *The Foundations of Language*, Oxford University Press 1971

'The place of language', *Educational Review*, **20** no. 2, 1968 (University of Birmingham)

Orders, teaching

The Society of Jesus (Jesuits) is the main order devised to teach outside the mission field, in the secondary sphere (boys). For the primary sphere the leading order is the Christian Brothers, formed in 1679. A leading order amongst nuns is the Sisters of Charity; but many other orders of monks and nuns are involved in teaching.

W. J. BATTERSBY, *The History of the Institute*, Waldegrave 1960

The New Catholic Encyclopedia, McGraw-Hill 1947

Ordinal number. *See* Cardinal number

Ordinary National Certificate, Diploma. *See* ONC, OND

Organization theory

The study of the structure and functions of organizations and the behaviour of groups and individuals within them. Organizations are groups of people whose activities are rationally coordinated, whose relationships are structured by a hierarchy of authority and which exist to achieve recognized goals, e.g. industrial firms, churches, schools, hospitals. In the general theory of organizations there has been a coming together of engineers, psychologists, mathematicians etc., in the search for general principles applicable to a wide range of organizations. An attempt is being made to articulate such principles into explanatory models.

N. P. MOUZELIS, *Organisations and bureaucracy*, Routledge & Kegan Paul 1967

P. W. MUSGRAVE, *The School as an Organisation*, Macmillan 1968

Organizer

A specialist engaged by an **LEA** to advise on the organization and teaching of a special subject or group of subjects in its schools, e.g. music, physical education. Usually a full-time post. Sometimes called an adviser.

Organismic age

An indication of the level of a person's general development arrived at by taking the average of a number of his 'growth ages' e.g. mental age, reading age, arithmetic age, weight age, height age.
See also **Age**

Out group

A symmetrical concept to **in-group**; the out group is any group considered to be 'them' as opposed to 'us'; to be 'the others'; and to be treated and viewed with reserve or even hostility.
R. K. MERTON, *Social Theory and Social Structure*, Free Press 1956, new edn, 1965

Out of school activities

Activities conducted in or for the school, out of school hours and on a voluntary basis, e.g. games, drama, music.
CENTRAL ADVISORY COUNCIL FOR EDUCATION, *Out of School*, HMSO 1948; reprinted 1959

Outward Bound School

A school whose object is the education of the 'whole man' having as one of its distinctive features a rigorous training in a sea and mountain setting. The origin of this development is in Dr Kurt Hahn's Salem School which he founded in Germany after the First World War. In 1933 he came to England and figured prominently in Gordonstoun School, Scotland. Other schools along similar lines have since been opened in different parts of Britain.
Outward Bound Schools run short courses (under the Outward Bound Trust) in such areas as the Welsh Mountains and the Lake District. The aim is to develop resource, self-discipline, a spirit of teamwork and adventure, as well as physical fitness.
Address: Outward Bound Trust, 123 Victoria Street, London, SW1

Overlearning

What is achieved by continuing to practise beyond what is needed for immediate recall or performance of a skill. Overlearning is usually necessary to ensure recall or recovery of a skill after a period of disuse, e.g. as with multiplication tables, or riding a bicycle.
E. R. HILGARD, *Theories of Learning*, Methuen 1959

Owen, Robert (1771–1858)

Radical mill-owner whose infant school for the children of his operatives at New Lanark greatly influenced infant education before Froebel's ideas became popular. The school was established in 1816 and stressed appropriate activities, singing, dancing and playing for children between two and six years. His ideas were propagated by Brougham, James Mill and others.
A. V. JUDGES, ed., *Pioneers of English Education*, Faber 1959, ch. 3
ROBERT OWEN, *A New View of Society, and other Writings*, Dent, Everyman's Library

Oxbridge

A term connoting the traditions, values, attitudes and methods of education which are common to the Universities of Oxford and Cambridge.
See also **Redbrick**

Oxfam

Oxford Committee for Famine Relief.
Address: 274 Banbury Road, Oxford.

P

Palsy, Cerebral
A general term describing various kinds of disability, due to brain damage usually associated with the **perinatal** period; the three main divisions, apart from the question of severity, come under **spastic, athetoid, ataxic.**
M. L. J. ABERCROMBIE, *Perceptual and Visuo-motor Disorders in Cerebral Palsy*, Heinemann for Spastics Society 1964
M. J. CARLSON, *Born That Way*, Evesham (Worcs), James 1957
HANDBOOKS OF BRITISH COUNCIL FOR THE WELFARE OF SPASTICS (13 Suffolk Street Haymarket, London, SW1), *Handbooks.*
K. S. HOLT, *Assessment of Cerebral Palsy*, Lloyd Luke 1965

Paper folding
1. A technique used in art and craft.
A. J. DUNCAN, *Education of the Ordinary Child*, Nelson 1942, ch. 7
M. GRATER, *Make it in Paper*, Mills & Boon 1961
2. An aid in teaching elementary mathematics, e.g. fractions or geometrical shapes and properties.
E. J. JAMES, *Teaching of Modern School Mathematics*, Oxford University Press 1958

Parameter (stats)
A measure describing a **population**, e.g. its average value as expressed in a **mean**; or its **standard deviation**. Exact measures of a 'population' are seldom possible but approximations are inferred from sample measures. We speak of 'the parameters of a population' and of 'the statistics of a sample'.
H. E. GARRETT, *Statistics in Psychology and Education*, 6th edn, Longmans 1966

Paranoia
A mental disease characterised by a highly organised set of delusions, particularly delusions of grandeur or persecution.
D. STAFFORD-CLARK, *Psychiatry Today*, Penguin (Pelican) 1952

Parent-teacher association
The combination of the teachers from a school with the parents of their pupils in order to cultivate the kinds of relationship and understanding that will make the education of the children a joint operation between home and school. The nature and degree of organisation of the association will vary from one place to another.

Advisory Centre for Education, 57 Russell Street, Cambridge.
National Federation of Parent-Teacher Associations, 127 Herbert Gardens, London, NW10

Parents' National Education Union. *See* **PNEU**

Parity of esteem
The view that different types of schools should enjoy equal social esteem. In **secondary education** this ideal underlay the **tripartite system** but was never achieved; it was held by many educationists that the lower esteem of the secondary modern school placed it at a disadvantage, and they argued that a unified Secondary system was the better solution.
O. BANKS, *Parity and Prestige in English Secondary Education*, Routledge & Kegan Paul 1955

Part or whole (method of learning)
The reference is usually to the memorising of a work (e.g. a poem) as a whole or by parts. Many factors are involved and the efficacy of the one method or the other will vary from person to person; with the amount to be learnt; the difficulty and complexity of the total task; whether the material possesses structure; the spacing of practices, etc.
E. A. PEEL, *The Psychological Basis of Education*, Oliver & Boyd 1956

Part-time day courses
Courses used mostly by students released by their employers for one or two days a week. These courses may include evening instruction as well.
See also **Day-release.**

Partially sighted
Having defective vision in an acute degree and needing special educational provision and care. This is one of the categories of handicap which **LEAs** are charged to provide for. There are **special schools** for the partially sighted, e.g. in Exeter.
W. HATHAWAY, *Education and Health of the Partially Seeing Child*, 4th edn, Columbia University Press 1959
W. LIGHTFOOT, *The Partially-sighted School*, Chatto & Windus 1948
The Education of the Visually Handicapped, HMSO 1972

Paternal deprivation
A child's loss of paternal care, guidance and affection due to prolonged absence or death of the father. Believed by some psychologists to be as important a factor as **maternal deprivation** in the causation of emotional problems and other difficulties arising in some children's development.

R. G. ANDRY, *Delinquency and Parental Pathology*, Methuen 1960

M. MEAD and K. HEYMAN, *Family*, Macmillan 1965

Pathological
Relating to structural and functional changes caused by disease.

Pavlov, Ivan Petrovich (1849–1936)
Russian psychologist and Nobel Prizewinner, 1904, for his work on digestion. From 1902 Pavlov studied systematically the conditioned reflex in dogs, which contributed greatly to the scientific approach to human mental disorders, and influenced learning theory. He sought to explain complex and higher mental processes by means of conditioning, but this aspect of his work has been criticised severely in the west.

H. K. WELLS, *I. Pavlov*, Lawrence & Wishart 1956

Payment by results
A system popularly attached to the Revised Code 1862 whereby **HMIs** examined children in school, the teachers' pay often depending in part or whole on their performance. The system, which was generally considered to be pernicious, was gradually modified during the next three decades.

G. A. LOWNDES, *The Silent Social Revolution, 1895–1965*, 2nd edn, Oxford University Press 1969

PE
Physical education: that part of education which concerns itself especially, but not exclusively, with the welfare of the body. Present day physical education is aware of the **psychosomatic** nature of persons and includes, as well as those physical activities associated with the gymnasium, games and athletics and tends to merge with movement connected with drama, music and biology.

A. BILBROUGH and P. JONES, *Physical Education in the Primary Schools*, 2nd edn, University of London Press 1963

PHYSICAL EDUCATION, Ling House, 10 Nottingham Place, London, W7: *The Yearbook of Physical Education*.

Pedagogy
The art and science of teaching.

A. PINSENT, *The Principles of Teaching Method, with special reference to secondary Education*, 3rd edn, Harrap 1969

Percentile (stats)
A point on a set of scores or measures arranged in rank order below which a certain percentage of the scores or measures appear, e.g. the twenty-fifth percentile, or P25, is that point below which 25 per cent of the scores appear.

D. M. MCINTOSH, *Statistics for the Teacher*, Pergamon 1963

P. E. VERNON, *Measurement of Abilities*, 2nd edn, University of London Press 1956

Percentile rank (stats)
A person's position or rank in a test on the supposition that there were 100 candidates, e.g. a PR of 60 means that the candidate is equal or better than 60 per cent of the candidates. Formula:

$$PR = 100 - \frac{(100R - 50)}{N}$$

e.g. A person who came 5th in a test in a class of 25 would have a percentile rank of:

$$100 - \frac{(100 \times 5 - 50)}{25} = 82$$

H. E. GARRETT, *Statistics in Psychology and Education*, 6th edn, Longmans 1966

Perception
In the more limited sense, awareness of things due to function of the senses; in the wider sense, includes the ability readily to understand, as in 'a perceptive mind'.

A. PINSENT, *Principles of Teaching Method*, Harrap 1941

M. D. VERNON, *A Further Study of Visual Perception*, Cambridge University Press 1954; ch. 2

M. D. VERNON, *The Psychology of Perception*, Penguin 1962

G. M. WYBURN *et al.*, *Human Senses and Perception*, Oliver & Boyd 1964

Percy Report
Higher Technological Education (1945), the Report submitted by a committee under the chairmanship of Lord Eustace Percy, recommended that a carefully selected and limited number of technical colleges should become

colleges of technology providing full-time courses of degree standard linked together by four regional advisory councils, the whole system coming under a National Council of Technology. Regional advisory councils were formed but it was another ten years before colleges of advanced technology appeared. *See* Appendix IIIA.

See also CAT

J. S. MACLURE, *Educational Documents 1816–1937*, 2nd edn, Chapman & Hall 1968

Perinatal
Referring to the period during or near birth.

Peripatetic teacher
A teacher who is not attached permanently to any particular school but who moves from one school to another teaching some subject or activity on a specialist basis, e.g. music, remedial reading.

F. W. KELLAWAY, *Part-time Teaching*, Bell 1952

Permissive attitudes
A relationship between teacher and child, parent and child, or therapist and patient, in which most (but not all) of the behaviour and speech of the latter is accepted by the former as being allowable in the therapeutic situation and for therapeutic purposes.

Permissive legislation
Legal powers granted by a central government to local authorities to carry out certain reforms, if they wish, but not compelling them to do so. For example, the raising of the school leaving age in Britain was made permissive in 1918 and in 1936 but few authorities availed themselves of the opportunity.

Perseveration
Basically refers to the persistence of a sensory image after the stimulus has terminated. More frequently in education refers to the marked tendency to persist in a task even when the stimulus has been removed, e.g. the tendency can be seen in the difficulty of switching from one task to another.

Personality inventory
A self report test where the subject replies to forced choice *pairs* of items or blocks of items; the tester is thus able to assess the response on various bipolar criteria such as neuroticism–stability, introversion–extraver-

sion, etc. Such inventories are specially useful in the diagnosis of abnormal patients; but they are also used as screening devices, e.g. in selecting applicants for jobs.

P. E. VERNON, *Personality Tests and Assessments*, new edn, Methuen 1953

Personality, Measurement of
That area of psychological measurement which is concerned with the qualitative and quantitative estimates of various personality traits and dispositions, e.g. interests, attitudes, emotional stability.

R. CATTELL, *Scientific Analysis of Personality*, Penguin (Pelican) 1965

H. J. EYSENCK, *Fact and Fiction in Psychology*, Penguin (Pelican) 1965

H. J. EYSENCK, *Scientific Study of Personality*, Routledge & Kegan Paul 1952

P. E. VERNON, *Personality Tests and Assessments*, new edn, Methuen 1953

Personality – types
Classification of individuals according to any outstanding trait or cluster of traits, e.g. Jung describes people as **introverts** or **extroverts** according to whether their interests are directed inwards to themselves or outwards to other people.

H. BRAND, *The Study of Personality*, Wiley 1954

R. B. CATTELL, *The Scientific Analysis of Personality*, Penguin (Pelican) 1970

E. R. HILGARD, *Introduction to Psychology*, Meuthen 1958, ch. 18

C. C. JUNG, *Psychological Types*, Routledge & Kegan Paul 1923

B. SEMEONOFF, *Personality Assessment* Penguin 1966

Pestalozzi, Johann Heinrich (1746–1827)
Swiss educator who, after the destruction of the town of Stans during the French invasion of 1798, began to care for orphaned and destitute children, and to investigate the problems of educating them in his school at Yverdon. In his main work *How Gertrude Teaches Her Children* (1801), he elaborated his theory of sense impression, the study of concrete, actual objects preceding verbal studies. His views influenced **Froebel** and **Herbart**, and, through Fichte, the Prussian elementary schools.

L. COLE, *A History of Education – from Socrates to Montessori*, Holt, Rinehart & Winston 1950, ch. 16

S. J. CURTIS and M. E. A. BOULTWOOD, *A*

Short History of Educational Ideas, 4th edn, University Tutorial Press 1965, ch. 13

Philosophy of education
The discipline which rigorously, logically and self-critically concerns itself with values, the self, truth, existence, reality, purpose, meaning, etc., in so far as they underlie educational concepts and practices.
R. F. DEARDEN, *The Philosophy of Primary Education*, Routledge & Kegan Paul 1968
W. H. KILPATRICK, *Philosophy of Education*, Collier-Macmillan 1963
D. J. O'CONNOR, *An Introduction to the Philosophy of Education*, Routledge & Kegan Paul 1957
R. S. PETERS, *Authority, Responsibility and Education*, 2nd edn, Allen & Unwin 1963
J. P. POWELL, ed., *Philosophy of Education: a bibliography*, Manchester University Press 1968
L. A. REID, *Philosophy and Education*, Heinemann 1962
J. W. TIBBLE, ed., *The Study of Education*, Routledge & Kegan Paul 1966

Phonic analysis
Opposite of **Phonic synthesis**. The breaking down of a word, or part of a word, into its constituent sound units (phonemes).

Phonic method
A method of teaching reading by teaching the sound values of individual letters, or groups of letters, and enabling the child to blend sounds to form words.
See also **Look and Say, Sentence method**
H. DIACK, *Reading and the Psychology of Perception*, Skinner 1960
W. S. GILL, *The Phonic Side of Reading*, Cassell 1952
F. J. SCHONELL, *The Psychology and Teaching of Reading*, Oliver & Boyd 1945

Physical education. *See* PE

Phonic synthesis
Opposite of **phonic analysis**. The blending of several sounds in sequence to form a word or part of a word: this is what happens when a child successfully uses his knowledge of phonics to read aloud a word that is new to his reading vocabulary.
V. SOUTHGATE and G. R. ROBERTS, *Reading – Which Approach*, University of London Press, 1970

Piaget, Jean (b. 1896)
Swiss scientist, philosopher and educator. Professor of Child Psychology and History of Scientific Thought at Geneva since 1929. Though his first interest was in zoology, he began from the task of standardizing Burt's reasoning tests for Parisian children to study the development of reasoning powers in children. Between 1925 and 1932 he continued to study the psychology of childhood, concentrating not on measurement and assessment of abilities but on the various kinds of thought activity which enter into intelligent behaviour. He studied his own and other children intensively as they developed, seeking to investigate stages of mental growth in various fields, such as language, reasoning, concepts of number and geometry and morality. English educationists who have shown interest in his work include Nathan Isaacs, E. M. Churchill, K. Lovell and E. A. Peel.
His publications include: *The Language and Thought of the child* (1926; 3rd edn 1959); *Judgment and Reasoning in the Child* (1928); *The Child's Conception of the World* (1929); *The Child's Conception of Physical Causality* (1930); *The Moral Judgment of the Child* (1932); *The Psychology of Intelligence* (1950); *Play, Dreams and Imitation in Childhood* (1951); new edn 1962); *The Child's Conception of Number* (1952); *The Origin of Intelligence in the Child* (1953); *The Child's Conception of Reality* (1955); **The Child's Conception of Space* (1956); **The Growth of Logical Thinking from Childhood to Adolescence* (1958); *The Child's Conception of Geometry* (1960); **The Early Growth of Logic in the Child* (1964); **The Psychology of the Child* (1969); *The Child's Conception of Movement and Speed* (1970) (all Routledge & Kegan Paul); and *Logic and Psychology* (Manchester University Press 1953).
* with **B. Inhelder** *Psychology and Epistemology*, Penguin University Books 1972
R. M. BEARD, *An Outline of Piaget's Developmental Psychology*, Routledge & Kegan Paul 1969
M. BREARLEY and E. HITCHFIELD, *A Teacher's Guide to Reading Piaget*, new edn, Routledge & Kegan Paul 1967
J. H. FLAVELL, *The Developmental Psychology of Jean Piaget*, Van Nostrand 1963
P. HALMOS and A. ILIFFE, eds, *Readings in General Psychology*, Routledge & Kegan Paul 1959

Pitman, Sir Isaac (1813–97)
Inventor of an English system of shorthand based on phonetics. Was very interested in the simplification of spelling. He was the grandfather of Sir James Pitman, the inventor of the **Initial Teaching Alphabet**.
A. BAKER, *The Life of Sir Isaac Pitman*, Pitman, 1930

Place value (notation) in arithmetic
The value imputed to a digit according to its position in relation to the other digits in the group, e.g. 2 means two units, but 2 in '23' means two tens.
L. W. DOWNES and D. PALING, *Teaching of Arithmetic in Primary Schools*, Oxford University Press, Unesco Handbooks 1958

Plateau of learning
A learning process will normally show an overall upward trend of improvement. But this upward curve will not always show a steady gradient and when the pupil, in spite of effort and practice, makes no perceptible progress he is said to be on a 'plateau of learning', which on a learning curve or graph would have a flat appearance.

Plato
Greek philosopher (427–348 BC). In his books *The Republic* and *Laws* he gave an account of educational theory in the Greek city-states, linking it with his political, social and philosophic beliefs. His works influenced early Christian educational thought, medieval views in some measure, and Renaissance attitudes profoundly. It is also still today the philosophic basis on which many ideas of a **liberal education** are founded. Many translations of his works are available.
W. BOYD, *An Introduction to the Republic of Plato* (1904), new edn, Allen & Unwin 1962
S. J. CURTIS and M. E. A. BOULTWOOD, *A Short History of Educational Ideas*, University Tutorial Press 1965, ch. 1
R. L. NETTLESHIP, *The Theory of Education in Plato's Republic*, Oxford University Press 1935

Play, Theory of
There is no completely satisfactory theory of play although the importance of play in the development of the child has long been recognised. Some of the best known theories of play are: (*a*) Superfluous energy theory of Spencer, (*b*) Preparation for life theory of Carl Groos, (*c*) Recapitulation theory of Stanley

Hall, (*d*) Recreation theory of William McDougall (*e*) Theory of Catharsis (*f*) Self-expression theory.
M. LOWENFELD, *Play in Childhood*, Gollancz 1935
E. D. MITCHELL and B. S. MASON, *The Theory of Play*, Barnes 1948
P. NUNN, *Education: its data and first principles*, 3rd edn, Arnold 1945, ch. 7
P. M. PICKARD, *The Activity of Children*, Longmans 1965
S. MILLAR, *The Psychology of Play*, Penguin 1968

Playway
A generic term to describe a wide variety of methods of teaching skills or subjects in which, at its best, the teacher conceives of the learning process as a game, which releases energies in the interests of education and provides the vital factor of motivation.
G. H. CALDWELL-COOKE, *The Playway*, Heinemann 1917

Plowden Report
Children and their Primary Schools (1967). A Report of the Central Advisory Council for Education (England). Lady Plowden was the Chairman. The terms of reference were 'to consider Primary Education in all its aspects, and the transition to Secondary Education'. The work was based on a large amount of detailed research and made many recommendations, some of the most important of which related to: Participation by parents; Educational priority areas; Future patterns of nursery education; Ages and Stages of primary education.
R. S. PETERS, ed., *Perspectives on Plowden*, Routledge & Kegan Paul 1969
See also Appendix IIIA.

PNEU
Parents' National Educational Union. A society founded in 1888 by Charlotte Mason with the aim of giving guidance to parents who wished to educate children in their own homes, and of supplying teachers and governesses for private schools which practised her educational theories.
Address: Murray House, Vandon Street, London, SW1

Polytechnic
The Regent Street Polytechnic, London – formerly a place of popular entertainment – was taken over in 1881 by Quintin Hogg as a

place of instruction for clerks and artisans. By 1897 the trend towards university type studies had become established in day classes, though the connection with trade and technical education was retained. Money from charities and London Companies became available after 1883 and many other polytechnics on the Regent Street model were opened to provide day and evening technical education.

R. PEERS, *Fact and Possibility in English Education*, Routledge & Kegan Paul 1963

Polytechnics (New)

A government white paper published in 1966 contained proposals for about thirty polytechnics to be based on existing regional colleges of technology, to which other institutions such as colleges of commerce or art might be amalgamated. Such polytechnics might undertake teacher training. Under the **binary system** such polytechnics would be controlled in matters of finance and general policy by **LEAs** but would have independent **governing bodies** and **academic boards** with responsibility for the day-to-day running of the college. Full-time and part-time courses are provided, and there is a bias towards science and technology. The first eight polytechnics were designated in 1969; others have been designated since then.

DEPARTMENT OF EDUCATION AND SCIENCE, *Plan for Polytechnics and other Colleges*, HMSO 1966

E. E. ROBINSON, *The New Polytechnics*, Cornmarket Press 1968

White Paper, *Education: a Framework for Expansion*, Cmnd 5174, HMSO 1972

Pool of ability

The idea that there is a definite limit to the proportion of people in a given population, who can profit from higher or academic education; and that this limit is imposed by biological factors. The argument is used in the discussion about the number of University places to be provided, etc. This view is countered by the argument that producing talent is a matter of creating good conditions for its development and early discovery.

Crowther Report, *15 to 18*, 1959

D. M. MCINTOSH, *Educational Guidance and the Pool of Ability*, University of London Press 1959

Robbins Report, *Higher Education*, 1963, ch. 6

Year Book of Education 1962, Section 3 annual

Population (stats)

As opposed to a sample, the complete set of observations that are relevant to the problem under consideration, e.g. the heights of *all* British children aged thirteen to fourteen; or the intelligence ratings of *all* the children in a particular school.

H. E. GARRETT, *Statistics in Psychology and Education*, 6th edn, Longmans 1966

Positivism

The philosophical point of view, elaborated by Auguste Comte, which dispenses with all inquiry into ultimate causes or origins, and which maintains that knowledge consists of positive facts, of the observation of sensory phenomena, of the objective relations of these phenomena, and of the laws which govern them.

Postgraduate degrees and qualifications

There are three major levels: diploma, master's degree, and doctorate. Diplomas may be had in education (at a higher level than the graduate certificate), usually by one year full-time course and examination. The degree of **MA** is conferred (*not* at Oxford and Cambridge) for research, and/or examination. (In Scotland the MA is the first degree.) The doctorate is granted after a further minimum two years, one of which must be residential in the university. In science, MSc is now less common than PhD, but the MA retains its place in arts and social sciences. Senior Doctorates (DD, DSc, etc) are awarded for outstanding works of scholarship. See various university prospectuses.

ASSOCIATION OF TEACHERS IN COLLEGES AND DEPARTMENTS OF EDUCATION AND CONFERENCE OF HEADS OF UNIVERSITY DEPARTMENTS OF EDUCATION, *Higher Degrees in Education* 1966

Postnatal

Referring to the period following birth.

Power test

A test whose content is arranged in order of increasing difficulty and whose purpose is to ascertain the testee's maximum level of ability, irrespective of time limit, e.g. Raven's Progressive **Matrices**.

Practice effect

1. Improvement due to repetition of the same or similar tasks.

E. R. HILGARD, *Theories of Learning*, Methuen 1959

2. The increase in score, without an increase in actual ability, resulting from the repeated use and practice of the same or similar tests.

P. E. VERNON, 'Practice and coaching effects in intelligence tests,' *Forum*, **8** 1966

P. E. VERNON, *Intelligence and Attainment Tests*, University of London Press 1960

Pragmatism, pragmatist

A philosophical position which closely relates ideas about truth and morality to conduct and practice, and states that the validity of such ideas is to be tested in terms of practical consequences. The philosophy is associated especially with the names of three Americans: Charles S. Pierce in relation to logic; **John Dewey** in connection with education; and **William James** in philosophy and psychology.

J. D. BUTLER, *Four Philosophies and their Position in Education and Religion*, Harper & Row 1968

W. JAMES, *Pragmatism*, new edn, Longmans 1943

A. V. JUDGES, ed., *Education and the Philosophic Mind*, Harrap 1957

Praise

As opposed to blame: an important factor in the learning situation in which the teacher endeavours to reinforce desirable responses in the child by giving him praise.

NATIONAL FOUNDATION FOR EDUCATIONAL RESEARCH, *A Survey of Rewards and Punishments*, Newnes 1952

Preceptors, College of

A non-residential college and examining institution founded in 1846 and given its Charter in 1849. It provides courses to improve the professional competence of teachers and grants the diplomas of Associate, Licentiate and Fellow to teachers who qualify. It also conducts certificate examinations which have been taken in private schools, overseas schools, in the Commonwealth, and, recently, in many **secondary modern schools**.

Address: The College of Preceptors, Bloomsbury Square, London, WC1

Prediction

Foretelling, especially in respect of a person's likely performance in the future on the basis of present assessment: this factor looms large in the validation of all selection processes, e.g. in **eleven-plus** selection.

Prefect system

The participation in parts of the school government by selected senior pupils. More loosely, the allocation of minor duties within the classroom to pupils. The system was regarded by **Thomas Arnold** as a most important facet of public school education.

R. WILKINSON, *The Prefects*, Oxford University Press 1963

DOVER WILSON, ed., *The Schools of England*, Sidgwick & Jackson 1928

Prenatal

Referring to the period preceding birth: foetal.

Prep

Short for 'preparation' in the sense that it represents an assignment of work to be done out of normal school hours. The expression is almost entirely confined to **preparatory** and **public schools**. The same type of assignment is more usually called **homework** in state schools. The term is also used in an abbreviation for preparatory school.

Preparatory school

Private schools catering for children between the ages of eight to fourteen, which prepare for **Common Entrance Examination** to **public schools**. They are fee-paying and offer a generally academic course; they are frequently residential and supported largely by the professional classes. They are subject to inspection and may apply for recognition as efficient by the **Department of Education and Science**. Incorporated Association of Preparatory Schools: for address see *Public and Preparatory Schools Yearbook*, A. and C. Black.

Primary education

Education covering broadly the age range five to eleven, especially in reference to the state system of education, and thus including the infant and junior stages.

BOARD OF EDUCATION, *Report of the Consultative Committee on the Primary School*, HMSO 1931

MINISTRY OF EDUCATION, *Primary Education*, HMSO 1959

Plowden Report, *Children and their Primary Schools*, 1967

Gittins Report, *Primary Education in Wales*, 1967

W. A. L. BLYTH, *English Primary Education*, (2 vols), Routledge & Kegan Paul 1965

R. F. DEARDEN, *The Philosophy of Primary Education*, Routledge & Kegan Paul 1968
A. M. ROSS, *The Education of Childhood*, Harrap 1960

Primary French
The teaching, usually by informal activity methods, of French in primary schools. Stimulated by the Leeds experiment in the early 1960s, a nationwide experiment sponsored by the Ministry of Education, began in 1963.
SCHOOLS COUNCIL, *French in the Primary Schools*, HMSO 1966
H. H. STERN, *Foreign Languages in Primary Education*, Oxford University Press for Unesco Institute for Education 1967

Private sector
Those schools which are outside the public system of education, viz. private, independent, preparatory and most public schools. They cater for approximately 5 per cent of the school population.
Statistics of Education, HMSO, annual
The Public and Preparatory Schools Year-book, A. and C. Black
Newsom Reports (1968–69), *Public Schools Commission First Report* and *Second Report*

Probability
The likelihood, in terms of chance, that any one event will take place in the context of a number of possibilities: for example, in the tossing of a single coin there is one chance in two of obtaining a head, or tail. The term is closely linked with inferential statistics, in which tentative conclusions are reached regarding the total group (height, reading ability, opinions, attitudes, etc.) on the basis of what has been discovered in a sample.
Measures obtained from a sample are unlikely to be exactly those of the total group (the population). Hence the statistician will express his findings e.g. average measure on the basis of a sample, as being true of the population (the total group) in terms of probability. These terms will express a 'degree of belief'. For example, the result of an investigation into the reading standards of ten-year-olds might yield a mean reading age of $10·00 \pm ·25$. This would mean that this reading age, based on the test results of a sample of ten-year-olds, is true of the total numbers of children aged $10·00$ within certain degrees of belief, i.e. accept $10·00$ years as being correct, with the proviso that

there are 34 chances in 100 that the true mean lies somewhere between $10·00$ and $10·25$, and that there are 34 chances in 100 that the true mean lies between $10·00$ and $9·75$.
H. E. GARRETT, *Statistics in Psychology and Education*, 6th edn, Longmans 1966
S. R. GRIFFITHS and L. W. DOWNES, *Educational Statistics for Beginners*, Methuen 1969

Probationary year
The first year's full-time service as a qualified teacher, in the course of which he must satisfy the **Department of Education and Science** of his practical proficiency as a teacher. The Secretary of State may, in exceptional cases, agree to a probationary period greater than, or less than, one year, or even waive it completely. The types of school in which probation can be served are: maintained, assisted, direct grant, or special chools to which the School Health Service and Handicapped Pupils Regulations 1953, no. 39 (12) apply.
See: *Education: a Framework for Expansion*, Ch. 8, HMSO 1972
G. R. BARRELL, *Teachers and the Law*, Methuen 1966
NATIONAL UNION OF TEACHERS and NATIONAL UNION OF STUDENTS, *Teachers and Probation*, Hamilton House
G. TAYLOR and J. D. SAUNDERS, *The New Law of Education*, 7th edn, Butterworth 1971

Probation officer
An officer employed by the Home Office to supervise persons who are awarded probation by a court of law. A statutory probation system was introduced in 1907 to replace the police court missionaries (Probation of Offenders Act). The profession set up its National Association in 1912, and was organised nationally between 1922 and 1926. The task of the probation officer is to use casework methods to build up a relationship with the offender within which he may offer advice, assistance and friendship.
Criminal Justice Act 1948, HMSO
J. F. S. KING, *The Probation and After Care Service*, 3rd edn, Butterworth 1969

Problem family
Term originated by family service units to describe families always on the edge of pauperism and crime, often with mental and physical defects, in and out of courts for child neglect, and needing the constant support and attention of welfare agencies.

R. WILSON, *Difficult Housing Estates*, Tavistock for Bristol University 1963

Problem solving

The mental process, typical of people at all stages of development, and of the higher animals, in which observed phenomena and relationships are used to find new relationships. The more developed stage of this process is characterised by the suggestion of one or more hypotheses to solve the problem and by methods of testing these hypotheses.
F. DEESE and S. HULSE, *The Psychology of Learning*, 3rd edn, McGraw-Hill 1967, ch. 2

Professional studies (of teachers)

A course of study in addition to academic disciplines, and including practice in schools, by which teachers are prepared for their work. Graduates follow a one-year consecutive course usually in a university department of education, whilst in colleges of education the professional studies are spread over the whole course. Professional studies are based academically upon child psychology and educational sociology, together with the history and philosophy of Education.
ATCDE, *Handbook on Education for Teaching*, Methuen, annual

Programmed learning. *See* Programming and Teaching machines

Programming

Breaking down complex tasks into their simple elements and presenting them in appropriate form, e.g. in a **teaching machine** or programmed texts, so that the learner can proceed to learn on his own and has immediate knowledge of his own success or failure with each element. Reinforcement is thereby effected.
Address: The Association for Programmed Learning, 6 Gardner Mansions, Church Row, London, NW3
A. A. LUMSDAINE and R. G. GLASER, *Teaching Machines and Programmed Learning*, National Educational Association, 1960
The Journal of Programmed Instruction (Quarterly): The Centre for Programmed Instruction of the Institute of Technology, Teachers' College, Columbia University, New York.
D. UNWIN, ed., *Media and Methods*, McGraw Hill 1964
H. KAY, B. DODD and M. SIME, *Teaching Machines and Programmed Instruction*, Penguin 1968

Progress class

A group of pupils, regarded as underfunctioning in some aspects of the *basic subjects* and brought together for an expected limited period in order to be given remedial help. It is normally hoped that they will return to their usual classes after a term or a year. The word 'progress' is used to indicate the more helpful diagnosis of **retardation** rather than **backwardness**.
Slow Learners at School, HMSO, ch. 4

Progressive school

A school which accepts and experiments in the more modern ideas of what constitutes education in one or more of these respects: curricula, methods of work, the general life and conduct of the school. Progressiveness in these senses is obviously a matter of degree.
W. B. CURRY, *Education for Sanity*, Heinemann 1947
A. S. NEILL, *A Dominie's Log*, H. Jenkins 1915
A. S. NEILL, *The Free Child*, H. Jenkins 1953
S. MARSHALL, *Experiment in Education*, Cambridge University Press 1963
R. SKIDELSKY, *English Progressive Schools*, Penguin 1968

Project

A unit of work having educational value and directed at a definite goal, e.g. a study of the village or town in which the school is situated or some aspect of the environment. The work will normally involve investigation, often outside school premises, collection of information and the solution of problems, and will often involve practical work, e.g. map-making or model-making. In projects the artificial boundaries of subjects disappear, teacher and pupils cooperate, group and individual work take the place of class activities, the classroom takes on the appearance of a workshop, and flexibility of timetable is a great advantage. (This is why projects are undertaken far more frequently in primary schools than in secondary schools).
M. S. FELLOWS, *Projects for Schools*, Museum Press 1960

Projection

A defence mechanism in which the person attributes to others the impulses and traits

which he has himself but cannot accept.
A. I. RABIN and M. R. HOWARTH, eds, *Projective Techniques with Children*, Grune 1960
J. C. RAVEN, *Controlled Projection for Children*, 2nd edn, H. K. Lewis 1957
K. YOUNG, *Personality and Problems of Adjustment*, 2nd edn, Routledge & Kegan Paul 1952

Projection test

A test which seeks to determine personality traits by getting the testee to let his ideas, wishes and fantasies flow freely but allowing the tester to measure and interpret the responses. Techniques used include **Rorschach** ink blots, sentence completion, interpretation by the testee of specially compiled pictures (Thematic Apperception Test or **TAT**) and the compilation of designs from special material.
J. BELL, *Projective Techniques*, Longmans 1948

Protestant ethic

The German sociologist Max Weber held that the early Calvinists saw wordly success as a sign of religious grace, and the work leading to worldly success as a religious vocation. Their discipline and enterprise were factors in the development of capitalism, and their ethic and outlook were a powerful stimulus to the growth of a modern rational, secular and worldly world-view (contrasted however because of its individualism, with the conformism of the modern organisation man). The protestant ethic is one of the hidden preconceptions underlying some aspects of the moral outlook in British and American education.
M. WEBER, *The Protestant Ethic and the Spirit of Capitalism*, trans. T. Parsons, Allen & Unwin 1930
W. H. WHYTE, *The Organization Man*, Simon & Schuster 1956

Psychiatry

The branch of medicine dealing with the study and treatment of mental disease and mental problems which may arise during or after organic disease. Also concerned with problems of personal adjustment.
P. HAYS, *New Horizons in Psychiatry*, new edn, Penguin (Pelican) 1964
MAXWELL JONES, *Social Psychiatry in Practice*, Penguin (Pelican) 1968
D. STAFFORD-CLARK, *Psychiatry Today*, Penguin (Pelican) 1952

Psychoanalysis

The theory of personality and the method of psychotherapy invented by **Sigmund Freud**. There are various psychoanalytic theories. The original Freudian school of psychoanalysis produced the divergent theories of **Adler** (individual psychology) and **Jung** (analytical psychology). More recently Klein, Fenichel and others have supported the orthodox libido theory, while the neo-Freudians, e.g. Fromm, Horney, Sullivan and Kardiner, have stressed the importance of social rather than biological factors in the development of personality.
Psychoanalysis emphasizes the dynamic aspect of mental life and lays particular stress on the importance of the unconscious. Therapy was originally based on the use of continuous free association.
J. A. C. BROWN, *Freud and the Post-Freudians*, Penguin (Pelican) 1961; Cassell 1963
H. CRICHTON-MILLER, *Psycho-analysis and its Derivatives*, 2nd edn, Oxford University Press (Home University Library) 1945
S. FREUD, *Two Short Accounts of Psycho-analysis*, Penguin (Pelican) 1962
C. RYCROFT, ed., *Psycho-analysis Observed*, Constable 1966; Penguin (Pelican) 1968

Psychology

The science which deals with the nature and functioning of the psyche or mind; with the ways in which the world is experienced subjectively. Beginning as a branch of introspective **epistemology**, it has, since 1879 when Wundt set up the first psychological laboratory, increasingly sought to use the methods of science, and to study the mind through behaviour. Hence (*a*) McDougall's definition 'the positive science of the behaviour of living things', (*b*) W. James's definition 'the description of and explanation of states of consciousness, as such'.
See also **Introspection**
C. J. ADCOCK, *Fundamentals of Psychology*, rev. edn, Methuen 1960; Penguin (Pelican) 1964
J. C. FLUGEL, *A Hundred Years of Psychology*, 3rd edn, by D. J. West, Methuen 1964
N. L. MUNN, *Psychology: the fundamentals of human adjustment*, 5th edn, Harrap 1966

Psychopath

A person having a pathological character disorder, showing as gross defects in judgment and emotional control; sometimes defined as 'moral imbecile.' No completely successful treatment has yet been discovered.

J. BOWLBY, *Personality and Mental Illness*, Routledge & Kegan Paul 1940

Psychosis

A mental disorder, organic or psychogenic affecting feeling and conduct, and causing behaviour problems serious enough to require treatment in an institution specializing in mental illness.

D. STAFFORD-CLARK, *Psychiatry Today*, Penguin (Pelican) 1952

Psychosomatic

A term which describes physical symptoms having their root in some psychological condition.

J. APLEY and R. M. KEITH, *The Child and his Symptoms*, 2nd edn, Blackwell 1968

Psychotherapy

One of the forms of treatment for mental illness. In the case of disturbed children, therapy is given normally in Child Guidance Clinics, or in schools for maladjusted children. Such help is given either by a child psychiatrist or by a psychotherapist. The latter, while not qualified as a doctor of medicine, will have received long special training to practise.

M. V. AXLINE, *Play Therapy*, Houghton Mifflin, 1947

B. M. FOSS, ed., *New Horizons in Psychology*, Penguin (Pelican) 1966, ch. 18

D. STAFFORD-CLARK, *Psychiatry Today*, Penguin (Pelican) 1954, ch. 7

Puberty

That period in life when the sex organs mature and secondary sex characteristics appear and which is considered to be the commencement of **adolescence**.

C. M. FLEMING, *Adolescence: its social psychology*, rev. edn, Routledge & Kegan Paul 1967, ch. 2

J. M. TANNER, *Education and Physical Growth*, University of London Press 1961

J. M. TANNER, *Growth at Adolescence*, 2nd edn, Blackwell 1969

Public schools

Usually private or independent schools, for pupils aged thirteen to eighteen, charging fees, usually non-coeducational, tending strongly to be academic in curriculum and, in most cases, residential. The criterion of the title 'public school' is whether the headmaster is a member of the Headmasters' Conference (**HMC**) or of Governing Bodies of Public Schools Association (boys and coeducational schools) and Governing Bodies of Girls' Public Schools Association. In this sense a number of semi-independent, or **direct grant schools**, are included in this category.

J. C. DANCY, *The Public Schools and the Future*, Faber 1966

Fleming Report, *The Public Schools and the General Education System* 1944

Newsom Reports, *Public Schools Commission*, *First Report* 1968, *Second Report* 1970, HMSO

V. OLGIVIE, *The English Public School*, Batsford 1957

Public and Preparatory Schools Yearbook, A. and C. Black

Public Schools Commission

The Commission was appointed, under the Chairmanship of Sir John Newsom, to advise on the best way of integrating the **public schools** with the state system of education.

A very brief statement of conclusions and recommendations, will be found on page 8 of the First Report: 'Our general conclusion is that independent schools are a divisive influence in society. The pupils, the schools and the country would benefit if they admitted children from a wider social background. We recommend a scheme of integration by which suitable boarding schools should make over at least a half of their places to assisted pupils who need boarding education. This change will take some time, and not all schools can be brought within the integrated sector simultaneously. The details should be worked out school by school, by a body we shall call the Boarding School Corporation.'

PUBLIC SCHOOLS COMMISSION, *First Report*, vol. 1 (Newsom) 1968; *Second Report* (Donnison) 1970

See also Appendix III

Punched card

A specially designed card in which holes can be punched, on a code basis, to record specific data. A number of such cards can then be sorted, counted, etc., or passed through a machine to produce statistical information.

Punishment

As opposed to reward: a penalty directed at an individual or group of individuals usually with deterrence as the aim. It might take the form of 'lines', detention, corporal punishment, etc., though, obviously, its most usual form is that of verbal rebuke.

NATIONAL FOUNDATION FOR EDUCATIONAL RESEARCH, *An Investigation into Rewards and Punishment in School*, Newnes 1952

Pupil-teacher

A young person who, by a scheme established by the Committee of the Council in 1846, trained to become a teacher by serving an apprenticeship of five years, after completing elementary education. A proportion proceeded to colleges of education, especially after the system of Queen's scholarships was set up. As secondary education developed and more colleges of education were established, the number of pupil-teachers declined, particularly after 1907; but residual vestiges of the system persisted for many years, some 'student-teachers' working in schools before attending college, until late in the 'thirties.

H. C. BARNARD, *A History of English Education from 1760*, University of London Press 1961, ch. 12

S. J. CURTIS, *History of Education in Great Britain*, 7th edn, University Tutorial Press 1967

Pyknic

A term used to describe a short, plump, barrel-chested type of physique. Kretschmer claimed that the pyknic physique was associated with the cycloid temperament, characterized by joviality, liveliness, moodiness, extroversion (*see* **extrovert**), and, in the case of mental illness, manic depressive psychosis.

E. KRETSCHMER, *Physique and Character*, 2nd edn Kegan Paul 1936

P. E. VERNON, *Personality Tests and Assessments*, new edn, Methuen 1953

Q

Q (stats)
The quartile deviation or the **semi-inter-quartile range.**

Qualified teacher
A teacher who has been recognized by the Secretary of State at the **Department of Education and Science** by satisfying the examination requirements of an **Institute of Education** and that particular unit of the institute (e.g. a **College of Education**) which he has attended.
There was previously, an automatic 'qualification' for graduates of a recognized university (even without training). Legislation to require training of graduates has been pressed for by the professional associations of teachers, for many years. After 1973 all graduates are required to complete successfully a course of professional training before entering the profession.
G. R. BARRELL, *Teachers and the Law*, Methuen 1966, ch. 3

Quality scale
A series of standard samples of schoolwork in a particular subject, e.g. handwriting, composition, etc., varying in excellence by fairly regular steps and arranged in order of merit, usually with a mark assigned to each, and used as a standard of comparison for evaluating pupils' work in that subject. Used especially where objective marking is difficult.
F. J. SCHONELL, *Backwardness in the Basic Subjects*, Oliver & Boyd 1942
F. J. SCHONELL, *Diagnostic and Attainment Testing*, 4th edn, Oliver & Boyd 1960

Quartile (stats)
A score in a frequency distribution, so chosen that 25 per cent of the scores are on one side of it and 75 per cent of the scores are on the other side. Q1, the first quartile, has 25 per cent of the scores below it, and Q3, the third quartile, has 75 per cent of the scores below it. Used in calculating quartile deviation or **semi-interquartile range.**
D. M. MCINTOSH, *Statistics for the Teacher*, Pergamon 1963
P. E. VERNON, *Measurement of Abilities*, 2nd edn, University of London Press 1956

Queen's scholarship
A scholarship, or exhibition, inaugurated in 1846 and tenable at a teacher's training college and awarded on the basis of a competitive examination held annually for **pupil-teachers** who had successfully terminated their apprenticeship. Hence Queen's Scholars.
S. J. CURTIS and M. E. A. BOULTWOOD, *An Introductory History of English Education since 1800*, 4th edn, University Tutorial Press 1966

Questioning
A classroom teaching technique whose function is to test the extent of the pupil's knowledge and understanding, to provide opportunities for the pupil to practise oral skills, and to promote rapport between teacher and pupils. Judicious use of questioning requires skill and experience, and is particularly important in teaching languages, including English in the junior school. If the questions are designed to draw the pupil towards a predetermined conclusion or insight step by step, the technique is known as 'socratic questioning,' a method once favoured in educational circles.
F. M. AUSTIN, *The Art of Questioning in the Classroom*, University of London Press 1949
A. G. HUGHES and E. H. HUGHES, *Learning and Teaching*, 3rd edn, Longmans 1949, ch. 19

Questionnaire
A list of written questions, directed at some central theme or topic, intended for submission to a number of people, with space for replies to individual questions. The questions may be in the form of statements which the respondent is invited to endorse or reject. A highly structured interview may be virtually an orally administered questionnaire.
A degree of literacy is normally postulated in respondents but it is possible, e.g. with a class of semiliterate children, to read the questions or statements aloud and let them indicate their written responses in some simple manner, e.g. with a tick or a cross.
R. BORG, *Educational Research*, McKay, New York 1963
C. SELLTIZ et al., *Research Methods in Social Relations*, Methuen 1960

Quintilian (AD 35–97)
Roman rhetorician, born in Spain, who was teacher to a number of pupils of note including Pliny the Younger. During his retirement, he wrote the *Institutio Oratoria*, for which he is best remembered. Quintilian is concerned with the education of the whole man and not merely the orator. Of the twelve volumes in

the work, Books I, X and XII are probably of greatest interest. In Book I, concerned with primary education, Quintilian stresses the important role the parents have to play in the education of their sons, and the need to keep the child's mind active. In Book X he emphasizes the importance of reading in the training of the orator, and in Book XII he points out the need for sound moral and intellectual qualities in an orator.

W. M. SMALL, *Quintilian on Education*, Oxford University Press 1938

Quota

Individual staffing establishments of schools introduced in the 1926 Code were abandoned at the outbreak of war, in 1939, but in 1941 each **LEA** was assigned a quota of newly trained teachers. In 1948 a quota scheme was introduced to control the distribution of women teachers. This was discontinued in 1956, but it was necessary to reintroduce quotas in 1958 so that **LEAs** in less attractive areas could secure a fair share of available teachers. The quota does not include occasional, temporary or part-time teachers.

MINISTRY OF EDUCATION, *Reports on Education*, Feb. 1964

NATIONAL ADVISORY COUNCIL FOR THE TRAINING AND SUPPLY OF TEACHERS, *The Demand for and Supply of Teachers, 1963–86: A Ninth Report of NACTST*, HMSO 1965

Quotient

A numerical index of the ratio of an individual's scores on two related age scales. It is frequently expressed as a percentage, e.g. Reading Age 12, Chronological Age 10. Ratio of RA to CA $= \dfrac{12}{10}$: expressed as a percentage, reading quotient $= \dfrac{12}{10} \times \dfrac{100}{1}$ $= 120$.

P. E. VERNON, *The Measurement of Abilities*, 2nd edn, University of London Press 1956

See also **Achievement quotient**; **Attainment quotient**; **IQ** (intelligence quotient)

R

r (stats)
The statistical symbol denoting the **coefficient** of **correlation**, a numerical index indicating the degree of correspondence between two sets of measurements. It ranges from $-1\cdot0$ to $+1\cdot0$.
H. E. GARRETT, *Statistics in Psychology and Education*, 6th edn, Longmans 1966
P. E. VERNON, *Measurement of Abilities*, 2nd edn, University of London Press 1940

Range (stats)
The difference between the two extreme scores of a distribution. It is the simplest numerical measure of dispersion but is greatly affected by one extreme score. Inclusive range is the difference between the largest and smallest score, plus one.
S. R. GRIFFITHS and L. W. DOWNES, *Educational Statistics for Beginners*, Methuen 1969

Rank order
The arrangement of a series of scores or measures from highest to lowest, in which case the emphasis is on position from top or bottom, i.e. fourth, sixth, tenth, rather than on actual marks or measures, e.g. Tom 40 per cent, John 74 per cent, David 60 per cent, would become in a descending order, 1. John, 2. David, 3. Tom. Rank order could also be thought of in the reverse form, i.e. from bottom to top.
P. E. VERNON, *Measurement of Abilities*, 2nd edn, University of London Press 1956

Rank order correlation
A method of determining **correlation** when the data are arranged in **rank order**, e.g. when comparing the orders of merit of a class on examination in any two subjects. The formula is as follows: rank order correlation coefficient $= 1 - \dfrac{6\Sigma d^2}{n(n^2 - 1)}$ where d stands for the differences between the two class positions, or rank orders, of each pupil, 6 is a constant, and n represents the number of cases involved. This correlation is often indicated by 'rho' or 'ρ' rather than by 'r'.
S. R. GRIFFITHS and L. W. DOWNES, *Educational Statistics for Beginners*, Methuen 1969

Rapport
Good personal relationships, especially with classes of children, conducive to an atmosphere of confidence, ease and trust within which effective teaching can take place, since communication is largely dependent on it for success. Rapport is an essential element in standardized testing procedures whether in the psychological clinic or in group testing in the classroom.
O. A. OESER, *Teacher, Pupil and Task*, Tavistock 1966

Rating
An estimate, qualitative or quantitative, of the degree to which a person possesses any given characteristic, e.g. a teacher might be required to give a child a rating for persistence on a **five-point scale**.

Rating scale
A device enabling the rater to measure defined traits in other people or in himself.
P. E. VERNON, *Personality Tests and Assessments*, new edn, Methuen 1953

Ratio, Teacher-pupil
The number of staff in relation to the number of pupils in a school, though usually expressed as an approximation and in terms of a proportion, e.g. 20 staff for 410 pupils would be described as a ratio of $1:20\cdot5$. The ratio is generally poorer in primary schools than in secondary schools.
Statistics of Education, HMSO, annual

Rationalisation
A defence mechanism in which the person justifies his actions by reasoning after the event. False but 'good' reasons are found to justify the person's acts or failure.
K. YOUNG, *Personality and Problems of Adjustment*, 2nd edn, Routledge & Kegan Paul 1952

Raw scores
The scores directly obtained from a test before they have been subjected to statistical treatment, e.g. (*a*) the number of words read correctly in a word recognition test before conversion to a reading age, or (*b*) the number of items answered correctly in an **intelligence test** before they are considered together with the child's **chronological age** and resolved into an intelligence quotient (**IQ**), **percentile rank**, or **standard score**.

Reaction
A response to a stimulus. May be taken in a narrow physiological sense as in **reflex** responses, or in the broader sense of personality responses, mental or emotional, to particular situations.

Readiness

A state of body, mind and feeling produced by a combination of growth and experience which implies fitness and ability to embark on some new task, e.g. a child's readiness to learn to read.

See also **Maturation**

N. L. MUNN, *Psychology: the fundamentals of human adjustment*, 5th edn, Harrap 1966, ch. 4

A. F. WATTS, *The Language and Mental Development of Children*, Harrap 1960

Reading (method)

There are three main methods (as distinct from schemes) of teaching reading.

1. **Alphabetic**, in which the child says the names of letters, e.g. see-aye-tee 'cat': completely out-of-date and most unhelpful to the child.

2. **Phonic**, in which the sounds (not names) of letters are used. If excessive use is made of this method in the early stages, reading for meaning is reputed to be slowed down and the child tends in future to read words rather than groups of words.

3. **Look and Say**, in which the child is taught to recognize whole words by their general shape and thus to concentrate on units of meaning from the start. A small initial and interesting vocabulary can be relatively quickly acquired by this method but soon the child will need to learn the phonic values of letters in order to avoid confusion between words of almost similar shape and in order to be able to attack new words.

The **Sentence method** is an extension of 'Look and Say' method. The child is taught to read whole sentences from the beginning.

See also **ITA**

J. C. DANIELS and H. DIACK, *Learning to Read: the phonic word method*, Chatto & Windus 1960

E. V. DECHANT, *Improving the Teaching of Reading*, Prentice-Hall 1964

A. J. HARRIS, *How to Increase Reading Ability*, 3rd edn, Longmans 1956

F. J. SCHONELL, *The Psychology and Teaching of Reading*, Oliver & Boyd 1945

A. E. TANSLEY, *Reading and Remedial Reading*, Routledge & Kegan Paul 1967

Reading speed

The speed at which a child can read a given passage usually with reference to a set of norms giving reading ages, corresponding to various speeds of reading, e.g. as in the **Neale Reading Tests**.

Reading speed tests for adults require a minimum understanding level before the norms can be interpreted. There has been considerable recent interest, particularly in America, in the possibility of achieving rapid increases in reading speed by the use of special techniques.

See also **Schonell Reading Tests**

M. DE LEEUW and E. DE LEEUW, *Read Better, Read Faster*, Penguin 1968

F. J. SCHONELL, *Backwardness in the Basic Subjects*, Oliver & Boyd 1942

Reading tests. *See* **Neale Reading Tests; Southgate Group Reading Tests**

Reasoning Tests, verbal and non-verbal

A term used synonymously with **intelligence tests**. The latter is now less widely used because of the doubts, expressed by many psychologists, about the meaning of the term 'intelligence' and what the tests really measure.

Recall

The aspect of remembering which requires the person to conjure up visual sound or other sensory images from past experience. Written composition and spelling are more difficult than reading because they require the ability to recall rather than to recognize.

F. C. BARTLETT, *Remembering: a study in experimental and social psychology*, Cambridge University Press 1932

I. M. HUNTER, *Memory, Facts and Fallacies*, Penguin (Pelican) 1957

Recapitulation theory of education

The theory, popularized by **Stanley Hall**, that children in growing up move through the same stages as humanity has witnessed in its own history; for some, this includes evolutionary development shown by the child in the womb. Many educationists have suggested that the curriculum should follow a similar development. The view is now questioned as being based on a false anthropology.

J. C. FLUGEL, *A Hundred Years of Psychology*, Duckworth 1964; Methuen University, Paperbacks

Recitation

A term that, at one time, indicated a poetry lesson, in which the main emphasis was on a stylised oral rendering of memorized verse or poetry by individual children.

Recognition
The aspect of remembering which is characterized by a feeling of familiarity when something which has previously been met is again perceived. Reading (as distinct from spelling and writing composition) is achieved by the process of recognition, i.e. the correct response of sound and meaning is achieved when visual patterns of words and letters are recognized from previous familiarity.
See also **Recall**
N. L. MUNN, *Psychology: the fundamentals of human adjustment*, 5th edn, Harrap 1966
F. J. SCHONELL, *Psychology and Teaching of Reading*, Oliver & Boyd 1945

Redbrick
A term used to designate universities in England and Wales other than Oxford and Cambridge (and possibly London) because of the widespread tendency to build with brick. The most recently built universities are sometimes, humorously, described as 'infra-red'.
W. H. G. ARMYTAGE, *Civic Universities*, Benn 1955
B. TRUSCOTT, *Redbrick University*, Faber 1943

Referral
1. In relation to examinations, or other qualifying procedure, the process of failing a candidate, usually with a view to requesting him to make another attempt.
2. The official procedure whereby a child is enabled to take advantage of special treatment such as that given at a child guidance clinic.
M. F. CLEUGH, *Psychology in the Service of the School*, Methuen 1951

Reflex
An involuntary and unlearned response which follows stimulation of a sensory area connected to the responding mechanism by a direct neural pathway. Sometimes referred to as an unconditioned reflex as contrasted with a conditioned reflex.
J. G. HOLLAND and B. F. SKINNER, *The Analysis of Behaviour*, McGraw-Hill 1961

Regional college
Institution of more advanced technical education, offering full-time courses at degree and HNC level, preparation for professional examinations, and similar opportunities beyond those available in local and area colleges. Some entered the field of teacher training. All have now been incorporated into **polytechnics**.

Registers
Records of attendance at school, at school meals, etc. Registers of attendance at school used to be of paramount importance since government grants to education authorities used to be conditional on satisfactory attendance.
G. K. BARRELL, *Teachers and the Law*, Methuen 1966
G. TAYLOR and J. B. SAUNDERS, *The New Law of Education*, 7th edn, Butterworth 1971

Regression
A reversion to modes of thought, feeling and behaviour which are more appropriate to an earlier stage in individual and social development. Regressive behaviour, usually traced to emotional immaturity, is often seen in young children when a **sibling** is born.
M. F. CLEUGH, *Psychology in the Service of the School*, Methuen 1951

Reinforcement
In the psychology of learning the process whereby the bond between the conditioned response and the original unconditioned stimulus is strengthened by the reintroduction of the unconditioned stimulus.
C. L. HULL, *Principles of Behavior*, Appleton-Century-Crofts 1943
B. SKINNER, *Science and Human Behaviour*, Collier-Macmillan 1953

Reliability (stats)
The quality of a test which indicates the extent to which it measures consistently. This quality is indicated by a **correlation** coefficient which has been derived on the basis of test-retest, or parallel-versions, or by the split-half technique.
H. E. GARRETT, *Statistics in Psychology and Education*, 6th edn, Longmans 1966
P. E. VERNON, *Measurement of Abilities* 2nd edn, University of London Press 1956

Religious education
Religious education in state maintained schools has been compulsory since the 1944 Education Act. It was previously carried out on a voluntary basis. **Aided schools** (e.g. Roman Catholic schools and some of the other denominational schools) have full freedom in their religious education: **County**

schools must conduct religious teaching on the basis of the **Agreed Syllabus; voluntary controlled schools** may conduct denominational teaching on two days of the week.

R. ACLAND, *We Teach them Wrong: religion and the young*, Gollancz 1963

G. R. BARRELL, *Teachers and the Law*, Methuen 1966

R. GOLDMAN, *Religious Thinking from Childhood to Adolescence*, Routledge & Kegan Paul 1964

G. TAYLOR and J. B. SAUNDERS, *The New Law of Education*, 7th edn, Butterworth 1971

Remand
After an initial appearance in court persons charged with an offence may at the discretion of the magistrate be remanded in custody to await trial at a higher court or for such purposes as medical or psychiatric reports. Children are usually held in remand homes; juveniles in remand centres where these are available. Remand centres are staffed by prison officers, but remand homes by teachers and house staff.

Remedial education
Education designed specifically for those who are considered to be **under-functioning** in one or more subjects. It is normally preceded by the application of attainment and diagnostic tests and often consists of individual work or work in a small group under a teacher who is skilled in this branch of education.

G. M. BLAIR, *Diagnostic and Remedial Teaching*, rev. edn, Collier-Macmillan 1956

M. F. CLEUGH, *The Slow Learner*, 2nd edn, Methuen 1968

G. M. DELLA-PIANA, *Reading Diagnosis and Prescription*, Holt, Rinehart & Winston 1968

A. E. TANSLEY, *Reading and Remedial Reading*, Routledge & Kegan Paul 1967

A. E. TANSLEY and R. GULLIFORD, *The Education of Slow-Learning Children*, Routledge & Kegan Paul 1960

Remembering
Recalling something previously learnt or experienced.
See also **Memory**

F. C. BARTLETT, *Remembering: a study in experimental and social psychology*, Cambridge University Press 1932

I. M. L. HUNTER, *Memory, Facts and Fallacies*, Penguin (Pelican) 1957

Reorganisation
The division of the former **elementary** schools into schools for **primary** (5 to 11+) and **secondary** (11+ to 15+) education. Recommended by the Hadow Report (*Education of the Adolescent*, 1926, *see* Appendix III), reorganisation made great progress after 1944 and was virtually complete by 1971. More recently the term has been applied to the reorganisation of secondary education towards a comprehensive system and has been extended to describe the processes by which first and middle schools have been set up.

DEPARTMENT OF EDUCATION AND SCIENCE, *Annual Reports*, HMSO.

Reorganised school
A school which, having formerly been all-age, has been divided so that it is either primary or secondary.
See also **Reorganisation**

Repetition
The act of repeating; also used more specifically to mean reciting something which has been learned.
See also **Rote learning.**

Report
In education it has three chief meanings:
1. a report on the school by HMIs;
2. a report on a pupil's work and progress made at the end of term or year and intended for parents' or guardians' perusal;
3. a government document on particular aspects of educational policy, e.g. the **Robbins Report on Higher Education.**

J. LELLO, *The Official View of Education: a survey of the major educational reports since 1946*, Pergamon 1944

Representative sample (stats)
A sample which possesses approximately the same proportions of constituents as does the **population** in general.

Repression
Applied by psychoanalysts to a mental process resulting from a conflict between the 'pleasure principle' and the 'reality principle': in this process, impulses and desires which conflict with accepted standards of conduct, together with their painful associations, are thrust out of consciousness into the unconscious: but in the unconscious they remain active and exert influence on the

individual's behaviour, mainly indirectly, and affect the content of dreams as well as tending to produce neurotic symptoms.

w. BROWN, *Psychology and Psychotherapy*, 5th edn, Edward Arnold 1947

s. FREUD, *Two Short Accounts of Psychoanalysis*, Penguin (Pelican) 1962

N. L. MUNN *Psychology: the fundamentals of human adjustment*, 5th edn, Harrap 1966

Research in education
Systematic inquiry related to the field of education. **NFER** keeps and publishes a record of current British researches in education and psychology. Blackwell lists researches already accepted as theses for **higher degrees**.

A. M. BLACKWELL, *List of Researches in Education and Psychology*, 4 vols, and suppls. for NFER, 1950–58.

w. R. BORG, *An Introduction to Educational Research*, McKay 1963

H. J. BUTCHER, *Educational Research in Britain*, University of London Press 1968

C. M. FLEMING, *Research and the Basic Curriculum*, 2nd edn, University of London Press 1954

NATIONAL FOUNDATION FOR EDUCATIONAL RESEARCH, *Current Researches in Education and Educational Psychology*,
NFER, *Educational Research*, periodical

Reserved teacher
A teacher who undertakes to give religious instruction in a **voluntary school or special agreement school**. He is not appointed by the LEA but by the **managers or governors**.

G. W. BARRELL, *Teachers and the Law*, Methuen 1966

G. TAYLOR and J. B. SAUNDERS, *The New Law of Education*, 7th edn, Butterworth 1971

Residential school
A school in which some or all of the pupils reside as well as study. Many schools in the private sector come under this heading as well as many schools for handicapped children.
See also **Public Schools; Preparatory School.**

F. G. LENNHOFF, *Exceptional Children* (*Residential treatment of emotionally disturbed boys at Shotton Hall*), Allen & Unwin 1960

Response (physical)
Broadly, the behaviour of an organism brought about by sensory stimulation. More narrowly, activity of the effectors (muscles

and glands), as a result of stimulation of the receptors (sensory cells).

Retardation
Often used synonymously with **backwardness** to indicate a level of performance in school well below what children of similar age are achieving. More precisely used (e.g. by Schonell) to describe the negative discrepancy between the child's attainments and what his intelligence rating had promised.

F. J. SCHONELL, *Backwardness in the Basic Subjects*, Oliver & Boyd 1942

Reversals
Reading or writing sequences of letters (or figures) backwards, e.g. reading or writing 'on' for 'no', or writing '71' when '17' was intended.

F. J. SCHONELL, *The Psychology and Teaching of Reading*, Oliver & Boyd 1945

M. D. VERNON, *Backwardness in Reading*, Cambridge University Press 1957

Reversibility
A characteristic, in Piagetian language, of logical thinking that enables a person to substitute an operation with an inverse operation, e.g. the young junior school child can add 3 to 4 and obtain 7. He can also reverse the operation by taking 3 from 7 and arriving back at the starting point, 4. The essence of reversibility at a very elementary stage can even be seen in the very young child who performs an action and retraces it by an opposite action when, for example, he moves an object away from himself and then deliberately pulls it back towards himself. At a more advanced level reversibility may be seen by the age of about thirteen when having tested an hypothesis a person may wish to retrace his steps and modify his hypothesis or substitute it with another.

R. M. BEARD, *An Outline of Piaget's Developmental Psychology*, Routledge & Kegan Paul 1969

J. H. FLAVELL, *The Developmental Psychology of Jean Piaget*, Van Nostrand 1963

Revised Code (1862)
The revised Code of Regulations made by the Committee of the Privy Council on Education for the administration of grants for elementary schools, chiefly the work of Robert Lowe, Vice-President of the Council and head of the Education Department. It terminated direct payment to certificated

teachers but made a single grant to school managers and incorporated the principle of **payment by results**.

See also **Newcastle Commission**

S. J. CURTIS and M. E. A. BOULTWOOD, *An Introductory History of English Education since 1800*, 4th edn (pp. 70–3), University Tutorial Press 1966

J. S. MACLURE, *Educational Documents: 1816–1967*, 2nd edn, Chapman & Hall 1968

Revision

Repetition of studies with a view to refreshing the memory and/or consolidating understanding, often in preparation for examinatons, or to provide the basis for new work.

In America the usual term is 're-view'.

Reward

What is awarded in response to certain actions or restraints in order to reinforce or perpetuate such responses, e.g. it is common in schools to reward excellence of work or industry with house points or with prizes on speech day.

NATIONAL FOUNDATION FOR EDUCATIONAL RESEARCH, *Survey of Rewards and Punishments*, Newnes 1952

Rhodes scholarships

Founded by Cecil Rhodes for students from countries of the British Empire, the USA and Germany, tenable at Oxford University. The scheme was established in 1904 but has been modified to some extent since then.

Rhythm

The regular recurrence of ideas, sounds or events, e.g. as in music or of the seasons.

Robbins Report

Higher Education (1963), report of a Committee appointed by the Prime Minister to review full-time higher education in Great Britain. The Report surveys the demand for higher education, costs, new forms of administration and courses; in general it calls for rapid and comprehensive expansion and the extension of degree courses inside and outside the universities, and for extraordinary measures to meet the crisis it envisages.

See also Appendix IIIA

J. LELLO, *The Official View on Education*, Pergamon 1964

Role

The ways of behaving which are expected of any individual who occupies a certain position (**status**) in the social scale. Role is the active and the dynamic aspect of status: e.g. what a policeman does (role) because of what he is (status). Learning a developing series of different roles is a key feature in the process of achieving social maturity.

M. BANTON, *Roles: an introduction to the study of social relations*, Tavistock 1965

B. J. BIDDLE and E. J. THOMAS, *Role Theory*, Wiley 1966

T. H. MARSHALL, *Sociology at the Crossroads*, Heinemann 1963, chs 8, 9

Role of teacher

In advanced societies teachers exist as a specialised profession, as opposed to the priests and the *literati*, who preserved the culture of earlier societies. Their role has developed from that of priestly adjuncts to that of autonomous professional persons. They frequently concern themselves, outside the classroom, with youth work, some aspects of therapy and social work, as well as teaching school subjects, sometimes to a high level of specialisation.

A. H. HALSEY, J. E. FLOUD and C. A. ANDERSON, eds, *Education Economy and Society*, Free Press, 1961, ch. 39

O. H. OESER, *Teacher Pupil and Task*, Tavistock 1966

A. K. C. OTTAWAY, *Education and Society*, 2nd edn, Routledge & Kegan Paul 1962, ch. 7

Role-set

The organisation of various roles around one particular central role, which is taken as the reference point. Around the teacher's role for example are arranged the roles, e.g. of headmaster, governor, parent, pupil, inspector, educational administrator, school welfare officer, etc.

R. K. MERTON, *Social Theory and Social Structure*, new edn, Free Press Glencoe 1968, ch. 9

P. W. MUSGRAVE, *The Sociology of Education*, Methuen 1965

Rorschach Test

A **projection test** devised by H. Rorschach, a Swiss psychiatrist (1884–1922). It consists of ink blot symmetrical patterns which the subject is invited to comment on in terms of what he can 'see' in them (in the sense of 'seeing' things when looking at the glowing embers of a fire). On the basis of his responses inferences are made about his personality.

J. E. BELL, *Projective Techniques*, Longmans 1948

B. KLOPFER and D. M. KELLEY, *The Rorschach Technique*, World Book Co. 1946

Rota or roster
A list or register of names with the duties assigned to each.

Rote learning
Learning which takes the form of mechanically committing to memory with little or no regard for meaning.

L. W. DOWNES and D. PALING, *The Teaching of Arithmetic in Primary Schools*, Oxford University Press, Unesco Handbooks 1958, pp. 292–4

Rousseau, Jean-Jacques (1712–78)
French philosopher. In his works, notably *Emile* (1763) and *La Nouvelle Héloise* (1761) he wrote at length on educational theory and practice, reacting violently against the prevailing tradition. One of his main contentions was that each child has an innate sense of what is right and wrong but that society thwarts this intuitive moral sense. His ideas reached and influenced a wide public; and, though often extreme and impractical, paved the way for fundamental reassessments of the nature and purpose of education.

W. BOYD, *Educational Theory of J. J. Rousseau*, Heinemann 1911; reprint

C. H. DOBINSON, *Jean Jacques Rousseau*, Methuen 1969

Royal Society
A society founded in 1660 to encourage and promote scientific research, its full title being The Royal Society of London for Improving Natural Knowledge. It received its Charter from Charles II in 1662.

Fellowship of the Royal Society (designated FRS) is one of the greatest honours bestowed on eminent scientists.

Address: The Royal Society, Burlington House, London, W1

Royal Society of Arts. *See* RSA

RSA
Royal Society of Arts: founded in 1754 for 'the encouragement of the Arts, Manufactures and Commerce of the Country'. It is still active and is best known for its conduct of school examinations (RSA) in a very wide range of subjects.

Address: 6–8 John Adams Street, Adelphi, London, WC2

Rural education
Education in schools in rural areas, in which education might differ from normal education in the following ways:

(a) the school, especially a **primary** school, might have small numbers of pupils and therefore a smaller number of classes, each taking in more than a one-year age-span.

(b) the school might show a bias towards rural studies in order to take advantage of the children's background of knowledge and experience.

R. BAILEY, *The Crisis of the Rural School*, SPCK 1955

H. E. BRACEY, *English Rural Life*, Routledge & Kegan Paul 1959

Russian education
Soviet education follows the line laid down by Lenin's *Manifesto* of 1919. It is a communist weapon; free, compulsory and polytechnic; secular, coeducational and extending to the widest range of workers, and under monolithic central control (though with divergencies in different Republics of the USSR). Established in the War Commission period of 1917–21, it developed through an experimental period to 1931; from then to 1956, as the economic plan was achieved, the formal backwardness of Education in Russia was seen, and there was a return to more severe and traditional attitudes of the Continental encyclopaedic curriculum. N. Khrushchev's 1958 theses mark a new phase designed to reemphasise the polytechnical and work-orientated aims.

There is a basic seven to eight year school for all, some pupils proceeding to a ten year school leading to the higher education at seventeen plus. There is an alternative ladder via officially sponsored correspondence courses. Evasions and lack of statistics in official publications prevent a genuine appraisal of the justice and efficiency of the Soviet system from a western standpoint.

G. S. COUNTS, *The Challenge of Soviet Education*, McGraw-Hill 1957

N. HANS, *Russian Tradition in Education*, Routledge & Kegan Paul 1963

B. KING, *Russia goes to School*, Heinemann 1948

D. LEVIN, *Soviet Education Today*, Staples 1960

N. GRANT, *Soviet Education*, Penguin 1970

S

Sadism
A term coined as a result of the writings of the Marquis de Sade to describe a condition characterised by the desire to obtain gratification by inflicting suffering on others. This tendency has been interpreted as a sexual perversion.
G. GORER, *Life and Ideas of Marquis de Sade*, Panther 1964
J. A. HADFIELD, *Psychology and Mental Health*, Allen & Unwin 1950

Salaries for teachers
For detailed information on current scales write to the National Union of Teachers, Hamilton House, Mabledon Place, London WC1, or to the National Association of Schoolmasters, 59 Gordon Square, London, WC1
See also **Burnham Committee**

Sample, Random (stats)
A sample selected in such a way that each member of the **population** stands an equal chance of selection.
H. E. GARRETT, *Statistics in Psychology and Education*, 6th edn, Longmans 1966
R. GOODMAN, *Statistics*, English Universities Press (Teach Yourself series) 1957

Sample, Stratified
A sample in which the sub-sample groups are proportional to the various groups in the **population**, e.g. if in a population there are 40,000 girls and 50,000 boys then a stratified sample should be in the proportion of 4 girls to 5 boys. It is usual, having decided on the appropriate proportion, to select members at random from within the strata.
H. E. GARRETT, *Statistics in Education and Psychology*, 6th edn, Longmans 1960
E. F. LINDQUIST, *Statistical Analysis in Education Research*, Houghton Mifflin 1940

Sampling
It is generally economical to examine only some elements in any statistical population, and the selection of representative elements is called sampling. The major methods are based on probability theory, and the concept of genuine randomness of selection. Simple random sampling (*see* **sample, random**) allows each element an equal chance of being selected and equalizes the chances of selection of each combination of elements. It is possible to forecast mathematically in these conditions the degree of reliability of the

sample as representative of the whole. In a stratified sample (*see* **sample, stratified**), simple random samples are taken separately with defined strata of the whole. There are also various kinds of accidental samples much less reliable for forecasting.
W. R. BORG, *Educational Research*, McKay 1963
H. J. BUTCHER, *Sampling in Educational Research*, Statistical Guides in Educational Research, no. 3, Manchester University Press 1966
H. S. GARRETT, *Statistics in Psychology and Education*, 6th edn, Longmans 1966
C. SELLTIZ et al, *Research Methods in Social Relations*, Methuen 1960

Sandwich courses
Full-time courses of study, broken by periods of industrial training which are an integral part of the course. If the period spent in college averages eighteen weeks or less per year the courses are regarded as **block release courses.**
P. F. R. VENABLES, *Sandwich Courses*, Max Parrish 1960
Year Book of Technical Education and Careers in Industry, A. and C. Black

Scaling of marks
The changing of marks and estimates to measures on a standard scale so that meaningful comparisons can be made between one set of estimates and another, e.g. the addition of pupils' **raw scores** in history and geography may be misleading unless we scale the marks obtained in each subject.
H. E. GARRETT, *Statistics in Psychology and Education*, 6th edn, Longmans 1966
D. M. MCINTOSH, *Statistics for the Teacher*, 2nd edn, Pergamon 1967
D. M. MCINTOSH, D. A. WALKER and D. MACKAY, *The Scaling of Teachers' Marks and Estimates*, 2nd edn, Oliver & Boyd 1962
P. E. VERNON, *Measurement of Abilities*, 2nd edn, University of London Press 1956

Scalogram
An **attitude scale**, pioneered by Guttman, whose construction is such that the person being rated will be favourable to all statements less extreme than the statement which characterizes his own attitude and unfavourable to all those statements which are more extreme.
A. L. EDWARDS, *Techniques of Attitude Scale Construction*, Appleton-Century-Crofts 1957

Scatter (stats)
The spread or **dispersion** of the scores or measures in a **distribution** around some measure of **central tendency**, e.g. as expressed in **average deviation**, **standard deviation**, or **semi-interquartile range**.
S. R. GRIFFITHS and L. W. DOWNES, *Educational Statistics for Beginners*, Methuen 1969
D. M. MCINTOSH, *Statistics for the Teacher*, 2nd edn, Pergamon 1967
P. E. VERNON, *Measurement of Abilities*, 2nd edn, University of London Press 1956

Scatter diagram (stats)
A double-entry diagram or graph in which a sign (dot, cross, etc.) indicates the point of intersection for each score or rank order position as indicated on the x and y axes respectively: the single point thus represents each person's pair of scores: frequently used in this way as visual representation of **correlation**.
D. M. MCINTOSH, *Statistics for the Teacher*, 2nd edn, Pergamon 1967
P. E. VERNON, *Measurement of Abilities*, 2nd edn, University of London Press 1940

Schedule
1. A form for filling in particulars, e.g. as in a questionnaire.
C. SELLTIZ *et al.*, *Research Methods in Social Relations*, Methuen 1960, Appendix C
2. An appendix to a main document, consisting of a list of particulars or details.

Schemata (sing. schema)
In **Piaget's** terminology the mental structures of thought and behaviour, which, beginning from primary reflexes, develop through sensori-motor and prelogical stages until they become complex systems. These complex mental structures are then used in what Piaget calls 'formal operations'.
R. M. BEARD, *Outline of Piaget's Developmental Psychology*, Routledge & Kegan Paul 1969
J. H. FLAVELL, *The Developmental Psychology of Jean Piaget*, Van Nostrand 1963
E. A. LUNZER, *Recent Studies in Great Britain on the Work of Piaget*, National Foundation for Educational Research 1964

Schizoid
Resembling schizophrenia. Of personality, tending to the characteristics shown by **schizophrenia**: an introverted and shut-in personality.

R. B. CATTELL, *The Scientific Analysis o, Personality*, Penguin (Pelican) 1965

Schizophrenia
An illness of the mind characterized by dissociation especially between the affective and intellectual processes. Sometimes used synonymously with **dementia** praecox.
R. D. LAING, *The Divided Self*, Tavistock 1960; Penguin (Pelican) 1967
R. D. LAING amd A. ESTERSON, *Sanity, Madness and the Family*, vol. 1: *Families of Schizophrenics*, Tavistock 1964
D. STAFFORD-CLARK, *Psychiatry Today*, Penguin (Pelican) 1952

Schonell, Sir Fred Joyce (1900–1968)
Australian Educational Psychologist. Professor of Education in the University of Queensland from 1956 before his election as Vice-Chancellor in 1962. Formerly Professor of Education in the Universities of Swansea and Birmingham. Particularly well known for his work on the diagnosis and treatment of backward children, on which he has written widely. His many publications include: *Essentials in Teaching and Testing Spelling* (Macmillan 1932); *Diagnostic Arithmetic Tests Manual* (Oliver & Boyd, 1957); *Backwardness in the Basic Subjects* (Oliver & Boyd 1942); *The Psychology and Teaching of Reading* (Oliver & Boyd 1945); *Diagnostic and Attainment Testing* (1949); 4th edn, Oliver & Boyd, 1960); *Diagnosis and Remedial Teaching in Arithmetic* (Oliver & Boyd, 1957); (with E. Roe and I. G. Meddleton) *Promise and Performance* (University of London Press 1962).
His wife, Eleanor, was closely associated with him in this work and herself made significant contributions to the study of children with cerebral palsy.

Schonell Reading Tests
A series of reading tests comprising attainment and diagnostic tests. The best known are the Graded Reading Vocabulary Test (reading age from 5 to 15), and the Silent Reading Tests A and B (the former having a reading age range from 6·9 to 12·8 and the latter from 6·7 to 13·9). There are separate norms for boys and girls in respect of the SR tests.
F. J. SCHONELL, *Diagnostic and Attainment Testing*, Oliver & Boyd 1949

School attendance officer. *See* **Welfare officer**

School boards

Elected *ad hoc* bodies of local people set up by the 1870 Education Act to receive and administer government grants and rates for school building and running costs, as and where schools were needed and where they were not provided by voluntary bodies. They were later superseded by the County and Municipal LEAs after the Balfour Act.

J. W. ADAMSON, *A Short History of Education*, Cambridge University Press 1919

School Certificate Examination

From 1902 it was recognised that the multiplicity of external examinations was harmful to the work of many schools. The Consultative Committee in 1911 recommended reform and coordination, and between 1917 and 1919 the First and Second School (Certificate) Examinations were introduced. The group principle was adopted. A certain level of performance in the First conferred Matriculation; the Second became known as the Higher School Certificate. In 1951 these examinations were replaced by the General Certificate of Education (Ordinary and Advanced Level) (*see* GCE), on a 'single subject' basis.

Spens Report, *Secondary Education*, 1938
Crowther Report, *15–18*, 1959

School histories

A list of the written histories of schools in England and Wales has been compiled by P. J. Wallis and is obtainable from the Education Department of the University of Newcastle.

School leaving age

The earliest legal age at which children may leave school. Lowe's **Revised Code** set it at, practically, 12; the 1870 Act gave permissive powers to make bye-laws raising the age to 13, with exceptions; the 1880 Act turned these powers into a duty. In 1900 the age was raised to 14 with very many exceptions; in 1918 (Fisher Act) it was then raised to 14 without exception. In April, 1947, it was raised to 15, and was due to be raised to 16 in 1970, until postponed in January 1968, as an economy measure, until 1972.

Hadow Report, *Education of the Adolescent*, 1926
Newsom Report, *Half our Future*, 1963
SCHOOLS COUNCIL, *Raising of the School-Leaving Age*, Working Paper no. 2, HMSO 1965

School Management Committee

A sub-committee of the Local Education Committee specially concerned with the day-to-day administration of schools.

School Mathematics Project (SMP)

A scheme directed by Professor Brian Thwaites of Southampton University to revise the English Secondary School Maths syllabus. Many schools are now associated with the project, which is assuming national importance. Some pupils now take alternative Modern Maths papers in the GCE Examinations.

See also **New Mathematics**
B. THWAITES, ed., *On Teaching Mathematics*, Pergamon 1961

School meals

Local authorities must by law provide milk (to seven years), meals and refreshments for pupils. For those in necessity (about 8 per cent) the meal is free; for the rest it is provided at cost. Nearly half of all children in maintained schools take school dinner. Teachers are required to supervise school meals, and have, through their professional associations, frequently protested in this connection; a sanctions campaign in 1967 was successful in removing the compulsory element in supervision.

G. R. BARRELL, *Teachers and the Law*, Methuen 1966
H. C. DENT, *Educational System of England and Wales*, rev. edn, University of London Press 1969
DEPARTMENT OF EDUCATION AND SCIENCE, *Annual Reports*, HMSO
G. TAYLOR and J. B. SAUNDERS, *The New Law of Education*, 7th edn, Butterworth 1971

School outing

A journey to some place of interest or enjoyment by the entire school or part of it, in which pleasure and social education are the chief aims.

Certain obligations are incurred by teachers and/or the LEA with regard to insurance against possible claims for accident etc.

Write for useful information to: School Journey Association of London, 23 Southampton Place, London, WC1

G. R. BARRELL, *Teachers and the Law*, Methuen 1966
G. TAYLOR and J. B. SAUNDERS, *The New Law of Education*, 7th edn, Butterworth 1971

School phobia

A condition caused by irrational fears of school, causing the child to persistently absent himself. The condition is often accompanied by psychosomatic illness for which medical or psychological help may be needed.

Schools Broadcasting Council

A body representative of teachers, **LEAs** and other educational organisations which advises the British Broadcasting Corporation on general policy for school broadcasting and on the scope and purpose of particular series of broadcasts on radio and television in schools. The council has its own permanent staff and a team of full-time education officers located in the various regions. (Scotland and Wales have their own separate Schools Broadcasting Councils.) The Council's advice is based on regular meetings and on surveys and reports coming directly from teachers in the classroom.

BBC Publications, Bond Street, London, W1A 1AR

K. V. BARLEY, *The Listening Schools*, BBC Publications 1957

Educational Television and Radio in Great Britain, BBC Publications 1966

Schools Council for Curriculum and Examinations

Set up in October 1964. It took over the function of the Secondary School Examinations Council which had existed since 1917, and also the function of the **Curriculum Study Group** which had existed since 1962. The Schools Council undertakes at primary and secondary levels fundamental reconsiderations of aims, scope and structure of the examination system, and of the schools' curricula. It publishes reports on its findings and recommendations in the form of bulletins and working papers, which may all be obtained from Her Majesty's Stationery Office.

DEPARTMENT OF EDUCATION AND SCIENCE, *Education in 1964*, Cmnd 2612, HMSO 1965, ch. 3

Schools Council Publications

Schools Council Publications have included a wide range of short reports on the **CSE** examination covering both general topics and individual subjects. (These continue the work begun by the **SSEC**). In addition several curriculum studies have been published as bulletins. Working papers designed to assist

the teacher in planning for the raising of the school leaving age have appeared regularly since 1965. All are obtainable at HMSO and in most educational bookshops.

Schools Inquiry Commission (Taunton Commission

A body set up by Parliament to inquire into the condition of endowed **grammar** and **elementary** schools and to find out how existing endowments could be used to increase their numbers. The Commission reported in 1868 and was followed by the Endowed Schools Act 1869 which set up the **Endowed Schools Commission** to carry on the work.

S. J. CURTIS and M. E. A. BOULTWOOD, *An Introductory History of English Education since 1800*, 4th edn, University Tutorial Press 1965, ch. 5

Science and Art. *See* Department of Science and Art

Scientific and Industrial Research. *See* Department of Scientific and Industrial Research

SCOLA. *See* Consortia

SEAC, South Eastern Architects Collaboration. *See* Consortia

Secondary education

Full-time educational provision for children between the ages of eleven and nineteen who are still at school.

J. W. B. DOUGLAS, J. M. ROSS and H. R. SIMPSON, *All our Future*, Peter Davies 1968

Crowther Report, *15–18*

Newsom Report, *Half our Future*

Secondary Education for All, HMSO 1963

Secondary modern school

The **Hadow Report** (*see* App. III) of 1926 recommended that there should be secondary education for all children and that there should be a minimum school leaving age of fifteen. In the years between 1926 and 1944, senior elementary schools appeared in increasing numbers, taking children from the ages of eleven to fourteen, who had not been admitted into **grammar schools**. The 1944 Education Act reorganized education in three stages: **Primary, Secondary**, and **Further education**.

Education was to be provided to suit 'the age, ability, and aptitude of the pupil'. Thus the secondary modern school appeared, as one of the three secondary schools in a tripartite system. Schools which had already appeared under the title of senior elementary schools were now to be called secondary modern schools, to distinguish them from the existing secondary (grammar) schools.

With the spread and growth of **comprehensive schools**, the secondary modern school, like the secondary grammar school, is in process of disappearing as a separate part of secondary education.

J. J. B. DEMPSTER, *Education in the Secondary Modern School*, Pilot Press 1947
W. TAYLOR, *The Secondary Modern School*, Faber 1963

Secondary Schools Examination Council

An advisory body on which the universities, the LEAs and the teaching profession were represented, set up by the **Board of Education** in 1917 to coordinate the work of the **School Certificate** Examining Bodies. The Council recommended the introduction in 1947 of the GCE. In 1958 it appointed a committee under R. Beloe, which produced the Report *Secondary School Examinations other than the GCE*. This led to the organisation of the CSE. The Council controlled such matters as definition of scope and standards of examinations, publication of results, rules and statistics. It also published reports and bulletins on examining in individual subjects and in CSE. The Council was wound up in 1964 and its functions taken over by the **Schools Council**.

S. J. CURTIS and M. E. A. BOULTWOOD, *An Introductory History of English Education since 1800*, 4th edn, University Tutorial Press 1966
DEPARTMENT OF EDUCATION AND SCIENCE, *Education in 1964*, Cmnd 2612, HMSO 1965

Séguin, E. (1812–80)

French psychologist who spent much of his life endeavouring to help handicapped children, particularly the mentally defective. His system of education was based on sensorimotor training. He spent the latter part of his life in the USA and had considerable influence on **Maria Montessori**.

Selection procedures

Procedures normally involving the use of tests enabling a choice of suitable candidates to be made, e.g. the selection procedures at eleven-plus usually include some or all of the following: Arithmetic test, English language test, Verbal reasoning test, Head's recommendation, interview.
See also **UCCA**
D. PIDGEON and A. YATES, *Admission to Grammar schools*, Newnes for NFER 1957
P. E. VERNON, ed., *Secondary School Selection*, rev. edn, Methuen 1957

Self-corrective apparatus

Materials which test and teach at the same time, e.g. a child might attempt to read the word 'dog' on one side of a card and turn the card over to check with the picture on the other side; or he might attempt the question, $4 \times 7 = ?$, given on one side of a card and check his answer with the complete version, $4 \times 7 = 28$, on the other. The recent developments in this direction are in terms of **programmed learning** and **teaching machines**.
L. W. DOWNES and D. PALING, *The Teaching of Arithmetic in Primary Schools*, Oxford University Press, Unesco Handbooks 1958
W. I. SMITH and J. W. MORE, *Programmed Learning*, Van Nostrand 1962

Self-expression

Expression of a person's own thoughts and feelings particularly in relation to creative activities in language, art and movement.
D. HOLBROOK, *The Secret Places: imaginative work in English in secondary school*, Methuen 1965
D. PYM, *Free Writing*, University of London Press for Bristol University Institute 1956

Semantics

The science or study of meaning especially in language: in language, the study of meaning as opposed to etymology, or the origin of words.
F. H. GEORGE, *Semantics*, English Universities Press (Teach Yourself series) 1964

Semi-interquartile range (stats)

Also called quartile deviation, or Q. It is a measure of the dispersion or scatter of a distribution and is equal to one-half the difference between the 75th and 25th percentiles of the distribution. In a normal distribution the semi-interquartile range becomes the probable error (PE), and is approximately equal to two-thirds the standard deviation of the distribution.
H. E. GARRETT, *Statistics in Psychology and Education*, 6th edn, Longmans 1966

P. E. VERNON, *The Measurement of Abilities*, 2nd edn, University of London Press 1956

Seminar
(From Latin 'semen' – a seed.) A discussion group comprising students and tutor(s) addressing themselves to subject(s) or topic(s) in which they have a common interest.
C. B. WELLINGTON and J. WELLINGTON, *Teaching for Critical Thinking*, McGraw-Hill 1960

Sense training
That part of the educational process which concerns itself with giving suitable experience to the senses, especially of eye, ear, and touch.
M. MONTESSORI, *The Montessori Method*, Heinemann 1912, 2nd edn, 1920; Bentley 1964
N. L. MUNN, *Psychology: the fundamentals of human adjustment*, 5th edn, Harrap 1966

Sensorimotor
1. The term used by **Piaget** to describe the stage of intellectual development in the first two years of life which manifests itself largely in motor responses to sensory impressions.
2. Referring to processes or experiences which involve sensory and motor factors of the psycho-organic system, e.g. perceiving the written word and reading it aloud.
Modern educational thinking is concerned with the use of as many of the senses as possible to reinforce learning, e.g. The sensorimotor factors would be used in helping a backward child to remember words not only by saying them but by tracing with the finger.
N. L. MUNN, *Psychology: the fundamentals of human adjustment*, 5th edn, Harrap 1966
E. A. PEEL, *The Psychological Basis of Education*, Oliver & Boyd 1956
J. PIAGET, *The Origin of Intelligence in the Child*, Routledge & Kegan Paul 1953

Sentence method in reading
Learning to read by reading whole sentences in the first instance rather than by (*a*) reading single words (**Look and Say**), or (*b*) combining phonic elements to form words (**phonic method**). Those who favour the sentence method proceed to help children to identify the individual words in the known sentences and, finally, to examine the phonic nature of some of the individual words.

E. LUKE, *The Teaching of Reading by the Sentence Method*, Methuen 1931
THE SCOTTISH COUNCIL FOR RESEARCH IN EDUCATION, *Studies in Reading*, vol. 1, University of London Press 1948
V. SOUTHGATE and G. R. ROBERTS, *Reading. Which Approach?* U.L.P. 1970

Set
1. A mathematical term for a group of items, symbolically enclosed in a bracket. It is possible to have an empty set or 'null' set containing no items.
D. PALING and J. FOX, *New Mathematics for Primary Teachers*, Oxford University Press, 4 books, 1968–69
R. R. SKEMP and J. S. FRIES, *Understanding Mathematics*, University of London Press, 5 books, 1964–69
2. Sometimes synonymous with '**attitude**' and meaning a predisposition to act and react in a particular manner in relation to some person, idea or situation.
N. L. NUNN, *Psychology: the fundamentals of human adjustment*, 5th edn, Harrap 1966

Sex instruction
Education in matters relating to sex. The main issue is whether parents or teachers are best suited to do this work and, if teachers, whether all children of the same chronological age are equally ready for education in sex matters. The best answer probably lies in healthy cooperation between parents and teachers.
C. BIBBY, *Sex Education*, Macmillan 1948
A. CHANTER, *Sex Education in the Primary School*, Macmillan 1966

Short division
That method of division in which the subtraction process is not written down and in which the remainders of the partial dividends may or may not be written before the next figure to be included in the partial dividend, e.g.

$$2)\overline{376}$$
$$\overline{188}$$

The answer may be written above or below the example.
See also **Division** and **Long division**
L. W. DOWNES and D. PALING, *Teaching Arithmetic in the Primary School*, Oxford University Press, Unesco Handbooks 1958

Sibling
A brother or sister; child, of either sex, of the same parents. Sometimes interpreted so as to include half-brothers and half-sisters.

Sight vocabulary
A person's reading vocabulary which he can read at sight, i.e. without having to use his knowledge of phonics.
G. M. BLAIR, *Diagnostic and Remedial Teaching*, rev. edn, Collier-Macmillan 1956, ch. 4
J. MCNALLY and W. MURRAY, *Keywords to Literacy and the Teaching of Reading*, 2nd edn, Schoolmaster Pub. Co. 1968

Sigma (stats)
This is a Greek letter used both in the lower case, ς, and in the uper case, Σ. In the former instance it stands for **standard deviation** and in the latter, for 'sum of'.
See also **sigma score**
D. M. MCINTOSH, *Statistics for the Teacher*, Pergamon 1963
P. E. VERNON, *The Measurement of Abilities*, 2nd edn, University of London Press 1940

Sigma scores or z scores (stats)
Scores expressed in terms of the **standard deviation**. In a normal distribution since the **mean** is expressed as O, almost all the individual marks or measures will fall within the range of three standard deviations (or z scores) above, and three standard deviations (or z scores) below the mean.
J. R. AMOS, F. L. BROWN and O. G. MINK, *Statistical Concepts*, Harper & Row 1965
H. E. GARRETT, *Statistics in Psychology and Education*, 6th edn, Longmans 1966
S. R. GRIFFITHS and L. W. DOWNES, *Educational Statistics for Beginners*, Methuen 1969

Significance (stats)
The degree to which a measure derived from a sample represents the corresponding measure in the **population**. The idea of significance thus extends to comparisons between populations which are based on samples of those populations; for example, it is possible to estimate the average height of girls or boys of a certain age by finding the average height of representative samples of boys or girls and one could then proceed to compare the average height of all boys and girls of this age on the basis of the measures derived from the sample means. There are statistical techniques for indicating what

degree of significance one is entitled to attach to calculations based on sampling.
H. E. GARRETT, *Statistics in Psychology and Education*, 6th edn, Longmans 1966

Sinistrality
Preference for using the limbs on the left side of the body. It can also apply to the eye and ear.
See also **Dextrality**; **Laterality**
M. CLARK, *Left-handed Children*, University of London Press for Scottish Council for Research in Education 1957

SISTER
Special Institution for Scientific and Technological Education and Research; proposed by Robbins Committee in Report *Higher Education*, 1963, to give prominence to technology and resemble the Massachusetts Institute of Technology (USA) or the technical high schools of Delft (Holland) or of Zurich (Switzerland). They were to be constituted as independent institutions of the university pattern.
Robbins Report, *Higher Education*, 1963, ch. 10

Sixth form
The upper part of a secondary school, which offers a one, two, or three year course after GCE O level. Except where a one-year (e.g. pre-nursing or general) course is offered, the work is of an advanced academic standard, confined usually to three main subjects for GCE A and S level and aiming at university or College entrance.
Crowther Report, *15–18*, Part V, vol. 1 1959
MINISTRY OF EDUCATION, *The Road to the Sixth Form: some suggestions on the curriculum of the grammar school*, Pamphlet no 19, HMSO 1951
A. D. C. PETERSON, *Arts and Science Sides in the Sixth Form*, Oxford University Press 1960
SCHOOLS COUNCIL, Pamphlet no. 16, *Some Further Proposals for Sixth Form Work*, HMSO 1967

Sixth-form college
A junior college taking the place of sixth forms. The idea of a sixth-form college has a history dating from a plan put forward, without success, by the Croydon education authority. It is now developing largely by the impetus of comprehensive secondary education. Comprehensive schools need to be very big in order to produce sixth forms

big enough to offer a wide variety of subjects, but a number of comprehensive secondary schools of moderate size in a neighbourhood between them can contribute to the formation of a large group of sixth form students who might be housed and taught together in a sixth-form college. The exact character of such colleges will vary from one **LEA** to another in two main respects:

(*a*) in the location of the college and its relationship to an already existing educational institution, e.g. the Mexborough College and the Mexborough grammar schools share the same locality and some amenities, and have the same headmaster; Exeter, on the other hand, has its college within the technical college.

(*b*) in the intake of pupils and the nature of the courses offered.

Colleges may restrict entry to pupils holding O level who wish to study for A level, or may broaden their scope of entry to pupils not holding O levels and provide a wider range of courses so as to meet the needs and interests of pupils of less academic ability.

Sizar

At the University of Cambridge and at Trinity College, Dublin, the name given to an undergraduate who receives an allowance from his college to enable him to study. Formerly, a sizar had to perform certain duties which are now carried out by college servants. The poet, Milton, for example, was a sizar at Cambridge.

Skeletal age. *See* Carpal age

Skills

Physical or mental abilities, acquired through knowledge and practice which can be exercised with relative ease and accuracy.

See also **Basic skills**

A. W. MELTON, ed., *Categories of Human Learning*, Academic Press 1964

Skinner, B. F.

Professor of Psychology at Harvard University. Particularly interested in the process of learning and is well known for his work on behavioural training, or operant conditioning accomplished by placing an organism in a carefully controlled environment in which a desired response can be reinforced. Has done extensive work with teaching machines and in the field of programmed learning. Publications include: *Science and Human*

Behaviour (Collier-Macmillan 1965) and *Walden Two* (Collier-Macmillan 1962), a Utopian novel embodying his ideas on learning.

E. R. HILGARD, ed., *Theories of Learning and Instruction*, University of Chicago Press 1965

Slow learners

Children of low ability and attainment, the least able in schools and those in **special schools**. Their education requires special techniques and skills, particularly of a remedial kind.

CHESHIRE EDUCATION COMMITTEE, *The Education of Dull Children*, 2 vols, University of London Press 1963

M. F. CLEUGH, *Teaching the Slow Learner*, 3 vols, Methuen 1961

F. J. SCHONELL, *Backwardness in the Basic Subjects*, Oliver & Boyd 1942

S. SEGAL, *No Child is Ineducable*, Pergamon 1967

SMP. *See* School Mathematics Project

Smoking

Following the publication in *Smoking and Health* by the British Medical Association of the results of their investigations into the relations between smoking and the incidence of lung cancer, there has been a strong pressure to use the schools, as a means to further the antismoking campaign.

G. JAMES and T. ROSENTHAL, *Tobacco and Health*, C. Thomas 1962

M. SCHRODER, *Better Smoking*, Allen & Unwin 1964

Snellen Chart

A printed chart with rows of letters of graded size designed to test distant vision (i.e. from a distance of twenty feet).

R. GAMLIN, *Modern School Hygiene*, Nisbet 1965

Social administration

Curiosity about society and its problems stimulated by the great pioneering social surveys of the late nineteenth century, led to the development of the systematic study of social administration as a university degree and diploma subject. Its subject matter is the great field of state activity designed to meet public needs and to solve social problems, e.g. services to maintain income, meet industrial conditions, exercise control over the physical environment by planning, promote health and provide public education. Special needs such as those of the handicapped, the elderly and offenders are also included in this field of study. This field of study is called 'Public Administration' by some teaching institutions.

D. C. MARSH, *An Introduction to the Study of Social Administration*, Routledge & Kegan Paul 1965

Social change

A more neutral sociological term which has largely replaced 'social progress', 'social evolution' or 'social development' because these imply a teleology or are value loaded. The term refers, for example, to changes in social structure (size, composition or type) or to changes in values or meanings held by large social groups. Sociologists work on the assumption that social change can be understood and its causes discovered, and that planned social change is possible.

O. BANKS, *The Sociology of Education*, Batsford 1968, ch. 10

G. BERNBAUM, *Social Change and the Schools, 1918–1944*, Routledge & Kegan Paul 1967

J. GOULD and W. L. KOLB, ed., *A Dictionary of the Social Sciences*, Tavistock 1964

Social interaction

The reciprocal behaviour of individuals towards one another within a social group, or of groups towards one another within a social system. This social behaviour, through communication in the form of action, speech, writing and gesture, sets up relationships capable of being systematically studied by social psychologists and sociologists; (cf. R. F. Bales technique of interaction process analysis, or sociometric methods). Enduring reciprocal actions are organised into **roles**, e.g. teacher to pupil, husband to wife, superior to inferior, etc. Relationships, patterns and processes of social interaction at the level of small group, the secondary group or at the level of the national, or **ethnic** community are the basic subject matter of **social science**.

D. CARTWRIGHT and A. ZANDER, ed, *Group Dynamics*, Tavistock 1968

G. C. HOMANS, *Social Behaviour*, Routledge & Kegan Paul 1961, ch. 10

T. M. NEWCOMB, *Social Psychology: a study of human interaction*, 2nd edn, Routledge & Kegan Paul 1966

A. K. C. OTTAWAY, *Education and Society*, 2nd edn, Routledge & Kegan Paul 1962

K.W.E.—7

Social maturity

The qualities displayed by the well adapted individual who acts confidently in, and accepts contentedly, normal group situations. It is characterised by the ability to cope easily with unfamiliar social situations, to manage personal relationships adequately and to exercise control over the self. The socially mature person is self-directing, accepts the consequences of his actions, is realistic about his capacities and the world in which they are employed, and is able to give and receive love. For children, Doll's **Vineland Social Maturity Scale** offers an assessment of development in this respect.

S. N. EISENSTADT, *From Generation to Generation*, Collier-Macmillan 1964

T. M. NEWCOMB, *Social Psychology: a study of human interaction*, 2nd edn, Routledge & Kegan Paul 1966

E. A. LUNZER, *The Manchester Scales of Social Adaptation*, NFER 1971

Social psychology

The study of individual social behaviour (response, interaction, development, motivation, etc.) against a background of social groups.

C. M. FLEMING, *The Social Psychology of Education*, 2nd edn, Routledge & Kegan Paul 1959

S. ISAACS, *Social Development in Young Children*, Routledge & Kegan Paul 1933

K. YOUNG, *Handbook of Social Psychology*, 2nd edn, Routledge & Kegan Paul 1957

Social science

The systematic study of man and society which comprises general and social psychology (sometimes called the behavioural sciences), sociology, economics, politics and social administration. The study of law is also included in this category by some writers.

D. C. MARCH, *The Social Sciences: an outline for the intending student*, Routledge & Kegan Paul 1965

T. RAISON, ed., *The Founding Fathers of Social Science*, Penguin (Pelican) 1969

Social studies

A school study which may include elements of history, geography, economics, political science, etc., designed to integrate the curriculum.

W. PHILIP and R. PREST, *Social Studies and Social Science in Secondary Schools*, Longmans 1965

Social survey

A method of investigating social conditions principally by description, observation and the gathering and analysis of answers to questionnaires.

M. ABRAMS, *Social Surveys and Social Action*, Heinemann 1951

Social worker

An employee of local, national or private bodies whose work is in the field of the special services.

Journal: *Social Work* (London)

Socialization

The total process by which an individual, usually the child, is inducted into group life; it consists of inculcating approved conduct, expectations, values, beliefs, etc., which enable the individual to interact harmoniously with his fellows.

J. H. S. BOSSARD and E. S. BOLL, *Sociology of Child Development*, 3rd edn, Harper 1960

S. ISAACS, *Social Development in Young Children*, Routledge & Kegan Paul 1933

Socio-economic group

A group within the national community assessed on both social prestige and income criteria, and forming a hierarchy; often a euphemism for social class.

GENERAL REGISTER OFFICE, *Classification of Occupations*, HMSO 1960

A. H. HALSEY, J. FLOUD and C. A. ANDERSON, eds, *Education, Economy and Society*, Free Press Glencoe 1961

Sociogram

A diagram illustrating a sociometric survey and showing a network of choices within a group, in response to some stimulus question. Responses are usually systematically recorded first in the form of a sociomatrix and then illustrated as a sociogram.

K. M. EVANS, *Sociometry and Education*, Routledge & Kegan Paul 1962

O. A. OESER, *Teacher, Pupil and Task*, Tavistock 1966

Sociology

The science of society, which studies the forms of social relationships, either in specific institutions, e.g. marriage, denomination, factory, or more abstractly, e.g. leadership and obedience relationships in management, government, etc. Sociology examines the way in which persons and groups act upon one another, together with the conditions and consequences of such activity: hence the nature of social change. It aims to describe the pattern of such relationships (social structure) and the way they operate (social function). There are special sociologies of large groupings: sociology of industry, administration, politics, religion, education, etc.

A. INKELES, *What is Sociology?*, Prentice-Hall 1964

G. D. MITCHELL, *A Hundred Years of Sociology*, new edn, Duckworth 1970

W. M. OGBURN and M. F. NIMKOFF, *Handbook of Sociology*, Routledge & Kegan Paul 1960

Sociology of education

The study of institutional forms of educational activity (schools, staff, administrators, pupils), which seeks to describe accurately a pattern of relationships and activities that can be submitted to deliberate analysis. Also the relationship of educational institutions with others, e.g. family, industry; and the conditions (economical, physical, etc.) in which educational institutions operate.

P. MUSGRAVE, *The Sociology of Education*, Methuen 1965

A. K. C. OTTAWAY, *Education and Society*, 2nd edn, Routledge & Kegan Paul 1966

M. D. SHIPMAN, *The Sociology of the School*, Longmans 1968

The Teaching of Sociology to Students of Education, Sociological Review Monograph, no. 4, Keele University 1961

Sociometry

A method of studying and investigating small groups of people by illustrating diagrammatically their preferred choices of companion within the group as shown by a questionnaire. A technique developed by Moreno and extensively used in research.

K. M. EVANS, *Sociometry and Education*, Routledge & Kegan Paul 1962

M. L. NORTHWAY, *A Primer of Sociometry*, University of Toronto Press 1967

O. A. OESER, *Teacher, Pupil and Task*, Tavistock 1955

Socratic method. *See* Questioning

Somatotype

Classification of people into personality types on the basis of physical characteristics.

E. KRETSCHMER, *Physique and Character*, 2nd edn, Kegan Paul 1936

P. E. VERNON, *Personality Tests and Assessments*, new edn, Methuen 1953

South Kensington
The profit of £180,000 made by the Great Exhibition of 1851 was used to bring together leading learned and artistic societies at South Kensington, London. They were: The Royal Albert Hall: The Imperial Institute; The Science Museum; The Natural History Museum; and The Royal College of Art, and the Victoria and Albert Museum.

Southgate Group Reading Tests
Test 1 is a Word Selection Test and Test 2 is a Sentence Completion Test. Test 1 is available in three forms and Test 2 is available in two forms so that they could be administered simultaneously to a whole class, desk partners using different forms.

Test 1 is most useful for average children aged 6–7½ years and includes a reading range from 5 years 9 months to 7 years 9 months.

Test 2 is considered most useful for average children of 7 years 0 months to 8 years 11 months, and includes reading ages between 7 years 0 months to 9 years 7 months.

V. SOUTHGATE, *Group Reading Tests*, University of London Press 1959, 1962

Spastic
A person who suffers from physical disabilities because of brain damage in the pre-natal or perinatal period. The severity of the disability and its exact nature vary considerably from one person to another. Until a relatively short time ago spastics were often mistakenly regarded as mentally subnormal but they in fact cover a wide range of intelligence.

See also the series *Little Club Clinics in Developmental Medicine*, Heinemann 1963

E. CARLSON, *Born that Way*, Evesham (Worcs) James 1953

F. E. SCHONELL, *Educating Spastic Children*, Oliver & Boyd 1956

Spatial factor (K Factor)
One of the abilities or group factors which Thurstone and others consider intelligence comprises. The other chief factors are – verbal, inductive reasoning, deductive reasoning; numerical, word fluency, rote memory and perceptual speed.

See also K factor; Deduction; Induction; Rote learning

I. MCFARLANE-SMITH, *Spatial Ability*, University of London Press 1964

P. E. VERNON, *Intelligence and Attainment Tests*, University of London Press 1960.

Spearman, C. E. (1863–1945)
English psychologist best known for his work on intelligence, in particular for his two-factor theory of **intelligence**. He was a pioneer in the field of factor analysis. After a short military career, worked with Wundt and others in Germany before returning to England and subsequently becoming Professor of Psychology in the University of London. Publications include: *The Nature of Intelligence and the Principles of Cognition* (Macmillan); *The Abilities of Man* (Macmillan 1927).

See also **Footrule**

Special agreement schools
LEAs are enabled to contribute by special agreement up to three-quarters of the cost of a new voluntary secondary school. Two-thirds of the Governors of such a school are appointed by the voluntary body and one-third by the LEA.

G. R. BARRELL, *Teachers and the Law*, Methuen 1966

G. TAYLOR and J. B. SAUNDERS, *The New Law of Education*, 7th edn, Butterworth 1971

Special Institution for Scientific and Technological Education and Research. *See* SISTER

Special place examination
A selective examination for children of 10 or 11 years for entry into **grammar schools**. Under the Board of Education Regulations 1907 there were to be in grammar schools 25 per cent free places (i.e. no fees); by 1930 the figure was above 50 per cent and under the 1944 Act, county grammar schools became 100 per cent free-place schools. The examination is now popularly called the **eleven plus**; formerly it was known as 'the scholarship'. With the spread of **comprehensive** secondary schools, the notion of selection at this age is becoming obsolescent.

Norwood Report, *Curriculum and Examinations in Secondary Schools*, 1943

Spens Report, *Secondary Education*, 1938.

P. E. VERNON, *Secondary School Selection*, Methuen 1957.

A. YATES and D. PIDGEON, *Admission to Grammar Schools*, Newnes 1957

Special schools
Schools for children suffering from various categories of handicap, e.g. blindness, maladjustment, mental subnormality.
Association for Special Education, 39, Little Common, Stanmore, Middlesex
S. JACKSON, *Special Education in England and Wales*, 2nd edn, Oxford University Press 1969
J. D. KERSHAW, *Handicapped Children*, Heinemann 1966
D. G. PRITCHARD, *Education and the Handicapped (1760–1960)*, Routledge & Kegan Paul 1963

Specialization
The practice of concentrating on a relatively small number of skills or subjects with a view to obtaining greater facility with greater speed in those areas of study or practice. In secondary schools the curriculum tends to take on a specialist nature, with teachers concentrating on one particular subject. In primary schools the teacher normally deals with all subjects though this is tending to change with demands at primary level for foreign languages, mathematics and physical education.
At the higher levels of learning this tends dangerously to a breakdown in communication between scholars in different fields and to the emergence of 'two Cultures'.
Crowther Report, *15–18*, 1959
C. P. SNOW, *The Two Cultures and the Scientific Revolution*, Cambridge University Press 1964

Speech therapy
Corrective or remedial training, usually given by a suitably trained person in a clinic, for those having speech difficulties of either a physical or emotional nature.
R. M. WILLIAMS, *Speech Difficulties in Childhood: a practical guide for teachers and parents*, Harrap 1962

Speed test or **Rate test**
1. A test designed to measure speed of work as distinct from other dimensions of performance (e.g. quality).
2. A test (e.g. **intelligence test**) containing many items of a similar level of difficulty which the subject must try to complete in a given time. The marking makes the assumption that the child who is quicker gets more correct responses and is therefore more intelligent.
Most modern tests are constructed on a combined **power** and speed principle.
P. E. VERNON, *Intelligence and Attainment Tests*, University of London Press 1960, ch. 2

Spelling
In language communication the act of recalling letters in their proper sequence to form words. More generally the method of representing words through visual symbols on the basis of an accepted orthography. English spelling is irrational and makes reading and writing unnecessarily difficult.
See also **ITA**
G. M. BLAIR, *Diagnostic and Remedial Teaching*, rev. edn, Collins-Macmillan 1956
G. HILDRETH, *Teaching Spelling*, Holt, Rinehart & Winston 1955
M. PETERS, *Spelling: Caught or Taught?*, Routledge and Kegan Paul 1967
F. E. SCHONELL, *The Essentials in Teaching and Testing Spelling*, Macmillan 1965

Spencer, Herbert (1820–1903)
English philosopher and writer on sociology and education. The son of a schoolmaster and largely self-educated, Spencer wrote voluminously about the social sciences of his day, including important essays on the curriculum, and on intellectual, moral and physical education (*Essays on Education*, Dent: Everyman). In demanding a realistic, practical, scientifically orientated education for both sexes and in his low esteem of classics and arts in education, he presents one extreme of Victorian educatonal theory; the other extreme is **J. H. Newman's** *Idea of a University*. Publications include: *Principles of Sociology* (ed. S. L. Andreski, Macmillan 1969).

Spens Report (1938)
A report of the Consultative Committee on Secondary Education published in 1938, under the chairman Mr Will Spens. Following on the **Hadow Report**, this Committee examined the grammar and technical high schools, with particular reference to those pupils not staying on beyond the age of sixteen. They examined the development of such schools' curriculum, its content, methods of examination, etc. The report had some influence on the 1944 Education Act particularly with reference to the development of technical education.
See also Appendix III
J. LELLO, *The Official View on Education*, Pergamon 1964

Split halves technique (stats)
A means of examining the reliability of tests containing many items. After the administration of the test, the items are divided into two halves (usually odd and even numbered items) so as to constitute two subtests. The scores of testees based on the odd items are then correlated with their scores on the even items.
w. R. BORG, *Educational Research*, New York, McKay 1963
H. E. GARRETT, *Statistics in Psychology and Education*, 6th edn, Longmans 1966
C. SELLTIZ *et al.*, *Research Methods in Social Relations*, Methuen 1960
P. E. VERNON, *Measurement of Abilities*, 2nd edn, University of London Press 1956

Sports
In schools, the reference is normally to school or district sports meetings in which individuals or teams compete in a wide range of athletic activities. Events are included to suit the ages of the children involved. It is usual, too, for the sports to be competitive, inter-house within a school, or inter-school in district sports.
Handbook of the Amateur Athletic Association, 54 Torrington Place, London, WC1
J. WOLFENDEN, *Sport and the Community*, Central Council of Physical Eduation 1960

'Spot' questions
1. Questions which those preparing for examinations anticipate will be asked;
2. Questions requiring answers of only a sentence or few lines of which a large number can be asked in a test. This enables the examiner to overcome some of the disadvantages of essay-type answers, in that a broader and more representative sample of skills and knowledge can be tested.

Standard deviation
Also SD or σ. An index of the spread of scores or measures above and below the *arithmetical mean* of these measures. In a normally distributed set of measures two standard deviations, one on either side of the mean will together include approximately 68 per cent of them; four SDs, two on each side, will together include approximately 96 per cent of them; and six SDs, three on each side of the mean, will together include practically all of the measures.
Most standardised tests produced nowadays for use in schools have a SD of 15.

SD is a useful descriptive and inferential index. It is needed to determine the standard error of the mean, is very useful in standardizing scores obtained in various subjects and is used in computing product moment correlation.
H. GARRETT, *Statistics in Psychology and Education*, 6th edn, Longmans 1966
S. R. GRIFFITHS and L. W. DOWNES, *Educational Statistics for Beginners*, Methuen 1969
P. E. VERNON, *Measurement of Abilities*, 2nd edn, University of London Press 1956

Standard error of the mean (stats)
A measure of the uncertainty inherent in a sample mean as an estimate of the **population** mean. It is computed by dividing the **standard deviation** of the sample by the square root of the number of items:

$$SE_m = \frac{SD}{\sqrt{N}}$$

If the sample mean was 100 and the standard error 2, then we could be confident at the 20 to 1 level of confidence that the population mean did not lie outside 100 ± 4.
H. E. GARRETT, *Statistics in Psychology and Education*, Longmans 1966

Standard progressive matrices
'A test of a person's capacity at the time of the test to apprehend meaningless figures, presented for his observation, see the relations between them, conceive the nature of the figures completing each system of relations presented, and, by so doing, develop a systematic method of reasoning', *Guide* (see below) p. 1.
The scale comprises sixty problems divided into five sets of twelve. It is an untimed test and can be given as an individual, a self administered, or as a group test. It should be considered together with the **Mill Hill Vocabulary Scale**, its verbal counterpart. The norms are supplied in both scales as percentile points.
J. C. RAVEN, *Extended Guide to Using the Mill Hill Vocabulary Scale with The Progressive Matrices Scale*, H. K. Lewis 1958
J. C. RAVEN, *Guide to the Standard Progressive Matrices*, H. K. Lewis 1960

Standard score
Test performance expressed in terms of standard deviation units from the mean. Basically it is computed by the formula

$$SS = \frac{X - \overline{X}}{SD}$$ where X = raw score, $\overline{X}$ = mean and SD = Standard Deviation.

There are various types of standard scores in use e.g. Z-scores; T-scores; Stanines; Deviation IQ.

H. E. GARRETT, *Statistics in Psychology and Education*, 6th edn, Longmans 1966

N. E. GRONLUND, *Measurement and Evaluation in Teaching*, Collier-Macmillan 1965

P. E. VERNON, *Measurement of Abilities*, 2nd edn, University of London Press 1956

Standardization of tests
The process of establishing **norms** or standards for a test; this might include norms of administration, size of print, spacing of words/sentences, duration of the test, marking or scoring instructions, and interpretation of scores.

P. E. VERNON, *Measurement of Abilities*, 2nd edn, University of London Press 1940

P. E. VERNON, *The Standardisation of a Graded Word Reading Test*, University of London Press 1938

Stanford-Binet
Stanford-Binet Test – The first important individual test of intelligence to be widely used in the USA. It was based on the work of **Binet** in France and was published in 1916 by **Terman** who was professor of psychology at Stanford University. This test is described by Terman in *The Measurement of Intelligence*, and subsequent revisions were widely used on both sides of the Atlantic particularly in child guidance work. Accurate results can only be obtained by people trained and experienced in the administration of the test. The later revisions of the test were made up of sub-tests arranged in the form of an age scale, there being six sub-tests at each age level. The test procedure is to establish the basal mental age, the age level at which all the sub-tests are passed, and continue testing until all the sub-tests at a particular age level are failed, adding two months to the basal mental age for each sub-test the child gets correct as he progresses through the test. There is a mixture of both verbal and non-verbal items in the test.

See also **L-M Intelligence Test**

L. M. TERMAN and M. A. MERRILL, *Measurement of Intelligence*, Harrap 1960

State system of education
Those non-fee-paying schools and colleges which receive support from local and central taxes exclusively. They are administered by county and county borough authorities (the **LEA**) and provide education at **primary**, **secondary** and **further** levels. They account for about 95 per cent of the whole system.

W. P. ALEXANDER, *Education in England*, Newnes 1965

J. ARMITAGE, *Our Children's Education*, Pall Mall Press 1960

TYRRELL BURGESS, *A Guide to English Schools*, Penguin 1964

Statistics
1. The collected numerical data relating to any sphere of activity, e.g. as in *Statistics of Education* (HMSO), or the history marks gained in any class in school .
2. A branch of applied mathematics concerned with organizing data so as to bring out their full meaning, e.g. taking a set of marks and arranging them in mark order of merit, finding the class average score, assigning **percentile ranks** to individual pupils, etc.
3. Measures describing a sample (e.g. mean; standard; deviation), as distinct from **parameters** describing a **population**.

S. R. GRIFFITHS and L. W. DOWNES, *Educational Statistics for Beginners*, Methuen 1969

Statistics for education
Statistics is normally regarded as a branch of applied mathematics and can be applied to many areas of study and investigation, e.g. education, industry and agriculture.

H. E. GARRETT, *Statistics in Psychology and Education*, 6th edn, Longmans 1966

S. R. GRIFFITHS and L. W. DOWNES, *Educational Statistics for Beginners*, Methuen 1969

D. M. MCINTOSH, *Statistics for the Teacher*, 2nd edn, Pergamon 1967

P. E. VERNON, *The Measurement of Abilities*, 2nd edn, University of London Press 1956

Statistics of Education
Compiled by the Department of Education and Science and published by HMSO. Separately-bound parts appear at intervals through each year. Formerly an appendage of the Ministry of Education's *Annual Report*, it now presents a comprehensive statistical account of the educational system from year to year. Though it used to deal exclusively with education in England and

Wales, it now includes data relating to Scotland and Northern Ireland.

Status

The value placed on position or rank in any group or community. Status may take the form of caste, or certain groups having legally defined and enforceable rights and duties, e.g. the 'estates' of lords, clergy, and commoners. Social class based on the individual's economic position is replacing these concepts in the industrialized nations. A person's standing in relation to other members of society is referred to as his 'social status' and rests on a consensus of opinion within the group. Thus it is difficult to judge objectively in many cases what a particular person's status is, but the main tests are wealth, occupation, parentage and education. The concept of status is very closely associated with that of **role**.

G. LINDZEY and E. ARONSON, *Handbook of Social Psychology*, 3 vols, 2nd edn, Addison Wesley 1968–69

A. K. C. OTTAWAY, *Education and Society*, Routledge & Kegan Paul 1962, ch. 6

Stern apparatus

Material made in wood, and devised by the American educationist, Catherine Stern, to help children in the acquisition of early mathematical concepts. It is produced in the UK by the Educational Supply Association.

C. STERN, *Children Discover Arithmetic*, Harrap 1953

Stimulus-Response (S-R), Theory

The theory of learning formulated by **E. L. Thorndike** which holds that learning consists of the formation and strengthening of bonds between stimuli and responses. Thorndike maintained that animal learning takes place purely by trial and error and does not involve insight or understanding.

M. B. R. BUGELSKI, *The Psychology of Learning*, Methuen 1957

E. R. HILGARD, *Theories of Learning and Instruction*, University of Chicago Press 1965

E. L. THORNDIKE, *Human Learning*, Massachusetts Institute of Technology Press 1966

Story-telling

An important element in education used very successfully in the education of the very young but tending to become more and more neglected with the older and/or the brighter pupils.

E. CLARK, *Stories and How to Tell Them*, new edn, University of London Press 1959

E. COLWELL, *A Story-teller's Choice*, Bodley Head 1963

Strabismus

Commonly called 'squint'. Owing to weakness and a consequent lack of coordination of the muscles of the eyeballs the person is unable to direct both eyes to the same object. Orthoptic treatment is often successful for this condition. Severe cases may need cosmetic operations on the eye muscles. Children with squint are liable to emotional disturbance.

E. E. MARTMER, *The Child with a Handicap*, Blackwell 1959

Streaming, stream

Dividing children in a school into two or more parallel chronological strata, or streams, on the basis of ability. The aim is to render teaching more effective by making classes more homogeneous in respect of ability. Opponents of streaming point to its social disadvantages and suspect that even intellectually it has a depressing effect on all except the brightest. Selection at eleven plus may be regarded as streaming on a big scale.

J. W. B. DOUGLAS, *Home and School*, MacGibbon & Kee 1964

B. JACKSON, *Streaming*, Routledge & Kegan Paul 1964

'Non-Streaming in the Junior School', FORUM, **7**, 1964 (PSW (Educational) Publications, 71 Clarendon Park Road, Leicester)

Structural apparatus (mathematics)

Apparatus which helps pupil/student to organise meaningfully mathematical data, the simplest and most original item of structural apparatus being one's fingers. Some well-known commercial structural apparatus are Stern, Cuisenaire, Avon, Dienes, Unifix, Structa.

See also **Tillich bricks**

J. B. BIGGS, *Mathematics and the Conditions of Learning*, NFER 1967

C. STERN, *Children Discover Arithmetic*, Harrap 1953

Student Examen

The Swedish final examination of the academic secondary school or gymnasium which admits to university and colleges of education. In Denmark the similar examination is called the Studenter.

See also **Abitur**

W. DIXON, *Schools and Progress in Scandinavia*, Pergamon 1965

Study, Methods of

Systematic ways of acquiring knowledge and understanding, e.g. methods of reading books, making notes, testing one's understanding of subject matter.

SIR JOHN ADAMS, *A Student's Guide*, English Universities Press (Teach Yourself series) 1938

R. D. BRAMWELL, 'Study skills and informal methods', New Era **40**, no. 2, 1959

J. S. BRUBACHER, *Modern Philosophies of Education*, McGraw-Hill 1969 ch. 3

C. A. MACE, *The Psychology of Study*, 4th edn, Methuen 1949; Penguin (Pelican) 1969

H. MADDOX, *How to Study*, Pan Books 1963

Study practice

A form of teaching practice now widely used by colleges of education, and considered to be of great value by those colleges which favour it. It is a preparation for teaching in which the emphasis is on the study in depth of one or more children for a whole school year, and on the trying out of educational theories, principles, and teaching methods in the practical situation. Normally a tutor and about twelve students will attach themselves to one class of children for the whole year for one half-day per week. Each student will be allocated his quota of pupils, and the tutor and students take over the teaching of the class. The bulk of the teaching will be on a tutorial basis, during which a student can try out various teaching methods and make an intensive study of his charges as individuals, but he will also observe his pupils as they react to the larger group situation, and as they react to the playground situation. He will make home visits to learn about the child's home and neighbourhood background and relevant details about his previous history. This work is carried on in close collaboration with the school staff. The work is supplemented by discussion among the group at college. Each student keeps a detailed diary of the school visits and at the end of the year writes a critical evaluation of the year's work and detailed studies of the individuals in his small group.

K. G. COLLIER, *Bulletin of Education 1953*, ATCDE

L. W. DOWNES and K. E. SHAW, 'Innovations in teaching practice', *Trends in Education*, 1968

Subculture

A subdivision of the larger national or community culture, restricted to one geographically, socio-economically or otherwise specially designated group, and which is recognisably a variation. Examples are: the slum subculture, teenage subculture, criminal subculture, immigrant subculture.

E. H. BELL, *Social Foundations of Human Behaviour*, 2nd edn, Harper & Row 1965, ch. 6

M. KERR, *People of Ship Street*, Routledge & Kegan Paul 1958

Subjective marking

Marking or scoring requiring complex judgments by the examiners, especially in marking essay type answers, and therefore tending to produce disagreements between different examiners, and even to fluctuation in standards in the same examiner; cf. **Objective marking**.

S. R. GRIFFITHS and L. W. DOWNES, *Educational Statistics for Beginners*, Methuen 1969

P. E. VERNON, *Measurement of Abilities*, 2nd edn, University of London Press 1956

P. HARTOG and E. C. RHODES, *An Examination of Examinations*, Macmillan 1936

Sublimation

The direction of undesirable or forbidden impulses into socially acceptable channels.

J. C. FLUGEL, *Man, Morals and Society*, Duckworth 1955

C. W. VALENTINE, *Psychology and its Bearing on Education*, 2nd edn, Methuen 1960

Subnormality

The condition in which mental capacity is so limited that the child needs special educational provision or is ineducable, and may require special medical and social care. Scientific terminology for mental deficiency used the three categories of idiot; imbecile; and feeble-minded (or moron). The Mental Health Act uses the two categories of 'severely subnormal' and 'subnormal'. Educational terminology uses the classification of 'unsuitable for education in school' and 'educationally subnormal'.

A. D. B. CLARKE, *Recent Advances in the Study of Subnormality*, National Association for Mental Health 1966

Subtraction

The act or arithmetical process of taking one number or quantity from another number or quantity: finding the difference between two numbers or quantities. For 'methods of' see **equal addition** and **decomposition**.

L. W. DOWNES and D. PALING, *Teaching of Arithmetic in the Primary School*, Oxford University Press, Unesco Handbooks, 1958

Suggestion

The process which involves the uncritical acceptance of ideas, beliefs or modes of conduct as the result of words, actions or attitudes of another person or persons. The suggestions may be actual or expressed in writing. In auto-suggestion, the process depends on conditions arising in the individual's own mind and is not motivated from without.

C. BAUDOUIN, *Suggestion and Autosuggestion*, 2nd edn, Allen & Unwin 1949

Suggestibility

A characteristic, permanent or temporary, of the individual which indicates his readiness to accept the ideas and modes of conduct of other people.

J. C. FLUGEL, *Man, Morals and Society*, Duckworth 1955

A. PINSENT, *The Principles of Teaching Methods*, 3rd edn, Harrap 1969

C. W. VALENTINE, *Psychology and its Bearing on Education*, 2nd edn, Methuen 1960

Sunday schools

Schools set up in the eighteenth century largely through the work of Robert Raikes to give instruction to children and adults who worked during the week. Their function is now limited to giving religious instruction to children, and they are organized wholly by individual churches.

Address: National Sunday School Union, Robert Denholm House, Nutfield, Redhill, Surrey.

C. BIRCHENOUGH, *History of Elementary Education*, 3rd edn, University Tutorial Press 1938

S. CURTIS, *History of Education in Great Britain*, 7th edn, University Tutorial Press 1966

G. KENDAL, *Robert Raikes*, Nicolson & Watson 1939

Superego

In Freudian psychoanalysis one of the three main divisions in the structure of the personality. The superego takes the place of the 'censor' of Freud's earlier formulations. It is the survival in the unconscious of the earliest pre-rational moral code of the child. It is an intolerant moral critic and is responsible for repression and feelings of guilt. The superego tends to cause most trouble when great moral pressure has been exerted on the child in his upbringing.

H. CRICHTON-MILLER, *Psychoanalysis and its Derivatives*, 2nd edn, Oxford University Press (Home University Library) 1945

S. FREUD, *Two Short Accounts of Psychoanalysis*, Penguin (Pelican) 1962

C. S. HALL, *A Primer of Freudian Psychology*, Allen & Unwin 1956

Supplementary courses for teachers

'Third year' courses of supplementary training taken immediately after the completion of two-year courses of initial training in most cases developed before 1939. After the war such courses were increasingly used to enable qualified teachers to receive specialized training in particular shortage subjects such as mathematics and science, handicraft, housecraft, and physical education. Some courses became established at universities and led to academic diploma qualifications, particularly in education, psychology and child development. The majority of supplementary courses were undertaken in colleges of education. College supplementary courses declined in the late 'sixties after the introduction of the three year course of initial training.

Annual Reports of the **Department of Education and Science** and (earlier) **Ministry of Education**.

Education: a Framework for Expansion, Cmnd 5174, HMSO 1972

Supplementary material

Material, e.g. in reading or arithmetic, designed to support and reinforce what has already been learnt. The less bright child needs more practice at each successive level than does the brighter child, e.g. supplementary reading books if they cover the same vocabulary as the basic readers are a valuable means of reinforcing words learnt in the basic readers.

Supply teacher

A teacher who is employed either on a short notice basis or normal contract to meet special demands caused by illness and absence of regular staff, within an **LEA** area.

G. R. BARRELL, *Teachers and the Law*, Methuen 1966

Syllabification (Syllabication)

The division of words, especially orally, into their component syllables. At the oral level this helps a child to improve his powers of aural discrimination and thus his abilities in reading and spelling.

E. W. DOLCH, *The Teaching of Sounding*, Garrard Press n.d.

Syllabus

Brief statement of a course of study.

Synapse

A neurological term to describe the point at which nerve cell fibres interlace and offer potential connections.

N. L. MUNN, *Psychology: the fundamentals of human adjustment*, 5th edn, Harrap 1966

Syndrome

A complex of related symptoms occurring together which characterize a particular physical or psychological condition.

T

Tachistoscope
A piece of apparatus designed to present visual material for a very short period of time so that perception takes place at a single glance. The actual duration of the exposure can be regulated by a diaphragm type shutter. Used particularly for the improvement of reading and spelling and for learning experiments.
See also **Flash card**
A. L. GATES, *The Improvement of Reading*, 3rd edn, Collier-Macmillan 1947, ch. 11
A. J. HARRIS, *How to Increase Reading Ability*, Longmans 1963, ch. 8

Tape recording
The use of tape-recorder to promote educational activities, e.g. in the teaching of foreign languages, to produce authentic pronunciation and accent, or in the production of radio drama in the classroom.
R. D. BROWN, *Tape Recording and Hi-Fi*, Arco 1968
R. HIRSCH, *Audiovisual Aids in Language Teaching*, Georgetown University Press; N.Y. Kraus Reprint Group 1954
J. G. JONES, *Teaching with Tape*, Focal Press 1962

TAT
Thematic Apperception Test: a projective technique used by the clinical and educational psychologist which collects the testee's comments on, or interpretations of, a series of standardized pictures.
J. BELL, *Projective Techniques*, Longmans 1948
P. E. VERNON, *Personality Tests and Assessments*, new edn, Methuen 1953
See also **Projection test**

Taunton Commission. *See* **Schools Inquiry Commission**

Taxonomy
A formal scheme for classifying objects, such that each class of objects is given a name, and the members of each class have something in common, e.g. classification of books in a library or plants in a collection.
B. S. BLOOM, ed., *Taxonomy of Educational Objectives*, Longmans 1964

Teacher-pupil ratio. *See* **ratio**

Teacher's contract of service
Under the state system, the contract exists between the teacher and the **LEA** even where the appointment has been made by the **managers** or **governors**. Excepting 'occasional teachers', teachers' contracts are in the form of a written agreement, if the appointment is to a particular school. It will define the conditions of service and indicate whether employment is on a full-time or part-time basis. Teachers will be supplied with two copies of the agreement, one of which will be signed and returned to the LEA. Termination of the agreement by either side is by two months notice terminating on 31 December or 30 April, or three months terminating on 31 August.
G. R. BARRELL, *Teachers and the Law*, Methuen 1960
G. TAYLOR and J. B. SAUNDERS, *The New Law of Education*, 7th edn, Butterworth 1971

Teaching Machines
The apparatus which houses the text of a programme (*see* **programming**). The machine may take the form of a specially designed book (e.g. scrambled text) or it may be a simple box with apertures and levers to enable the learner to read the questions and make the responses. It may also be a highly complex piece of electronic apparatus involving computers and feedback mechanism.
M. GOLDSMITH, *Mechanisation in the classroom*, Souvenir Press 1963
R. GOODMAN, *Programmed Learning and Teaching Machines*, 3rd edn, English University Press 1967
A. A. LUMSDAINE and R. G. GLASER, *Teaching Machines and Programmed Learning* (Dept. of Audio-Visual Instruction, NEA)
B. SKINNER, 'Teaching machines', *Scientific American*, Nov. 1961
H. KAY, B. DODD, and M. SIME, *Teaching Machines and Programmed Instruction*, Penguin 1968

Team teaching
The technique being developed, particularly in the UK and USA, which recognizes that a number of different teachers, even within a specialist subject, may each have something special to contribute to the teaching and learning of a particular topic. The teaching is planned by the team. The plan may consist of 'lecturing', demonstration, or exposition by one or more teachers to a large group of children, followed by discussions or practical work in small groups. The technique can be effective and economical since it combines large scale instruction by modern

visual aids, with concern for children as individuals.

M. BAIR and R. G. WOODWARD, *Team Teaching in Action*, Houghton Mifflin 1964

D. P. CHURCH, H. I. GARRITY and G. JAMES, 'Team teaching'; *Forum*, **8**, no. 1, Autumn 1965

K. LOVELL, *Team Teaching*, Leeds University Press 1967

UNIVERSITY OF EXETER INSTITUTE OF EDUCATION, *An Experiment in Team-Teaching* 1970

Technical education

The universities of technology (formerly colleges of advanced technology) form the apex of a structure of **polytechnics**, regional, area and local Colleges. Regional technical colleges offer courses to degree, HNC and HND levels, and advanced awards of professional associations in science and technology. Though they have many full-time students, most are on part-time or **sandwich** courses. Area colleges offer some HNC together with ONC and other intermediate courses including commerce, languages and general studies. Local or district colleges (now sometimes 'of further education') prepare students for City and Guilds, ONC 'O' level of GCE examinations, and accept day release students. Some have incorporated **sixth form colleges**; the classification is flexible. Few technical schools remain at the secondary level; technical education thus forms a major part of Further and Higher Education provision. The Universities of Technology are self-governing, but the others are administered by the **LEA** and supported financially by the central government.

Crowther Report, *15 to 18*, 1959

H. C. DENT, *The Educational System of England and Wales*, University of London Press 1961

MINISTRY OF EDUCATION CIRCULAR 305/56

Robbins Report, *Higher Education*, 1963

E. VENABLES, *The Young Worker at College*, Faber 1967

Television (educational)

Television is playing an increasing part in the educational processes whether incidentally at home or through educational broadcasts directed at schools. It is having an impact both on what children learn and on educational method in the schools. While the effects on levels of children's literacy are not certain it may be worth noting that many less able children are having increasing access to literature and drama through the spoken word and the visual image.

Television for schools was set up, after pilot experiments by the BBC and by ITV networks in 1957. It has grown immensely in size and importance. For information teachers should write to the Education Officer of the BBC or ITV in their own region.

Closed circuit television (CCTV) is being increasingly set up and used by schools, colleges and universities. In some instances LEAs are feeding CCTVprogrammes to their schools via landlines.

H. T. HIMMELWEIT, A. N. OPPENHEIM and P. VINCE, *Television and the Child*, Oxford University Press 1958

D. UNWIN, ed., *Media and Methods*, McGraw-Hill 1964

Temperament

The affective or emotional aspect of personality, with particular reference to the mood-states of the individual.

H. H. EYSENCK, *The Scientific Study of Personality*, Routledge 1952

P. E. VERNON, *Personality Tests and Assessments*, new edn, Methuen 1953

Temper trantrum

A violent outburst of anger, usually in a young child, triggered off when the child is thwarted, especially in social situations. Temper tantrums may be observed along with other traits like **enuresis**, thumbsucking etc., in many older children who are emotionally disturbed or maladjusted.

W. M. BURBURY, E. M. BALINT and B. J. YAPP, *Introduction to Child Guidance*, Macmillan 1945

M. F. CLEUGH, *Psychology in the Service of the School*, new edn, Methuen 1951

C. W. VALENTINE, *The Normal Child and some of his Abnormalities*, Penguin 1956

Tension

A psychological state of expectancy usually accompanied by corresponding biological factors, e.g. heightened reflexes, pronounced heart-beats.

Tenure, Security of

A teacher's security of tenure is qualified by the terms set out in the rules of management or articles of government.

A teacher has the right to be present at any meeting of **managers**, **governors** or **LEA** at which his suspension or dismissal is being considered and he has the right to be accompanied by a friend. He must be given seven days' notice of such a meeting. Dismissal may be challenged only on the grounds of *ultra vires* or bad faith.

G. R. BARRELL, *Teachers and the Law*, Methuen 1966

F. TAYLOR and J. B. SAUNDERS, *The New Law of Education*, 7th edn, Butterworth 1971

Terman, Lewis M. (1877–1956)

US Psychologist, Professor of Psychology at Stanford University. Author of Stanford Revision of Binet Scale (1916). Introduced the term 'Intelligence Quotient' (**IQ**). He was largely responsible for first group intelligence tests, Army Alpha and Beta (1917). His great research work from 1921 for 35 years until his death was concerned with early identification of and suitable educational provision for gifted children. His many publications include: *Genetic Studies of Genius* (1926); Stanford University Press.

Terman collaborated with Maude Merrill, who later became his wife, in much of his work; in particular, the revisions of the Binet-Simon intelligence scale.

See also **Mentally gifted; Stanford-Binet**

Tests

Techniques and/or published material whose aim is to measure or assess: the purpose of the test may be classification, diagnosis, comparison with established norms, checking of knowledge and/or understanding.

R. D. SAVAGE, *Psychometric Assessment of the Individual Child*, Penguin (Science of Behaviour ser.) 1968

F. J. SCHONELL, *Diagnostic and Attainment Testing*, Oliver & Boyd 1949

P. E. VERNON, *Measurement of Abilities*, 2nd edn, University of London Press 1956

P. E. VERNON, *Personality Tests and Assessments*, new edn, Methuen 1953

P. E. VERNON, *Intelligence and Attainment Tests*, University of London Press 1960

T groups

Training groups brought together especially in business and management specifically for the purpose of studying the participants' own behaviour. The technique stems from the work of Freud and K. Lewin, and is intended to promote insight into social relationships by exposing individuals to 'feedback', i.e. processes by which the effects of their behaviour on others is made clear to themselves.

C. ARGYRIS, *Interpersonal Competence and Organisational Effectiveness*, Tavistock 1962

W. R. BION, *Experiences in Groups*, Tavistock 1968

L. P. BRADFORD, *et al*, *'T' Group Theory and Laboratory Method*, Wiley 1964

Thematic Apperception Test. *See* TAT

Therapy

The special treatment or practices designed to cure or alleviate a disorder of the body, mind or personality.

See also **Occupational therapy**; **Psychotherapy**

Thomson, Sir Godfrey H. (1881–1955)

Professor of Education, Newcastle, 1920, Professor of Education, Edinburgh University and Director of Moray House Training Centre, 1925. Produced first British group intelligence tests for use in **Special Place Examination** in Northumberland in 1921. At Moray House established a testing unit which became the largest producer of tests in Europe. Profits from tests were used for further production and research. Originally a scientist and mathematician, he aimed to make research in Education more rigorous through the application of statistical techniques. His main contributions to Education and Psychology have been on the mathematical side. His works include: *A Modern Philosophy of Education* (Allen & Unwin 1929), and *Factorial Analysis of Human Ability* (University of London Press 1939).

Thorndike, Edward Lee (1874–1949)

American psychologist whose main interest lay in the field of learning. In World War I he was concerned with the classification of personnel in the US Army and the methods he used set the pattern for personnel selection and vocational guidance in the years which followed. Publications include: *Educational Psychology* (1903); *Mental and Social Measurement* (1904); *Psychology of Learning* (1914); and *Fundamentals of Learning* (AMS Pr. New York Teachers College, 1932); *The Psychology of Wants, Interests and Attitudes* (Appleton-Century, 1935); *Thorndike Junior Dictionary/Senior Dictionary* (Ryerson Press, 1935, 1941).

Three Rs

*R*eading, (*W*)*r*iting and (*A*)*r*ithmetic, i.e. The 'basic subjects'.

M. C. AUSTIN and C. MORRISON, *The First R*, Collier-Macmillan 1963

C. M. FLEMING, *Research and the Basic Curriculum*, 2nd edn, Methuen 1946

J. C. GAGG, *Common Sense in the Primary School*, Evans 1951

Plowden Report, *Children and their Primary Schools* 1967

Tibble, John William (1901–72)
Professor of Education, University of Leicester from 1946; Director of University of Leicester School of Education. Formerly editor of *Education for Teaching*. Editor of Students' Library of Education (Routledge & Kegan Paul). His many publications include: *Physical Education and the Educative Process* (Evans, 1952); *John Clare* (Heinemann 1956); and *The Study of Education* (Routledge, 1966).

Tillich bricks
Rods in vogue early in this century designed to help children in the introductory stages of number. May be regarded as leading to the modern spate of mathematical structural apparatus in the form of rods.

M. PUNNETT, *The Groundwork of Arithmetic*, Longmans n.d.

Tinbergen, N.
Zoologist, Reader in Animal Behaviour in the University of Oxford. Working on lines developed by Lorenz, he has made significant advances in the study of social behaviour amongst animals; his work is considered by many to be relevant to learning theory in education. Publications include:
Social Behaviour in Animals, 2nd edn, Methuen 1965

B. FOSS, *Determinants of Infant Behaviour*, 4 vols, Methuen 1961–69

Tolman, Edward Chase (1886–1959)
American psychologist; Professor of Psychology, University of California, 1918–54. Tolman's approach to psychology was eclectic, but he became identified with a form of behaviouristic psychology known as purposive or molar **behaviourism**. This theory rejected the conditioned reflex as the unit of behaviour and substituted the ideal of goal-directed action, guided by cognitive processes. His major work, published in 1932, was *Purposive Behaviour in Animals and Men* (Appleton-Century 1932).

Training college, college of education
Colleges for the education and training of teachers are associated with universities through area training organisations. There are General, Froebel, Domestic Science, Physical Education, Art and Technical Training Colleges, offering a three-year course, in main subjects, curriculum subjects and Education. About one-third are **grant-aided** (Church) colleges, the rest are **LEA** controlled. Most are residential but there are several day colleges.

ATCDE, *Handbook on Training*, Methuen Annual

McNair Report, *Teachers and Youth Leaders*, 1944

James Report, *Teacher Education and Training* 1972

F. H. PEDLEY, *A Parent's Guide to Examinations*, Pergamon 1964

Some colleges offer two-year shortened courses for 'mature' students, and one-year post-graduate courses. An increasing number offer four-year courses leading to the degree of Bachelor of Education.

Transfer of training
The influence, negative or positive, that the possession of one habit, skill, idea or ideal may have on the acquisition or performance of another allied characteristic: e.g. the influence of one's training in methodical and systematic consideration and arrangement of data in mathematics on one's methods of organizing data in physics, or geography. The amount of transfer from one subject or skill to another depends upon how far there is a similarity of content, technique or principle.

E. A. PEEL, *The Psychological Basis of Education*, Oliver & Boyd 1956

R. E. RIPPLE, *Readings in Learning and Human Abilities*, Harper & Row 1964

Translation class
A class thought of as a bridge between one stage of education and the next, e.g. a class for seven-year-olds at the bottom of the junior school who have recently completed the first part of their education in an infant school.

E. MELLOR, *Education Through Experience in Infant School Years*, Blackwell 1950

Transport, School
The local authority must by law provide transport for children to reach school if it is

three miles or more (in case of children under eight, two miles or more), from home. Fares are paid or transport is hired by the **LEA**.

H. C. DENT, *Educational System of England and Wales*, rev. edn., University of London Press 1969

G. TAYLOR and J. B. SAUNDERS, *The New Law of Education*, 7th edn, Butterworth 1971

't' Ratio

Statistically similar to the **critical ratio**, the value of 't' indicating at what level of probability (e.g. 5 or 1 per cent) the difference between two sample means is **significant**.

H. E. GARRETT, *Statistics in Psychology and Education*, 6th edn, Longmans 1966

P. E. VERNON, *Measurement of Abilities*, 2nd edn, University of London Press 1956

Trauma

Any injury or shock, physical, mental, or emotional, resulting in a more or less persistent mental or emotional disturbance.

Treasure chest

A simple **projection test** for getting to know young children quickly. Their attention is drawn to a 'treasure chest' which they have longed to explore and which, they are told, they can now in imagination open and examine. They describe the contents of the chest thus revealing to the teacher many of their interests and feelings. This can help the teacher to establish close personal relations with the child quickly. The technique is capable of interpretation in depth in the hands of a psychologist.

J. E. BELL, *Projective Techniques*, Longmans 1948

J. C. RAVEN, *Controlled Projection for Children*, 2nd edn, H. K. Lewis 1957

Treasure Chest for Teachers

A publication of the Schoolmaster Publishing Company which lists the sources teachers can use to obtain teaching materials cheaply or free.

Address: Hamilton House, Hasting Street, London, WC1

Tripartite system

The division of **secondary education** into **Grammar**, **Technical** and **Modern** schools, with a selective examination. The system took

shape between the **Hadow** Report (1926) and the 1944 Act. It is now developing into a multipartite system with the introduction of **comprehensive** and other new forms of secondary organization.

S. J. CURTIS, *History of Education in Great Britain*, 7th edn, University Tutorial Press 1967, chs 10 and 11

F. M. EARLE, *Reconstruction in the Secondary School*, University of London Press 1944

Norwood Report, *Curricula and Examinations in Secondary Schools*, 1943

Spens Report, *Secondary Education*, 1938

Trivium and quadrivium

The branches of the medieval curriculum of Western Europe, i.e. grammar, logic, and rhetoric; arithmetic, geometry, astronomy and music. Often known as the Seven Liberal Arts.

Truancy

Deliberate absence from compulsory school attendance without medical or other adequate cause. The **LEA** has a duty to enforce regular attendance and may institute proceedings against parents. The child may in addition be brought before a juvenile court for truancy, and the court may make an order committing the child to an **approved school**. It may issue a **Fit person order** or make other arrangements for supervision, to ensure attendance.

Persistent truancy is often symptomatic of more serious problems involving the child and may be associated with maladjustment (as **school phobia**) or delinquency.

G. LUMMIS, 'School attendance', *British Journal of Educational Psychology*, **12**, 1946, part 1.

M. J. TYERMAN, *Truancy*, University of London Press 1968

True-false test

A type of test in which the testee is required to indicate whether each of a number of statements is true or false.

P. E. VERNON, *Measurement of Abilities*, 2nd edn, University of London Press 1940, pp. 234–6

Tutor

Generally, a teacher, though usually restricted to college or university staffs. More particularly the lecturer/professor in his capacity of teacher to an individual or small group.

Tutor text
A *teaching machine* in the form of a book: for example, N. A. Crowder and G. C. Martin's *Adventure in Algebra* (English Universities Press 1962) and
J. R. AMOS, F. L. BROWN and O. G. MINK, *Statistical Concepts: a basic program*, Harper & Row 1965

Twins
Two children of the same mother, either **dizygotic** (two-egg) or **monozygotic** (one-egg), conceived and born together

See also **Fraternal twins; Identical twins**
J. SHIELDS, *Monozygotic Twins*, Oxford University Press 1962

Two-factor theory of intelligence
The theory first enunciated by **Spearman** early in this century that mental abilities give intercorrelations which can be accounted for by a general factor, 'g', corresponding to what we generally mean by general intelligence, and various specific factors (S_1, S_2, etc.)
C. E. SPEARMAN, *The Abilities of Man*, Macmillan 1967

U

UCCA
Universities Central Council on Admissions. A clearing house to help universities to facilitate the application and admission of student candidates to appropriate universities and faculties. UCCA publishes reports on its activities, and an annual handbook to help schools and intending students.
Address: 29–30 Tavistock Square, London WC1

UEI
Union of Educational Institutions. An examining body operating mainly in the Midlands. The academic standard of examinations is rather lower than that of GCE O level.
Address: Norfolk House, Smallbook Ringway, Birmingham, 5.

UGC
University Grants Committee. A group of people, knowledgeable in matters relating to universities, and independent of the Government, who advise on Government grants to the universities and on their development plans. The grants are made on a five-year basis, or quinquennium. The Committee was first set up in 1919.

UKRA
United Kingdom Reading Association: a body formed in 1964 as an affiliate of the International Reading Association, to encourage the study of reading problems at all levels; to assist in teacher-training; to publish research findings and to sponsor Conferences.
Address: 2 Taviton Street, London, WC1

ULCI
Union of Lancashire and Cheshire Institutes. A regional examining body for school and commercial subjects at a level somewhat lower than GCE O level.
Address: Africa House, 54 Whitworth Street, Manchester, 1

Unconscious
In psychoanalytic theory, a postulated region of the mind which is inaccessible to a person himself but which is more or less accessible to the psychoanalyst. It is supposed to be that area of the mind in which are lodged repressed ideas and memories of past experiences together with, and often in conflict with, the basic human drives such as sex, aggression, etc.

J. A. C. BROWN, *Freud and the Post-Freudians*, Penguin (Pelican) 1961; Cassell 1963
A. CRICHTON-MILLER, *Psychoanalysis and its derivatives*, 2nd edn, Oxford University Press (Home University Library) 1945
E. JONES, *Life and Work of Sigmund Freud*, Penguin 1967
D. STAFFORD-CLARKE, *What Freud Really Said*, Macdonald 1965; Penguin 1967

Under-achievement
1. Generally the negative discrepancy between a child's school achievements and those of his contemporaries.
2. The gap between his achievements and his potential (as determined by intelligence tests).
S. R. GRIFFITHS and L. W. DOWNES, *Educational Statistics for Beginners*, Methuen 1969
F. E. SCHONELL, *Backwardness in the Basic Subjects*, Oliver & Boyd 1942

Underfunctioning
A child in the school situation is considered to be underfunctioning when the level of his attainments (usually with reference to the basic subjects, i.e. reading, writing, mathematics) seems to be below what is considered to be his potential, e.g. Intelligence Quotient 130; Reading Quotient 100. The term is applicable equally to mentally bright and to mentally dull children.
See also **Backwardness; Retardation**
F. J. SCHONELL, *Backwardness in the Basic Subjects*, Oliver & Boyd 1948
S. R. GRIFFITHS and L. W. DOWNES, *Educational Statistics for Beginners*, Methuen 1969

Underwood Report. *See* Appendix III

UNESCO
United Nations Educational, Scientific and Cultural Organisation, created under the Charter of the United Nations as a specialized agency to promote 'international cultural and educational cooperation'. Its constitution provides that it will consist of a General Conference composed of representatives of member states; an executive board of eighteen members; and a secretariat composed of a director-general and staff.
Unesco's programme is being carried out in six main areas of activity: education; social sciences; natural science; cultural activities; mass communications, and technical assistance.

Uniform (school)
The dress usually consisting of a blazer, hat, tie, and prescribed colour of dress, skirt or trousers required by many secondary and an increasing number of primary schools. The badge or device of the school is usually incorporated. The higher the social status of the school, in England, the more rigid is likely to be the requirement for uniform.

Union of Educational Institutions. *See* UEI

Union of Lancashire and Cheshire Institutes. *See* ULCI

United Kingdom Reading Association. *See* UKRA

United Nations Educational Scientific and Cultural Organisation. *See* UNESCO

Universities Central Council on Admissions. *See* UCCA

University Grants Committee. *See* UGC

University college
During the period of the expansion of civic universities new institutions of university rank which had not the power of granting their own degrees were set up. Usually the degrees of London University were granted. Except in the case of the University of Wales, which is federal, the former university colleges now have full charters as autonomous institutions.
W. H. C. ARMYTAGE, *Civic Universities*, Benn 1955
S. J. CURTIS and M. E. A. BOULTWOOD, *An Introductory History of English Education since 1800*, 4th edn, University Tutorial Press 1966

University Entrance
There is a general academic requirement, usually based on performance in the O and A levels of the GCE, for university entrance, which is stated in the respective Prospectuses. Applications are made through the Office of the Central Council on Admissions.
See also UCCA
ASSOCIATION OF COMMONWEALTH UNIVERSITIES, Committee of Vice-Chancellors, *A Compendium of University Entrance Requirements*, Annual
NATIONAL UNION OF TEACHERS, *University*

and College Entrance, Schoolmaster Publishing Co.
F. H. PEDLEY, *Parent's Guide to Examinations*, Pergamon 1964

University Extension Movement
At the instigation of James Stuart of Trinity College, the University of Cambridge set up in 1873 a syndicate to provide courses of lectures to be given by university teachers to local bodies. Oxford followed with a Delegacy in 1878. Lectures were given to mechanics' institutes, cooperative societies, etc.
New universities followed in the tradition, and were in turn stimulated by extention lectures arranged by the older universities. Higher learning throughout the country was greatly stimulated and advanced by this movement in the period before the 1944 Act.
R. PEERS, *Adult Education in English Education*, 2nd edn, Routledge & Kegan Paul 1959
R. PEERS, *Fact and Possibility in English Education*, Routledge & Kegan Paul 1963

University training department. *See* **Education department**

Unstreaming
The process of grouping children into classes on the basis of chronological age instead of abilities.
J. W. B. DOUGLAS, *The School and the Home*, MacGibbon & Kee 1964; Panther 1969
Forum (magazine, 7)
Plowden Report, *Children and their Primary Schools*, 1967, ch. 20

Upper-case letters
Capital letters, as opposed to small or **lower-case** letters. Words spelt in upper-case letters are not as readily recognised as those composed of lower-case letters: it will have been noted that words on signposts on new motorways are in lower-case letters. Parents purchasing plastic letters for their children should bear this in mind.

Urban geography
The systematic study from the geographical point of view of built-up areas, cities, city regions, conurbations. The discipline overlaps with kindred social studies, such as public administration, statistics, sociology and town planning. It is of interest to educationists in offering a systematic analysis of conditions influencing the educability of urban children.

AMA, *The Teaching of Geography*, 4th edn, 1958

Urban society
In contrast with primitive societies, advanced industrial societies have been increasingly centred on cities, particularly in western Europe. The education of children living in large cities presents special problems, noted by the **Newsom** and **Plowden Reports**. The study of social conditions in cities and conurbations has made an increasing contribution to the sociology of education and kindred disciplines.

J. F. EGGLESTON, *The Social Context of the School*, Routledge & Kegan Paul 1967

J. B. MAYS, *Education and the Urban Child*, Liverpool University Press 1962

Usage
The customary way in which a language – vocabulary, syntax, idiom, etc.—is used, i.e. 'common usage'. More particularly the reference is to the common usage as established and illustrated by speakers and writers of repute.

H. W. FOWLER, *Dictionary of Modern English Usage*, rev. Sir E. Gowers, Oxford University Press 1965

E. GOWERS, *The Complete Plain Words*, new edn, HMSO 1957; Penguin (Pelican)

S. POTTER, *Our Language*, Penguin (Pelican) 1950

Utilitarian education
The Utilitarians were a group of the Philosophical Radicals led by J. Bentham and J. S. Mill in the first half of the nineteenth century. They entered the controversy about the value of the classics, which stemmed from R. L. Edgeworth's *Practical Education*, and they used the Press and Parliament to demand reforms. **H. Spencer**, who called himself a 'rational utilitarian', was perhaps their most influential writer in the strictly education field, but it was **T. H. Huxley** who finally was able to use his membership of various commissions and the London School Board to secure curriculum reform. The opposing views were voiced by **J. H. Newman** and **Matthew Arnold**.

E. HALEVY, *Growth of Philosophical Radicalism* 2nd edn, Faber 1954

D. M. TURNER, *History of Science Teaching in England*, Chapman & Hall 1927

Utopianism
1. The tendency amongst speculative writers to construct ideal fictitious societies to embody and illustrate their preferred values (cf. Moore's *Utopia*).

2. Any speculative plan which seems over-idealised or detached from reality.

K. MANNHEIM, *Ideology and Utopia*, trans. Wirth and Shils, Routledge & Kegan Paul 1954

E. SKINNER, *Walden Two*, Collier-Macmillan 1962

V

Valentine, C. W. (1879–1967)
British educational psychologist. Professor
of Education, University of Birmingham
1919–46. Editor of the *British Journal of
Educational Psychology*, 1931–55.
Publications include: *The Psychology of
Early Childhood* (Methuen, 1942); *Psychology and Mental Health* (Methuen, 1948);
Psychology: and its Bearing on Education
(1951; 2nd edn, Methuen 1960); *The Normal
Child and Some of His Abnormalities*
(Penguin, Pelican 1956).

Validity (test)
The extent to which a test or measuring
device measures what it purports to measure,
e.g. a weighing machine can normally claim
complete validity. A test of attainment can
be seen to have a high measure of validity,
but the extent to which eleven-plus tests
measure fitness for one form or another of
secondary education can be questioned
statistically as well as educationally. Tests
can be validated statistically by correlating
the scores on the test with some criterion
measure, e.g. scores deriving from other
tests in the same field, teacher's ratings, etc.
H. E. GARRETT, *Statistics in Psychology and
Education*, 6th edn, Longmans 1966
P. E. VERNON, *Measurement of Abilities*, 2nd
edn, University of London Press 1956

Value judgment
To make a *value* judgment is to assess an
issue or to argue on the basis of precon-
ceived and personally decided ideas, rather
than on empirically tested facts.
See also **Values**
J. WILSON, *Thinking with Concepts*, Cambridge University Press 1963

Values
Principles which in order of worthiness give
direction to human thought and action; they
are cultural standards which meet with wide
agreement, and enable people or groups to
compare and judge their experiences and
objectives. By reference to value systems an
order of priorities for action, and a criterion
of relevance can be set up, so that human
activity can be organized and understood,
analysed and planned. The value systems will,
of course, vary from individual to individual
and from culture to culture.
J. HOSPERS, *An Introduction to Philosophical
Analysis*, 2nd edn, Routledge & Kegan Paul
1967

G. E. MOORE, *Ethics*, Oxford University Press
(Home University Library) 1912

Vernon, M. D. (b. 1901)
Professor of Psychology in the University
of Reading 1956–67. Particularly interested
in the fields of perception and reading. Sister
of **P. E. Vernon**.
Publications include: *Backwardness in
Reading* (Cambridge University Press, 1957);
and *The Psychology of Perception* (University
of London Press 1965; Penguin 1970).

Vernon, P. E. (b. 1905)
Professor of Educational Psychology at
University of Calgary, Canada; formerly at
the Institute of Education, University of
London and at Psychology Department,
Glasgow University. Brother of **M. D. Ver-
non**.
Publications include: *The Measurement of
Abilities*, 2nd edn (University of London
Press, 1956); *The Structure of Human
Abilities* 2nd edn (Methuen, 1950); *Person-
ality Tests and Assessments*, new edn
(Methuen, 1953); *Intelligence and Attainment
Tests* (University of London Press, 1960);
Personality Assessment (Methuen 1964)

Vineland Social Maturity Scale
An inventory devised by E. A. Doll for
assessing what a child can do in real life
situations, the result being given in terms of
a social age level. This scale has been adapted
for use in Britain by M. Kellmer Pringle.
E. A. DOLL, *Vineland Social Maturity Scale:
Manual of Directions*, Minneapolis, Educational Test Bureau, 1936
E. A. LUNZER, *The Manchester Scales of
Social Adaptation*, NFER 1970

Visiting teacher. *See* **Peripatetic teacher**

Visual aid
Any method of helping or stimulating learning and understanding whose appeal is to
the sense of sight: e.g. film, picture, map,
graph, and blackboard.
National Committee for Audio-Visual Aids
in Education: 33 Queen Anne Street,
London, W1
Visual Education Year Book. Also monthly
magazine.

Vocabulary
Words and verbal expressions that can be
recognized or recalled, in the oral and aural

sense or in writing or print. Thus there is a basic fourfold way of considering vocabulary which, in the main, coincides with the sequence of the child's linguistic development: (a) listening vocabulary, (b) spoken vocabulary, (c) reading vocabulary, (d) written vocabulary.

A. F. WATTS, *Language and Mental Development of Children*, Harrap 1960

Vocabulary test

Usually a test of the extent of a person's understanding vocabulary with a view, inferentially, to establishing that person's intelligence, e.g. Crichton Vocabulary Test; Mill Hill Vocabulary Test; the vocabulary tests included in the Terman-Merrill (**Stanford-Binet**) scale or the Wechsler Intelligence Scale for children (**WISC**)

P. E. VERNON, *Intelligence and Attainment Tests*, University of London Press 1960

Vocational guidance

Expert guidance given to help individuals to select areas of work for which their talents, training and interests will suit them best.

Careers Guide, HMSO, annual

M. GRAINGER, ed., *Careers and Vocational Training*, 16th edn, Arlington Books 1969

A. MACRAE, *Talents and Temperaments*, Cambridge University Press

The Careers Master and *The Careers Mistress*, Assistant Masters' Association.

Voluntary controlled school

Schools in which two-thirds of the Managers are appointed by the **LEA** (one-third being appointed by the voluntary body). The **Agreed Syllabus** is followed in controlled schools, but parents have the right to ask that their children shall take not more than two periods per week of denominational instruction (given by teachers specially appointed for the purpose).

G. R. BARRELL, *Teachers and the Law*, Methuen 1966

G. TAYLOR and J. B. SAUNDERS, *The New Law of Education*, 7th edn, Butterworth 1971

Voluntary schools

Schools run by voluntary bodies (almost invariably the Churches are implied) who provide part or all of the cost of building, but who receive government aid and are liable to inspection. A number of **colleges of education** and **approved schools** are similarly administrated.

See also **Aided School**

VSO

Voluntary Service Overseas. The initials are also used to described the people who give this service, which is usually for one or two years in an under-developed country.

Address: 18 Northumberland Avenue, London, WC2

W

WAIS
Wechsler Adult Intelligence Scales: the most effective individual intelligence tests for use with adults. Like the **WISC** it involves verbal and performance items and provides separate scores for the verbal and performance scales, in addition to the full-scale **IQ**.
D. WECHSLER, *Measurement of Adult Intelligence*, 4th edn, Williams & Williams 1958

Washburne, Carleton W.
American educationist who was superintendent of schools in Winnetka, Illinois, when the procedures characterized as the **Winnetka Plan** were developed in the early 1920s. Publications include: *A Living Philosophy of Education* (Day 1940).

Wastage
Term used to denote the loss of trained teachers from the profession during their early years of employment. It refers in particular to the loss of young women teachers due to marriage and childbearing. The average teaching 'life' of young recently trained women teachers is between three and four years but something like 6000 are returning annually after bringing up their families.
Kelsall Report, MINISTRY OF EDUCATION, *Women and Teaching*, 1963
NATIONAL ADVISORY COUNCIL FOR THE TRAINING AND SUPPLY OF TEACHERS, *Demand for and Supply of Teachers 1963–86*; Ninth Report *of NACTST*, HMSO 1965

Watson, John Broadus (b. 1878)
American psychologist, the leader of the behaviourist school of psychology, was Professor of Experimental and Comparative Psychology and director of the psychology laboratory at Johns Hopkins University. He carried out a large number of experiments with children. His experiment on the acquisition of emotions by conditioning with the child 'Albert B' is quoted as a classic, though later experimenters have challenged his findings. His books include: *Psychology from the Standpoint of the Behaviourist* (1959) and *Behaviourism* (1925).
B. B. WOLMAN, *Contemporary Theories and Systems in Psychology*, Harper & Row 1960

WEA
Workers Educational Association. The **University Extension movement** did not successfully reach artisans and less skilled workers. Albert Mansbridge, a Cooperative Wholesale Society clerk, inspired a new movement to bring these in. As a result of articles in the *University Extension Journal* in 1903 a new body was created. It was helped by the financial provisions offered to adult education by the Education Act of 1902. Branches were linked together in districts, and a tutorial class system replaced lectures. The movement grew rapidly, as did **LEA** grants in support. Many WEA students became prominent in Trade Union and political life.
National Address: Temple House, 27 Portman Square, London, W1
R. PEERS, *Fact and Possibility in English Education*, Routledge & Kegan Paul 1963

Weaver Report
Report of the Study Group on the Government of Colleges of Education, published by the **Department of Education and Science** (HMSO 1968). The main recommendations were: (*a*) that the governing bodies of colleges should be reconstituted to include representation of **LEAs**, universities, college staff, and the teaching profession; (*b*) that academic boards should be established in the colleges; (*c*) that the instrument and articles of government should be drawn in accordance with national legislation. The Report was implemented in Education (No. 2) Act in 1968. Its major intention was to increase the independence of colleges, and to secure more broadly based governing bodies on which staff were more fully represented.

Wechsler Adult Intelligence Scales. *See* **WAIS**

Wechsler Intelligence Scale for Children. *See* **WISC**

Weighting
Assigning statistical weight to indicate the relative importance of an item in a test, or of a single test in a battery of tests, when a composite score is required, e.g. in an examination the candidate might be told that some question carries more marks than others in the same test; or in the eleven-plus selection process, the LEA might place more stress on **IQs** by doubling whatever mark the candidate received in the intelligence tests.
P. E. VERNON, *The Measurement of Abilities*, 2nd edn, University of London Press 1956

Welfare Officer
1. School: an official of the **LEA** formerly known as the school attendance officer, whose responsibility is to visit schools and homes on matters arising from the non-attendance of pupils at school.
Plowden Report, *Children and their Primary Schools*, 1967, vol. ii, Appendix 8
2. Welfare Department: an official of the Welfare Department of a local authority responsible ultimately to the medical officer of health, and concerned mainly with work arising from the care of the elderly, and with advising and assisting destitute or evicted families especially in the matter of housing.
3. National Assistance Board: Officer concerned with advice and assistance to destitute persons, discharged prisoners, and similar persons in need.
4. Home Office: officer of the Home Office until 1965 concerned with **aftercare** of persons licensed from Approved Schools and Borstals: the functions of this Officer have since been taken over by the **Child Care Officers** or **Probation** Officers.

Welfare services
These consist mainly of:
Financial benefits: unemployment, sickness, retirement, death, maternity, injuries.
Health benefits: medical and hospital care, home nursing, home help. Measures to control nuisances, and to deal with offences against the Food and Drug Acts. Provision of ante-natal clinics and infant-welfare foods.
Legal benefits: Legal aid, implementation of the Rent Acts, legislation to ensure adequate conditions of work.
General benefits: Education, Municipal Housing, Youth Services and Children's Welfare.
P. ARCHER, *Social Welfare and the Citizen*, Pelican 1957

Where? Information on Education
The quarterly publication of the Advisory Centre for Education (ACE). Subscribers are entitled to copies of WHERE? and may for a small charge, put questions to the Advisory Centre which are answered confidentially.
Address: Advisory Centre for Education (ACE) Ltd, 57 Russell Street, Cambridge.

White Paper
Term used to describe the written version of any important piece of government policy to be presented to Parliament. White papers are published by HMSO and are available to the public. An example is given below.

White Paper, *Education: a Framework for Expansion,* Cmnd 5174 1972
This document visualizes the expansion of the education service in the next ten years and makes special reference to:
(a) schools: nursery, primary, secondary and special
(b) the in-service training of teachers
(c) the institution of a three year course leading to B.Ed. and qualified teacher status
(d) the introduction of two year courses leading to a Diploma in Higher Education
(e) an appreciable expansion in the Polytechnics
(f) an expansion, but smaller growth rate than had been anticipated, in student and post-graduate numbers in the Universities
(g) the establishment of new regional committees to coordinate the education and training of teachers.

Whitehead, Alfred North (1861–1947)
British philosopher and mathematician, from 1924 Professor of Philosophy at Harvard University. He defined education as 'the acquisition of the art of the utilisation of knowledge', and opposed the formalistic transmission of 'inert ideas'. He advocated overlapping cycles in learning: romance, precision, generalization. He wrote strongly in favour of technical education. Publications include: *Aims of Education* (Benn, 1929); *Adventure of Ideas* (Cambridge University Press, 1933).

'Whole' method of learning
Learning (e.g. a poem) by memorizing as much as possible of the poem in its entirety rather than section by section or stanza by stanza.
N. L. MUNN, *Psychology: the fundamentals of human adjustment*, 5th edn, Harrap 1966
A. PINSENT, *The Principles of Teaching Method*, 3rd edn, Harrap 1969

Wilderspin, Samuel (1792–1866)
Samuel Wilderspin worked out a system of infant education which influenced the curriculum and buildings of **elementary** schools in the middle of the nineteenth century, mistakenly introducing children too early to

formal instruction. The 'gallery' is characteristic of this type of school.

Wing college

A college designated by the then Minister of Education to specialize in some branch of work and study (e.g. PE or Science) and thus to provide a special supplementary third-year course for suitable candidates. The term is now obsolescent.

ATCDE, *Handbook on Training for Teaching*, Methuen, annual

MINISTRY OF EDUCATION, *Annual Report*, 1960, HMSO

Winnetka Plan

A scheme drawn up by **Carleton W. Washburne** in 1919 for organizing the more basic parts of the school curriculum on an individual basis and gearing the work to suit individual needs and abilities. It was introduced into the junior and senior high schools of Winnetka, Illinois, and is still used in those schools. The other parts of the curriculum involving social and creative activities, are organized on group or class basis.

C. WASHBURNE, *A Living Philosophy of Education*, Day 1940

WISC

Wechsler Intelligence Scale for Children. An individual test of intelligence providing verbal, performance and full-scale **IQs** for ages from 5 to 15·11. It was standardized in America. The manual and performance material with standard modifications for use in Britain can be obtained from the National Foundation of Educational Research **(NFER)**.

P. E. VERNON, *Intelligence and Attainment Tests*, University of London Press 1960

Withdrawal

A passive **defence mechanism** taking the form of response to frustration by avoiding the situation or object causing it. For example, satisfaction is obtained in fantasy by daydreaming, or by substitutes such as drugs or alcohol. The withdrawn person reduces his social interaction. In children, withdrawal in the school or social situation may be a symptom of more serious emotional disturbance. The danger is that the disturbance is frequently overlooked since the withdrawn child is not normally a source of disciplinary trouble.

J. R. STRANGE, *Abnormal Psychology*, McGraw-Hill 1965

Word-blindness (dyslexia)

A disability supposedly resulting from lesions in some part of the brain, which interferes with the ability to read. The organic disability is probably found very rarely but the phrase is used far too readily to rationalize other difficulties in learning to read.

MACDONALD CRITCHLEY, *Developmental Dyslexia*, Heinemann 1964

A. W. FRANKLIN, *Word-Blindness or Specific Developmental Dyslexia*, Pitman Medical Publishing Co 1962

M. D. VERNON, 'Specific dyslexia', *British Journal of Educational Psychology*, June 1962

Word recognition test

Usually a standardized test of a person's powers to read isolated words aloud. The words are graded in difficulty and the tests yield scores which can be converted into Reading Ages. Most widely used in UK are the tests compiled by **Burt, Vernon, Schonell**. Tests are individually administered. They correlate highly with tests of speed, fluency and comprehension in reading. **Neale's Reading Tests** combine these factors.

An experienced tester can gain much diagnostic information from the administration of a WR test.

R. D. SAVAGE, *Psychometric Assessment of the Individual Child*, Penguin 1968

P. E. VERNON, *Intelligence and Attainment Tests*, University of London Press 1960

Words in colour

An attempt to facilitate the early stages of reading by giving each of forty-eight sounds a colour, regardless of its particular spelling in any one word.

See also **Gattegno**

Work card

A card given to a pupil indicating some particular assignment of school work, e.g. in mathematics or history, or as part of a project.

A. W. ROWE, *The Education of the Average Child*, Harrap 1959

Workers' Educational Association. *See* WEA

Working class

A broad term used to describe the social group which is neither professional nor clerical. It is overwhelmingly the largest social group and is usually divided into the skilled, semiskilled, and unskilled subgroups.

A. M. CARR-SAUNDERS, *A Survey of Social*

Conditions in England and Wales, Oxford University Press 1958
R. HOGGART, *The Uses of Literacy*, Chatto & Windus 1957; Penguin (Pelican) 1969
S. ZWEIG, *The Worker in an Affluent Society*, Heinemann 1961

Working mothers
Mothers who have a part-time or full-time paid job in addition to looking after the home. Some social workers believe that there is a high correlation between the increase in the number of working mothers in recent decades and the increase in juvenile delinquency.
V. KLEIN, *Britain's Married Women Workers*, Routledge & Kegan Paul 1965
A. MYRDAL and V. KLEIN, *Women's Two Roles*, Routledge & Kegan Paul 1968
S. YUDKIN and A. HOLME, *Working Mothers and their Children*, M. Joseph 1963

World technique
A projective technique helping the skilled observer to distinguish between retarded or neurotic children on the one hand, and normal children on the other. The child is given 150 objects and is invited to construct a town, village, farm, zoo, etc., usually on a sand tray.
M. J. BELL, *Projective Techniques*, Longmans 1948
M. LOWENFELD, 'The nature and use of the Lowenfeld World Technique in work with children and adults', *Journal of Psychology*, **30**, 1950

World Yearbook of Education
The *Yearbook of Education* was founded in 1953 by Sir Robert Evans and is published annually by Evans Bros, London. Editorial responsibility is shared by London University and Columbia University, New York. Reports from many countries on a common topic or theme are combined with a series of theoretical and comparative articles to form an authoritative source book of comparative education. From 1965 the publication has been called the *World Yearbook of Education*.

Y

Young person
A person over compulsory school age who has not yet attained the age of eighteen years.

Youth Centre
An establishment (e.g. housed in a school or a separate building) usually run by e.g. an **LEA** or a church, in which young people can congregate for social and for educational purposes. Membership may be restricted, for example to young people attached to a particular church or chapel, or may be open. There will be a **youth leader** who may or may not have received special training and who may be working part-time or full-time.
Albermarle Report, *The Youth Service in England and Wales*, 1960
MINISTRY OF EDUCATION WORKING PARTY (Chairman, G. S. Bessey), *The Training of Part-time Youth Leaders*, HMSO 1962
McNair Report, *The Supply, Recruitment and Training of Teachers and Youth Leaders*, 1944

Youth Employment Service
A service designed to provide guidance to school leavers, to find openings for them. It is administered locally by the **LEA** or by local officers of the Department of Employment and Productivity. Centrally this work is organized by a Central Youth Employment Executive responsible to the Department of Employment and Productivity and which includes representatives of the Department of Education and Science and of the Scottish Education Department.

Youth leader
A person who has undertaken to provide and foster leadership in a **Youth Centre**. He or she may be the representative of a voluntary body, e.g. a church or chapel, or he may be in the employ of an **LEA**. If the latter he will be paid, and may be employed on a part-time or full-time basis. He may or may not be trained.
Full-time one-year courses are provided by the National College of Youth Leaders at Leicester and many **LEAs** acting on the recommendation of the Bessey Report have provided courses of their own for the training of part-time Youth Leaders. Some Colleges of Education are also including courses in Youth Leadership as part of their teacher-training courses.
Albermarle Report, 1960
Bessey Report, 1962
McNair Report, 1944

Youth Service
The Youth Service was officially called into being in 1939 with the issue of the Board of Education circular 1486. The circular drew together into the 'Youth Service' the three parties who had for a number of years been helping young people between fourteen and twenty during their leisure hours, namely, the Central Government, the LEA's and the Voluntary Organisations. The McNair Report of 1944 was concerned particularly witn the provision of Youth Leaders.
Albermarle Report, *The Youth Service in England and Wales*, 1960
McNair Report, *Supply, Recruitment and Training of Teachers and Youth Leaders*, 1944

Y

Z

'z' Scores. *See* **Sigma scores**

Appendix I

The law of the land, as set out in the Education Act of 1944, makes parents responsible for the education of their children. It does *not* compel them to send their children to school but it does insist that the children get a suitable education between the ages of 5 and 16*. How that legal duty of the parent is carried out is characteristically left to the individual. A parent may, if he is rich enough, employ private tutors, he may teach the child himself, or he may choose to pay fees at private schools. He may, as does the vast majority (94 per cent) of the population, make use of the educational facilities provided by the state. But failure to provide adequate education for their children may result in parents being fined or imprisoned or in having the children taken away as 'being in need of care and protection'.

The state system of education, as shown in the accompanying diagram, is thought of as organized in three main stages, Primary, Secondary and Tertiary (higher education and further education).

The Primary stage indicates the legally required first period of children's schooling between the ages of 5 and 11 years, but it also loosely embraces the preschool period for the small percentage of children who attend *nursery schools* before the age of 5. Children between the ages of 5 and 7 may be educated in separate Infant Schools which will cater for boys and girls together. Such children would then go on from 7 to 11 to junior schools which may be for both sexes or (more rarely) for boys and girls separately. *The primary school* which caters for the whole range from 5 to 11 is usually coeducational and the work of the early years is organised as a separate department within the same building.

In some areas a system of *first schools*, *middle schools* and *high schools* is being developed.

For most children educated in the state system, *secondary education* begins normally in the autumn term following their eleventh birthday. In areas where selection still takes place allocation to various types of secondary school is usually made following selection procedures which take place in the preceding year. This is popularly known as 'the 11-plus

* As from 1972–73.

examination' which varies with the area in which it is operating but which is usually a compound of objective tests of reasoning, of competence in Arithmetic and English, and of subjective assessments by teachers based on school records over several years. Under pressure from some educationalists who doubt the validity of the tests and suspect the harmful effects of the 11-plus examination on the curriculum of primary schools – and under protest from many parents who complain of the harmful physical and psychological effects of the examination on their children, an increasing number of local authorities are abandoning the formal examination and substituting other procedures for allocating children to the various types of Secondary School in their area.

On an average for the country as a whole 45 per cent to 50 per cent of the children go to *secondary modern schools* while approx. 20 per cent go to some form of grammar or technical school. In an increasing number of areas, various forms of *comprehensive* secondary education are being set up which enable selection procedures to be eliminated since children from primary schools, whatever their academic attainment or potential, may all go to the same secondary school. In 1970 the proportion of children in comprehensive schools exceeded 30 per cent.

One interesting plan to eliminate premature selection is being carried out in Leicestershire, where the whole range of children are transferred from primary schools at the age of 11 to the buildings of former secondary schools until the age of 14. These 'middle' schools are called *high schools*. After 14, any child, whatever his ability or attainment, whose parents are prepared for him to stay at school till the age of 16, may then go to a grammar school to pursue an academic type of education. It is claimed that such schools, catering for the later stages of adolescence, have an increased motivation, and that they provide full opportunities for children who tend to develop later than is normal.

Another development is the plan being worked out in the West Riding of Yorkshire. The idea here is to change the existing structure of primary school provision by creating 'middle' schools which have an age range from 9 to 13 (similar to that of the preparatory schools in the private sector). This would, of course, mean extending the range of the present infant course to cover the ages 5 to 8, a reform long suggested by many

The Educational System in England and Wales

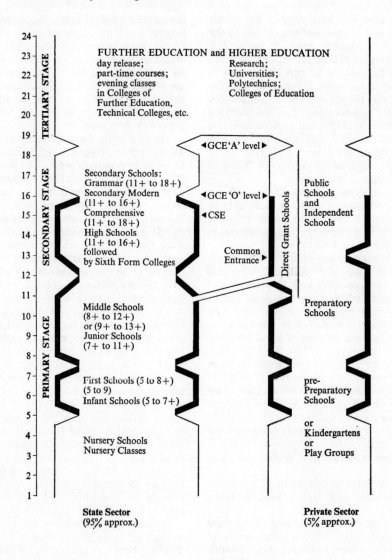

FURTHER EDUCATION and HIGHER EDUCATION
day release;   Research;
part-time courses;   Universities;
evening classes   Polytechnics;
in Colleges of   Colleges of Education
Further Education,
Technical Colleges, etc.

TERTIARY STAGE

◄GCE 'A' level ►

SECONDARY STAGE

Secondary Schools:
Grammar (11+ to 18+)
Secondary Modern
(11+ to 16+)
Comprehensive
(11+ to 18+)
High Schools
(11+ to 16+)
followed
by Sixth Form Colleges

◄GCE 'O' level ►
◄CSE

Common
Entrance ►

Public
Schools
and
Independent
Schools

Direct Grant Schools

Middle Schools
(8+ to 12+)
or (9+ to 13+)
Junior Schools
(7+ to 11+)

Preparatory
Schools

PRIMARY STAGE

First Schools (5 to 8+)
(5 to 9)
Infant Schools (5 to 7+)

pre-
Preparatory
Schools

Nursery Schools
Nursery Classes

or
Kindergartens
or
Play Groups

State Sector
(95% approx.)

Private Sector
(5% approx.)

educationists concerned with the welfare of younger children. Under this reformed plan, children would then begin their Secondary education in a Comprehensive type of school after the age of 13.

In some areas (e.g. Exeter, Southampton) the LEA has set up a *sixth-form college*, which children enter from their comprehensive or grammar school after the age of 16.

Most children leave *secondary modern schools* at the end of their compulsory period of education (i.e. at the end of the spring or summer term following their sixteenth birthday). But there is an increasing tendency for boys and girls to stay on, after the compulsory period, when they may take a school-leaving examination, such as the CSE (Certificate of Secondary Education) or GCE (General Certificate of Education).

Approximately a fifth of the population now go to *grammar schools* after the age of 11. Some of these are very old foundations dating back to the Middle Ages but the majority were built in the years following the 1902 Education Act which required the newly constituted local authorities to provide facilities for secondary as well as elementary education. The grammar school offers a curriculum which is deliberately academic and sets out to prepare its children by a general (non-vocational) approach for eventual entry into technical, professional, and commercial posts at any time after the age of 16, or for eventual entry to universities at the age of 18 to 19. After four or five years of a grammar school course most pupils take the examination leading to the General Certificate of Education (GCE) at Ordinary Level. Those who stay on beyond 16 to work in a sixth form normally take the GCE at Advanced Level two years later. It is on the results of this examination that selection for entry to universities, polytechnics and colleges of education is normally made.

Tertiary education is deemed to begin when secondary education is concluded. This category covers a wide variety of studies at different levels. It includes those designated under the title of 'higher education', such as courses at university, polytechnics and colleges of education; and those which are designated under the title of 'further education' which includes those courses at technical colleges and other educational establishments which are designed for people, older than secondary school age, who are not involved in 'higher education'. Courses of 'further education' may be full time, or part time. They may lead to awards and qualifications or may be taken without any qualifications in view.

The *private sector* of education, catering for approximately 5 per cent of the child population, consists mainly of independent schools which are financed by fee-paying parents and/or by ancient foundations, and donations from industry. The majority of these independent schools are small preparatory schools whose aim is to prepare boys (after the kindergarten stage) for the Common Entrance Examination into the public schools at the age of 13. Since 1957 all schools in the private sector are liable to be inspected by the Department of Education and Science, and to be 'recognized as efficient'.

Though some public schools such as Winchester, Eton and Harrow have ancient foundations, the majority were founded and grew during the nineteenth century in order to provide boarding education for the sons of the aspiring and prosperous industrialists and merchants. The importance and influence of the public schools is far-reaching and quite disproportionate to their numbers.

Some characteristics
of British schools and education

a Though a few schools existed for a tiny minority of the literate population from the sixteenth century onwards, the masses of the country did not get the opportunity for school education until the latter part of the nineteenth century when schools were set up mainly by religious bodies to provide free elementary education for poorer children. It was soon realized that sufficient schools of the required quality for all children could not be provided by voluntary agencies alone and during the second half of the century the state became progressively interested both financially and educationally in school provision. This led to a great deal of dissension and antagonism from religious bodies but compromises were gradually worked out, so that a *dual system* of schools exists which enables 'Church' schools to be included in a state financed system.

b The administration of the educational system is also characterized by another form of dualism. Unlike the system in many other countries, the administration is not centralized but exists through a partnership between the central government (the Department of Education and Science) in London and the local authorities in approximately 150 towns or counties throughout the land. The administration and conduct of schools is supervised by civil servants at the national and local level, aided by Her Majesty's Inspectors and by local inspectors, advisers and organisers.

c The schools and, in fact, the whole system has a tradition of academic freedom and individual liberty which is probably not matched anywhere else in the world. Teachers, though paid by the state through the local authorities, are *not* civil servants and are thus not subject to detailed day-to-day direction and regulation as to how their work is carried out. General national polices are, under this system, carried out by the use of 'suggestions to teachers' from Her Majesty's Inspectorate and by help given to schools by 'advisers' and local organisers.

Each school is free to plan its own curriculum and syllabuses (with the exception of Religious Education) and to choose its own textbooks. The influence of external public examinations (e.g. GCE) tends towards standardization, but even here schools are able, if they wish, to develop particular topics within a subject in their own way and to arrange for special papers to be taken to fit their own chosen syllabuses.

d The headmaster or headmistress in the British educational system has an importance and a responsibility rarely found in other systems. This is largely a consequence of the lack of a tight central direction of education and results in remarkable differences in character between one school and another and in their approach to educational problems.

e Most visitors from other countries are struck by the quality of the relationship between teachers and children in most British schools. While schools are not 'child-centred' in the American sense, there is strong pastoral concern by teachers for their children which extends beyond subject matter and the learning process. Schools are regarded as communities where social responsibility and the development of individual personality are as important, if not more important, than academic achievement.

f The Education Act of 1944 laid down the egalitarian principle that each child is entitled to the kind of education for which he is qualified by 'age, ability and aptitude'.

Though there has been considerable progress in this egalitarian direction since 1944, many circumstances such as overcrowding of classes, poor school buildings, shortage of teachers, have so far prevented the realisation of equality of opportunity for all. Theoretically, however, educational opportunity for all is open even beyond the university stage, in the sense that the able children of poor parents are not prevented from such education by reason of their poverty. All students who qualify are eligible for government grants.

Education in Scotland

Educational provision in Scotland has much in common with that of England and Wales but Scotland has its individual traditions which affect its approach to education at all levels. Education is administered by the Scottish Education Department under the general aegis of the Secretary of State for Scotland.

Primary education is broadly similar to the English and Welsh pattern, but there are fewer separate infant schools and the children stay in primary schools one year longer, i.e. until the age of 12 plus (seven years in all).

Secondary education is largely coeducational and takes place in:

a Junior secondary schools for those children who will leave at 15 having completed a three-year course.

b Senior secondary schools for those who intend to leave later at 16, 17 or 18, having completed at least a four-year course.

c Comprehensive-type schools which may be similar to those set up in England or may be merely a convenient way of accommodating a and b on the same site.

Transfer to secondary education is rather easier and less controversial than in England, because there is more senior (i.e. grammar) accommodation and because the system of transfer is more flexible. A parent who wants a more ambitious education for his child can usually get it, provided the child is reasonably suitable for it.

The Scottish Certificate of Education (Leaving Certificate) is open to pupils in Senior Secondary Schools and to students in Further Education establishments. It is taken in two grades: Ordinary (cf. 'O' level GCE) taken by pupils at 16 plus, and Higher (rather lower than 'A' level) taken by pupils at 17 plus.

All men who intend to become teachers in Scotland must be university graduates unless they are holders of recognized diplomas in educational handwork, physical education, art, music or other technical subjects. The professional and practical training of all teachers is undertaken in colleges of education. University departments of education are concerned only with the academic study of the subject.

Teachers' salary scales negotiated by a separate body in Scotland have consistently been superior to those in the rest of Great Britain.

The development of Scottish education has perhaps been comparatively smoother than the English since historically it has not had to contend with the problems of dualism. The tradition of state education developed much earlier than in England where the voluntary agencies (in particular, the religious bodies) were predominant for most of the nineteenth century.

Appendix II

The more important Education Acts in England and Wales

1840 *Grammar Schools Act*
Enabled grammar schools to teach subjects other than the classical languages and literature.

1844 *Factory Act of 1844* (Sir James Graham)
One of a series of Factory Acts. Required parents of children who worked in textile mills to make them attend schools on three full days or six half-days in each week. Extended to cover non-textile factories and workshops in 1864 and 1867.

1856 Government established an Education Department by an Order of Council.

1868 *Public Schools Act*
Outcome of the Clarendon Commission's Report on the nine large public schools in 1864. The Act required each school to make its governing body more representative by including members nominated by Oxford, Cambridge and London Universities and various learned societies. The governing body was given full powers in connection with fees, curriculum and the appointment or dismissal of the headmaster.

1869 *Endowed Schools Act*
Followed the issuing of the Taunton Commission's Report on Secondary Schools in 1868. The Act set up the Endowed Schools Commission, which in 1874 merged with the Charity Commission, to draw up new schemes of government for secondary schools. It also abolished the custom whereby all masters in grammar schools were required to hold a licence to teach granted by the bishop of the diocese.

1870 *Elementary Education Act* (W. E. Forster)
Established school boards, elected by the ratepayers, to build and maintain public elementary schools with rate aid, in addition to Government grant and school fees. School boards were given wide powers, e.g. they could levy a local rate for the building of schools; they could make education compulsory in their area; they were free to decide whether religious instruction should be given in their schools. The Act instituted the 'dual system' with the undenominational board schools on the one hand and the denominational voluntary schools on the other.

1876 *Elementary Education Act* (Lord Sandon)
Set up School Attendance Committees in districts where there were no School Boards and established the principle which made it the duty of the parent to see that his child received 'efficient elementary instruction in reading, writing and arithmetic'. The Act also made it illegal to employ any child under the age of 10, or a child between 10 and 14 who had not reached a certain educational standard. Children who lived more than two miles from a public elementary school were exempt from the provisions of the Act.

1880 *Elementary Education Act* (Mr Mundella)
Required all school boards and school attendance committees to draw up by-laws making school attendance compulsory for all children between 5 and 10; after 10 exemption based on educational attainment could be obtained.

1888 *Local Government Act*
Established county and county borough councils which were to become important in the subsequent development of public education.

1889 *Technical Instruction Act*
County and borough councils were given power to levy a rate not exceeding one penny in the £ for aiding and supplying technical education.

1893 *Elementary Education (Blind and Deaf Children) Act*
Empowered school boards to provide education for blind and deaf children resident in their areas.

1898 *Elementary Teachers' Superannuation Act*
Enabled teachers to secure an annuity through the payment of voluntary contributions.

1899 *Board of Education Act*
Incorporating a number of the recommendations put forward by the Bryce Commission (1894–95), the Act established a Board of Education to 'superintend matters relating

to education in England and Wales'. The Board, headed by a President appointed by the Crown, replaced the Education Department, the Science and Art Department, and took over those activities of the Charity Commission concerned with educational matters. The Act also set up a Consultative Committee, of the present-day pattern.

1902 *Education Act* (sponsored by the Prime Minister, A. J. Balfour)
Established 330 local education authorities to replace 2,559 schools boards and 788 school attendance committees. The LEAs were empowered to provide not only elementary education but also 'education other than elementary', including secondary, technical, teacher training and adult education. Board schools became 'provided', or often 'council', schools. Voluntary schools became 'non-provided' schools and received rate aid. The Act perpetuated the 'dual system' and was also responsible for setting up the Part II and Part III authorities. This subsequently led to administrative difficulties.

1904 *Education (Local Authorities' Default) Act*
If an LEA refused to make adequate grants to non-provided schools in its area, this Act enabled the Board of Education to deduct the required sum from the government grant to the authority and pay it direct to the managers of the schools.

1906 *Education (Provision of Meals) Act*
LEAs were given authority to provide premises and facilities to help voluntary organisations with the provision of school meals.

1907 *Education (Administrative Provisions Act)* (R. McKenna)
Provided for the medical inspection of school children and empowered LEAs to provide evening play-centres for children or to assist voluntary organizations in providing them. The Act also introduced the free place system whereby some of the yearly intake into secondary schools should be pupils from elementary schools. LEAs were also given power to acquire land for building new secondary schools.

1918 *Education Act* (H. A. L. Fisher)
Gave increased power to LEAs, but a great weakness of the Act was that many of the clauses were not mandatory and the final decision was left to the LEA, for example the school leaving age was raised to fourteen, without exemption, but LEAs were empowered to raise it to fifteen. The employment of children was restricted and no child below the age of 12 could be employed. Another recommendation was that day continuation schools should be established for pupils who had left elementary school at 14. LEAs were also empowered to set up nursery schools and nursery classes for children between 2 and 5 years old. Medical inspection and treatment were extended to pupils in maintained secondary schools.

1918 *Teachers' Superannuation Act*
Introduced a scheme whereby every teacher in elementary and secondary schools was entitled to a lump sum and pension based on length of service and the salary earned during the last five years of service. At first the scheme was non-contributory but from 1922 all teachers were required to pay 5 per cent of their salaries towards superannuation. Further amendments were introduced in the Superannuation Acts of 1925, 1956 and 1972.

1921 *Education Act*
Consolidated the recommendations of the 1918 Act.

1936 *Education Act*
Stated that the school leaving age would be 15 after 1 September 1939. Some pupils were to be permitted to leave at 14 provided they entered employment which the LEA considered beneficial. Managers of non-provided schools could apply, within a stated period of time, to receive grants of between 50 and 75 per cent of the cost of new buildings for senior pupils. These schools were to be known as 'special agreement schools'.

1944 *Education Act* (R. A. Butler)
The Board of Education was replaced by a Ministry. The Minister's task was to see that local authorities put the national policy for education into effect. The consultative committee of the Board of Education was replaced by two Advisory Councils, one for England and one for Wales. Part III authorities were abolished and the number of LEAs reduced to 146, but to placate the former Part III authorities 171 divisional executives and 44 excepted districts were established.

Provided schools were to be known as

county schools and non-provided schools reverted to their former title of voluntary schools. There were to be three types of voluntary school – the special-agreement school, the aided school, the controlled school.

Religious education and collective worship became compulsory in all schools, although no teacher is compelled to give religious instruction. Similarly, parents can withdraw their children from religious education lessons and school worship, if they so wish.

'The statutory system of public education shall be organized in three progressive stages to be known as – Primary Education, Secondary Education, Further Education'. LEAs were required to provide boarding education for pupils 'for whom education as boarders is considered by their parents and by the authority to be desirable in boarding schools or otherwise'. It was also made the duty of LEAs to provide nursery schools or nursery classes where a sufficient number of parents wish their children to have nursery education.

The school-leaving age was raised to 15 from 1 April 1947.

1946, 1948, 1952 *Education (Miscellaneous Provisions) Acts*
These were amending Acts which ironed out certain irregularities in the 1944 Act without altering its main structure.

1956 *Teachers (Superannuation) Act*
The contribution of both teacher and employer was raised to 6 per cent.

1959 *Education Act*
The grant payable towards the cost of new voluntary (aided) schools or to increases in the buildings of existing schools was raised from 50 to 75 per cent.

1962 *Education Act*
Made law the recommendation of the Crowther Report that the number of leaving dates should be reduced from three to two – Easter and July.

1964 *Education Act*
1. Enabled new schools to be established for certain age groups of children which was not possible under existing post-war legislation.
2. Removed an anomaly in law relating to the payment of maintenance allowances by LEAs for handicapped pupils who were over compulsory school age.

1967 *Education Act*
Made provision for increase of grant to educational institutions such as 'aided' and special agreement schools.

Extended the power to require LEAs to defray expenses of establishing 'controlled' schools.

Made provision for loans in respect of capital expenditure for colleges of education.

1968 *Education Act*
1. Amended the law as to the effect of, and procedure for, making changes in the character, size or situation of county schools or voluntary schools, to enable special age limits to be adopted to existing as well as for new schools.
2. Made further provision for the government and conduct of colleges of education and of other institutions of further education maintained by LEAs, and of maintained special schools.
See also Weaver Report

Appendix III

basic salary scale but extra increments should be paid for additional qualifications and experience. Allowances were also to be paid to teachers holding posts of special responsibility.

The 'pledge' system, whereby a student, starting a course in a training college or a department of education, promised in writing to enter the teaching profession, should be abolished.

The two-year training colleges course should be extended to three years.

A three-year course for full-time youth leaders was recommended. To facilitate transfer between youth leadership and teaching, salaries in the two professions should be comparable.

(Committee appointed by the President of the Board of Education to consider the supply, recruitment and training of teachers and youth leaders.)

1944 The Public Schools and the General-Educational System (Lord Fleming)

The Board of Education should draw up lists of public schools who would be willing to accept girls and boys from LEA schools.

There were two abasic schemes:

Scheme A—Direct Grant Schools. LEA would pay tuition fee and boarding fee if necessary and recover the appropriate amount on a graded scale from the parents.

Scheme B—Public Boarding Schools. Board of Education would award bursaries to qualified pupils who had attended a grant-aided primary school for at least two years. Bursaries would depend on the income of parents.

(Committee appointed by the President of the Board of Education.)

1945 Higher Technological Education (Lord Eustace Percy)

A small number of the larger technical colleges should be selected to run courses roughly equivalent to university degree courses. These colleges should be called Royal Colleges of Technology. There should be the greatest possible degree of self-government and responsibility.

A small number of national schools of technology to cater for the needs of small but important industries should be established within existing colleges.

Regional advisory councils and regional academic boards of technology, composed of college and university staffs and representatives of industry should be set up. There should be a central, coordinating council, a National Council of Technology.

(Committee appointed by the Minister of Education)

This report was followed by two other reports on the supply and training of people in science and technology – the Barlow Report and the Wakefield Report (Scotland), both published in 1946.

1946 Scientific Manpower (Sir Alan Barlow, Bt)

Recommended that university provision should be expanded to double the output of scientists (though not at the expense of the humanities) and, at the same time, to raise standards. The report had a great effect on the growth and development of post-war university education and, in turn, on the nature of secondary grammar education.

(Committee appointed by the Lord President of the Council, Cmnd 6824.)

1955 Report of the Committee onMaladjusted Children (J. E. A. Underwood)

The 97 recommendations of the report fall under three headings:

1. The Child Guidance Service, including the training and supply of staff.
2. Other forms of day treatment and residential treatment including aftercare.
3. Other measures of prevention.

(Committee appointed by the Minister of Education.)

1959 15 to 18 (Sir Geoffrey Crowther)

The school-leaving age should be raised to 16 and the most favourable time for doing this would be between 1965 and 1969, i.e. between the two bulges which affect secondary schools. This should come before the establishing of county colleges.

As a preliminary step towards the raising of the school leaving age the number of leaving dates in the school year should be reduced from three to two – at Easter and in July.

The Minister should reaffirm his intention to implement, at the earliest possible date, the provision of compulsory part-time education for all young persons of 16 and 17 who are not in full-time education.

Concerning the development of further education there were three main recommendations:

(*a*) There should be a greater degree of integration between schools and further education.

(b) To reduce the failure rate more time should be allowed in all courses.

(c) 'Block release' should wherever possible be substituted for release on one day a week.

The supply of teachers should be increased, to reduce the size of classes and to meet the demand brought about by the raising of the school-leaving age.

(Report of the Central Advisory Council for Education (England) Vol. 1, *Report*, 1959; Vol. 2, *Surveys*, 1960.)

1960 *Grants to Students*
(Sir Colin Anderson)
State scholarships should be abolished and replaced by open entry scholarships offered by the universities. The holder of an open scholarship would be able to keep up to £100 of the scholarship without deduction from the government grant.

The scale of parent contributions should be revised so that 40 per cent instead of the previous 25 per cent of students can obtain the full Government grant.

(Committee appointed by the Minister of Education and the Secretary of State for Scotland. Cmnd 1051.)

1960 *The Youth Service in England and Wales*
(The Countess of Albemarle)
The Youth Service should be extended to all young people between the ages of fourteen and twenty.

A Youth Service Development Council of not more than twelve members should be set up.

The Youth Service should provide young people with opportunities for 'association, training and challenge' of the right kind.

There should be increased grants to cover salaries, buildings, etc.

An emergency training college offering a one-year course in youth leadership for men and women should be set up.

LEAs should organize part-time training for part-time leaders.

(Committee appointed by the Minister of Education. Cmnd 929.)

1960 *Secondary Schools Examinations other than GCE* (R. Beloe)
The Minister should accept the examination for the Certificate of Secondary Education (CSE).

External examinations should not be taken by pupils before the end of the fifth-year course.

All examinations should be subject rather than group examinations.

More able pupils should receive a credit award.

General responsibility for the examination should be undertaken by about twenty Regional Examining Boards but the form and content of the examination should be in the hands of teachers.

NB. At the request of the Minister the Secondary Schools Examination Council was reconstituted in 1961 and in August 1962 published its fifth report – 'Examinations in Secondary Schools – the Certificate of Secondary Education'.

(Committee appointed by the Secondary Schools Examination Council.)

1963 *Half our Future* (Sir John Newsom)
An immediate announcement should be made that the school-leaving age will be raised to 16 for all pupils entering the secondary schools from September 1965 onwards

A special body of teachers who are ready to go where they are needed in return for financial compensation may be the only solution to easing the problem of 'bad areas' which feel the effects of the teacher shortage most acutely.

Greater demands both in the nature and amount of work required, should be made on the pupils, and a realistic and practical approach should be made to the curriculum.

Pupils in the last two years at school should have some choice in their programme of work and should work a longer school day.

Positive guidance to adolescent boys and girls on sexual behaviour is essential and this should include the biological, moral, social and personal aspects.

All graduates entering the profession should be trained, and untrained graduates already in the profession should attend in-service courses to help them to deal with the problems they encounter in the schools.

(A Report of the Central Advisory Council for Education (England).)

1963 *Higher Education* (Lord Robbins)
There should be a unified system of higher education but at the same time there should be considerable academic freedom.

Higher education should be available to all those qualified to profit by it. By 1980–81 there should be 350,000 places in universities, 145,000 places in Colleges of Education and 65,000 places for full-time advanced students in further education.

Training colleges should be renamed colleges of education. The three-year course leading to professional qualification should continue but there should also be available a four-year course leading to professional qualification and to a B Ed. degree of the university to which the college is attached.

There should be five Special Institutes for Scientific and Technological Education and Research. They should each contain 3500–4500 students and approximately half should be post-graduate.

Colleges of Advanced Technology should in general be designated as technological universities, with power to award both first and higher degrees.

(Committee appointed by the Prime Minister. *Report*, Cmnd 2154; *Appendices*, Cmnd 2154 I–V; *Evidence*, Cmnd 2154 VI–XII.)

1967 *Children and Their Primary Schools* (Lady Plowden)

Terms of reference were 'To consider primary education in all its aspects and the transition to secondary education'.

The Report considers a mass of evidence and gives its recommendations and conclusions on the following topics; Participation by parents; Educational priority areas; Children of immigrants; Health and social services and the school child; Primary education in the 1960s, Its organization and effectiveness; Providing for children before compulsory education; The ages and stages of primary education, long-term recommendations; Selection for secondary education; Continuity and consistency between the stages of education; The size of primary schools; Education in rural areas; Children learning in school; Religious education; The child in the school community; How primary schools are organized; Handicapped children in ordinary schools; The education of gifted children; The staffing of the school; The deployment of staff; The training of primary school teachers; The training of nursery assistants and teachers' aides; Independent primary schools; Primary school buildings and equipment; The status and government of Primary Education.

There were also a number of minority conclusions reached on religious education, nursery education and corporal punishment.

(Report of the Central Advisory Council for Education (England). Vol 1, *Report*; Vol. 2, *Research and Surveys*.)

1967 *Primary Education in Wales* (Professor C. E. Gittins)

Report of the Central Advisory Council for Education (Wales), with the same terms of reference as for the Plowden Committee (above)

There was a great deal of common ground between the two enquiries, and close contact was maintained by the inclusion on the Council for England of two members of the Welsh Council. Recommendations on many fundamental issues are common to both reports but on certain matters their recommendations differ, e.g. recommendations relating to educational priority areas are accepted in the Welsh (Gittins) Report but with certain qualifications; the Welsh Report, unlike the Plowden Report recommends the relaxation of the statutory requirement making religious education compulsory. In addition the Gittins Report gives particular attention to special circumstances in Wales and therefore, for example, deals at some length with the problem of bilingualism in Wales. The report shows different emphasis in other respects, too, for example in devoting a large section to the handicapped child and the child with learning difficulties in the ordinary school.

1968 *Public Schools Commission* First Report: Sir John Newsom; 1970 *Public Schools Commission* Second Report: Professor David Donnison

The Commission's terms of reference were to advise the best way of integrating the public schools within the State system of education. Its principal recommendations were that:

An integrated sector should be set up into which any suitable independent boarding school might enter on the condition that half its places would be allocated to assisted pupils from maintained schools (i.e. from the state system).

Such schools should admit a wider range of ability, i.e. any pupil capable of taking a course to CSE.

Coeducational boarding schools and boarding schools for young children should be encouraged and developed.

Assisted pupils should come mainly from those needing boarding conditions, as this alone justified public expenditure.

There should be close association of integrated schools with LEAs by giving the schools an 'aided' status.

A Boarding Schools Corporation should be set up to guide regional groups of LEAs in handling applications.

Parental contributions should be required at a rate similar to that of the present University Awards scheme for that part of the cost which goes above the average cost of maintained day schools.

There should be an Education Act to enable an integrated sector to develop.

First Report: 2 vols., *Report* and *Appendices*, 1968.

Second Report: Vol. 1. *Report on Independent Day Schools and Direct Grant Grammar Schools*; vol. 2, *Appendices*, Vol. 3, *Scotland*, 1970.

1972 *Teacher Education and Training* (Lord James of Rusholme)

This report, against a changing national educational background, e.g. increasing numbers leaving school with two or more GCE A levels, proposed far-reaching changes in the arrangements for the organization of education and training of teachers. The proposals, in the main, subsumed under three 'cycles' or stages:

1. The personal (academic) education of students, most of whom would elect to take a further 'cycle' or stage in order to become teachers. This first cycle would last two years terminating with a qualification entitled diploma in higher education, and would include students who intended to terminate their higher education at this point.

2. Pre-service education and induction: students accepted for cycle two would in their first year study educational theory and carry out a teaching practice of at least four continuous weeks: If successful, the student would then become a 'licensed' teacher, in the second year of the second cycle (i.e. in the student's fourth year). He would then be in a position to be employed in a school teaching four-fifths of his time, spending the other fifth of his time following courses at nominated centres which were appropriate to his needs as a teacher in his first year. On the successful completion of a year as a 'licensed' teacher, he would qualify for the status of 'registered' teacher and would be awarded the degree of BA(Ed).

3. Inservice education and training. 'The third cycle comprehends the whole range of activities by which teachers can extend their personal education, develop their professional competence and improve their under-

standing of educational principles and techniques' (p. 5).

Teachers and full-time staff in further education colleges would be entitled to release with pay for not less than one school term in every seven years of service for the purpose of cycle three.

(Report by a Committee of Inquiry by the Secretary of State for Education and Science.)

Other Educational Reports, published by HMSO

1943 *Report on Post-war Agricultural Education* (Lord Justice Luxmoore), Cmnd 6433

Training in Child Care (Dame Myra Curtis) Cmd 6922 (interim Report, Cmd 6760)
Report of the Committee on Higher Agricultural Education in England and Wales (Dr Thomas Loveday) Cmd 6728

1947 *Interim Report on Agricultural and Horticultural Institutes* (Dr Thomas Loveday) (Min. of Agriculture and Fisheries)
School and Life (Sir Frederick Clarke) Min. of Education; Central Advisory Committee for Education (England)

1949 *Education for Commerce* (Sir Alexander Carr-Saunders) Min. of Education, Special Committee
The Future of Secondary Education in Wales (Professor R. I. Aaron) Min. of Education; Central Advisory Council for Education (Wales)
Interim Report on the Provisions of Part-time Instruction by Local Education Authorities for Agriculturalists, Horticulturalists and Domestic Producers (Dr Thomas Loveday) Min. of Agriculture and Fisheries

1954 *The Organization and Finance of Adult Education* (Dr Eric Ashby) Min. of Education
Early Leaving (Sir Samuel Gurney-Dixon) Min. of Education; Central Advisory Council for Education (England)

1957 *Supply and Training of Teachers for Technical Colleges* (Sir Willis Jackson) Min. of Education Special Committee.

1958 *Education for Agriculture: Report of the Committee on Further Education for Agriculture provided by LEAs* (Earl De La Warr) Cmnd 614
Training for Skill, Recruitment and Training

of Young Workers in Industry (Robert Carr) (Min. of Labour)

1959 *Social Workers in Local Authority Health and Welfare Services* (Miss Eileen Younghusband) Min. of Health and Dept. of Health for Scotland, Working Party.

1960 *Sport and the Community* (Sir John Wolfenden)
Education in Rural Wales (Alun Oldfield-Davies) Central Advisory Council for Education (Wales)
Report of the Committee on Children and Young Persons (Lord Ingleby), Cmnd 1191
National Advisory Council on Art Education: First Report (Sir William Coldstream),

Appointed to advise the Minister on all aspects of art in further education.

1962 *Training of Part-time Youth Leaders and Assistants* (G. S. Bessey). Ministry of Education Working Party

1963 *Women and Teaching* (R. K. Kelsall). Report of an Independent Nuffield Survey.

1968 *Report on the Government of Colleges of Education* (T. R. Weaver). Department of Education and Science Study Group

1969 *The Open University* (Sir Peter Venables). Report of the Planning Committee to the Secretary of State for Education and Science

Appendix IV

Education Journals

AMA, The Journal of the Incorporated Association of Assistant Masters in Secondary Schools. Gordon House, 29 Gordon Square, London WC1

Adult Education, 35 Queen Anne Street, London, W1, bi-monthly

Art and Craft Education, Evans Bros. Ltd, Montague House, Russell Square, London WC1

Bible Story, New Fleetway House, Farringdon Street, London EC4

Birmingham University Historical Journal, The School of History, The University, Birmingham 15

Books: *The Journal of the National Book League*, 7 Albemarle Street, London W1

British Journal of Educational Psychology, Scottish Academic Press, 25, Perth St, Edinburgh

British Journal of Educational Studies, Faber, 24 Russell Square, WC1

British Journal of Sociology, Routledge & Kegan Paul, Carter Lane, London EC4

Catholic Teachers Journal, St Mary's College, Strawberry Hill, Twickenham, Middlesex

Comparative Education, Pergamon Press, Headington Hill Hall, Oxford

Child Education, Evans Bros Ltd, Montague House, Russell Square, London, WC1

Conference Journal of HMC, The Master, Wellington College, Crowthorne , Berks, 3 times a year

Discovery, Professional and Industrial Publishing Co. Ltd, Mercury House, 109–119 Waterloo Road London SE1

Education, 10 Queen Anne Street, London, W1

Educational Research, NFER, The Mere, Upton Park, Slough, Bucks, 3 times a year

Educational Review, University of Birmingham

Education for Teaching, ATCDE, 151 Gower Street, London WC1

English, the Magazine of the English Association, 1 Brockmere, Wray Park Road, Reigate, Surrey

English Language Teaching, Oxford University Press, Dover Street, London W1

Family Doctor, 47–51 Chalton Street, London, NW1

Film User (incorporating *Industrial Screen*), PO Box 109, Croydon, Surrey

Forum, 86 Headland Road, Leicester

Froebel Journal, 2 Manchester Square, London W1

Forward Trends, 7 Albemarle Street, London W1

Health Education Journal, Central Council for Health Education, Tavistock Square, London WC1

Hibbert Journal, Manchester College, Oxford

Higher Education Journal, NUT, Hamilton House, Mabledon Place, London WC1

Historical Journal, Cambridge University Press, Euston Road, London, NW1

History Today, Bracken House, 10 Cannon Street, London EC4

Housecraft, Journal of Association of Teachers of Domestic Science, 10 Queen Anne Street, London W1

International Journal of Adult and Youth Education, UNESCO House, Place de Fontenoy, Paris, 7e

ITA Journal, 9 Southampton Place, London WC1

Journal of Biological Education, Berkeley Square, London W1

Junior Bookshelf, Tower Wood, Windermere, Westmorland

London Teacher, Hamilton House, Bidborough Street, London WC1

Look and Learn, New Fleetway House, Farringdon Street, London EC4

Mathematics Teaching, Vine Street Chambers, Nelson, Lancs

Mind, Magdalen College, Oxford

Mental Health, 39 Queen Anne Street, London W1

Modern Languages, 2 Manchester Square, London W1

Music in Education, 27–8 Soho Square, London W1

Music Teacher and Piano Student, Evans Bros Ltd, Montague House, Russell Square, London WC1

New Education, Bracken House, Cannon Street, London EC4

New Era, 32 Earl's Road, Tunbridge Wells, Kent

New Schoolmaster, NAS, Swan Court, Waterhouse Street, Hemel Hempstead, Herts

New Society, Cromwell House, Fulwood Place, High Holborn, London WC1

Parents' Review, Parents' National Educational Union, Murray House, Vandon Street, London SW1

Physical Education, Ling House, 10 Nottingham Place, London W1

Pictorial Education, Evans Bros Ltd, Montague House, Russell Square, London WC1

Preparatory Schools Review, The, 22 Shaftesbury Avenue, London WC2

Programmed Learning, 27 Torrington Square, London WC1

Review of the Incorporated Association of Headmasters (private circulation)

School and College, 18–20 York Buildings, Adelphi, London WC2

School Government Chronicle and Education Review, 50 Clifton Road, London N22

School Librarian and School Review, 150 Southampton Row, London WC1

Science Teacher, 60 Paddington Street, London W1

Scottish Educational Journal, 46 Moray Place, Edinburgh 3

Sociological Review, Managing Editor, University of Keele, Keele

Special Education, 12 Park Crescent, London, W1

Speech and Drama, St Bride Institute, Fleet Street, London EC4

Teacher, The, Hamilton House, Hastings Street, London WC1

Teacher of the Blind, School for the Blind, Liverpool 15

Teacher of the Deaf, Oak Lodge, 192 Nightingale Lane, London SW12

Teacher's Work, The, The Richview Press, Clonskeagh, Dublin 4

Teachers World, Evans Bros. Ltd, Montague House, Russell Square, London WC1

Teaching Arithmetic, Pergamon Press, Oxford

Technical Education and Industrial Training, Evans Bros. Ltd, Montague House, Russell Square, London WC1

Technical Journal, The, Journal of the Association of Teachers in Technical Institutions, Hamilton House, Mabledon Place, London WC1

Times Educational Supplement, The, Printing House Square, London EC4

Higher Education, The Times Newspapers Ltd, Printing House Square, London EC4

Treasure, New Fleetway House, Farringdon Street, London EC4

Trends in Education, Department of Education and Science, HMSO

Universities Quarterly, Turnstile Press, 10 Great Turnstile, London WC1

Use of English, The, Chatto & Windus, 40 William IV Street, London WC2

Visual Education, 31 Queen Anne Street, London W1

Where? Advisory Centre for Education Ltd, 57 Russell Street, Cambridge

World's Children, The, 29 Queen Anne's Gate, London SW1

Youth Employment, 9 Carmelite Street, London EC4

Youth Service, Department of Education and Science, Curzon Street, London W1

Notes

Notes

Notes

Notes

Notes

Notes

Notes

Notes

Notes

Notes